A Life with History

A Life with History

JOHN MORTON BLUM

University Press of Kansas

Chapter 14 of this book was published in a slightly different form by the *Yale Review*, which has kindly permitted the reprinting here.

© 2004 by the University Press of Kansas

Published by the University Press of Kansas (Lawrence, Kansas 66049), which was organized by the Kansas Board of Regents and is operated and funded by Emporia State University, Fort Hays State University, Kansas State University, Pittsburg State University, the University of Kansas, and Wichita State University.

Library of Congress Cataloging-in-Publication Data

Blum, John Morton, 1921–
    A life with history / John Morton Blum.
        p.   cm.
    Includes index.
    ISBN 0-7006-1338-2 (alk. paper)
    1. Blum, John Morton, 1921–   2. Historians—United States—Biography.
3. Historiography—United States—History—20th century.   4. United States—
Historiography.   5. United States—Politics and government—Historiography.   I. Title.
    E175.5.B59A3   2004
    973′.07′202—dc22   2004004567

British Library Cataloguing-in-Publication Data is available.

Printed in the United States of America

10 9 8 7 6 5 4 3 2 1

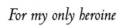

For my only heroine

Contents

Preface, *ix*

Acknowledgments, *xiii*

Prologue: Background, *1*

1 Andover, *3*

2 Veritas, *20*

3 269416, *38*

4 Apprentice, *61*

5 In Clio's Active Service, *78*

6 Extracurricular, *93*

7 The Institute, *103*

8 Professional Engagements, *120*

9 At Home at Yale, *136*

10 Undertakings, *151*

11 In King Arthur's Court, *165*

12 Chairman, *175*

13 Double Trouble, *191*

14 Yale Students and Harvard Fellows, *206*

15 The Busy Hum of Academe, *226*

16 Changes Large and Small, *243*

Epilogue: The Great Adventure, *259*

Index, *269*

Preface

I have long believed that the act of observing the past—the historian's calling—alters the past under examination, just as the process of observing the behavior of subatomic particles affects their behavior. That is not to say that there is no actual past, but that the past is far too complex to be reconstructed fully in any historical account. At best, historians reconstruct selectively and interpret some part or aspect of the past that interests them. To that process historians bring their biases, political and cultural, and the influence of their personal experience in their own time. Those who remember some part of the past ordinarily see it differently from those without that memory. Indeed that difference explains in large part the revisionism that occurs as generations of historians succeed each other. I have tried to place myself in my own time and within my own culture in order to assist any reader curious about the biases that I bring to my recollections and reconstructions of things past.

I began to write about my youth at the request of my older daughter. But I had kept few records of that time, or of any other period of my life. It was writing that made my memory work. I discovered that I recalled some conversations so vividly that I felt secure in quoting them directly. I also found a few letters, to which I have referred when I have quoted them. Writing this book made me realize how long and how inextricably I have been involved in the academy. I studied first at Phillips Academy and then at Harvard University; those years were punctuated by military service in the United States Naval Reserve, during which I learned much about writing history and much about myself. Then I taught at the Massachusetts Institute of Technology and Yale University, and as a visiting professor at Williams College and in England at Cambridge and Oxford — all wonderful places to teach. I have also been a trustee of the Buckingham School, the Hotchkiss School, and Harvard — all outstanding seats of learning, respectively for children, teenagers, and adults.

But it would be incorrect to say that I have always wanted to be a historian. When I was ten I wanted to grow up to play second base for the New York Yankees. At thirteen I saw myself as a future Speaker of the House of Representatives. I also thought I might enjoy writing stories. By the time I was seventeen I knew that the stories I most enjoyed writing were true stories. It was then that I realized I wanted to be a historian, and since then I have never really wanted to be anything else. I had found my calling. So I agree with my good friend and distinguished colleague Edmund S. Morgan, who on retiring said that it had always been a wonder to him that he was paid to do the only thing he wanted to do. *"Now* you tell me!" exclaimed A. Bartlett Giamatti, then president of Yale. Bart knew that both Ed and I were paid comparatively well. He knew, too, that one reason academic salaries are lower than salaries in other callings is the delight of academicians in earning a living by doing what they would in any case elect to do.

Yet professors of history, no matter how strong their affection for their field, spend much of their time on matters that have nothing to do with the past. Academic historians, like others in the academy, find their working hours crowded with committees, faculty and departmental meetings, the necessary tasks of finding jobs first for themselves and then for their students, and decisions regarding promotion for their junior colleagues. Those and other activities constitute the necessary impedimenta of academic life. Teaching and preparation for teaching, private discussions with students, grading papers, scholarship, and reviews of the scholarship of others consume only a fraction, though a substantial fraction, of one's time.

Academic life only poses as a refuge from the getting and spending of most other careers. It is no less demanding than they are, no less crowded or competitive. Still, for the generation of Americans who emerged from the terrors and dislocations of World War II — for my generation — academic life had immediate attractions. Many veterans believed that the educational benefits of the GI Bill promised entry into a clean world, a quiet world, a world safe for privacy and the life of the mind. Of course veterans seeking higher education had other motives, too. Some had parents who had pointed them toward the academy. Others were resolved to avoid careers in business, which had shattered their fathers' spirits during the Great Depression. Most veterans who started toward the Ph.D. thought of the university as essentially a grown-up school where they could play Mr. Chips.

Only a small percentage of the GIs enrolled in doctoral programs had even the faintest idea of what was involved in writing a book. Relatively few of them ever did write one, for they soon learned that scholarship was something to do or not to do in a teacher's spare time. And there was little spare time. For the most part, the academic "refuge" attracted innocent refugees. But they could not long remain so.

Satisfaction with academic life required adaptation to its folkways. The academy provided not a refuge from reality, but an alternative reality — in my case, a reality grounded in teaching and writing history. That reality, as well as the long road to and through academic life and the great satisfactions the academy provided, have been essential to my life.

Acknowledgments

Memory serves at best as a shaky platform on which to rest a book, and the memory of one principal in a relationship may vary from that of another. So I have been eager to test my recollections by asking friends, old and young, to comment upon them. They have done so with effect, correcting errors and omissions, and reminding me of other ways to assess our past. Their comments have much improved this book. Any remaining mistakes or infelicities are exclusively my own.

My cousin, William J. McKee, informed me beyond my previous learning about the LeVino family, into which were born his mother and mine. Four Andover classmates — Henry Terrie, Gordon Tuttle, George Wagoner, and Jack Walsh — suggested appropriate modifications in my account of our years together at Phillips Academy. Carl Schorske improved the first six chapters with his predictably insightful suggestions. The late Georges May reminded me of some significant aspects of the episode at Wright Hall. The entire manuscript benefited from the meticulous corrections of Richard W. Leopold, who has been a constructive critic of my work for sixty years. Marie Borroff, Mary Louise Brewster, Lewis L. Gould, Laura Kalman, Howard R. Lamar, Sharon Oster, and Gaddis Smith also assessed an early draft and identified ways to enhance it, some of which I did not undertake. Sam Chauncey, a wise critic, continually urged me to "think bigger." I hope he understands that I tried. My agent, William B. Goodman, served as a learned editor of my prose and cerebration, as did my publisher, Fred M. Woodward, and my wife, Pamela. Ever my shrewdest critic, she held me to my statement that our family was not a subject of this book. Nevertheless, in print as in life, she is my only heroine.

Prologue: Background

"Andover," my brother once said, "turned your life around." He was correct. It was at Andover that I first realized that I could make a career of teaching and writing history, and that I wanted to. It was at Andover that I first met overt anti-Semitism, but also at Andover that I first made lifelong friends. It was at Andover that my adolescent naïveté began to yield to more mature thinking. So I begin this book with Andover.

I cannot confidently begin any earlier, as the eminent American novelist and playwright Thornton Wilder once warned me. Thornton was a familiar presence at New Haven literary gatherings, where on several occasions we met. At one such affair I was chatting over cocktails with several acquaintances when I happened to remark that I had little memory of my childhood. I felt a light tap on my shoulder. It was Thornton, who had been standing behind me, eavesdropping on the conversation. "What a shame, John," he said, "for then you had no childhood."

I had had a childhood, of course, a contented but apparently not a memorable one. Born in 1921, I read the books American boys read during the 1920s and early 1930s, especially adventure books. I dreamed of glory on the playing field, but I was too small and awkward to perform athletic feats. I became a good student once I fell under the spell of good teachers. I enjoyed the company of my younger twin brother and sister, and I loved my parents, who loved me. Until 1939, when all of us children had departed, our family lived either in New York City or on Long Island.

Like their forebears, my parents were decent, though undistinguished, people. My paternal grandparents were immigrant Jews:

my grandfather, Gustave Blum, was a French-speaking Alsatian who fled the Bosche in 1871; my grandmother, Laura Klee, was German. Both my maternal grandparents, Rose Rice and Alexander LeVino, were born in Virginia. ("LeVino" was a variant of Levin or Levine.) My father, Morton G. Blum, a remote but caring man, had a small talent as an inventor but none as a salesman, his primary occupation. He never completed high school. My mother, Edna L. Blum, attended Hunter College for a year or two and harbored large ambitions for her children, ambitions requiring higher education for their fulfillment. Both my parents rejected Judaism and never practiced it. My mother found a substitute for spirituality by joining the Ethical Culture Society, an essentially secular organization that endorsed the Ten Commandments. Bourgeois to the core, and Republican, my parents identified with common American middle-class values and aspirations even after the Great Depression left them just about penniless. My father managed after a fashion, partly by borrowing money and partly by running up debts, which he did not repay.

A friend of my mother's recommended that she try to obtain a scholarship for me at Phillips Academy in Andover, Massachusetts. She did; I was accepted; and in 1935 I left home for school, never wholly to return. So my history with history began at Andover.

I

Andover

Founded in 1778, Phillips Academy in Andover, Massachusetts, had a long history and a deserved reputation as a leading
American boarding school for boys. Every year since its founding
it had enrolled some boys who needed financial aid to attend, as I
did. The school, as big as any of its rivals while I was there, included
some seven hundred students with about a hundred of them in the
junior, or first, year. (The ensuing years were called lower middle,
upper middle, and senior.) Andover had strict rules of behavior and
high academic standards, but within those constraints it cultivated
a studied regard for the independence of its students. The juniors
were subjected to more supervision than the older classes and to a
more systematic introduction to the mores and expectations of the
institution. But even the juniors had to handle their peer relationships and their emotional problems on their own. Half the class was
segregated in Williams Hall, a dormitory equipped with its own dining hall, supervised by a master, his wife, and two proctors. They
presided at meals, where any lapse in table manners resulted in ex-
pulsion from the hall, a punishment I was subjected to on several
occasions when I refused to eat beets or turnips.

Andover was then quintessentially male, Victorian in its values
and Republican in its politics, though some of the younger masters
were quietly New Dealers. Calvin Coolidge, argued headmaster
Claude Moore Fuess in his biography of that president, was a great
and good man. Students were to address the masters as "sir"; or by
their family name—for example, "Mr. Ling"; or, where applicable,
as "Doctor"—as in Dr. Darling, a history master. (We did not then
know that the younger faculty considered the insistence on the title

"Doctor" an affectation on the part of those with a Ph.D.; nor did we know that that usage was considered gauche at universities.) Phillips Academy was established to teach its students "the great end and real business of living," as its founder said, and to produce "the better sort of men." In 1935 it still believed in the stiff upper lip, hard work, clean living, and high character. One respected Latin master explained the school's mission: to educate "a handful of men who . . . are able to make their own decisions and are willing to abide the consequences." The headmaster made frequent, mumbled comparison at daily chapel of "Andover men and Pomfret boys" (Pomfret being a small boarding school in Connecticut). We all understood what he meant. An Andover man was to do his job, no matter how hard, and to do it well.

Fortunately I had the rudimentary qualities for survival at Andover: I came from a loving and supportive family. My parents had instructed me in proper deportment and rewarded academic performance. I had also had some experience in living away from home, and I had enjoyed it. Though something of a loner, I had made my way among my peers. And I had a sound grounding (though no more than that) in the subjects that I would have to study. More important, books—especially fiction and works of history—had already become a significant element in my life.

I realized, however, that I lacked the qualities most important to some of my fellow students. Most of the wealthier students valued social standing and money, which translated as being upper middle class and WASP; appearance, which included proper clothing and a handsome visage; and athletic prowess. The most favored contests occurred in football, baseball, and track and field—the "major sports" in which Phillips Academy (in Andover, Massachusetts) and Phillips Exeter Academy (in nearby Exeter, New Hampshire) battled every year before a partisan assembly composed of all the students of both rival schools. Participation in those contests was beyond my reach. And I had none of the other desirable attributes. My family lived in genteel poverty, and was no less Jewish for its rejection of Judaism; at Andover Jews were admitted, but were not yet first-class citizens. My wardrobe was as sparse as my purse was inadequate. As one classmate and lifelong friend fondly reminded me years later, I "didn't have two nickels to rub together."

In 1935 I was also just about the smallest boy in the school, though thereafter I grew a little and some students matriculated who were even smaller than I. Worse, I had no athletic talents, not even reliable eye-to-hand coordination. For intramural athletics the school divided students into four clubs —Gauls, Greeks, Romans, and Saxons. Early in the first term, the juniors stood alongside a wall in the gym while the head of each club selected his new members. Predictably, I was among the last four chosen, and went by default to the Gauls. Also of necessity glued much of every day to my studies, I was an outstanding candidate for becoming known, in the parlance of the day, as a "drip." In short, at first I was a marginal member of the Andover community. As a result, socially I found the first year a struggle. After two years, however, I felt very much at home.

In those first two years at Andover I distanced myself from my parents sufficiently to fit on my own terms into my society of peers. Though this process of maturation is normal for adolescents, my mother fought a rearguard action against it. She wanted me to be content and successful at Andover, but at the same time she wanted to keep me in her grasp. She clung to her sons. So it was on the afternoon my parents delivered me to Williams Hall. As I settled into my assigned room, my father gave me five dollars for expenses and my mother made me promise to write twice every week. (I did so until 1946, always avoiding mention of anything truly meaningful to me, dutifully reporting some academic triumph or the score of a recent sporting event.) They then departed, as soon did I, joining two other new boys for a walk to the nearest stationery store, where most of my five dollars evaporated.

On returning I was astonished to find my parents. Mother had persuaded my father to return and check to be sure I wasn't homesick. I wasn't, nor was I ever. But I was glad for the opportunity to request another five dollars. Later during that school year Mother visited for two days, living in some local bed-and-breakfast and interrogating the dean and several instructors about my performance. She approved, she told me—especially of my English teacher, a recent Harvard graduate who brushed his hair back on both sides, as I should. Though I agreed with my mother's assessment of my English teacher—I admired his crisp manner and neat bow ties—I was mortified by her visit. Perhaps sensing my discomfiture, perhaps satisfied by her reconnaissance, she returned to Andover only once more before my commencement in June 1939.

My father asked me no questions, ever, even on our drives to or from Andover. I gradually discovered that his financial arrangements with the school were parlous at best. Room, board, and tuition came to $1,100 a year, and some pocket money was essential for books and supplies, as well as for an occasional hamburger and Coke. I received no allowance, and responses to my requests for cash were erratic. After the Christmas holidays I found myself a job in the alumni office and thereafter I earned my own pocket money, about which my embarrassed father never inquired.

On Prize Day, the last morning assembly of my first year, I was awarded a scholarship of $300 for the next year. When I reported the news to my parents, I could see at once that they were crestfallen. In the weeks that followed, I learned by repeated questioning of my mother that Father was essentially broke. He had prospered briefly in 1934 and 1935, but had never received most of his commissions from his employer. During my first year he had depended on a $500 scholarship to meet my Andover expenses. For my lower middle year, the school was going to reduce my scholarship to $300 but would assign me a regular responsibility that paid $300 into my account —thus $600 in all. Father was to pay the balance, but he could not afford to, so he fell into debt to the school. I knew nothing of that debt.

Needing to make money, I contrived ways to do so. At that time scholarships at Andover depended partly on need but heavily on grades. So it was essential for me to maintain an average of at least 85, the minimum requirement for making the second honor roll. (I never dared aspire to the first honor roll, which required an average of 90.) My anxieties about grades were not misplaced: I ordinarily did little better than 80 in science and foreign languages, so I had to compensate by excelling in math, English, and history. For me, attaining good grades required steady, hard work, and I spent my abundant energy at my desk and in the library. Linking financial aid to academic performance, I was to discover, distorts the learning process: too much depends on grades and too little on intellectual discovery.

I also sold contracts for a nearby laundry service and subscriptions to the *New York Herald Tribune*. I sold and delivered firewood. I hawked hot dogs at football games and ice cream at baseball games. In my senior year, I was hired by a General Motors vice president to tutor his son, a fellow student, in American history. In most of these enterprises I worked as a junior partner of an impecunious classmate, a natural entrepreneur who became not a business executive but a social worker.

I was earning enough in 1937 to take about $200 to the school treasurer for deposit in my account. It was then that I learned about my father's growing debt to the school, which would total about $1,800 by the time I graduated. The treasurer made it clear that he did not trust my father, so I said I would assume the debt. He also told me that I would not receive my diploma until I had repaid the debt. (I did so in 1945, while the United States Navy was providing me with a generous monthly check for which I had little use in the western Pacific.) After my meeting with the treasurer, I discussed the matter with my father. He told me he was sorry, that he had a sick wife (which was true—a heart attack and a stroke) and two other children to support, so he simply could not afford Andover. He also said that I was free to do as I pleased about the school. He was being honest with me, and I was grateful, for my knowing the facts cleared the way for me to continue at Andover, my first objective, and reduced the financial pressure my parents felt then and thereafter.

Of course I remained a minor, dependent still on my parents during summer months and needing their support as I always had. The summers of 1936 and 1937 I spent with my brother at the beach or on the tennis court. In the summer of 1938 I lived at home, then in Manhattan, where I worked at the Metropolitan Museum of Art. In 1939 I worked at the *Herald Tribune* in the circulation department (I remember that our sales objective was always to beat the *Times*).

But at Andover I was glad to be on my own. My sense of financial independence soared when I undertook the job the school assigned me in 1936–37 and again in 1937–38. The school considered me too small to wait on tables, so instead every evening I delivered infirmary slips. The master in charge of each dormitory was responsible for knowing the whereabouts of all the students in his charge. So when a student was admitted to the infirmary, a slip was sent so informing the student's dormitory master, a process repeated when the student was discharged. It fell to me to deliver those slips, which gave me the opportunity to walk about the glorious campus, beautiful in both setting and architecture. The sky, too, was often beautiful, with the northern lights sometimes illuminating the sky on crisp autumn evenings and a bright moon often erasing the stars over the winter snows.

My job allowed me ample time for reflection and took me in a typical week to every corner of the campus, which I came to know and savor, indeed in a private sense to possess. I moved briskly in order to get back to my studies, but I relished the routes down Main Street and School Street, where some of the lower middle houses stood. I circled the upper middle quadrangle and strode along the paths that connected the senior dormitories, two of them handsome early-nineteenth-century structures, and brought the main classroom buildings into view. In the process I passed under the arch of elms fronting the art museum and the library, crossed over toward the gymnasium and the satisfying symmetry of Bulfinch Hall, named for its great architect. I doubled back toward his other building, Pearson Hall, and thus to the quadrangle behind it and forward of the Commons. Along my route, high on the campus, I could see from almost any angle the glowing blue clock that shone on four faces from the tower atop Samuel Phillips Hall. The palpable, physical aspect of my increasingly beloved school engraved itself in my consciousness. I was becoming—I could feel it—an Andover man.

Central to that development were my classmates, especially those who became my friends, some for life. In my junior year I made no close friends. But another Jewish boy, an excellent student, and I spent some time together and decided to be roommates the next year. We were drawn to each other initially by our common response to the aggressive anti-Semitism of two Williams Hall neighbors, who were roommates. Bullying was not uncommon at the school, but the boys who attacked me made it clear that they disdained Jews. The Williams Hall pair always attacked a single victim. They began with verbal abuse, which soon escalated to physical attacks. Since both were bigger and stronger than I, there was little point in resisting. When I tried to, I was quickly subdued or, in one instance, blamed by a proctor for creating a disturbance. Of course the unwritten student code ruled out reporting the matter to any master.

My two attackers in our lower year were assigned to Abbot House — the same dormitory as I was. I told them at once that I would tolerate no more physical punishment, and to my surprised gratification, thereafter they left me alone. (In retrospect I should have struck the same posture a year earlier.) But now they picked on another Jewish boy, who reported their conduct to his mother. She in turn asked my mother about anti-Semitism at Andover. To my chagrin, Mother arrived at the school to interrogate both the headmaster and me about the issue. I denied that there was a problem, and so did Claude Fuess, the head, who may have been self-deluded where I was instead simply a liar, protecting my privacy. I was resolved to handle anti-Semitism my own way in my own time. The student on whom my former tormentors had fastened left Andover at the end of the academic year.

In my remaining years at the school I experienced little anti-Semitism, though to my knowledge no Jewish student was invited to join a fraternity. Perhaps to spare my feelings, I attributed that exclusion not to my classmates but to the alumni of the various fraternities. Still, the abolition of fraternities after World War II did serve democracy at Andover. Among the faculty I sensed no prejudice except in the case of one mathematics master of German descent. He went out of his way to tell me when the Munich agreement was announced in 1938 how pleased he was with the resulting German gains. I swore at him — a dumb move: he reported me to the dean, the head summoned me, and in private in his office heard my account, awarded me a painless demerit, and sent me on my way.

But Andover, like most — perhaps all — other boarding schools at that time, had no Jews on the faculty and, to my knowledge, no Catholics as well. Indeed, there were few if any tenured Jews or Catholics on the arts and sciences faculties of elite colleges — Harvard, Yale, Princeton, and Dartmouth, for examples. On Sundays Phillips Academy required attendance at morning chapel with its Congregational service. Catholic students were allowed instead to go as a group to a church in town, but no Jewish services were available. Though that was a matter of indifference for me, it offended some other Jewish students and was another example of the prejudice that made Jews at Andover uneasy.

The friends I began to make in Abbot House, I was happy to note, treated me no differently from the way in which they treated each other. We were high-spirited fifteen-year-olds, for the most part conspirators determined to have a somewhat naughty good time. Abbot House contained about eight double rooms on two floors above the residence of the presiding master, who was by reputation something of a tyrant and who happened to have a wooden leg. We suspected that his reputation was mythic, for at one house meeting he asked us please not to throw empty Coke bottles out the windows for, as he put it, "my wife makes me pick them up." He served us cider and doughnuts while we listened to his radio on election night in 1936 when it became apparent by ten o'clock that Franklin Delano Roosevelt would win reelection in a landslide. Hardly the behavior of a tyrant!

But we pretended to dread him, which gave an extra thrill to our successful efforts quietly to break all the school rules we disdained. So it was that several of us, myself included, regularly smoked cigarettes—forbidden fruit—while lying with our heads in the fireplace and blowing the smoke up the chimney. Two roommates on the third floor now and then sipped Scotch whiskey, also of course forbidden, to the strains of the 1812 Overture. (The school outlawed radios but allowed victrolas, most of which were committed to contemporary swing music.) One memorable Saturday evening, after the weekly movie, Jack Walsh, our most handsome and gallant housemate, used a window fire escape—a rope with a sling on it by which a student could lower himself to the ground—to hoist up a young woman, a student at nearby Abbot Academy who lived at home in town. She sat for about ten minutes in a morris chair in Jack's room while we took turns saying hello and watching the stairway on the chance that the dormitory master might materialize. Then we lowered her down and celebrated our success in having had a pretty girl in a dorm where the only women allowed were mothers. Tobacco, booze, and our best approximation of sex—no wonder that in our class book at graduation a group of us defined Abbot House as our greatest experience at Andover.

Abbot House brought our group together and we moved on, still together, to dormitories for upper middlers and then for seniors. The others all went to Yale for their undergraduate degrees, whereas I went to Harvard. During our Andover and college years, I spent many vacation evenings with Jack Pulleyn, notable for his bawdy songs and unfailing good humor. Our families resided in New York City, mine from 1937 through 1941. Our paths crossed only once after World War II, in the New Haven railroad station, where Jack was running to catch the train from which I had disembarked. "Hey," he called out, "are you still a Yankees fan?" "Of course!" I answered before he disappeared. Obviously the Yankees had become part of my identity at Andover. As students Jack and I rode the New York subways to their various destinations, boarded the upper decks of Fifth Avenue buses for cooling rides to Washington Heights, and downed Scotch whiskey with no chasers, twenty-five cents a drink, at the Silver Dollar bar in Times Square. Both of us were tone deaf, but this did not deter our robust singing of football fight songs.

On occasion in New York we were joined by Gordon Tuttle, who came in from suburban New Jersey. Later a lawyer and corporate counsel, Gordon was an incomparable listener, a wise man who was at once quietly intelligent and equally laid back. He and Jack and I, with different friends as a fourth, frequently played bridge together, almost invariably on the train from Boston to New York for vacations. Two other close friends from Abbot House were George Wagoner and Jack Walsh, both later insurance executives, both handsome youths whom girls found attractive, George imperturbable, Jack volatile. For more than sixty years we four remained as companionable as we had always been. We came in time to meet the wives our friends had wooed. At school, in twos and threes and fours, we engaged in "bull sessions," talking about girls but not about sex, for we did not know much about sex. We listened to Walsh as he read aloud selections from the letters he had received from any number of girls. We were, I think, at once admiring and a mite jealous of his distant harem. We talked about sports. And we talked about our schoolmates and our teachers, comparing views about who was and who was not a "good guy" and why.

We attended athletic events in twos and threes to cheer Walsh, who won varsity letters in football, track, and baseball, and to cheer Pulleyn, who set a school record in the fifty-yard free-style swim. On those occasions, and simply walking to and from Commons or later relaxing outside of the senior dorms, we teenagers gradually bonded. In the usage of a later time, we hung out together. Though we had in common our shared experience, we were very different from each other. Pulleyn and Walsh were gifted athletes, Tuttle and Wagoner were competent at recreational sports, and I was a klutz. Three of us needed financial aid while two were comparatively rich. Two of the group were Catholic and the others (except for me) were Protestant, but religion never seemed to matter. I made other good friends at Andover, two of them later successful academicians: Elias Clark, who became a professor of law at Yale, and Henry Terrie, a Dartmouth professor specializing in American literature.

The aim of Phillips Academy, according to its founder, was to prepare its students for the serious business of living. That objective required more than just studying. Serious living, as we were told again and again, entailed a readiness to assume and discharge responsibilities to oneself and to one's community, whether family or school or ultimately town and country. *Finis origine pendet*, read the school's motto: "The end depends upon the beginning." And *non sibi* — "not for oneself." Andover provided various opportunities for its students to meet these expectations. As a senior I was assigned as a clerk in the office of the registrar, a gentle lady of many years. She could seem formidable but treated me always like a valued nephew. More important, I was proud that the work I did really helped her manage her office. Eager for at least a vicarious role in varsity sports, I also volunteered to become an assistant manager of the soccer team, and was elected by the team to be manager in my senior year.

That year I was also associate editor of the literary magazine, *The Mirror*. The other senior editors did most of the work while I went along for the ride. The magazine had published a short story I wrote in 1937, inspired by Nathaniel Hawthorne's notebook writings, which I had discovered while browsing in the school library. Hawthorne mused about how a soft breeze could have at once a casual and a profound meaning, for example to a farmer who watched it winnowing his grain and to the captain of a schooner trying to outrun a pirate ship. I stole his idea without attribution, though I wrote the story in my own words. Publication of my work thus provoked conflicting feelings of great joy and great guilt.

Also in our senior year I was a member of the debating team that beat Exeter, but that victory owed most to my teammate, an accomplished orator. In the spring of 1939 he and I took the affirmative on the question of whether, in the event of war, Great Britain and France could defeat Germany without American participation. We won, but an Exeter master came up to me afterward to tell me that we would prove to be very wrong. He was correct, of course, as I came to realize within the year.

My extracurricular experiences were surely useful, but Andover was above all a school, with formal education central to its mission. And formal education was central to my life in my four years there. Some of the ablest teachers at Phillips Academy — dynamic, talented, generous men — introduced me to the life of the mind. That introduction affected the rest of my days and began to shape my choice of profession.

The Andover faculty included some dull and ineffective time-servers, some classroom characters, and perhaps a dozen outstanding teachers. In my first two years at the school I studied under dull men except for a few characters. My first-year math instructor, a man of some sixty years, improved algebra with his quiet wit. In my second year Richard Gummere, Jr., a recent Harvard graduate, tried to teach Latin, largely Caesar, without addressing syntax, an omission for which we were all grateful at the time. Eager to avoid the scrutiny of his elders, "Buzz," an elegant young man, often arrived at morning class through a basement window and in his dinner jacket after a night on the town in Boston. We enjoyed reading Shaw's *Caesar and Cleopatra* aloud with him while the subjunctive languished. Twenty years later my wife and I briefly visited Buzz at Bard College, where he was then dean of admissions, an office he later held at Teachers' College, Columbia. "John," he told me during that visit, "every morning I wake up, go in to shave, look into the mirror, and say to myself: 'Buzz, you lucky bastard, you don't have to teach today.'" Like many other young, educated, and able men, he had had to teach during the 1930s because there were no other available jobs.

In my second year at last I had one teacher who made an intellectual difference: A. Graham Baldwin, the school's gentle Congregational pastor, who taught a mandatory Bible course. Gray Baldwin, in later years a personal friend, presided at Sunday chapel, where he frequently sermonized on themes related to the Social Gospel, which mixed "muscular Christianity" with social reform. That outlook, ebullient in 1900, by 1936 was in a state of entropy. In Bible class Gray treated both Old and New Testaments as literature to be understood, not as sacred script. He sensed without my informing him that I was uncomfortable with the texts we examined, mainly because they were largely new to me. So he soon provided opportunities for us to chat privately. By the end of the term I had told him how much I disliked the God of the Old Testament, the God who punished Job for no good reason, who was said to set one people apart as his chosen few, who inspired prophets to rant about the kind of human behavior that remained common as reported in the daily press.

I had then, and ever since have had, trouble with the concept of sin and even more trouble with the idea of salvation. I wanted no part of any supernatural force, which I certainly could not worship. So I was equally uncomfortable with the God of the New Testament, who led his supposed son to death in order to save true believers from an eternal damnation in which I could not believe. And the miracles—the virgin birth, the resurrection, the loaves and fishes—struck me as mystical, metaphysical myths, incomprehensible to me in my secular outlook. Bible study set me against organized religion in the Judeo-Christian tradition but not against the ethical principles of the Decalogue, which seemed to me to prescribe sensible rules for communal behavior.

Gray and I talked about such matters as long as I was at school. He made a strong case for the historical bases of the Old Testament and for the metaphorical significance of the articles of Christian faith. But I remained unconvinced, and he accepted this. Indeed he enrolled me in Circle A, an organization of students over which he presided. The only duty of Circle A was to meet with distinguished visitors to Andover, listen to them talk, and ask them questions. This gave me the chance to sit at the feet for an hour or so of several extraordinary men—Robert Frost, Frank Lloyd Wright, and Henry Stimson, then Andover's senior trustee, a man whose public career had already evoked my admiration.

One day in my senior year Gray Baldwin quoted a prayer that expressed the secular spirit he rejected. "Oh, God," that prayer began, "if there is a God, I feel no need of Thee." I wrote him a note that afternoon to say that these words encapsulated my own thinking. Thanking me for my letter, he wondered how long I would continue to feel as I did. The answer, though I did not then know it, proved to be about six years, until naval duty in the Pacific. In the interval I wrote Gray a letter of utmost importance to me. I asked him if it was proper for me, an unbelieving Jew, to propose marriage to an Episcopalian woman who had never experienced anti-Semitism. He replied that if I loved her, of course it was all right. So a month later I proposed to the young woman and we were married within the year. I hope that my soliciting Gray's support for the major decision of my life made Gray realize how much I valued his counsel.

In my upper middle year at Andover five times a week I trembled at the figure of Frank Benton, a veteran teacher of Latin and Greek who served also as line coach of the football team. On autumn afternoons you could hear Porky Benton's stentorian, southern voice for miles around shouting out to one of his linemen: "Yo' base, Lyford, yo' base!" At the foot of his desk I heard him shout at me: "Yo' voibs, Mister Blum, yo' voibs!" I was paying my dues to Porky and Cicero for a lazy preceding year of Caesar, but I learned from Porky enough Latin for any three years. "Man's greatest blessing," Porky told me as I worried through his exams, "is that he can't see the future." I did not want to see my grade. Then in his forties, Frank Benton was tough in manner but soft inside, and no boy who studied under him ever forgot his manner. "You call me sir," he said, "and I'll call you sir." He did and we did.

During that year a required course was the history of art, for which Andover provided an extraordinary facility, the Addison Gallery of American

Art. It also provided two splendid teachers. Charles Sawyer, director of the gallery, taught us architecture in one term and painting in the next. He gave particular attention to the Parthenon and the cathedral at Chartres, and to the painting of the Florentine Renaissance and the French Impressionists. Art became a part of my life. It was Charles who arranged my summer at the Metropolitan Museum. As a senior I elected a course Sawyer shared with Bart Hayes, who at that time was in charge of studio art. Later, at Harvard, I enrolled in several semesters of art history, one of them on twentieth-century painting. And on my second date with my wife-to-be, we spent an afternoon at the Museum of Modern Art in New York. We have since spent many afternoons in many cities in the same way.

I learned from Bart Hayes that I had no more talent for creating works of art than I had for playing baseball. In neither activity could I approach the major leagues. But Bart did teach me to see. One day he held up a water-color, a seascape by John Marin, and asked us to comment about it. At first it simply puzzled me. Then Bart suggested different ways of looking at it. He pointed to Marin's use of a glasslike plane to indicate perspective. He suggested the importance of the visual relationships among colors. Within fifteen minutes of observation and discussion under his tutelage all four students in the class had become converts. From that day forward contemporary painting has afforded me the special satisfactions arising from visual understanding based on close examination.

The teacher who most influenced me at Andover was Alan Blackmer. A slender man of middle height, a graduate of Williams College, Alan was a schoolmaster later much honored for his contributions to secondary education. In the 1950s Alan and I became personal friends; in the 1930s he was one of my mentors. Officially Alan taught third-year English, but his true calling was teaching his students how to think. He did so as we sat around an oblong table in a newly refurbished seminar room. Along the way we read great literature, *Macbeth* and the *Alcestis* of Euripides, for example, and *War and Peace*, on which we spent some weeks. Like Tolstoy, Alan made the novel much more than the story of Natasha and Pierre. He made it a laboratory for the study of love, power, and war. I recall reading it with fascination late into the night, so late one cold winter evening that my house master knocked on my door, entered, and scolded me for not getting enough sleep.

Alan taught ideas. Under his guidance we studied the *Meditations* of Marcus Aurelius. It was my first exposure to philosophy. The tenor of the text fit the outlook of the academy and communicated Alan's intended message for his students: "If you apply yourself to the task before you, following right reason seriously, vigorously, calmly . . . you will live happily" and "The mind that is free from passion is a citadel." For me, trying at that time to understand what formal religion had never told me, Marcus Aurelius offered reassurance: "I am a part of the whole that is governed by nature." He also reinforced a secular connection Andover was trying to communicate: civic virtue was anchored in the personal virtue of each citizen.

Another text Alan assigned was James Harvey Robinson's *The Mind in the Making*. It left an enduring impression on my developing consciousness, precisely as Alan had intended. Rereading that book many years later, and reading also my marginalia, I was stunned to realize how much I had begun at seventeen to absorb a manner of thought that I retained, though not without some severe doubts and modifications, for the rest of my life. Published in 1921, *The Mind in the Making* became a best seller at a time when debunking conventional thinking was a major intellectual exercise. Robinson's outlook was shared by other distinguished thinkers of the time, including historian Charles Beard and philosopher John Dewey. He and they were in vogue while Alan Blackmer was in college. So in assigning Robinson in 1938 Alan was flattering his students with an author who had spoken importantly to him. Perhaps in the culture of Phillips Academy both were at least mildly subversive.

A professional historian, Robinson also spoke to me. He rejected western religion as based upon superstition. He looked instead to rationality, specifically to the inductive method — the method of the natural sciences — as the appropriate basis for understanding. For him the dispassionate writing and study of history provided a telling example of induction. His kind of "scientific" history, I came to see, would conform to the reigning standard, history as it actually was — von Ranke's *"wie es eigentlich gewesen ist."* That was the kind of history I aspired to write for the next several years, until I realized it could not be done. Robinson's kind of history had a mission: to relate the past to the present, especially to the obtrusive issues of the present. That purpose made dispassionate history even more difficult to write than it would otherwise have been, a fact I had yet to realize.

Robinson critiqued acquisitive society, specifically America in the age of the robber barons and the renaissance of that age in the America of the 1920s. He fashioned a proudly anti-business tract, which resembled Beard's work, and which was spiritually the precursor of the dominant academic culture of the New Deal years. He also attacked prejudice, especially anti-radical prejudice, which was expressed in his day during the Red scare that had followed World War I. The intellectuals with whom Robinson associated himself included Marx, Freud, Keynes, and Lippmann, all of them soon to become familiar to me, all of them in Robinson's view "scientific" thinkers. Later, at Harvard, studying the writings of those titans, I leaned to two of them, Keynes and Lippmann. But I had absorbed from Robinson a more general message. Then and later Robinson — and Alan Blackmer, too —were for me apostles of a self-consciously skeptical intelligence, the kind of intelligence I was eager to develop.

In retrospect I realize that James Harvey Robinson, through Alan Blackmer, unknowingly shaped my part of the dialogue I engaged in the following year with Gray Baldwin. Alan's immediate influence grew in my senior year when he and his wonderful wife, Josephine, on whom I had a powerful crush, invited me to join the company that met on some Sunday evenings for supper in their home. One other senior was among that group, an exchange student who had just completed his studies at Christ's Hospital, a secondary school in England. Years later he became the obstetrician for Queen Elizabeth II. To the best of my memory, the others at the table were young members of the faculty.

Alan and Jo Blackmer set the informal agenda for those evenings of good conversation. They were a revelation for me, for I had never before participated in anything like them. We talked about current issues, among them the trembling peace in Europe and the currents of contemporary literature. Alan one Sunday mentioned a poem by T. S. Eliot and suggested we all read some of that author's early work. The next time we met, *Prufrock* and *The Hollow Men* provided the subjects of discussion, which led to an evening on Freud's theory about the interpretation of dreams. Eliot and Freud, and with them Ernest Jones, never previously my acquaintances, were heady stuff, and I listened much more than I contributed to the discourse during and after dinner. I was learning that one could really live the life of the mind, in one's home and with friends. It was my first, inviting exposure to genteel intellectuality.

In my fourth year at Andover I had the good fortune to study with two other men who made a lasting difference in my life — Arthur W. Leonard and Wilbur Bender. Mr. Leonard, the chairman of the English department, was then approaching retirement. Behind his back his colleagues called him "Honey" because he was so sweet. In class he focused on great literature and careful exegesis of the text. So it was that we spent three months of concentrated study on *Hamlet,* with Mr. Leonard joyfully rendering Polonius. Toward the end of the fall term I participated in an annual contest in declamation. Each contestant was to read an original essay he had written. The faculty judges, of whom Mr. Leonard was one, awarded the prize to another senior. As we started back to our dormitories, Mr. Leonard asked me to come to see him after class the next day. When I did so, he said to me, "You don't know how to speak, do you?"

Always loquacious, I was stunned by his remark. Mr. Leonard offered to spend an hour privately with me one evening a week. During these sessions he had me talk into a wire recorder, then a new device, and he corrected my pronunciation. He was my Henry Higgins. Mr. Leonard's generosity still moves me deeply. We put in several months with the wire recorder while he reminded me to sound the first "h" in "which," to say "you" with a long "u" and not a flat "a" — and much more that was designed to expunge New York from my speech. He taught me to modulate my voice, to pay attention to proper breathing, pace, and elocution. Playing back to me what I had said into the wire recorder, correcting it, and having me say it again, Arthur Leonard taught me how to speak.

When he was satisfied, about the time the spring term began, he conscripted me for the debating team, from which an experienced member had been removed for failing grades. Debating bothered me because the rules forced participants, regardless of their beliefs, to take either side of a stipulated question. But I would have done anything in gratitude to Mr. Leonard. And my gratitude increased when I won a declamation contest in June, a contest requiring each contestant to recite from memory an essay he had written. Mine was entitled "The Luxury of Integrity." And I recalled Mr. Leonard in 1957, when I began to lecture to hundreds of undergraduates for an hour three times a week at Yale, a role for which natural ease and clarity in speaking were essential.

Some thirty years younger than Mr. Leonard, Wilbur Bender instructed me in American history during my senior year. Andover had made that subject the centerpiece of the senior curriculum. Wilbur, in later years a friend, made the subject throb. He was an unlikely Andover master, a stocky and irreverent Mennonite from Ohio, a Harvard graduate and candidate for the Ph.D. in history, a degree he never completed because after World War II he became an administrator and ultimately a widely celebrated dean of admissions to Harvard College. As a teacher at Andover he interpreted the American past through the liberal lens of historians who were avid Roosevelt Democrats. He assigned mostly textbooks, though on every issue a variety of textbooks so as to expose differences in historical interpretation. Wilbur, I later came to realize, had found his preferred interpretations in books by Claude Bowers on the Federalist era and Reconstruction, Matthew Josephson on the age of the robber barons, and in works by the eminent progressive scholars Charles Beard and Vernon Parrington. The views of those historians and their disciples dominated the profession until my generation of historians came of age after World War II. They saw conflict in the national past, conflict between the people and the moneyed interests, and thus between good and evil; conflict rooted in economic inequality. The past, I would learn after World War II, was more complex than that interpretation allowed.

At Andover Wilbur gently dominated the classes he taught, teased his students to venture interpretations of their own, threw his stocky trunk into the body language of discourse as he threw it across the tennis court, his favorite place — the place where, at the end, rushing to the net, he died. He tolerated discussion of some outlandish student views but not any defense of slavery or attack on FDR. I relished every minute of American history classes, admired Wilbur and his ideas, and did my best work at Andover in his course.

He must have thought highly of me, for he invited me to call on him one evening in January and then brought up the subject of college. I told him that I had no firm plans for college. I had supposed in the worst case that I could get some scholarship at Columbia and live with my parents, who at that time resided across the street from the campus. He rejected that idea. I was going, he told me, to Harvard. Indeed he had made an appointment for me on the next Wednesday afternoon to see his friend, Henry Chauncey, the Harvard dean of major scholarships. Mr. Chauncey would tell me what steps to take.

I had dared only to dream of going to Harvard, a university I held in awe but, as I saw it, could not possibly afford. Henry Chauncey explained that I could. If I did well on a set of examinations he described, among them the ordinary college board exams of that era and the then-new scholastic aptitude tests, Harvard would award me a scholarship of $500 and a job waiting on table that paid $300. This income would cover room, board, and tuition, including the infirmary fee. I would need another $200 for personal expenses, but if I could not earn that during the summer, Mr. Chauncey held, I had no business thinking about Harvard anyway. It worked out exactly as he said it would. And I knew then and always that for my Harvard admission and scholarship the indispensable agent was Wilbur Bender.

By commencement time I was looking forward to college but already felt nostalgic, for Andover had been very good to me and for me. At the final morning assembly I was awarded two prizes for excellence in American history and the scholarship from Harvard that Mr. Chauncey had proposed. My mother, present at the occasion, was all tears when she met me after the assembly adjourned. A week later, following commencement exercises and the completion of my college board examinations, I left Andover to return to New York. In September I would move on to Cambridge and Harvard. But the years at Andover never left me. Over sixty years later I remember best a few good friends and a few splendid teachers. I also believed when I graduated from Andover that I might like to teach history, in which I intended to major at Harvard, but I presumed that, as a Jew, I could not expect employment at Phillips Academy.

That exclusion seemed to me at the time a tolerable liability. It was offset by the results of the polls taken by the editors of the class yearbook. Those results, to my surprise and delight, revealed that my classmates by and large respected me. They considered me an able student, a young man destined for success, and even the head of an unnamed political party. The liability was also offset by the legacy the school had deeded me. I tried to describe that legacy in an essay I contributed to a small book Claude Fuess edited in 1959, *In My Time: A Medley of Andover Reminiscences.* What I wrote then still expresses my memory of the Phillips experience:

> There were the blue clock, praetorian of punctuality; the Palladian windows, signatures of measured grace; the rows of elms, testament to grace's age; the ashen stands, coliseums for the passive. . . . Above all . . . was the vista, the long prospect turning out and back again into the life of the mind. That was Andover: an end to innocence.
>
> Innocence did not crumble. It retreated in a series of identical engagements, each a sequence of resistance first, then confusion, then excitement, then perception. . . . One [master] stood four yards away from us, a seascape in his hands. It seemed a maze of blues and greens and planes of glass. Marin was not art, we said. Art rang eight bells, or placed a lintel neatly on two posts, or stroked a canvas with the fullness of a brush. He . . . pointed to this line, that space. We . . . saw. . . .
>
> Around an oblong table Natasha met Pierre, Aurelian mused, Alcestis dared. Neither memory nor rote replaced elucidation at that table. Disarmed, we stumbled . . . surprised ourselves, and thought. In other rooms America expanded beyond the Hill. The record of the past, no longer only names and dates, received its shape from current ruminations. It could change . . . and we could change it. . . . The mind contains the past but may not safely live there.

That was the mark of Andover.

2

Veritas

We were the perfect class in number, exactly 1,000, so President James B. Conant told us when we first assembled, standing in the dining hall of the Harvard Union in September 1939. Then he introduced Archibald MacLeish, eminent American poet, Harvard Law School graduate, Librarian of Congress. MacLeish, a distinguished veteran of World War I, greeted us: "Gentlemen, you are the class of 1918." The war in Europe had just begun with Hitler's invasion of Poland and the British and French decision to fight rather than yield again. When I had listened at home to radio reports of the invasion earlier that month, for the first time in my life I had seen my father weep. Now, newly arrived at Harvard, I heard some of my classmates boo MacLeish. They did not want to go to war. No sane man could have wanted to. But a small minority of the class, of which I was one, could foresee no way to avoid war without surrendering to fascism. I had abandoned my earlier hope that England and France could manage without American aid and involvement. I feared Japan, too, exactly as Henry Stimson had warned us to in his discussions at Andover. Indeed as a freshman I predicted that we would be at war with Japan before my class graduated.

It was an unpopular forecast, but appeared more and more likely as the months passed. The war sat like a growing weight on our college years. With the German advance in western Europe in the spring of 1940, the war became for me something of an obsession, as it did for many Jews, potential victims of Nazi persecution, and eventually for all Americans who were friends of freedom. Gradually the war entered our undergraduate lives, our hopes and fears.

We could not avoid the penumbra of the war, but at the same time we had to manage the business of growing up while attending college.

I had looked forward to Harvard with great expectations. My decision to apply there was the most important decision I had made. I acted without consulting my parents, for I knew they were uninformed about higher education and, with Harvard's help, I would be paying my own way. I also decided on Harvard without exploring alternatives. I did not even visit other campuses, though I could have joined more than a hundred of my Andover classmates in going to Yale, which offered me a generous scholarship. But as much as possible (and although thirty-four of my Andover classmates also chose Harvard), I wanted to strike out on my own. When I first informed my parents of my choice in April 1939, my mother took my word for it that Harvard was the best place for me, but my father objected, saying that among the businessmen he knew, the Yale graduates stood out. I replied that I had no intention of becoming a businessman, though I refrained from saying that I wanted a less risky and more intellectual career as a historian. In my naïveté, I believed that academic life would assure such qualities. I also believed—again naïvely—that Andover had prepared me to handle with ease whatever Harvard, or for that matter life, might demand of me.

As a result, I had a great deal of growing up to do during my freshman year. The year crawled by while I made one adolescent mistake after another, usually wrongly assuming that someone else was at fault. In my senior year at Andover, I had belatedly realized that I wanted some nice girl to care about me. But I knew no girls except for my sister and a few of her friends, none of whom I found appealing. I arranged several dates with a girl I had known in junior high school, but she clearly had other interests.

At Harvard, I yearned for a friendship with a pretty, bright, sympathetic young woman. Finding none, I blamed my awkwardness on four years at an all-male school. Andover, I concluded, had not prepared its students for normal heterosexual society, or for the emotional aspects of life in general. On the former score, I may have been correct. Eventually the school merged with its neighboring Abbot Academy, to the benefit of students at both institutions. But as a collegian I had yet to learn that no formal education prepared one for handling emotional problems. I would have to work those out on my own.

In fact, I did not work hard at anything during my freshman year at Harvard. As a student waiter in the Harvard Union, my performance was rather reluctant and sometimes desultory, though not so bad as to cause any trouble. It was the same with the athletic program. I should have taken advantage of the splendid facilities for tennis and squash, or some other recreational sport. Instead I hung out with the track squad. I tried to qualify as a sprinter, but I was too slow, cut too many practices, and smoked too many cigarettes to make the grade. I counted on Andover momentum to see me through Harvard courses, but they required more effort for success than I expended. In retrospect I can conclude only that I was in the midst of a silent adolescent rebellion against the rigors of academic excellence.

But all was not lost. Among the other student waiters and their friends, a talented and ambitious group, I came to know half a dozen with whom I discussed history during the rest of our days as undergraduates. So it was also at track practice. Though I could not perform at varsity standards, I met classmates who could. Several of them became my closest friends at Harvard. They included Truman Mitchell Ford, "Mike" to us and his many fans, a nationally ranked pole-vaulter and a housemate of mine in our senior year. Mike and I played bridge, ate meals, and drank many beers together. Mike introduced me to the frivolous but attractive young ladies at the Garland School of Homemaking in Boston and later, at Smith College, to my future wife. He and two or three others from the track squad moved in and out of my life for many decades, as did several members of the Signet Society, a literary and intellectual club to which I was elected in my junior year.

But as a freshman I had yet to meet the most outstanding members of the class. They included Ben Bradlee, later the courageous editor of the *Washington Post*; Norman Mailer, one of the most talented writers of the century; Eric Larrabee, critic, historian, Centurian extraordinary; Bruce Barton, Jr., later a senior editor of *Time* while still a young man; and Abram Chayes, an international lawyer who served admirably on the New Frontier. Harvard's class of 1943 was a great collection of men, as time would demonstrate; but as a freshman I had yet to realize how able were my classmates and how hard I would have to work to keep up with them.

Harvard was not free of anti-Semitism, but after Andover I was more or less inured to it. Still, it bothered me that I could identify no tenured faculty member who was Jewish except for the professor of Semitic studies. That would change slowly only after the war. Further, Harvard had openly discriminated against Jews in its admission policies in the 1920s, and these policies had been approved by then-President A. Lawrence Lowell. Even in 1932 it was a college, as one of my proper Bostonian friends put it, of "cousins and uncles." President Conant, striving for geographical diversity in admissions, designated national scholarships — sizeable grants of $1,200 a year — for western applicants only. That designation, perhaps not accidentally, ruled out eastern applicants, of whom many were Boston or New York Jews. Indeed, as late as the 1950s President Pusey attempted, in the end unsuccessfully, to forbid Jewish marriages in Memorial Church. But anti-Semitism did not warp my daily life as an undergraduate, partly because I met only one faculty member who was anti-Semitic and partly because I had learned that among contemporaries, there was none worth knowing who was prejudiced against Jews or Catholics, or black or Asian Americans.

As with friends, so with studies: my freshman year exposed only a small fraction of what Harvard offered. I selected an unimaginative academic schedule. In later years I would advise freshmen to seek out courses in fields they had never studied — in geology or astronomy to satisfy a science requirement, in Italian or Russian or Chinese as a new foreign language, in anthropology or sociology for a social science. But as a freshman, badly advised, I elected courses that kept me on paths I had already explored at Andover. On one final exam in June 1940 I proved conclusively that the best of all possible governments for France was the Third Republic. I received an A, my only A that year; the Third Republic vanished forever less than two weeks later. Excused from freshman English, I made the mistake of selecting no literature course at all; instead, I enrolled in a writing course that expected a thousand words of fiction a week from each student, or the equivalent in poetry. For the first semester I alternated between fiction and verse and did equally poor work in both. Disturbed by the negative assessments I received, I asked the instructor for his advice. "Blum," he said drily, "why don't you try expository writing?" The rest of the year I did, with somewhat better results, earning a final B for the course. I should have learned a permanent lesson, but in later years I would occasionally try fiction and poetry again, always with the same result.

Still, the writing course exposed me to the prose of my contemporaries, some of them juniors and seniors, who were taking as their models writers I had not yet read. Moved by their example, I spent many evenings reading for edification and reward, particularly James Joyce's *Portrait of the Artist* and *Ulysses* (with which I struggled), the plays of Thornton Wilder, the novels of Scott Fitzgerald and Ernest Hemingway, and essays by Ralph Waldo Emerson and Henry David Thoreau. It was not the faculty but my classmates who were leading me toward a literary education. At Harvard, as in all colleges with high standards of admission then and now, students can learn as much from their peers as from the faculty.

The great academic disappointment of my freshman year was the introductory history course, a survey of European history from the fall of Rome through World War I. Professor Roger Merriman gave lectures twice weekly during the fall semester. A historian of the Renaissance, "Frisky" Merriman put on British airs, worshipped the British aristocracy, played showman on his stage, bellowed at the thousand students in his class, and pronounced broad generalizations that could stand little scrutiny. "The Middle Ages," he roared again and again, "were slow, slow, slow, inconceivably slow." They were indeed, for the students who were forced to listen to him. Even worse was the course's textbook, a history of medieval Europe. Reading that text every week, that compendium of data little interpreted, almost soured me on history forever.

But the weekly third required hour of the course placed students in discussion sections, which were taught by recent recipients of the Ph.D. in history or aspirants to that degree. They were an able lot, most of them soon to become prominent within the profession. I was assigned to one of the best, Carl Schorske, an outstanding teacher and intellectual who after the war became a popular, respected, and sensitive professor successively at Wesleyan, the University of California at Berkeley, and Princeton. (Carl was then "Mr. Schorske" to me. Indeed "Mister" or "sir" was the preferred Harvard mode of student address for all faculty members, regardless of rank. In this memoir I have used first names of those who later became my friends.) Carl met his honors group, about eight students, one evening a week in his residence, a house not far from the Harvard Yard. Even as a young man in 1939, he had a commanding interest in the history of ideas. He used our honors section to introduce us to political theory, a new subject for me. One of us would report on a text we had all read, and Carl would then lead a general discussion, with his own illuminating remarks setting a stunning standard of analysis.

I no longer recall all that we studied, but I remember that during the winter I rendered a report on Thomas Hobbes's *Leviathan*. The book impressed me; it offered the first argument I had met that ran counter to the assumptions and conclusions of John Locke and, in his wake, the American Jeffersonians. Hobbes postulated an angry and chaotic state of nature, peopled by timorous men who irrevocably surrendered their personal independence to an autocratic ruler in return for social and political tranquillity. That theoretical state seemed to me accurately to forecast the real world as it had come to exist in 1940 in Hitler's Germany and Stalin's Soviet Union. The past was relevant to the present, even though the present should not provide the basis for interpreting the past. But Americans, so I then believed, had a mission to preserve the freedoms the dictators denied their people, a mission therefore to demolish the partners to the Nazi-Soviet pact.

Carl Schorske had no argument with my recapitulation of Hobbes, but he had tried to preserve neutrality about current affairs in his discussion group. Opposed to American intervention in the war, he kept his opinions to himself while he met his classes. In an autobiographical essay, he later explained his position as an assistant in the introductory course: "Merriman . . . believed . . . that the instructors had a public responsibility to get in there and tell the little gentlemen what the war was all about, to make them realize the importance of America's intervention. A few of us, across the often bitter barriers of political division, joined hands to resist the use of the classroom as an instrument of political indoctrination. . . . The experience taught me how shared academic values could sustain friendships that political differences might destroy." As I came to understand when I began to teach, Carl was correct, though his objective was difficult to achieve. In 1940 it was not he but I who brought the current war in Europe into an analysis of a seventeenth-century political pamphlet. And worse, in 1940 I falsely attributed his position to his isolationist beliefs, which he did not hide outside of his classes. So I went on through the dreadful spring of that year to make my irrelevant, interventionist points with an unbecoming irritability. The lecturers in that spring by and large shared Merriman's opinion about the war, thereby unknowingly encouraging my unexpressed argument with Carl, an argument he never joined. I brought the war into every answer I wrote to the questions on the final exam. My passion about intervention overwhelmed my limited understanding of European history. Carl was generous to grant my performance in the course a B.

The grade bothered me less than did the course itself. It seemed to me to lack structure and cohesion. I had studied the American past at Andover with a growing sense of its contours. The basic relationships among the major developments of American history became familiar to me. Not so with the European past, for which the introductory history course as I absorbed it provided few clues. Carl was not to blame. Placed in an honors section, we were supposed to be able to comprehend the course on our own. Carl's task was to supplement the lectures and assigned reading. He decided to focus his section on political theory, at which he shone. But the course as a whole left me dissatisfied, as did the entire freshman year, as did also my unremarkable grades. I had not come to Harvard to dislike my only history course or to achieve a record of three Bs and one A.

Depressed, I wrote Wilbur Bender to confess my disappointment with Harvard and with myself and to ask him whether he thought I should continue at Harvard, perhaps with a major in government, or start looking for a job. Familiar with the doldrums so common among freshmen and sophomores, he replied with an encouraging proposal. Go on in history at Harvard, he advised, and if after another year I were still unhappy, he would find me a position in New York. His confidence in Harvard and in my ability to recover gave me needed heart. And my wounded pride fed my determination to conquer Harvard in my sophomore year.

During my sophomore and junior years, resolved to prove myself, inspired by some extraordinary teachers, blessed with a job that exactly suited me, I discovered how wonderful an education Harvard College offered an undergraduate who knew what he wanted to learn. And more emphatically with each passing week, I wanted to learn to become a professional historian, a historian of the United States who would feel at home also with the history of other times and places, a teacher and a scholar, though I was only beginning to understand what scholarship entailed.

The Harvard system of residential houses, established in the early 1930s, abetted the learning process while also lending grace to undergraduate living. Each "house," modeled on the colleges at Oxford and Cambridge, had a master, residential and nonresidential tutors, and about two hundred undergraduates. Each house, named after a former Harvard president, also contained a dining hall, a library designed for student use, squash courts, and single, double, and triple suites for students. Much of undergraduate social life centered in the houses. They brought together members of all three upper classes. My roommate and I shared a four-room suite (two bedrooms, a living room, and a bath) on the fifth floor of Lowell House. Across the hall from us were three seniors, all outstanding academically. One of them generously instructed me in squash, which I played thereafter at an intense but mediocre level. He and his suitemates urged me to follow their example of serious commitment to academic excellence, just as the Lowell House shield proposed: *"Occasionem cognosce"* (recognize opportunity).

Lowell House also provided its student members with an introduction to patrician manners, though that objective went temporarily by the boards after the United States entered the war. Each student was invited at least once every year to sherry with the master, and once also to high table, which required a dinner jacket, expected also of all those in the dining hall on high table evenings. Until the war came, waitresses served à la carte meals three times a day, and a maid cleaned the student suites. Jackets and ties were required in the dining hall, in classes, and in the libraries. Some of the tutors were sartorially elegant, and we, gripped by admiration, thought one day to follow exactly their example.

My tutor was less elegant than he was athletic, and he and I had at each other at squash about once a fortnight. Those contests, as well as occasional evenings of bridge, nurtured my growing friendship with Barnaby Conrad Keeney, a medievalist who later became a war hero, professor and president of Brown University, the first head of the National Endowment for the Humanities, and Provost of Claremont College. Barney was precisely the kind of tutor that Woodrow Wilson had called on Princeton preceptors to be: "guides, philosophers, and friends" to the undergraduates they instructed. Like Carl Schorske, Barney kept the war out of his teaching, but privately we wholly agreed about American policy. Indeed Barney helped me to see the continuities in Anglo-American legal and constitutional history.

He also assisted me in selecting courses for both semesters of my sophomore and junior years. To encourage my interest in history, Barney felt that I should enroll in the American history survey even though I had covered much the same ground at Andover. I did so both semesters of my sophomore year and learned much that I had not previously known. In 1940–42 I also took two semesters of Latin American history (a field new to me), two of introductory economics, a semester course on the American empire, one on the Roman republic, one on English constitutional history, one on Greek culture, one on modern French painting, and other courses as well. As a senior I studied American foreign policy and American constitutional development. In economics my section instructor had little use for the superannuated textbook, saturated as it was with outmoded assumptions about an automatic marketplace. So he bootlegged the theories of John Maynard Keynes to a few of us who were doing well in the course. He also enjoined us to stick close to the textbook in writing our exams and to seize any chance to audit the lectures of Joseph Schumpeter, the great Austrian economist then at Harvard, where he propounded his case for the entrepreneur.

Joseph Schumpeter was only one of the distinguished émigrés who had reached Harvard in their flight from fascist Europe. The Italian medievalist George LaPiana and the Italian statesman Gaetano Salvemini had fled from Mussolini's fascism; and Werner Jaeger, an eminent classicist, had run from Hitler. I did some errands for Salvemini, a kind man who never felt at home in the United States; and I took a course on Greek humanism from Jaeger, whose English, though imperfect, was clear enough to convey the ideas about Greek concepts of virtue for which he was celebrated.

But American scholars in my experience proved to be more powerful teachers. The most engaging was Charles MacIlwain, then in his mid-sixties, a scholar without peer in the field of British medieval constitutional history. Mac did not perform; he talked. He engaged in a commanding exegesis of British constitutional texts, written in Latin, which he assigned for us to study and to interpret in class. Always precisely on time, he would enter the classroom, place his pipe along the crease in his fedora, open his copy of Stubbs's charters, suck in his dental plates, and resume his exegesis where he recalled (sometimes in error) that he had left it at the previous meeting.

His comments, replete with learning and bibliographical references (to Maitland in particular) drew meaning from the texts. He dwelt on Magna Carta for weeks. Under MacIlwain's direction Barney Keeney had written his dissertation on the meaning of "vel . . . vel" in Chapter 24 of Magna Carta. That issue, typical of Mac's thinking, was no small matter. Did the conjunctions mean "either . . . or" or "both . . . and" in the phrase about trials based upon the law of the land and/or judgment by peers? Only if the meaning was "both . . . and" was there implied a rule of law; and, as he did not need to tell us, the rule of law had become an issue of moment in the twentieth-century politics of Europe. Later, in discussion groups at MIT and Yale, I tried to follow Mac's example, talking with students about texts, eliciting meaning as the class moved along.

The model lecturer in my undergraduate years was Frederick Merk, a disciple of Frederick Jackson Turner, the renowned historian of the American West. Merk had come from Wisconsin to Harvard with Turner in the 1920s, and he succeeded his mentor in teaching the history of the American frontier, which in his version covered a multiplicity of subjects. Then in his forties, Fred was a superb lecturer. He followed exactly the outlines he wrote on the blackboard, began always with the phrase "At the last hour," and finished on time. He expected his students to understand how things worked, so he carefully explained such things as the mechanics of the cotton gin and the process by which the Second Bank of the United States rediscounted a note. His examinations were imaginative. In my year in his course, he wrote "Wyoming" on the blackboard and instructed us to give the topic three hours. His choice of exam topic expressed his geographical determinism. His physical determinism led him after one major blizzard to snowshoe the five miles from his house to his class in the Harvard Yard. Only six of some sixty students showed up that day, and Fred never forgot any one of them.

Fred struck me as a latter-day Whig in the guise of a contemporary New Dealer. He was organized, lucid, imperturbable, eloquent in his obvious enthusiasm for his subject, righteous in his wrath about slavery, his reedy voice holding the attention of his large audience as he moved across the continent with the frontiersmen. In 1946 Jim Field, then at the outset of his career as a historian of the American navy, happened to meet Fred in Widener Library one bright Saturday afternoon. "What are you doing here, Jim?" Merk asked. "A young man has to make his way in the world," Jim answered. "But what are you doing here, Mr. Merk?" "Ah," Fred replied, "an old man has to prepare to die." He lived another two decades, a dedicated scholar and craftsman, a teacher who, as his many doctoral students agreed, taught integrity

—thoroughness and honesty with the sources, care and clarity in prose, characteristics I tried to stress when I began to work with graduate students. And when I came to lecture at Yale I found myself using the blackboard as Fred had, striving for lucidity and completing my lectures on time—though unlike Fred, who lectured behind his lectern, I paced as I talked.

Courses provided only part of the education available to history majors at Harvard. A larger part derived from the tutorial system that the major required. Tutorials were designed to prepare undergraduates for their junior and senior departmental examinations and for writing their senior essays. The undergraduate major was a smaller and less taxing derivative of the doctoral program. The junior departmental examination tested the student's learning in three fields—mine were American history since 1789 (my speciality), modern Latin American history, and the history of the Roman republic; the senior departmental exam tested the student's special field; both exams tested the student's understanding of major historical interpretations. Tutorials in the sophomore year focused on either ancient or medieval history; in the junior year, on historical interpretations; in the senior year, on the required research essay.

The system had one glaring fault: it was only as good as the tutors made it, and not all tutors were equal. Mine as it happened were outstanding, without exception major players in the profession of history as their careers unfolded. Barney Keeney started me off in Greek history, which was enriched by the course I was taking from Werner Jaeger. Once a week I met Barney either alone or in company with a classmate who was exploring the same subject. Together we read translations of Herodotus, Thucydides, some Plato, and some modern texts about the Greeks. Each week we also read an interpretative paper we had written.

Somewhat subdued in his comments during joint tutorials, where severe criticism would have embarrassed a student, Barney showed little restraint in one-to-one sessions. Those were the most educational tutorials, though they also tested one's resilience. I have never forgotten my first assignment with Barney. I was to write a short paper addressing the question of whether Solon the Athenian went to Egypt before or after he wrote the Athenian constitution. There remained extant only two relevant sources, both available in translation, one a fragment by Solon, the other a short passage from Herodotus. After pondering them both, I wrote a page that proved to my satisfaction that Solon had been to Egypt before he wrote the constitution. With some pride I read the paper to Barney—who forthwith directed me to destroy it, start the assignment all over again, and return a week later with an acceptable paper. Stunned, I repaired to the library and reread the sources, which had not changed. For five days I worried about the question until suddenly, late one night, inspiration struck. The sources, I then wrote for Barney, permitted no firm conclusion about the order of the events. "Mr. Blum," he said after I had read my new offering, "there is an outside chance that you may someday become a historian."

The following spring I enrolled in a course entitled "The Ethics of Democracy" in which the lecturer was the philosopher Ralph Barton Perry, a favorite student years earlier of William James and who later became James's biographer. Perry was also a leading Harvard interventionist, and I expected that his course would provide philosophical confirmation for my views. But he proved to be at best a middling lecturer, and his weekly sections, as well as all the grading, fell to a disheveled graduate student imbued with rigid, Marxist doctrine. I suffered through the term, hoping to rescue a B. The night before the final examination I studied late in Widener Library. Walking to Lowell House to go to bed, I met Barney at the gate. Soon to be married, he was emerging from a bachelor party, well into his cups. We had a short conversation. Where have you been, he asked. Studying for a philosophy exam, I replied. What do you think of philosophy, he asked. I think it's a lot of crap, I replied. When you come to me and tell me that about history, Barney said, grinning, I shall recommend you for a summa. It was just the right note on which to end my sophomore year, a year in which I rediscovered history and developed my lifelong feelings of gratitude, affection, and admiration for Harvard College.

During my junior year Barney's tutorials turned to theories of history, especially to Marxism, which both of us rejected as we also rejected all determinism, Hegelian or otherwise. We both believed in agency, in the importance in history of contingency, and in the complex and multiple nature of causation. Before Christmas, our tutorials had become compatible discussions of historical issues.

Just after Christmas 1941 Barney enlisted in the army. Before leaving Cambridge he arranged for Myron Gilmore, probably the foremost history tutor at Harvard then, to let me join his tutorial group, which was really a seminar. The group met one evening a week at Gilmore's home, where Alfred North Whitehead, a relative of his wife's, silently joined the undergraduates. I could not decide who was the more impressive, Gilmore, who led the discussions of the papers read after we assembled, or Whitehead, who provided, on request, his own summary comments after coffee and soft drinks were served. Whitehead met us, one by one, as we emerged that spring from our long departmental examination. One by one he asked us what questions we had answered and how we felt about our efforts. We were enormously gratified to have so famous a philosopher inquire about our work. He had become an intellectual hero to me, a status confirmed when I read his *Aims of Education*. In 1940–41 he had debated the question of American intervention in public forums against Ernest Hocking, a Harvard philosopher and isolationist. On one memorable evening, embarking on his rebuttal, Whitehead said softly, "Hocking, Hocking, he says what he knows but he doesn't know what he says." That sentence became my mantra for many months.

Myron Gilmore, then in his early thirties, was a "faculty instructor," a rank unique to Harvard, where President Conant had invented it as a substitute for assistant professor. My new tutor and I were to become friends during the war, but in 1942 I knew Myron primarily as a teacher. A graduate of Amherst with his doctorate from Harvard, a specialist on the French and Italian Renaissance, he later became the head of I Tatti, Bernard Berenson's former residence near Florence, Italy, which had become the Harvard Center for Renaissance Studies. Myron brought a learned elegance to scholarship, as he did to life. He was a graceful raconteur, a gourmet, a lover of good wines, a winning hand at martinis, and incidentally a devoted husband and father with a fascinating and unconventional wife. As a tutor in the winter and spring of 1942, he led us through theories of history. So it was that we read Tolstoy on the nature of warfare and then tested his theses by examining a war we had studied in a lecture course. I wrote about Andrew Jackson's war against the Georgia Indians, a choice that entertained Professor Whitehead, who had never previously heard of the episode.

Mostly Myron concentrated on the ideas of Vilfredo Pareto, then very much in vogue among Harvard historians. Pareto, an Italian economist and sociologist, had greatly influenced L. J. Henderson, a Harvard professor of medicine and sociology and an intellectual force in the Harvard Society of Fellows. Economists knew Pareto for his theory of equilibrium. Henderson looked primarily to Pareto's sociology, which he summarized in a short, pithy book. Henderson's book introduced and explained the abstruse vocabulary Pareto employed. But Pareto was comprehensible without the "sentiments" and "persistent aggregates" he referred to in his writings. He was concerned with the importance of the irrational in human affairs, in history not the least, and with the complex nature of causation. Pareto thus offered a refutation of Marx's dialectical materialism. Because of this, some scholars, Marxists especially, assumed erroneously that Pareto was a fascist.

Others found Pareto inspirational, as did Crane Brinton, a Harvard historian of ideas who wrote two books popularizing Pareto's approach. One examined bastardy in the French revolution. Brinton found that the French courts would not enforce revolutionary statutes giving bastards rights to inherit equal to those of legitimate children. From this finding Brinton demonstrated the unchanging view of the nature of family—a "persistent aggregate" in Pareto's terms. Brinton's other Pareton book, *The Anatomy of Revolution*, was a comparative study of the revolutions in the North American colonies, France, and Russia, and was a standard assignment in Harvard history tutorials in the early 1940s. Myron Gilmore's influential tutorials drew me into the Pareton camp. Indeed as a professor at Yale I came to say every year in my first lecture, borrowing from Pareto and Henderson, that understanding history required understanding "the simultaneous interaction of mutually interdependent variables"—but, I added, we could talk about these variables only one at a time.

The war and the question of American intervention commanded my attention. I followed the daily news about the Italian and later German campaigns in Greece. I wondered, as did other Americans, how long Great Britain could take the blitz and whether lend-lease would draw us into the war. Indeed I was working to that end for three hours every weekday afternoon. Waiting on table served as a job for scholarship students only in the freshman year. Thereafter each needy student was assigned to some task for which he was paid thirty-five cents an hour, which in fifteen hours a week covered the costs of board. It was my great good fortune my sophomore year to be assigned as an errand boy for American Defense: Harvard Group, a faculty organization active in the cause of immediate aid to England and ultimate partnership in the war. Ralph Barton Perry was the head of the group for which during term time I became a kind of clerk.

This was for me a perfect job. I believed firmly in what I was doing. My task required for the most part reading letters to the editor in dozens of daily papers from cities all over the country. I was supposed to clip all letters opposed to aid to England, which in the winter of 1941 included those opposed to lend-lease, and refer those letters to the office manager. She in turn arranged for the press committee to draft answers, which were signed in the names of men and women who had agreed to let American Defense use their monikers in the papers published in their home cities. I was then to look for those replies and clip them. So, for example, a letter to the *St. Louis Post Dispatch* opposing lend-lease would evoke a reply written by an American Defense author but signed by a housewife in Missouri. Some replies received an anonymous signature, such as one published by the *Boston Herald* signed "A Lonely Widow."

The office of American Defense had ample space for the volunteers who met every afternoon to file correspondence and type letters and essays designed for publication to advance the cause. These volunteers, my company at my job, were mostly faculty wives, and I came to know them, and through them their husbands, quite well. As it worked out, from sophomore year forward I spent more time with faculty, particularly young faculty, and with their wives than I did with my classmates. I knew that they referred to me behind my back as "Little Blum," but the nickname was affectionate, and I was, after all, not quite five feet seven and not quite 135 pounds.

But I was large enough in the spring of 1941 to draw the fire of the Harvard Young Communist League. Two of its members objected to my assignment to American Defense. I was working on what Harvard called a Temporary Student Employment job. The funds for TSE jobs came from the National Youth Administration, an agency of the federal government within the Works Project Administration. The Young Communists argued that I was assisting propaganda efforts in behalf of a belligerent foreign country, Great Britain, which they considered to be an illegal use of federal funds. They protested to the office of the Dean of Harvard College, who heard them out, gave me a chance to respond, and decided in my favor. The protesters continued to complain until June 1941, when Germany invaded the Soviet Union and they found themselves suddenly on my side. By that time I had developed a considerable and lasting antipathy to members of the Communist Party of the United States. Some of them were doubtless worthy, if deluded, people, but their methods were nasty and their objectives skewed.

On December 7, 1941, I completed a paper I was writing on the vulnerability of the Philippine Islands before going out to play bridge at the Keeneys'. The New York Philharmonic was softly playing in the background when the radio broadcast was interrupted for a portentous announcement: the Japanese had attacked Pearl Harbor. Barney proposed at once that we volunteer for the tank corps. He envisaged himself driving a tank with me standing on his shoulders, firing the canon. That evening I called my father, who persuaded me to defer any military decision until I arrived at home for Christmas vacation two weeks hence. Barney enlisted in the infantry with assurances that he would qualify for officer training, as he did. He went on in field intelligence, eventually working ahead of Patton's army to capture German prisoners and interrogate them — very tough duty.

In 1941 my parents had moved again, this time to South Norwalk, Connecticut, where my father spoke with the local navy recruiter about me. Both of them urged me to go up to New Haven to enlist in the naval reserve before I was drafted. I had romantic notions about naval air, but I enlisted instead in V-7, a reserve program for college students who were close to graduation and would receive training to become officers in the fleet. At once I received orders to return to Harvard on an accelerated schedule that was to include mathematics and physics. My undergraduate glory days were drawing to a close.

The pressures of war affected Harvard only marginally until June 1942, when we returned for the new summer semester, the first semester of our senior year. Officers training for the navy supply corps filled the dormitories in the Yard; freshmen were moved into the houses. That crowded the suites: four rooms now held three rather than two residents. With the waitresses of earlier days gone into war work, the dining hall introduced trays and served meals cafeteria style. More important, conscription or enlistment had taken several Lowell House tutors and some of my classmates into the army. In the fall I joined three friends in a small frame house we rented together. My curriculum as a senior included calculus, physics, and astronomy. The navy demanded those courses, though none of them later mattered at sea.

The best lectures I heard as a senior were on American foreign policy since 1898. Richard W. Leopold, a faculty instructor, delivered them in high style in his last term before leaving for military service. A graduate of Phillips Exeter and Princeton, Dick had written his dissertation under the direction of Arthur Schlesinger, Sr., Harvard's prominent social historian and master of that field. But Dick had left the field for foreign policy, the speciality he pursued thereafter. He was a friend and contemporary of both Myron Gilmore and Wilbur Bender, who had asked him in 1939 to keep an eye on me. He became my tutor in the summer of 1942, and was later for many years my close friend. He had the good sense to realize that we were all fixated on the war. We worried about the grim American defeats in 1942: the perilous invasion of Guadalcanal that August and the earlier loss of the Alaskan islands Sitka and Attu to Japan. (The United States Navy had yet to reveal the great Allied victory at Midway.) In his lectures Dick gave special attention to Woodrow Wilson and the prospect of peace after the current war ended.

In our tutorial, which was directed to finding a topic and preparing for my senior essay, Dick led me to American naval history, a new field for me, and to my essay topic, "The Problem of Guam in American Naval Policy." This topic was the best substitute for a uniform. It made me feel almost on active duty, the topic was so timely. The Japanese had taken Guam at the outset of the war, and Roosevelt's earlier recommendations for fortifying the island with harbor improvements had been turned back by Republican isolationists. The topic also opened up larger questions about the strained relations of the United States with both Japan and Great Britain during the interbella years, 1919–39. My research required extensive work in congressional documents, experience that proved important for my whole professional life. Though Dick Leopold reported for duty at the end of the summer, the senior essay he helped me shape became my intellectual preoccupation for the rest of my undergraduate days.

There were of course other academic assignments, some in the tutorials of my last semester with Oscar Handlin, another young instructor, as distant to his students as Dick was accessible. Though without interest in naval or diplomatic history, Oscar was a man of deep learning and intelligence. He was celebrated for his laconic and inscrutable manner. Certainly he wasted no time, either his or his students'. At our first meeting in September, I asked as I departed whether he had an assignment he wanted me to prepare. "Read Parrington," he said. I knew that Vernon Parrington had written three volumes on American intellectual history. "Which volume?" I asked. Oscar shrugged, a typical response. "Read Parrington," he repeated. So I did, all three volumes in the next week, and I wrote a report criticizing the author for slighting the Whigs. That approach apparently suited Oscar, who in later years helped me in many ways.

During my senior year I also had new duties in my TSE job. Military service had removed most graduate students from universities. As a consequence, Harvard was finding it hard to recruit enough instructors for Frisky Merriman's introductory course. To relieve the shortage, the department chairman, Fred Merk, asked me to take charge of the grading of all map questions. That was a great compliment, for Fred placed a high value on maps and the ability to use them, no matter what the course. Though I knew I would be very cheap labor, I welcomed the chance for this kind of ancillary teaching. Merriman, whom Fred obviously disliked, silently tolerated my presence. Like all courses that summer, History 1 was offered concurrently to Radcliffe women as well as Harvard men, an unprecedented arrangement. Frisky went out of his way to insult the women attending his lectures. But in grading maps, I found the top student in the course to be a Radcliffe freshman, who compiled a perfect record on her map questions. Frisky complained to Fred that I must have erred, but Fred backed me up.

In my spare time I remained involved in typical undergraduate pastimes. Mike Ford and I played pinball for an hour or so many evenings, often after drinking a beer at a nearby bistro. As stags he and I attended several dances, including a notable ball at the Signet Society and another, less formal affair at Lowell House, where my brother came along. Bill had a two-day pass from nearby Fort Devens, where he was awaiting orders after enlisting in the army. I was not to see my brother again until he returned from Alaska after the war.

My desk was my anchorage. There I labored at writing my senior essay, my first serious scholarly venture. Eager to do a professional job, I worked hard on my prose as well as at understanding my subject. In later years when I reread the essay I realized how primitive it was, but that rereading provided a standard for grading the senior essays that came my way. And Dick Leopold's direction, clear to me even after he had departed, provided a splendid model for directing those seniors at Yale who later turned to me.

As the term drew to its end, the effort I had made at Harvard after my freshman year paid satisfying dividends. In October I was elected one of sixteen seniors — eight classmates had preceded us — inducted into Phi Beta Kappa, for me the academic equivalent of a varsity letter. In January I was called in for an oral examination on my senior essay. The leading examiner was Payson Wild, a professor of government and a specialist on international affairs, who would soon become dean of the graduate school of arts and sciences at Harvard. After asking me to elaborate on the disagreements I had described between the state and navy departments, disagreements that muddled foreign and military policy, he told me to suggest ways in which the federal government could avoid such problems in the future. Uninformed about arrangements in wartime Washington, I suggested a standing committee on foreign and military policy, a committee with its own staff, with senior representation from the state, war, and navy departments that would be responsible directly to the White House. I was closer to postwar reality than I knew. Wild must have liked both the essay and my answer, for I received my A.B. summa cum laude in history and a prize for the best undergraduate essay that year on a subject relating to American government. So my undergraduate years ended on a personal high.

But we were still, as MacLeish had warned us, the class of 1918. My orders called for me to report for duty at the United States Navy Midshipman School at Columbia University on February 22, 1943. That allowed me a month of leisure, which I spent mostly loafing impatiently at home. One weekend Mike Ford telephoned from his home in Albany to suggest we engage in a last civilian fling at Smith College. There we proceeded to Wallace House, where Mike's fiancée had arranged for her roommate to join us. The four of us were playing bridge when a trim, stylish, lively brunette came downstairs and stopped to chat. I was at once much taken with the handsome newcomer, Pamela Zink, who at my request agreed to join us after my bridge partner left for a previous engagement with her singing group. Bright, responsive, companionable, Pamela spent the evening with us, to my continuing delight. Smitten, I told Mike later that evening that faint heart ne'er won fair lady, so he had to support me. He looked puzzled until I said, "I'm going to marry that girl." He laughed. Though I could not have predicted it, the pursuit and achievement of that objective was to make life in the navy tolerable for me.

At the time I met Pamela, I was sure I could conquer the world, as I felt I had conquered Harvard College. I had little sense of my limitations, my weaknesses, my naked and vulnerable self. Indeed, like most young men just out of college, like most on the brink of military service, I was still an arrogant innocent. I still believed I could plan my life and by hard work execute my plans. At Andover and at Harvard I had absorbed much — more than I yet realized — about learning and teaching. I had begun to understand history. I had made friends with men, not the least my tutors, whom I would see and admire throughout our lives. But I still knew little about my emotions and about life. In the next three years I was to learn much more about the world and about myself.

3

269416

Training for the United States Naval Reserve imposes upon recruits a certain deliberate anonymity, not unlike that of prisoners. Prisoners lose control of their lives; so do sailors and their junior officers. Prisoners receive numbers, by which at times they are known; so, too, midshipmen. *"Name and number!"* an officer would demand of a recalcitrant recruit. And if I were that recruit, the reply would be: "Blum, J. M., sir, 269416." A number never to be forgotten. "Keep your finger on your number," one Annapolis man told another, for the number marked seniority. In the regular navy a deed well done might result in a promotion ahead of the normal time when your number was to come up, and a misdeed could lead to a loss—a downgrading—of your number. It was with the latter that 269416 was occasionally threatened during all but the last four months of his active service. Some men of my generation remember their active service in World War II as the most exciting and rewarding period of their lives. Not I. My memory of this time, in both training and at sea, is one largely, though not exclusively, of boredom, of nostalgia for my bride, and of anxiety punctuated a few times by fear—all redeemed by a final assignment in the autumn of 1945.

On February 22, 1943, at the USN Midshipman School at Columbia University, in a room that looked across West 114th Street at the windows of an apartment my parents had once rented, I began my training. Like the others in my regiment, I quickly learned to call John Jay Hall, where we resided, "the ship" with walls that were bulkheads, floors that were decks, stairways that were ladders. I also memorized my number. But inadvertently I fell out of step. About two weeks after we reported as apprentice seamen, my regiment underwent a scarlet fever epidemic, but I caught lobar pneumonia. An ambulance took me to the naval hospital at Saint Alban's on Long Island. There, high fever, hallucinations, and an oxygen tent kept me out of trouble for several days.

I came to my senses late one March afternoon when I heard my father's voice. He found me in a room off a ward where the presiding doctor was an orthopedic surgeon who had not so much as seen a case of lobar pneumonia since medical school. The other patients in the ward doubtless bored him: they were there because they had just been circumcised. That doctor and that ward gave me my first experience with navy snafus. Early in April I was sent home to get in shape to return to duty. Eating five meals a day, exercising vigorously, I worked at recovering my normally excellent health, succeeded, and received orders to report on May 30, 1943, at the USN Midshipman School at Notre Dame, Indiana. My pneumonia and its aftermath had consumed three months.

Those months, when I should have been at war or preparing to go to war, gave me a priceless opportunity to court Pamela Zink. While I was at the hospital, delirious, I must have mentioned her name, for my father, saying nothing, one day handed me a copy of a *New York Sunday Times* magazine. One page contained a photo of Pam next to her written description of proper fashion for a young woman making the transition from college to war work. I began writing her letters as often and as intimate as I thought appropriate. More important, though our epistolary courtship was to continue for many months, in May I arranged two dates with her, our first dates, both marvelous. On one we went to the circus at Madison Square Garden. Emmett Kelly as "Weary Willie" played solitaire on the floor while on the high wire a cyclist, balancing with a long bar, rode back and forth between his colleagues at either end of the course while the band played "You'd Be So Nice to Come Home To," exactly my feeling about Pamela. On our other date we went to the Museum of Modern Art for tea and then to a bistro in the Village for a quiet, joyous dinner. The memory of those evenings provided a leitmotif for our letters during the next four months. To that correspondence I gave as much time and thought as I could wring from my military obligations.

All midshipman schools offered substantially the same curriculum, though local circumstances made idiosyncratic differences. At Notre Dame, the navy, emulating the host university, stressed athletics and physical fitness. As midshipmen we ran relay races against Marine trainees through an obstacle course that included a wall twice my height over which we had to maneuver. I managed—as I also managed the academic work, which was for the most part dull but easy, though curiously abstract and unreal. We studied seamanship and damage control without boarding a ship. We studied gunnery in the absence of a live cannon, navigation without a sextant.

The experience of military training, so often described in memoir and fiction, was about the same for everyone. The description in Herman Wouk's *Caine Mutiny* aptly characterized my life at Notre Dame. I was punished when a white glove inspection located a dead fly at the bottom of the globe of the light on my desk. I was punished for berating a training film by Frank Capra that made good old apple pie the reason for fighting the war. Why not, I was heard to opine, good old bird's nest soup? The U.S. Navy had no use for irony. As punishment, I (like all offenders) had to march for two or three hours at night around the lake separating Notre Dame from St. Mary's College. The lake, we agreed, served as the largest chastity belt west of Europe. Discipline, like close order drill, seemed rather silly, though we knew we were supposed to learn to react to orders at once and without thinking. And we accepted that we were at the mercy of the navy in order to reach our target of assisting in what we all agreed was a necessary war.

Once, after a fashion, I was rewarded. I could not understand the fire control textbook, which tried to explain the workings of automated naval gunfire. What was essentially an electronic device — a prototype computer — measured the speed of a ship, its course, any offsetting currents and winds, and the speed and course of the target airplane or vessel. The machine then calculated the appropriate aim and elevation of the ship's guns and fired them. Thus, we were told, did the Mark V director operate; but we had no model of it, and the book was for me an inadequate substitute. Unable to understand the textbook description for the predictable exam with its standard questions asking for the exact words of the text, I memorized the book, which mercifully was short, and received a high grade on the exam. The commanding officer, an Annapolis graduate, called me in, congratulated me, and invited me to remain at Notre Dame to teach the subject to the next contingent of midshipmen. I replied that I preferred to go to sea and had applied for submarine duty — his former duty. Of course, he said, but we need instructors. "But sir," I pleaded, "I don't know anything about fire control. I memorized the book. Please test me." He did. He read aloud several sentence fragments from the book and I went on to complete each sentence. "Well," the captain said, "I'll be goddamned! Where did you go to college?" "Harvard, sir," I said. He replied, "I might have known. Dismissed, mister."

But I did not get submarine duty. I passed the written and the physical examinations for qualification for submarine training, but the last hurdle, a psychological interview with a medical officer, tripped me up. In the allotted time, I simply could not put together a rectangular block from a dozen fitted pieces. (I still can't.) The naval commander, commissioned from civilian life, patiently explained that a reliable three-dimensional sense was necessary in a submarine. He then asked me why in the world I had asked for submarine duty, a hazardous assignment that carried extra pay. He himself, he said, was claustrophobic. I replied that I was not concerned about either the danger or the pay. I wanted primarily to find a ship without the kind of chickenshit that had characterized midshipman training. The officer replied that he didn't blame me and that he could write me orders for anti-submarine training, which would result in duty aboard a ship smaller than a sub. Was there anything else he could do for me? Yes, I replied. Could he write me orders to delay thirty days before reporting? There was a girl I wanted to propose to. He said he could, and he did.

On a chill September day my fellow recruits and I were commissioned ensigns in the U.S. Naval Reserve — made "officers and gentlemen" by act of Congress and certification of the Secretary of the Navy. In a last act of midshipman naughtiness I asked the Texan who commanded our battalion what a gentleman was. "Wha, don't you know?" he said. "A gent'eman lats a lady's cigarette." Then he embarrassed me by congratulating me on standing seventeenth in the regiment. He was serious while I had been frivolous. Further, I had cared too little about the academic side of training to work hard at it or even to look at the published class ranking. It did make a difference. When a new officer, a Notre Dame classmate, joined our ship a year or so later my superior standing in class made me the more senior officer. As a midshipman I had not known what was important.

During my months at Notre Dame I had spent most of my time thinking of Pamela. I had written her several times a week, sent her a book of Conrad Aiken's love sonnets, telegraphed a dozen red roses to greet her after her tonsillectomy. Now, a day after reaching home after Notre Dame, I set out for Northampton. Pam met me at the train station. We walked to a spot she knew alongside Paradise Pond. There I proposed to her. We had our first kiss, and she did not reject my proposal. Within a week we became engaged, to the tearful dismay of my mother and the anti-Semitic anger of Pamela's father. When I entrained for Miami and the Submarine Chaser Training Command, we felt for the first time the intimation of mortality that parting inspires in lovers.

SCTC believed in hands-on training. Early each morning I left the Bachelor Officers Quarters, where I was billeted in Miami, for breakfast at the navy mess and then classes on anti-submarine warfare, particularly the use of newly developed sound gear for echo ranging to detect and attack submarines. Sound officers, of whom I was to be one, often served also as communications officers, so training involved exposure to various encryption devices. The most useful was the secret electrical enciphering machine, or ECM, a forerunner of electronic technology, which operated according to a setting of controls that changed every day at 12:01 a.m. Greenwich Meridian Time. Sound officers were trained as jacks of all trades, so we had a two-day course for ships without doctors and a week's course in navy courts and law. I learned to administer sulpha drugs and morphine, to speed to a hospital ship when a sailor needed a real doctor, and never—absolutely never—to attempt, Hollywood-style, to perform operations on my own. I also learned as much as the navy knew about the prevention of venereal diseases. The course on naval law taught us how to help an accused enlisted man to cop a plea and how to differentiate between a charge, a general accusation, and a specification (a particular violation that supported a charge). All of that learning had a future utility.

We spent a couple of days a week on the water on a submarine chaser, an SC, a small wooden ship that normally carried three officers and about twenty enlisted men. We practiced drills—rescuing a man overboard, docking, anchoring, getting under way, simulated attacks. They all looked easier than they turned out to be when for a few minutes each of us played officer of the deck. We were a mixed lot. Several officers in my group had had no experience at sea, while others were combat veterans now undergoing further training, as was Lieutenant Commander Franklin D. Roosevelt, Jr., who had been a hero of the landing operation at Anzio beachhead in Italy. No one was more approachable and outgoing than he.

After Christmas life accelerated. Pamela arrived, as planned, for a week. I was on temporary duty in a summary court, a soft job, and therefore able to join her and some friends every afternoon at the officers' club on Miami Beach. On January 3, 1944, Pamela left for home—another shattering parting—with plans for us to be wed as soon as I could get to her home in Summit, New Jersey. The war, we felt, would never end, so we had decided to get married as soon as we could. The day she left I received orders for temporary duty as observer at sea on a destroyer escort (DE). That ship returned to Miami within a week. Orders awaited me to report at once to the PC 616, a steel patrol craft, in Panama. My training was over at last, some two years after the attack on Pearl Harbor, two years of tough fighting on and across both oceans, both the fighting and its accompanying dangers I had missed.

Boarding a PBM flying boat in Miami, I flew as a passenger—my first flight—to Kingston, Jamaica, and thence to Cristobal-Colon on the Caribbean side of the Panama Canal. I had no confidence in my readiness for the tasks that lay before me. As I had feared, book learning was inadequate for use at sea. It was only learning by doing that differentiated salty veterans from raw trainees. So also, as I was later to discover, with history. It was one thing to read and absorb a scholarly book. It was quite another to grub in the archives and manuscript collections for the data that permitted the writing of a book, and going on over several drafts to write it. The true professional historian had continually to write as well as to read; the true naval officer had to go to sea.

The USS PC 616, one of a class of several hundred, looked rather like a scale model of a fleet destroyer, one inch of PC to one foot of destroyer. As I recall, the PC was some 163 feet long overall, 23 feet abeam at its widest measurement, displacing when loaded about 300 tons, roughly the weight of Columbus's *Nina*. Like any sailing canoe, the PC rode roughly, rolling in even a slight sea, pitching or yawing in heavier weather, but holding its course while churning its crew. It was my great fortune never to be seasick, not even during the two typhoons we weathered. The propensity for seasickness varies directly with sensitivity to music, and I was just about tone deaf. At sea that was an advantage. But because I never felt ill at sea, I had little patience for those who did. The ship had a complement of five officers and sixty men, and almost all of them soon became conditioned to movements at sea.

Like a minority of its class, the 616 had two Fairbanks-Morse opposed piston diesels as main engines, a sturdy pair capable of remaining at sea indefinitely. The auxiliary engines, General Motors pancake diesels, provided the energy for electricity, much in demand for the gyrocompass, radio, radar, power steering, and other electrical uses. But the auxiliaries proved less reliable than the mains, and the mains had two problems. The slowest speed at which the ship was capable of maintaining way was several knots, too fast for a comfortable approach to docking. So we had to cut the engines as we slid alongside a dock or dropped anchor. Worse, the main engines were started by compressed air, but the air compressor could build up to only about six starts, after which there was no way to start again without a considerable wait, a liability in an emergency requiring tight maneuverability abetted by the engines.

Over time I had battle stations at various guns. The PC 616 was a floating arsenal. The ship carried a forward cannon, a three-inch 50 using fixed ammunition, as well as two 20-millimeter and one aft 40-millimeter machine guns, two depth charge racks astern, two other depth charge projectors, one port and one starboard, and a set of forward rockets fired from electrical launchers. Since the forecastle was underwater in even a slight chop, the electrical contact points for firing the rockets quickly rusted. As a consequence, we never succeeded in firing a complete pattern of eight rockets, though now and then two or three responded properly. Under pointer control only, our forward cannon was noisier than it was dangerous. The crews at the anti-aircraft guns received little practice and only rarely managed to lead an aerial target enough to bother its pilot. Essentially our effective weapons were the depth charges, which we used primarily to frighten away any submarine thought to be lurking near our convoys. We were not bad at protecting those convoys, but we were woefully inadequate in the "hunter-killer" operations we undertook. PCs and SCs, manned as they were by reservists, struck those in the regular navy as Mickey Mouse. Indeed the regulars referred to us as the Donald Duck Navy, and some PCs painted a mouse cartoon on their bow. I and my shipmates did not, for however inept we were, we took our duties seriously.

The ship, about a year old when I came aboard, was based in the Canal Zone in Panama where it nested alongside docks near the Gatun Locks. Like other PCs there, its mission primarily was to accompany merchant vessels to and from Guantánamo Bay, an American naval station on the south coast of Cuba. Traffic was heavy from New York and New Orleans to Guantánamo Bay, or "Gitmo" in our usage, for much of the materials of war for the Pacific moved through the Panama Canal, just as Theodore Roosevelt had long ago predicted they would. We met the New York to Panama convoys in Cuba and took them to Panama, with ships for the most part in ballast in our convoys in the other direction. Now and then we were diverted with convoys to other Caribbean ports, to Santiago, Cuba; to Kingston, Jamaica; to Puerto Limón, Costa Rica; to Cartagena, Colombia. Now and then we were sent on "hunter-killer" missions, efforts by our task unit of PCs to find and sink German submarines operating in the waters off Panama. We did not then know it, but the top secret compromise of the German submarine code permitted British and American cryptographers to locate those and other U-boats when they surfaced to charge their batteries and to radio for orders. So the locations where we were to seek out the submarines were bona fide, but we never found one.

Between January and June 1944, I saw enough Caribbean ports to convince me to avoid Latin America in the future. The Canal Zone, American territory, was officially Jim Crow, a disgrace, and unofficially every port we entered practiced some degree of apartheid, a function of social class as well as racial prejudice. Caribbean baroque architecture offended my taste, as did Caribbean music. More important, the poverty of the places we visited exceeded anything I had ever seen at home, even in the heart-breaking photographs by Walker Evans of the rural South. Worse, the Latin American middle class seemed not to care. In Santiago we met executives of the Bacardi Company, the local rum distillery and brewery, who displayed only disdain for the impoverished in their back yards. In Puerto Limón the streets were filthy and the people both poor and ill. I had studied Latin American history at Harvard and had thought of working after the war as a journalist in Argentina, a position an uncle could arrange for me through a friend of his at McGraw, Hill. Though I knew Argentina did not much resemble the Caribbean countries, I decided to eschew all of Latin America because conditions there, in part a function of U.S. exploitation, made me uncomfortable and guilt-ridden. The only joyful experience I had ashore was charging with a shipmate up the San Juan Ridge in Santiago along the tough path Theodore Roosevelt had blazed in 1898 against Spanish fortifications.

I was fortunate in my shipmates. Officers lived very close to each other on a PC. There were two small staterooms below deck, each with tight space for two officers, the captain sleeping when he could in the wardroom on the main deck. The wardroom served also as the decrypting and dining area. When I reported for duty the captain was Bill Porter, a lieutenant junior grade, Yale '41, salty after a year or so at sea. The executive officer, Ted White, also a lieutenant junior grade, University of Pennsylvania '41, I found to have a more compatible temperament, as did the other officers. With never a spat we sailed together through most of 1944. We got along with each other partly because we had to, but without becoming friends. While we were aboard we needed to work together, to trust each other with our lives, and to tolerate each other's limitations and idiosyncrasies.

The burden of sixty-five lives fell most gravely on the skipper. Bill Porter carried that weight with anxious efficiency. Ashore he acted the jaunty womanizer. At sea he expressed his anxiety through surliness and impatience with mistakes. Only months after he left the ship did I realize how good a captain he had been, especially in dealing with an inexperienced and clumsy officer like me. The lessons he taught had an immediate but lasting impact. He began by making me the ship's first lieutenant, the officer responsible for the hull and its appurtenances. That assignment forced me carefully to learn my way about the PC and to work closely with our boatswain mate (second class), a confident young fellow with little use for officers. Further, Porter ordered me for three months under no circumstance to put any enlisted man "on report" — that is, to discipline no one. That order forced me to figure out how to get along with the crew. I suspect that I never became a beloved officer; few did. But I never had trouble with the enlisted men, and at a cautious remove that excluded personal matters, I eventually came to enjoy an informal camaraderie on watch at sea with several of the petty officers whom I had trained as signalmen or quartermasters.

At the start it was I who needed training. The PC 616 normally sailed under "Condition 3M"—the M stood for "modified"—meaning that a third of the crew was to be on duty at any time, with one officer in charge on the bridge. (Condition 1 meant general quarters with all personnel at battle stations; Condition 2 had half the crew and officers on duty with the other half off.) The captain did not stand watch but had to be available at all times and in command at general quarters and when shoving off or returning to port. Until I qualified to stand watch alone, the three other officers were on one and off two watches of four hours apiece. Once I qualified, the duty became one on and three off, a more relaxed schedule.

Normally we followed a set procedure for convoying merchant ships. The PCs in our task unit sailed out beyond the harbor's anti-submarine nets and swept the area where the merchants were to gather. Sweeping involved echo ranging: a ship sent out a sound signal— "ping" — and listened for an echo. An echo— "pong" —indicated the presence of a solid object underwater. The Doppler effect—the sound of the "pong" rising or falling, the frequency of the sound waves increasing or decreasing—indicated whether the object was moving respectively toward or away from the ship. A moving object, unless otherwise demonstrated, was assumed to be a submarine, and on detecting one the watch officer informed the captain, who called general quarters and took command. The PCs had to "keep station" with each other so that their echo ranging would cover the entire area for the sortie without interruption; otherwise a submarine could sneak through an uncovered patch of ocean. Keeping station required maintaining a course and speed common to the other ships in the unit, a task demanding continual adjustments. I had a lot to learn.

The lessons became more difficult after the convoy had formed and started underway. The escorts then spread out into a formation that placed some escorts on both bows of the convoy and some at both flanks. Keeping station with each other, the PCs moved out in a kind of ballet away from and back toward the convoy while they echo ranged, looking for submarines coming toward the convoy. Because German subs, few any longer on the prowl in the Caribbean, at that time could not sustain speeds for catching the convoys from behind, no escorts sailed on the quarter of the convoy or trailed it. Now and then a straggler had to receive a special escort to protect it from being picked off. We lost a few merchant vessels in 1944, all of them stragglers that ignored orders and wandered across coral reefs, where we could not properly echo range. All the vessels in the convoy had to keep station, which meant that the convoy had to move at the speed of the slowest merchant in it, usually about six knots. The PCs, sailing in and out as they were, needed to move in phase so as to cover the area of search fully, and also had to keep up with the convoy by sustaining a higher speed, usually about eight knots. Wind, sea, currents, and human error affected the movements of all the ships, so the need to adjust speed and course was continual, and the watch officer had to stay alert.

Within my first month I erred notably. During one evening watch, about 2200 hours (10 p.m.), Porter came up onto the flying bridge, where I was trying to regain my proper position relative to the convoy and other escorts. Visibility was poor, but a report I had requested from radar had informed me that I had gone out too far from my station. So I had changed course and increased speed to compensate. The sound of the engines changing speed had awakened Porter, who came up to see what was going on. Believing that I had the situation under control, I had sat down on an ammunition box near the voice tube to the wheel house. As Porter arrived I stood up and walked to his side. He asked why I had left station, nodded when I explained the course I had taken, and remained until I had the ship back where it belonged and had adjusted course to stay there. But when near midnight I went below to write up the log, I found Porter awaiting me. He gave me the worst tongue-lashing I have ever received. Never again, he growled, was I for any reason to sit down on watch. Didn't I know what *standing* a watch meant? No one could be alert, he said, sitting down. All I could say was, "Yes, sir!" Without further comment, Porter left. I followed his order for the rest of my time at sea. And that saved me and the ship many months later on a black night off Iwo Jima when another ship on patrol lost position and came only inches from our bow before I saw it and turned away, emergency full speed.

We sailed out one afternoon from Panama for target practice. A friendly airplane towed a sleeve well astern. We were to hit the target with fire from our several machine guns. My station was at the aft 40-millimeter gun, next to the ready box that encircled it. Only seconds into the drill that gun had a hang fire. A shell was stuck somewhere between the breech-block and the muzzle. It was my duty as the officer there to clear the hang fire, a potentially dangerous procedure because a live shell might explode at any time. I started, following doctrine, by using a special implement through the muzzle to unscrew the business end of the shell from the breech end where the projecting head had been stuck. (I later learned that sea water had led to rusting of the shells' breech ends.) I could not budge the connection, which (I also learned later) had been fixed when the shell had been manufactured. After about ten minutes of futile effort on my part, Porter began to shout down from his aft position on the upper deck to warn me that the ship could not return to port until I had cleared the gun. I would be punished, he said, if he missed the movie that evening on the base. The warning made no difference. The gun did not hear it, and I was so fearful of a hang fire explosion that my knees were trembling.

No other officer volunteered to come to my assistance, but after another half an hour or so, the chief machinist mate came on deck. Porter ordered him, as I urged him, to stay away. But the regular navy chief, our only regular, Chief Tony Manalia, "Tony Bananas" as the fleet knew him, marched slowly right up to me. "Hey, Mr. Blum," he said, "you ain't got the strength to clear this fucker. I'm going to help you." I told him that the responsibility was mine. "Who the hell cares?" Tony said. "You been in this here navy maybe a couple of months. I've fired more guns than you've met." (Tony had been at Pearl Harbor when the Japanese struck.) So we went to work together with no protest from Porter, who was still worried mostly about his movie. Tony gave me courage. He also persuaded me to work from the breech end. We each grabbed a marlinspike and began to pry at the edge of the jammed shell. If we could force it out backwards, it would drop into my arms, or so we reasoned, and I could throw it over the side. That is, if it didn't explode. I remained anxious but willing, for there was no apparent alternative. After half an hour of shoving, the shell suddenly gave, sprang backward out of the breech into my chest, and at once I rushed to the starboard railing and threw the shell into the drink. The crew clapped. I thanked Tony. Porter canceled the firing exercise, took the ship in, and got to his movie on time.

Soon thereafter Porter announced that as long as he was skipper, he would do everything he could to prevent his officers from getting married. Married officers, he asserted, were too eager to get home to take the risks necessary for winning the war. Of course we were doing nothing critical for victory. Further, White was already married, and neither of the others had steady girlfriends, so Porter's threat was obviously directed against me.

An unfriendly truce arose between the captain and me. It escalated to anger during an assignment that took the PC 616 to Talara, Peru, an oil port dominated by Canadian-American interests. We were to meet two Peruvian submarines there and escort them back to Panama for repairs, which were to be paid for by lend-lease. It was a ridiculous mission. The United States had given the Peruvians the subs, which they used as gunboats near the headwaters of the Amazon to resist Brazilian incursions. Once the repairs were made, they intended to return the ships to the same duty. Under no conditions, they told us, would the subs dive; they never had. On the way down to Peru, we had trouble transiting the Panama Canal where the pilot put aboard did not know how to handle our engines. He crashed into one of the locks at Gatun. The resulting damage to the hull was too minor to abort our mission, but Porter went into orbit, where he stayed for the rest of the trip.

As we approached the Talara harbor, an Argentine passenger ship started out, setting a course that would cross our bow. Incensed, Porter warned the Argentine, a neutral vessel, to stand clear. The Argentine ignored him. Porter ordered the forward three-inch 50 cannon to ready for fire. Again he warned the Argentine to stand clear; again he was ignored. My station when we were about to anchor happened to be at the forward gun. I stood there, appalled by the situation. Without orders from Porter, I told the gun crew to load an illuminating shell. When Porter then ordered the gun fired, there resulted not a shell across the neutral's bow but a Fourth of July display of fireworks. Nevertheless this caused the Argentine to change course and steam away. That satisfied Porter enough to persuade him to withhold punishing me until he had first enjoyed a night of liberty ashore.

The PC's small boat took the officers ashore except for one who had the watch. I was to relieve him at 2345 (11:45 p.m.), so the boat remained on the beach to await me. That gave the boat crew a chance to look around. Porter would signal for the boat when he was ready to return, probably an hour after I had taken the watch. But the party we were invited to attend by oil company executives proved to be bibulous, and our plans changed. I discovered that the port director was a Harvard contemporary whom I had known casually. He was as dismayed as I was by Porter's approach to the Argentine. While we had a couple of drinks, talking as we sipped, I lost track of time and neglected to eat. Then I hurried back to the ship and, testing my sobriety, went to check the bearings of our anchorage.

In his haste to go ashore, Porter had dropped the anchor in an area with a shifting bottom. When I checked, it was clear that the bottom was not holding, for we were drifting much too close to the shore. So I ordered the crew to raise the hook and headed the ship out to sea. It was much too dark to try to find a new anchorage in the crowded harbor. We sailed back and forth about a mile out to sea until just before dawn. As I later heard the story, Porter was drunk, incredulous, and enraged at 0215 (2:15 a.m.), Easter morning, when he could not locate the PC 616. He hired a Peruvian boat to search the harbor. Porter was standing in the bow, arms akimbo, like a small George Washington, when he spotted us just after daybreak, hull down, moving toward the harbor. By this time his hangover had become brutal and he was having a fit. He ordered preparations for liberty for the crew. "Go to your quarters," he then shouted at me. "And Blum, you are to hold Easter services at 1500" (3 p.m.). Then he went to the wardroom to sleep it off. Porter probably meant to embarrass me by making me, for that Easter at least, the ship's pastor, but I had attended Easter services at Andover and knew how to proceed. More important, though Porter did not know it, I had become friendly with Father O'Reilly, a Jesuit at the mission in Kingston, Jamaica. He told me and the sailors whose confessions he heard that in the absence of a priest aboard, while we were at sea, attendance at any formal service the ship held would absolve sins until a Catholic church and confessor became available ashore. So on Easter Sunday especially, I felt, the crew's Catholic sailors deserved a service, even the kind of low church Protestant service I could manage.

The rest was easy. I knew one of the men could play the accordion. He and I remembered the words to the first stanzas of dozens of hymns. Relying on first stanzas only, we could provide two hymns, separated by a brief sermon. And I knew the call to service that Claude Fuess had used at Andover, as well as the Lord's Prayer, which would follow the second hymn and precede a blessing. The only problem was the sermon. The navy supplied every ship with a book of canned sermons. I looked up Easter Sunday and found a text of about three hundred words focused as ever, even though it was Easter, on the evil of venery. So I substituted words of my own that associated Easter with the renewal of spring, the season of rebirth. Some fifteen men, most of them Catholics, attended the service that afternoon. Afterward the Polish shipfitter came up to thank me. Porter apparently considered my own sins absolved, for he said nothing about the ship's disappearance the previous night. On Monday we started back to Panama with the two subs. How to characterize the wars of Talara — opera bouffe? More likely Mickey Mouse.

On June 6, 1944, Allied forces invaded Hitler's fortress Europe. We heard the news at Guantánamo Bay, Cuba. Never had I felt more useless. And I was to feel much the same way when American forces invaded Guam and Saipan. The Donald Duck navy was not heroic. Two weeks after D-E day we were in Cuba again when Ted White relieved Porter of command. I liked Ted, who believed in marriage. This was an important quality, since we were going on to Key West, where our ship was to be retrofitted for duty in the Pacific. I needed a commanding officer sympathetic to my plans, as Ted was. He and I went on leave the day we arrived in the United States. On June 28, 1944, Pamela and I were married in a small wedding at her family's home in Summit, New Jersey. The minister, my mother's brother-in-law, used the Book of Common Prayer, as modified by Pam. Perhaps most notably, she removed the word "obey." My mother and sister cried throughout the ceremony, to my great annoyance. Pam looked wonderful in her gown, and I wore my whites for the first time. We spent five days in the Berkshires and then traveled to Key West, where we took a room at a beachside hotel for the two weeks the PC 616 would be in port. We were fortunate to have had these days together. It was a bittersweet time, every moment delicious but shadowed by the recognition that going to the Pacific meant a long tour of duty. Parting left us both feeling hollow.

Ted White was a good sailor and a gentle captain, but he had bad luck as skipper. Leaving Key West, we were ordered to escort a single ship, the SS *Hindoo* — American owned, of Panamanian registry, with an American gun crew aboard — a freighter in ballast, from Guantánamo to Cartagena, Colombia. The night before we were to make landfall the sky was clear when I reached the bridge for the midwatch. Radar reported a large blip, moving fast, on our port bow. Seeing nothing, I concluded it was a dirigible, a common visitor to the area. But a few minutes later we could see a ship, hull down, off the port bow and moving toward us and the *Hindoo*, which was on our starboard quarter. So I called the captain, who on arriving on the bridge took command, though I remained there to assist him when called upon. White ordered the signalman to raise the ship, now with its hull in sight, by Morse code on the flashing light. He also summoned another signalman to raise the *Hindoo* on our other light. White and I were quickly puzzled. The *Hindoo* was not responding, though we kept trying. We later learned that there was a fire in the *Hindoo*'s hold, which the captain and most of the crew were trying to extinguish. The helmsman, alone in the wheel house, saw our signals but could not read them.

Concurrently our signals to the oncoming ship were receiving an odd response. Each word we sent was acknowledged, but when we asked for acknowledgment of a sentence, we received only a signal to "repeat." It later developed that the approaching ship was the MV (motor vessel) *Australia Star*, out of Liverpool on its maiden voyage via the Panama Canal to Sidney. A young midshipman was working the light and did not know Morse code. He dutifully flashed his light after each word, but he did not understand that our messages were warning his ship that it was on a collision course with our convoy. Merchant skippers hate to change course, so the *Australia Star* plowed along, turning on its running lights, passing us to our starboard. On it went, crashing into the *Hindoo* amidships, killing the gun crew, who were asleep in the cabin where the collision occurred, and sinking the ship, which foundered in a few minutes. On a clear night, two ships in sight of each other for at least ten minutes on a collision course, had both failed to alter course and collided. And we were responsible for the safety of the ship that sank!

Aghast, we turned to assist in the rescue of the *Hindoo*'s crew, as did the *Australia Star*. White ordered me to join him in our small boat, which took us to board the *Australia Star*. It was hard to say who was angrier, White or the captain of the MV whose brand-new ship had suffered extensive damage. The captain of the *Hindoo* was desolate. Conversations among the captains established the facts—the fire, the untrained midshipman—which we had had no idea of. Then we escorted the *Australia Star* to dry dock in Panama.

The navy at once ordered a Board of Inquiry. I was not personally responsible, for Ted White, the captain, was in command once I had called him to the bridge. But I was a witness, and I felt for Ted. The board interrogated me twice. I later learned that, asked on both occasions what running lights I had seen on the *Australia Star*, I testified the first time to a combination of lights that I contradicted the second time. White did much the same. Obviously in just three days after the collision, we did not really remember what we had seen. The board heard also from witnesses from both merchant ships. Soon thereafter we were simply told to forget the matter and proceed with our preparations for Pacific duty.

Some years later, in 1947, when the matter of the collision became an admiralty case in a United States district court, Ted and I had to testify again. We then learned that the Board of Inquiry had found us both "criminally negligent" for not firing a green Very shell, an emergency signal for all ships in the immediate area to come right. It had never occurred to either of us to use that simple device. But the board also declared us "not actionally liable" because of our youth and inexperience at sea. (Mickey Mouse!) I had been at sea only seven months; Ted, about a year and a half. The district court in 1947, in a decision ultimately confirmed by the Supreme Court (338 U.S. 823, 1949) ruled that the escort did have a responsibility for its convoy. Therefore, in the calculus of admiralty law, the value of the escort had to be added to the value of the *Hindoo* in determining the American debt to the British government, the owner of the *Australia Star*. (The damage suffered by that ship exceeded the combined value of escort and convoy, so Uncle Sam had to make up the difference.)

After the inquiry about the collision we received our orders to transit the canal and escort a fleet tug towing two barracks barges from Panama to New Guinea. That was a long way to go, some 4,000 nautical miles, especially since the tug, with its large load, was capable of only six knots. The barracks barges were floating hotels, each three stories, each complete with doctors and medical facilities, each loaded with fuel oil. They were to serve as dormitories for American troops. We would have to come alongside the after barge, take on fuel as needed, move up to fuel the tug, and drop back to fuel our PC. That action would theoretically expose the whole convoy to submarine attack, but the Japanese had no known submarines in the south Pacific. Before we left Panama at least a third of our veteran crew were transferred and replaced by mostly teenage seamen. So training became a necessity as we moved west. Many afternoons I taught algebra on the after deck to petty officer aspirants. They were eager to learn enough to pass their qualifying tests, and I, in my first experience with teaching, enjoyed my work. All day, every day, we young officers were learning more about our ship, the ocean, and ourselves.

But we were still babes at sea. Two days beyond Tahiti our auxiliary engines began to throw out black exhaust, indicating incomplete combustion and the need for us to make repairs. But the engines worked through a regulator, a sealed, clocklike mechanism that was beyond the capacity of any small ship to repair. The regulator had to be replaced in a shipyard that had the necessary part. Some destroyer escorts nearby agreed to take over our convoy while we steamed ahead to Funa Futi in the Ellice Islands to seek help. We were to keep in touch with the DEs and pick up the convoy within a few days. At Funa Futi, while the local yard cut through our main deck, lifted out the auxiliary engines, and replaced them, I went ashore to the communications shack to sustain radio contact with the DEs.

The base officer assisting me accompanied me back to the PC. He was hoping to buy some bourbon or Scotch whiskey. It was illegal for any navy ship to carry liquor. But the officers of the PC had together purchased several cases from what seemed a safe source, the regular navy captain in charge of the port at the Pacific end of the Panama Canal. We were resolved to keep the cases sealed until we reached a permanent base. When my Funa Futi companion asked to buy a few bottles, he was refused. "This whiskey," White told him, "is not for sale at any price, not even a hundred dollars a bottle." Disgruntled, the officer departed. The episode would soon haunt us.

We returned to our convoy. The auxiliary engines installed at Funa Futi soon proved as faulty as those we had given up, and the Commandant of the South Pacific Theater ordered us to put in at Florida Island in the Solomon Islands for an overhaul. A substitute PC would escort the tug to its destination. We were at a dock on Florida Island on Christmas Eve 1944. I had the watch and retired early. While I slept, White decided to celebrate the holiday by opening the whiskey and sharing it with the crew. I awoke to find half the crew and the other officers sleeping it off. I made it clear that I disapproved of the Christmas Eve party, but White only laughed and said there were three bottles of Scotch remaining and I could have them all.

Two days later there arrived at the gangway two strangers, lieutenant commanders, who asked to come aboard. They said they had heard we had liquor for sale. Fed up with the whole liquor business, I said I would sell them a bottle of Johnny Walker Black Label for less than its wholesale price, $5.00. They bought it. In another two days White and I were served with papers informing us of a pending court-martial "for carrying liquor aboard ship for sale at exorbitant prices." Either the Panama captain who sold us the liquor had put the Funa Futi officer up to charging us, or the officer had done so on his own, but either way Admiral Halsey was calling us to account. The admiral had a billboard in the Tulagi harbor reading: "Kill Japs! Kill more Japs! You will be doing your part if you help to kill those yellow bastards! Signed: Bull Halsey." Did he care about an insignificant ship like ours? And could it be said that this was not a racist war?

"No" to both questions. Halsey surely cared nothing about the local proceedings in the Solomons. Further his local legal office had stubbed its toe. As I knew from my course in naval courts and boards, a charge and the specifications supporting it had to be separated to assure a conviction. The charge against us was not separated from its specifications. Indeed there were no specs. Rather, the charge combined two specifications, one of them patently false. I so informed the lieutenant commander who had bought the Scotch from me. "You know very well," I told him by telephone, "that we were wholly overt about the whiskey, and you bought it for $5.00, a bargain." He replied: "Overt means hidden." And then he hung up.

Ted White reluctantly left our defense to me. I think he had visions of naval prison. But when we stood before the court-martial in Tulagi, I asked to approach and then requested a private audience with the presiding captain of the court, White, and the accusing lieutenant commander. The request was granted. I then asked the lieutenant commander to confirm that he had paid $5.00 for his bottle. He did so. I then asked the presiding captain if he considered the price exorbitant. He did not. So, I pointed out, we did not do as charged. You had liquor aboard ship, the captain replied. Yes, sir, I said, but not for sale at an unreasonable price. And the charge requires proof of both its parts. You have issued no specifications, so we are not guilty as charged, and I see no reason for a trial.

The lieutenant commander was angry, but remained quiet. The captain reflected a few minutes. "You're correct, Ensign Blum," he said. "But watch yourself in the future. Keep your finger on your number!" Ted and I were then dismissed. We would have liked a stiff drink to celebrate our escape, but there was obviously no way we could do that. And, equally obviously, the war had gone north. The Solomons by early 1945 were little more dangerous than the Caribbean.

Shortly thereafter we were to go north, though first Ted White was replaced as skipper by Charles Harris, who had been aboard since before I had reported. I became executive and communications officer. Harris ran a tauter ship than White had, a change we needed. And Harris handled the ship with enviable skill. We went on several kinds of assignments. Frequently we had convoy duty within the archipelago, sailing like Mr. Roberts from ennui to tedium and back. More often we were on ping patrol, sound searching to locate two-man Japanese submarines that were trying to sneak down "the slot" west of Savo Island and into the harbor at Guadalcanal in order to pick off a ship staging there for an invasion further north.

The people of the Solomon Islands, Melanesians all, could not have been stranger to Western eyes. The women traded with us, providing fresh pullet eggs in return for empty tobacco tins that they used to make jewelry. The men, inveterate sailors in their dugout canoes, had devised a way to find a celestial fix at night. They did so by getting a reflection of Orion in a gourd, which had been carved with one-quarter removed, then hollowed and filled with water up to the level of the resulting lip. I tried to learn their method but failed. At night Orion dominated the gorgeous southern skies. Its orbit across the heavens provided a recurrent natural wonder that elevated any midnight watch. For me, the beauty and the vastness of the ocean resonated in transcendental empathy with "Katahdin," an essay by Henry David Thoreau that I was then reading. Katahdin was of course a mountain in Maine, but it was a great work of nature, like the sea. So Thoreau's words: "We have not seen pure Nature, unless we have seen her thus vast . . . and awful, though beautiful . . . made out of Chaos and Old Night. . . . Talk of mysteries!"

Mysteries imbued that time. Wonder at the ocean. Wonder about the jungle, where we took on water from a river that ran down from Guadalcanal highlands, filled with strange wildlife, where American Marines had so recently spilled their blood. Missing Pamela sorely, I wondered, too, about the mystery of love. Like nature, love was transcendent. And that April, with the shocking news of the death of Franklin D. Roosevelt, the only president most of the crew remembered, we confronted the mystery of death. I had been holding services at sea since we had left Peru. Attendance was small, seven or eight sailors each Sunday. Now I planned a memorial service for Roosevelt by adapting a passage of Thomas Wolfe, whose novels I had been reading. Wolfe's protagonist, returning from his father's funeral, memorialized his father; by capitalizing "Father," I could use the passage, slightly modified, as a sermon memorializing FDR. So I did, and that Sunday we sang the Navy hymn "Eternal Father Strong to Save" with special fervor. One other officer came to that service as well as thirty-nine sailors, the largest number ever to attend, even on later Sundays after Japanese aerial bombings or a typhoon.

Young Americans far from home, we mourned our president. And I began to reformulate my ideas about religion. I felt the presence of a force greater than man. I felt that force in all things. But I still rejected the concepts of an anthropomorphic god and a revealed truth. I rejected then and later both Judaism and Christianity. Though I could not then yet define it, in later years I could describe my faith. I was neither atheist nor agnostic, nor was I in the least evangelical. Increasingly as the war went on, I was becoming a pantheistic transcendentalist, a child of Emerson and Thoreau, a believer in mysteries inherent in experience.

About a fortnight after the president's death, we received orders to escort a troop transport to Saipan via Eniwetok. The voyage to Eniwetok was without event. That atoll, one of the Marshall Islands, a large, curvilinear coral reef protruding from the ocean, was years later blown to bits in an atomic test. While we lay over a day to take on fuel and water, for the first time in weeks we received mail from home. There had never been a mail packet like this one. I went below to savor a shower of letters from Pamela. Putting them aside for further readings later, I opened a few packages that contained my Christmas presents from her, the best a small photo volume with snapshots of her. Only after examining those pages again and again did I turn to the rest of my mail. There was an unexpected letter from Fred Merk. He urged me to use the benefits in the GI Bill to finance graduate work in history at Harvard, and he spelled out the reduced criteria for former Harvard students with outstanding undergraduate records to earn a Ph.D. It all felt so remote to me that I put the letter in my sea bag for a closer reading after the war, which then seemed years away.

There was also a surprise letter from Myron Gilmore. He had been writing logistics history for the navy, he reported, but was now about to undertake a new assignment. Would I, he asked, be interested in relieving him and completing the study he had begun. *Would I?* The thought of duty in Washington, DC, provoked instant euphoria. I wrote Myron at once. I also wrote a brief note to Fred Merk, promising to see him when I reached home. And, wonderful to recount, in the same mail I received orders to await the arrival of my relief and then depart for thirty days' home leave. I daydreamed of exploring life in Washington with Pamela. Then I began waiting for my relief—and waited and waited.

On reaching Saipan we were ordered immediately to proceed alone to Guam for duty with the submarine contingent there. That night, as we sailed south and approached the latitude of the island of Rota, one of the Mariana Islands that the navy had bypassed, we came under attack from Bettys, two-engine Japanese bombers flying at about 1,500 feet, beyond range of our guns. They dropped small bombs that descended so slowly we could dodge them. But they kept at it all night, holding us at general quarters until dawn. There was little danger, but I found, as I did whenever thereafter we were under similar attack, that my knees turned to water until I left the bridge. Once I could no longer see the bombers I was totally cool—and occupied intellectually, for my battle station allowed me to remain on the bridge with the captain or, at my discretion, to go below to plot on a mooring board radar information about the course and speed of the incoming aircraft we intended to evade. I needed an intellectual occupation to stay cool. So I preferred the radar and mooring board below deck to the sights and sounds of the open bridge. No one shared my preference, but no one questioned it.

We reached Guam early the next morning. While there we reported to ComSubPac, the Commander of Submarines in the Pacific. Our job was to leave the harbor nightly to rendezvous at dawn with an American submarine returning from a tour at sea. The sub would not surface until it reached the area for the meeting, so precise navigation on our part was essential. We never missed a rendezvous. We escorted the sub to harbor to protect it from American aircraft, which might otherwise have attacked it. As they entered the harbor, the returning submarines flew a flag hoist indicating their kills, or hoisted a broom to show a clean sweep—all their torpedoes had scored hits. The ships in the harbor responded by blowing their whistles or sounding their horns. We escorts felt very puny. But Admiral Nimitz, the commander of the forward area, had moved his headquarters from Pearl Harbor to Guam, where the mail from home arrived daily and we enjoyed the amenities of a swanky officers' club, so we were sorry to leave, as we had to when ordered to Iwo Jima.

At Iwo Jima, where Japanese soldiers remained hidden in the many caves of the island, the harbor was artificial, merely a small bay, dredged and closed off by an anti-submarine net, lacking a protective lee. The Japanese now and then sneaked out of their caves and swam into the harbor with the hope of tossing a hand grenade onto a ship at anchor. At night we kept a patrol from dusk to dawn with orders to shoot whenever a strange sound or sight suggested the presence of the enemy. The island, scarred by the terrible battle that had raged over it, was a desolate place, a large airstrip useful only as an emergency landing field for the huge B-29 Super Fortresses that returned, crippled, from bombing Japanese cities. We went on ping patrol to protect the harbor from Japanese submarines, we took convoys back and forth to Saipan, and we joined a few hunter-killer groups. At sea at night off Iwo Jima we were often at battle stations, as Bettys flew down from Chichi Jima, just north of Iwo and still in Japanese hands. The Bettys were a nuisance. The B-29s, though we did not realize it, were helping to bring the war to an end.

Soon after we reached Iwo Jima, a new captain, whom I shall call Joe T., relieved Harris. I was to remain as executive officer until my elusive relief arrived. Joe T. had served on a PC in Alaska, but he had no experience with celestial navigation because of the constant cloudiness of that area and had little skill in ship handling. Certain that our real enemy was the Soviet Union, he expected the war to go on until we took Moscow. He and I did not get along, though both of us tried to make the best of an awkward situation. It was awkward because the crew knew me and my ways, which were the long-standing ways of the ship, whereas Joe T. had ways of his own that he was eager to impose.

In July 1945 a typhoon came roaring toward Iwo Jima. We were at anchor in the harbor when all ships there were ordered at dawn to get underway and proceed to evacuate the harbor before the expected winds could blow them ashore. A dangerously disorganized exit took perhaps an hour. By the time we were at sea, the wind had reached speeds of more than 100 knots and waves were breaking over our radar dome some ten feet above the flying bridge where I was standing watch, soaked, hanging on to the 20-millimeter gun. The storm was so fierce that the USS *Baltimore*, a heavy cruiser nearby, sustained serious damage. We were like flotsam and jetsam on the turbulent sea; but I tried, as we had learned, to take the sea on our quarter. We were doing well enough until a small tanker, anchored near the south face of the island, sent a light message asking for help to pull itself out to sea.

Small though it was, the tanker was twice our size and roiled in the surf. Against my advice, Joe T. decided to attempt a rescue. I went below to the wheel house while he ordered the PC 616 to go into the surf, approach the tanker, and toss it a messenger — a weighted rope — attached to our heaviest line. Maneuvering to a few feet from the tanker, we were thrown up and slammed into it as the messenger dropped, useless, into the surf. As I felt the impact of the collision, I called the engine room and ascertained that we had only two remaining starts. Before Joe T. could give another order, I seized the engine room telegraph and signaled for emergency, both engines full astern. We backed down at once, away from the surf and into the sea again, with our stem post, the forwardmost part of our keel, broken from the collision. Afraid of further damaging that crucial strength member, I continued backing down while trying to avoid the worst of the sea. Joe T., seasick like almost everyone aboard except for the senior shipfitter and me, went down to the wardroom and closed the doors. I asked one of the other officers to take the deck. Brave fellow, though violently ill he had himself tied to the 20-millimeter gun and took over the watch.

I raced with the shipfitter and two other sailors to the paint locker, the most forward compartment of the ship, to inspect the damage to the stem post. We found it broken about five feet from its peak, with its lower part wiggling like a loose tooth. The crew's head lay aft of the paint locker and the forward crew's quarters aft of the head. Together the shipfitter and I decided to take a mattress from one of the bunks and shove it into the growing gap in the stem post. Mirabile dictu, the mattress stayed there until we were ready to remove it several days later. With the mattress in place, I ordered the others to shore the door and after bulkhead of the paint locker so that if we took water, the water could not get into the head. They worked on this task for the next half an hour. Exhausted, I then slept for an hour.

Back on the bridge, I took over the watch and had the radioman raise Saipan, explain that our stem post was broken and we were backing down, and ask for orders. The reply directed us to proceed on our own to Saipan. Joe T. was still locked from the inside in the wardroom and uncommunicative. We headed for Saipan as best we could. As we sailed south, the sea and winds receded. We arrived at our destination in about two days. Repairs began right away.

Curiously, Joe T. and I never discussed the episode. He left his isolation only as we approached the harbor at Saipan, where he took charge of the repairs. For many years I felt that I had been mutinous. My engine order in the surf had no authorization, but it was never overruled. Joe T. had closed himself in the wardroom, where we then left him. One day it occurred to me that Joe T. must have realized that my order to the engine room had been necessary. It was his order, not mine, that had led to the broken stem post, and my order, not his, that had started the ship to safety. Less said, sooner mended, he may have decided. Whatever the case, he never accused me of mutiny. He also never openly explained the cause of the damage. Indeed he remarked not at all about that morning of terror in the typhoon.

It was sheer terror that I felt from the time we entered the surf until we started for Saipan — though at least my terror was punctuated by action. For months after the war I was ashamed of my fear. Then one afternoon in 1951, I read *The Caine Mutiny*, which described a ship during a typhoon, and I realized that almost everyone felt fear in such a sea, as also in battle. I knew I was not a brave man. But I now recognized that I had been able to function in the face of danger, and I wept in relief.

After the stem post was repaired we returned to Iwo Jima, where my replacement arrived almost at once. Like Odysseus, I took a long time getting home, for junior naval officers had to hitchhike. A Marine pilot gave me a lift from Iwo to Saipan. There I found space on a transport carrying B-29 crews to Honolulu for rest and recreation. I had marveled at their courage; now I marveled at their youth. The bombs were dropped at Hiroshima and Nagasaki before we reached Pearl Harbor. In the crush of officers seeking transportation to California, I bribed a WAVE officer to put me on a baby aircraft carrier en route to San Francisco. She received my last bottle of Johnny Walker Black in return for her favor. I swore a private oath to myself as we sailed under the Golden Gate Bridge that never again would I willingly go to sea. (I kept that oath until 1963.) In September 1945 I met Pamela in New York. I was not happy about the navy and not happy about myself, but I was vastly relieved to be done with war. Though I had further duty ahead, I rejoiced in the arms of my wife. Number 269416 was home again.

4

Apprentice

Like most veterans returning from war, I was as eager to get home as I was to leave the armed services. Home meant two things to me. The first was Pamela. Where she was, there was home. The second was Harvard, the last place where I had lived and thrived before donning a uniform. Pamela looked forward to a life with me in Cambridge even before she had experienced that beguiling city. When I had graduated from Harvard College I could not afford to contemplate further formal education. But the navy years had made me comparatively comfortable. I had saved almost all of my monthly salary, which was swollen after marriage by a family allowance. There was little to buy at sea except for cigarettes at five cents a pack, drinks at officers' clubs at ten cents, and postage stamps. So I could pay off my debt to Andover and hold some war bonds as an emergency reserve. Commuting from her family home, Pam had worked as a junior corporate trust administrator at the Guaranty Trust Company in New York City and was prepared to find a job as soon as our plans were settled. My return to the academy was made possible by the GI Bill. I was eligible for four years of educational benefits, which included tuition and a family allowance, about $100 a month.

As my naval orders stipulated, in September 1945 on my arrival in New York I reported to the Commandant of the Third Naval District. At his office I learned that my orders to return to the Pacific had been canceled. I had too few "points" (credits for discharge) for immediate demobilization, but I could look forward to that event in December. My interim orders would come through in three weeks; my leave would terminate in thirty days. I called Myron

Gilmore in Washington at my first opportunity to ascertain whether he still expected me as his relief. It had been a long time since his letter had reached me in Eniwetok. Myron explained that the details had yet to be arranged. He suggested that Pam and I come to Washington for a day and that we have dinner with him and his wife the evening we arrived and an interview with my prospective commanding officer the next morning. If the interview went well, Myron was sure I would receive official orders to complete the history he had begun. We agreed on a date about two weeks away.

Meanwhile Pamela and I visited Cambridge to see whether Harvard Law School would admit me or whether I should instead begin the program for the Ph.D. in history that Fred Merk had described in his letter to me, which I had kept, unexamined, since Eniwetok. Pam and I arrived in Cambridge, I in uniform, to confront the wartime problem of finding a place to stay. While from a drugstore phone Pam called various landladies who listed temporary accommodations — an arduous task — I walked up to the law school, where I learned that I could count on admission in January 1946 or at certain intervals for a year thereafter if I wished to begin in the History Department. The university was planning three terms a year; my GI eligibility allowed me four years or twelve terms, so I had plenty of latitude.

With Pamela still on the phone, I went to keep an appointment with Fred Merk. Obviously glad to see me, he greeted me with a strong handshake. At once I felt very much at home, very much back to my roots. Fred explained the details of the graduate program I would undertake if I decided to matriculate. Characteristically he advised me while still on active duty to brush up on my foreign languages and to think about a topic for my dissertation. Then he sent me to call on Oscar Handlin, who was also welcoming. As I left the building, I was leaning strongly toward history rather than law, but I had not quite made up my mind.

Just then I almost literally bumped into Elliot Perkins, master of Lowell House and a lecturer in eighteenth-century English history. He invited me to join him in the master's residence for a glass of sherry. Perkins was a Boston Brahmin through and through, the son of a former fellow of Harvard College (a member of the Harvard Corporation). He had married an outgoing English woman, and had assumed British manners, an Oxbridge accent, and a generous use of "ain't," an affectation he considered aristocratic. He was also a famously uninformed and dull lecturer. Once we arrived at his study he asked me what brought me to Cambridge. I had come, I said, to decide whether to enter law school or the doctoral program in history. "You better go to law school," Perkins replied. "Hebrews can't make it in history." I thanked him for his advice, met Pamela for lunch, and informed her that I was going to enroll in the history program. Perkins's comment had clinched my decision.

There remained the matter of my orders. As planned, we went to Washington to meet Myron. I was anxious over the prospect of having to make a good impression on senior officers who would quickly discover that I had only an A.B. degree. But a thoughtful friend who drove us to dinner cheered me. "Don't worry," he said. "You've done something the rest of them have not." "What's that?" I asked. "You've been to sea," he replied. That answer lifted my morale and kept it high during the evening with the Gilmores and their other guests, all Harvard historians and their wives whom I had known before we went to war. Myron, I learned, was now relieved of his historian's duty and was instead writing testimony for naval officers of flag rank to take to the Senate committee on unification of the armed services. The testimony put forth the navy's reasons for opposing that prospect, a sensible proposal of the air corps to which the navy bitterly objected because unification threatened that department's traditional independence.

The next morning Myron took me to meet his friend and former commanding officer, Lieutenant Elting E. Morison of the U.S. Naval Reserve. Elting was a second cousin of Admiral Samuel Eliot Morison, the great Harvard historian of the colonial period whom President Roosevelt had selected as the official historian of the navy during World War II. Admiral Morison was writing about strategy and naval engagements. His was a history of valor, battle, and glory. Elting, in contrast, presided over half a dozen professional historians, reserve officers in their thirties as he was, who were writing a classified history of naval logistics during the war. It was supposed to provide an account of the difficulties the navy had overcome, a lesson for the future in what not to do as well as what worked. Myron had completed about half of a proposed study of naval logistics planning, which he hoped I would finish. But he admitted that he had forgotten that I had only a bachelor's degree. The others in Elting's office, mostly Harvard graduates, had either completed their doctorates or at least had begun their graduate studies. So I had reason to worry about my credentials.

But I had yet to know Elting Morison, Harvard '32, schoolmaster briefly at St. Mark's, assistant dean for a year at Harvard College, disciple of Fred Merk. He was unlike any naval officer or any professional historian I had ever met. When we arrived at his office, Myron introduced us and then departed. Elting was seated at his desk in what I soon learned was his characteristic posture: leaning back in his chair, hands locked behind his head, feet on the desk, with both shoes separated at the soles, which he was wiggling with his toes. I was to discover that his officer's raincoat lacked a belt. In or out of uniform, it made no difference to Elting. He asked me the topic of my doctoral dissertation. I admitted I had yet to begin graduate work. Undeterred, he asked me the topic of my senior essay and who had directed it. I told him about my study of Guam, which seemed to please him, and about Dick Leopold's role, of which he enthusiastically approved. "You'll do," he said. "Report here when your leave expires." My official orders were written accordingly.

I reported early in October 1945 and began at once to submerge myself in my new duty as apprentice historian working for Elting Morison, an unconventional master of the craft. He was also, as I was to discover, an old friend not only of Myron Gilmore and Dick Leopold but also of Wilbur Bender and Henry Chauncey. I had stumbled into a special Harvard old boys' network. Most of my new colleagues were also from Harvard, among them Duncan Ballantine, a doctoral candidate in English economic history, already designated to write a summary, declassified version of the findings of the whole group. He did so in his *U.S. Naval Logistics in the Second World War,* published by Princeton University Press in 1947. Each of us had a slice of naval logistics as his preserve, and duty otherwise only to rotate in attendance at the morning meetings of the staff of Vice Admiral F. J. Horne, VCNO (Vice Chief of Naval Operations), Elting's reporting senior. Horne for his part reported to Admiral Ernest J. King, CNO and COMINCH (Chief of Naval Operations and Commander in Chief, U.S. Fleet). Junior officers in Washington were sure that King reported, if at all, only to God.

Elting's office resembled a small history department rather than a naval command. He thrived on informality. Rank mattered to him not at all. Good conversation engaged him more than did the progress of the work. He had no peer in the navy as a raconteur. And he knew the navy inside out, for he had written a masterful biography of Admiral William Sims, his father-in-law, who had been a key innovator of the modern navy. In his research Elting had interviewed the captains who had served under Sims, men now admirals who knew and respected him. Day after day, often all day long, they came to consult with him or just to gossip or talk shop. My desk was just to one side of Elting's office, with only an open door between us, so I could not help but hear much of the conversation at which he excelled.

Responding to questions from the admirals, Elting picked up useful information wherever he conveniently could. One morning soon after I had joined his outfit, he asked me what I knew about fleet communications. I began to explain some of the difficulties we had had with NPM JUMP, the radio from Pearl Harbor. We had carried a communications allowance similar to a cruiser's and had served as communications center for our whole task unit. Elting listened, asked informed questions, and took me alone to lunch, where the conversation continued. I surprised myself by the range of my learning. After luncheon we returned to Elting's office. Almost at once there was a knock at his exterior door, the door opened, and in walked an admiral. I jumped to attention while Elting, his feet as ever on his desk, called out, "Hello, Betty! Come on in and sit down." His visitor was Admiral Harold R. Stark, who dutifully sat in the chair I had vacated as I went to my desk. Through the open door I could hear Elting say, his sharp voice rising, "Now, Betty, about fleet communications, as you asked me . . ." He went on to tell Admiral Stark what I had told Elting at lunch. I was amazed that my report, the view of a junior lieutenant, was reaching flag rank. And I had expected the floor to collapse when Elting had greeted an admiral as he had. Instead, the admiral was listening to a lecture for which I had been a major source.

That episode was a first step in my conversion from suspicion of high rank to admiration for most of those who had gained it. I met them largely through my research, but now and then unexpectedly face to face. I had on occasion in furthering my research to talk with Vice Admiral Horne, about whom nobody had warned me. He had lost three fingers on his right hand when a gun exploded. He gesticulated with the stump, from which I could hardly move my eyes. When I could, they became fixed on his waistcoat, his own design, for admirals were allowed to wear finery of their chosing. Horne's vest looked exactly like the vest of a train conductor, so that to me he looked like the operator of a streetcar. Still, he proved to be easy to talk to. Another day, Admiral W. F. Halsey, a controversial hero, came walking toward me down a long corridor. I froze at attention. Still yards away, he called out, "As you were, lieutenant, as you were!" No sign of a misdirected court-martial in that demeanor. Admiral King started across Constitution Avenue one day when I was crossing with some other officers in the opposite direction. Every one of us stopped and snapped to a crisp salute. King was by nature imperial.

I had been crossing Constitution Avenue on my way to the Federal Reserve building, which during the war had been the home of the Joint Chiefs of Staff. In that building were some top secret papers I needed to examine. My business, after all, was research and writing, the perfect combination for an apprentice historian. How to go about it? Myron had let me read as much manuscript as he had completed. It defined naval logistics for me: the organization of the procurement, transportation, and delivery of supplies for both the fleet and the areas it helped to invade and support. Elting intended to write a summary study of logistics but never got beyond a first sentence:

"Logistics is the third dimension of modern warfare." Asked why he could go no further, he replied simply, "That sentence says it all." Perhaps it did for insiders, but I had much more to write about logistics planning, and Elting and Myron simply let me loose to probe the record, literally hundreds of documents, most of them classified.

It soon became apparent that most of my contribution, in the end a manuscript of about 150 pages, would focus on two developments: a reorganization of the logistics for the invasion and support of advanced bases, and a proposed reorganization of the naval districts. Myron had begun to write about the former; his work now fell to me. I took over with a discussion of the problems inherent in adapting the units the navy had planned to the actual conditions they found at advanced bases. In planning, the bases had been organized in units of three standardized sizes: Lions, which included future major bases such as Guam; Cubs, smaller naval bases; and Acorns, air bases. But from 1942 onward local conditions required changes in the materials intended for the various units. As Duncan Ballantine, borrowing from my manuscript, later summarized the issue: "Few of the Cubs which were sent out followed exactly the lines on which they had originally been assembled. . . . Repeated requests were received from area commanders that Lions and Cubs be reshuffled in their composition." The navy would have to plan smaller, more adaptable, and more flexible assemblies.

To meet that objective the VCNO promulgated in March 1943 a "Catalogue of Advanced Base Functional Components," which listed components — in all, 79 in 1943 and almost 250 in 1945 — "each designed to fulfill a necessary function at an advanced base." Taken together (again quoting from Ballantine's summary), "the components represented the sum of individual units constituting a major base, but the components could be selected individually, combined, and regrouped" with ease. Consequently planners could tailor advanced base assemblies to varied operational needs. By the end of the war the catalogue ran to 479 volumes, weighed 250 pounds, and indicated the requirements of each component down to the last wrench and cotter pin. The planner or area commander needed only to list the components he needed; the details provided the information for supply officers in charge of procurement, shipping, and assembly.

This new system worked. Without it the United States could not have won the war in the Pacific as quickly or efficiently as it did. Yet the new system involved changes in the ways the navy had traditionally operated, and it therefore threatened officers accustomed to the old ways and the perquisites accompanying them. The innovators met resistance. That pattern of innovation and resistance was to become years later the focus of Elting's historical interests. It was the stuff of history, but in my case, it was history for confidential, internal use only, and history therefore written as much as possible without proper names. So, for example, Admiral Horne ordinarily appeared as "VCNO."

A plan originating in the office of the VCNO for the reorganization of the naval districts had potentially major significance. Naval districts were the basic administrative divisions, most of them within the United States (such as the Third District in New York), within which operated the supporting functions for all of the bureaus of the Navy Department. The district commandants had lines of authority that intersected the lines of authority of the bureaus (such as the Bureau of Ships or the Bureau of Ordnance). The resulting conflicts hindered the functions of the VCNO, who had overall responsibility for navy logistics. Organized largely for purposes of local defense, the districts had not accommodated to the logistic requirements of the world war. Admiral Horne therefore supported a general order to increase the authority of the bureaus and reduce the responsibilities of the districts. But that proposal raised anew the ancient question of civilian or military control of national defense, for the bureaus were under the military, reporting ultimately to the Chief of Naval Operations. The President had long resisted allowing the bureaus to gain authority at the expense of the Secretary of the Navy, a civilian officer. He saw the aggrandizement of the bureaus over the districts as analogous and rejected the proposed general order.

My work was done with a degree of circuitousness and speculation that my final manuscript left out. Puzzled by the failure of the district reorganization, for which I could not find a satisfactory paper trail, I enlisted Elting to ask Admiral Horne what had gone wrong. Elting then reported back to Duncan and me. Horne had told Elting that a copy of the plan was in the briefcase of Secretary of the Navy Frank Knox on the weekend in 1944 during which Knox had died. Elting then asked Horne whether he had brought the matter up with Knox's successor, James Forrestal. He had not, Horne said, because Forrestal had told him he was enjoying a honeymoon period with Admiral King, a notably prickly officer. "What I want to know," Duncan asked Elting, "is who was getting screwed?"

We assumed that King had blocked the plan. But I wanted to know why and how, so I asked a WAVE archivist for the Chief of Naval Operations for the full files of the relevant documents. She told me to come back the next day. Minutes after I had returned to my desk, a lieutenant commander from Admiral King's staff came into our offices, asking for me. I rose to attention.

"Lieutenant Blum?" he inquired. "Yes, sir," I replied. "I have a message for you," he said. "Keep your finger on your number!" And with that he wheeled around and left.

I proceeded then to write a draft in which I stated categorically that Admiral King had rejected Admiral Horne's plan. As always, Elting reviewed my draft. An incomparable editor, he made his usual comments, calling for me to shorten my draft by at least a quarter, to reduce the number of adjectives and adverbs, to come up with stronger verbs and more precise nouns —though as ever he left the revisions wholly to me. He liked my draft, he said, but he was uncomfortable approving my account until I had personally checked it directly with Admiral Horne. Usually Elting undertook that kind of checking himself, and I was anxious about asking the admiral about his own past. But Admiral Horne, who had read my account, cooperated without reserve. Everything he had told Elting about Knox, King, and Forrestal had been true, he said, but he had not told Elting the whole story. Admiral King, he now informed me, had himself taken the district reorganization plan directly to President Roosevelt. It was the president who had killed it. King was trying to protect the memory of his late commander-in-chief.

I rewrote my account accordingly, and Duncan in using it gave the question of civilian or military control its due. Elting and I enjoyed reconstructing the conversation we imagined King to have had with Roosevelt. The president had been assistant secretary of the navy during the administration of Woodrow Wilson. Proud of that experience, Roosevelt, once he became president himself, was wont to remark that he knew more about the navy than did anyone else in Washington. In a way he had proved his point by reaching down through the officers' ranks to promote King over a dozen more senior men. Roosevelt also knew many retired admirals whom he had met when they had less rank during his time in the Navy Department. During World War II, many of those old friends had been called back to active duty as commandants of naval districts. Elting and I assumed that the president, eager to reward them, wanted to keep them where they were. But we doubted he had said so to Admiral King. Rather, so we supposed, Roosevelt, presented with the proposal for reorganizing the districts, had thrown back his majestic head, removed his pinch eyeglasses, and said: "Why Ernest, I know more about the navy than anyone else in this town, and this plan won't work!" But of course I did not include any such surmise in my history, though Elting might very well have approved of it if I had. Working in Elting's group gave me a taste of writing what was essentially political history, a taste I found to my liking for the next half century.

While I was writing history, I was also learning about history as a profession. Almost every day the officers in Elting's command ate lunch together at the cafeteria on the top floor of the Department of the Interior, just across Constitution Avenue. Other historians who were also naval officers frequently joined the group. It was at lunch that I first met Lieutenant Commander Vann Woodward, who was at that time writing his book on the battle of Leyte Gulf. A native of Arkansas, thoroughly Southern, Vann hated the apartheid of his region, about which he was later to write famously. In later years we became friends, collaborators, and colleagues. In 1945 he was already impressive, a handsome naval lieutenant whose bright blue eyes took in everything that was going on. Probably the foremost historian of the United States of his generation, he had when I met him published only one book, his stunning biography of Tom Watson, the influential Georgia Populist. He was wary of the Harvard contingent, who in turn were wary of him.

Conversation at lunch frequently turned to professional issues. The others, all older than I, were preparing to return to their civilian careers, so talk naturally moved to jobs, to professional reputations, and to one book. Arthur Schlesinger, Jr., had just published his striking *Age of Jackson*. We all read it. I was in awe at the ease of the author's prose, his depth of learning, and the significance of the historical revisions that he had brought to his work. None of us was surprised when we learned in October 1945 that Harvard had made Arthur, who was only five years my senior, a tenured associate professor.

His reputation soared during 1945. We talked about others who had enjoyed a similar experience years earlier. Many of them were historians whose names were new to me or whose work I had not read. So at our lunches I accumulated a personal reading list that lasted me for at least five years. The consensus among the historians at lunch ranked at the top of living American historians Admiral Samuel Eliot Morison and rated as his greatest accomplishment his two-volume biography of Christopher Columbus, *Admiral of the Ocean Sea*. I found that splendid work a rewarding place to begin my reading, not the least because Morison necessarily placed so much of his account in parts of the Caribbean I had so recently visited. When I returned to Harvard, my expectations high, I enrolled in his course on colonial history. He was majestic, in uniform or out; the course, however, was less so.

In Washington I also set about executing Fred Merk's mandate to find a topic for my dissertation. I knew I wanted to focus on some aspect of United States history. Before the war I had imagined writing about the Wyandotte Indians whose land lay athwart the transcontinental railway route Stephen Douglas had had in mind when he introduced his Kansas-Nebraska bill. But that topic no longer interested me, though Merk would have applauded it.

Myron suggested that my part of our joint study — M. P. Gilmore and J. M. Blum, "Aspects of Logistic Planning" (1946) — would qualify as a dissertation, but I felt uncomfortable with that shortcut. Dick Leopold advised me to look for a subject in twentieth-century history, a field not much explored at that time, though Arthur Schlesinger, Jr., was about to begin work on his *Age of Franklin D. Roosevelt.* Elting, whom I consulted at length, reflected for some days and then simply suggested that I seek inspiration by reading Thomas Beer's elliptical *Mauve Decade.*

Beer's book, an impressionistic and idiosyncratic meditation about the culture of the 1890s, contained many allusions for which my thin learning about the period was inadequate. But of course I could fill in the gaps of my knowledge. More important, my explorations and the book itself were engaging. I was reminded that history was enjoyable, indeed the most fulfilling thing I knew. That was the main reason that had made me decide to enter the doctoral program at Harvard. Other reasons also influenced me. The experience of war had strengthened my desire to live my life in the academy, as a college professor. History had at that time something of a grip on the academic imagination. College departments taught the history of literature, of art and architecture, of music, of economic thought. My work on the history of logistics planning demonstrated that history could also be useful by exposing the past for the lessons it could teach for the future. But, most of all, I simply wanted to do history for the fun of it. And I wanted to focus, in the phrase of Frederick Scott Oliver, on "the endless adventure of governing men."

Beer's book stimulated the imagination, and in my case inspired my thinking about dissertation topics. One Saturday afternoon, reading Beer, I was freely associating unrelated ideas. Pamela was at work at Garfinkle's, a Washington department store, where she had escaped the boredom of housekeeping by taking a job for the Christmas season selling jewelry. When she returned, we went out for cocktails with neighbors. Our host had regaled us often with stories about his office, a room in the suite of Joseph P. Tumulty, who had been Woodrow Wilson's political secretary. That evening I asked my host whether he would introduce me to Joseph P. Tumulty, Jr., who was then in charge of the family law practice. He said he would, and he did a few days later.

The office of Tumulty and Tumulty, near the corner of 14th and F Streets in downtown Washington, contained dozens of framed and signed photographs of Democratic bigwigs as well as most of the files from the senior Tumulty's White House years. I had come upon a treasure. With the permission of Joe, Jr., I had also found my topic, my commanding occupation

for the next several years. Writing a biography of Joe Tumulty, a talented political operator, would put me into twentieth-century political history, just
where I wanted to be. In January 1946 I began my terminal leave. My navy
days were over, but they had ended with a portentous assignment, the beginning of my professional career and a first collaboration with Elting Morison. The Harvard Graduate School of Arts and Sciences lay ahead.

The Harvard program in history, except for one seminar each term, put
graduate students in undergraduate lecture courses, with the graduate students required to write course papers, theoretically papers based on research
and reflection. As much as possible, I selected courses I knew to have excellent lecturers, of whom the best was David Owen in English history since
1815. For that course I wrote my best paper, a study of the thinking of Frederick Scott Oliver. He had been a member of the group who founded the
Round Table, a journal devoted during the decade before World War I to the
examination of British imperial problems, especially the problem of Ireland.
Both an imperialist and a federalist, Oliver wrote a biography of Alexander
Hamilton that accorded with his scheme to solve the Irish question by making Ireland a free state within a federated British government. Owen liked
the paper enough to suggest that I change my major to modern English history; though flattered by his suggestion, I was committed to American history. A year or so later, a graduate student in English history did write his
dissertation on the *Round Table*.

Most of the lecture courses I took as a graduate student did not shine. An
exception was colonial history with Samuel Eliot Morison, a detached lecturer but a wonderful historian. For him I wrote a paper about the raid on
Cartagena by Sir Francis Drake. "Purple," he commented about my prose,
"but I love it." I had hoped for that response. But I was surprised and flattered when Admiral Morison, still in uniform while on terminal leave, invited a fellow student and me to tea at his old family home on Brimmer
Street in Boston. We went, we listened to the admiral's stories about his
family and his war, we were impressed.

During the winter of 1946 I sat in a seminar conducted by Fred Merk.
Each week one of us presented a progress report on his research; the last report was to be devoted to his conclusions about his topic. Each week every
student would comment on the paper just read, with Fred providing a summary view. In later years I was to adopt that pattern in seminars I taught.
The topics covered a broad range of history as well as my own area, a study
of progressivism in New Jersey in the decade before 1910, the year Wilson
ran for governor of the state. Joe Tumulty at that time was a rising young

Democratic reformer. Fred Merk knew nothing about my subject, but he was a shrewd critic whose comments helped me define the issues I had to address. I intended to carry on in the fall of 1946 with Tumulty's career as Wilson's political secretary in Trenton. But Oscar Handlin, whose permission I solicited to join his seminar, advised against it. I would have no future as an American historian, he said, unless I took a seminar with Arthur Schlesinger, Sr., the outstanding American social historian in the profession. But I had found Schlesinger to be a mechanical lecturer and his nominalistic social history not particularly to my taste. More important, I wanted to work on my dissertation topic. Reluctantly, Oscar yielded and let me join his seminar on immigration and ethnicity in the United States.

Oscar ran his seminar in a pattern similar to Merk's, but by September 1946 the war veterans' rush to Harvard crowded all courses. About sixteen of us met at the Handlin home one evening a week. As we delivered our research reports, ordinarily two at each meeting, Oscar almost invariably seemed to fall asleep, his eyes closed. It became something of a game to try to make a point that would awaken him. Still, the seminar exactly suited my purposes. There were several papers about political bosses in major cities, all of them rather like "Little Bob" Davis, for whom Tumulty had worked in Jersey City. Oscar's comments on my early draft sent me to sources I had not known, most usefully documents of the New Jersey legislature. Those sources, and newspapers in New York City and Jersey City, supplied most of my data, for Tumulty had kept no records of his own until 1913.

On the whole, however, my first year of graduate study offered few moments of joy. For me, a Harvard alumnus, the lecture courses, which made up three-quarters of the program, had no novelty and transmitted learning in a clumsy way. I learned much faster by reading the books listed in the course bibliographies or recommended by fellow students. In later years at Yale, like my colleagues there I taught doctoral candidates only in seminars, some of them focused on research, the others devoted to discussions of historical works that raised questions of interpretation or method—a marked improvement over the Harvard program.

The graduate students in American history at Harvard had a club, the Henry Adams Club, which supplemented their courses. The club rarely held a general meeting. Instead members formed "cells" of four or five students, who read learned papers to each other. The cell I joined included Alfred D. Chandler, Jr., G. Wallace Chessman, and Sydney Ahlstrom. Wally and I had overlapped at Andover. He later became the dean and the official historian of Dennison College, as well as the biographer of Theodore Roosevelt for a series edited by Oscar Handlin. Sid, later a colleague at Yale, won a National Book Award for his history of religion in America. And Al Chandler, already exploring the history of American business, became the foremost scholar in his field, winner of a Pulitzer Prize, and so good a friend that he agreed to serve as my son's godfather. Over the years, beginning in 1946 and continuing thereafter, I learned more about history from Al than I did from any other contemporary.

I also learned much about the role of a dean of students. In addition to serving as a teaching assistant, I accepted a position as assistant graduate secretary of Dudley Hall. That institution, a weak imitation of the residential houses, provided a one-room social center for students who commuted to Harvard from communities in Greater Boston. For the most part Irish or Jewish, these students would have preferred to live at Harvard with the other undergraduates, but their families could not afford to pay the necessary fees. Presiding over Dudley was Charles W. Duhig, who in earlier years was an assistant dean of the college and now was the gentle but voluble autocrat of the Dudley luncheon table. Charley, as best I could tell, wanted me as an assistant largely for company at lunch. We became good friends, and Charley told me again and again to become a lecturer as soon as I could, because, said he, I had a resonant voice, like his own bass.

I also spent time every weekday with Dudley's students. Some of them had academic or family problems with which I tried to help. I recall tutoring one veteran in Roman history, for which I was at best the proverbial one-eyed man instructing the blind. When he passed his exam, in gratitude he gave me a fifth of Ballantine Scotch, the best whiskey we drank that year. Another student confessed confidentially that his girl was pregnant and said he was the father. A law student I consulted wisely recommended a blood test, which proved conclusively that my Dudley lad was not that child's father, after which the girl admitted that several others might have been. At Dudley I learned about advising undergraduates, about their typical preoccupations, about their uncertainties in choosing a career. I was also discovering that I had no interest in a career of my own as a dean of students.

After my first year, I spent most of my days in the library, usually until it closed. Like other veterans, I was eager to complete my doctoral program as quickly as possible. That would provide at least a partial exit from genteel poverty. More important, a real job might make life easier for my overburdened wife. Pamela had become a grader in courses on marketing and finance at the Harvard Business School, a job that filled her days. But I worked almost every evening, as most doctoral students did, with an occasional Saturday night off for the movies. So our social life was negligible, though we did now and then share a meal with Fay and Al Chandler or Barbara and

Peter Solomon, the latter couple neighbors we met because Barbara was in Oscar's seminar with me. Every graduate student imposes on the spouse who stands by. Certainly I did. My absences from domestic responsibilities became more onerous for Pamela when our first child, Pamela Powell, arrived in January 1947, just as my last course exams began.

Through the following August I spent my working hours reading everything I could find in Widener Library about American cultural and political life during the first two decades of the twentieth century — memoirs and biographies of politicians and journalists, the *New York Times* day by day, periodicals, general histories. I was trying to immerse myself in what Douglas S. Freeman, the great biographer of Robert E. Lee, had called "the fog of history." The past on which I was at work had to become as familiar to me as the present — perhaps even more familiar, since I spent most waking hours every day with the people and issues of the early part of the century. As the fog of history enveloped me, I hoped to recognize where Tumulty fit in his times. I did not then have teaching in mind, but of course a comfortable familiarity with a period of the past would enhance both lectures and seminars. I knew I was approaching my goal when I began inadvertently dating my correspondence not 1947, but 1913.

Supported by a Harvard fellowship, in September 1947 I went to Washington, my Mecca. In the Manuscripts Division of the Library of Congress were the collections I most needed. Though Woodrow Wilson's widow refused to open the Wilson papers to anyone at that time, and though her own papers were also closed, I found pay dirt in Wilson's letters and memoranda to his Cabinet officers whose papers were available. More important, the Tumulty papers were fully available in his law offices, where Joe, Jr., treated me royally. He and I became friends, he introduced me to some of the Tumulty family, and he asked Warren Johnson to help me out. Johnson had been Tumulty's secretary in the White House. He knew the old-timers still in Washington who came by now and then to visit, among them Senator Joseph Guffey of Pennsylvania and Attorney General Thomas Clark. Warren also knew where the secrets were, and he directed me to some Tumulty papers in a warehouse in the northeast section of the District.

There I came upon some important material about a wartime rumor, false but common, that Tumulty had been shot or imprisoned as a German spy, and about the interview Wilson had given Louis Seibold of the *New York World* just before the Democratic convention in 1920. A brief history of the rumor gave me the content for one of the first articles I published in a learned journal, the *Journal of Abnormal and Social Psychology*. The Seibold material would have been of use to Arthur Link in his mammoth project editing the papers of Woodrow Wilson. But after my work with them was completed, the files from the warehouse were somehow lost when the Tumulty family gave the rest of Tumulty's records to the Library of Congress.

Palm Sunday in Washington in 1948 was a beautiful day for walking Pammy in her stroller at the zoo. Even better, I could tell Pamela that I had completed my research in the archives and papers relevant to my dissertation. We had used up our wartime savings, and our household budget was out of balance. The time had come for me to find an academic job. We planned to spend a month in Summit where Pamela could help her father ready his house for sale, then a month with my father in South Norwalk; and then we hoped to move on to a paying position wherever I could find one. Amherst was looking for an assistant professor in American history, but its new president, a Columbia man, wanted a fellow alumnus. Harvard offered me a place as a tutor, but at a salary too small to support my family. The Mississippi State College for Women expressed interest, but I had resolved not to live in the segregated South. I had work to do in New Jersey interviewing Tumulty's brother and reading local newspapers, and I looked forward to starting to write my dissertation, but otherwise the immediate future appeared bleak.

Then there arrived a letter from Elting Morison asking me to meet him a few days later at the Washington Hotel, where he was to be briefly in residence. He did not say why, but I looked forward to conversation with Elting just as so many admirals once had. Though we both lived in Cambridge, we had been out of touch except for a few brief greetings at a popular bookstore. At his hotel we spent a few minutes catching up with each other. Elting, as I had known, was at MIT, where he was teaching English literature part time and otherwise occupied editing the letters of Theodore Roosevelt. He had recently, he told me, applied for a grant to make possible the completion of that project. It was too big a task for any one person, he had concluded, so he planned to recruit a staff. He did not yet know whether he would receive the grant. In the event he did, he wanted to ascertain whether I would be interested in becoming associate editor. I said at once that in principle I would, though first I would have to learn the details of the offer. We agreed to keep in touch. I departed with a sense of anticipation much greater than I had let on to Elting. But it would be some time before I heard from him again.

In April Elting asked me to come to Cambridge for an interview about the Roosevelt letters. At that meeting he made firm the offer he had outlined in Washington. I would be associate editor of the Roosevelt letters and, after a year, I would also teach one course for the humanities department of the Massachusetts Institute of Technology. In order to use my eligibility under the GI Bill to the full, I would begin my editorial work in September but read what little Elting had already completed during the summer while I also wrote as much as I could of my dissertation. The proposed salary, supplemented by the GI family allowance for the three summer months, was $3,500, in those days and by my standards a generous sum.

I intended to accept Elting's offer but asked for several days to think it over. Fred Merk and Dick Leopold, both of whom knew Elting well, supported my inclination to join him. David Owen agreed I needed the income. But every other Harvard historian I consulted advised against both MIT and the Roosevelt project, which they forecast would never reach completion. To them, MIT was beyond the professional pale for historians, and Elting was a maverick who had not even bothered to take the special, postdissertation oral exam required for the Ph.D. Oscar Handlin argued strenuously that it would be a mistake for me to decline the tutor's job at Harvard. If you say "no" now, he warned, it would be "no" forever. But Pamela rejoiced at the prospect of returning to Cambridge and her friends there, and I trusted Elting. He had been, after all, a most satisfactory commanding officer. He had seen the logistics history to completion. He had taken a chance on me, and I was fully prepared to take a chance on him. Further, Theodore Roosevelt had been the most popular American in public life during the first two decades of the century, the period in which I had been immersing myself. The prospect of getting to know him through his letters excited me.

So did my writing on Tumulty. By the end of the summer I had finished three chapters of my dissertation and had drafted a fourth. As I had hoped, Tumulty and his period were blending in my account; and, though I knew I would have to make some revisions, I was happy with my draft. I found writing to be exhilarating; I took satisfaction in struggling with a difficult paragraph or chapter until it fell into place. I realized that I was not producing great history, but I was striving to become a competent craftsman, and I felt that I was on my way. I also enjoyed my weekday afternoons, as I reviewed Elting's editing of Roosevelt's correspondence through 1900. There was much yet to be done on those years, but the existing manuscript revealed a fascinating man, a Roosevelt quite unlike the man his detractors had drawn. By Labor Day, when Elting returned from a summer in New Hampshire, I looked forward to editing Roosevelt's letters during the day and writing Tumulty's biography on weekends and evenings.

There would be costs in that schedule for Pamela and our daughter. I read aloud to Pammy every evening, and Sunday afternoons were reserved for excursions — to Watertown by trolley, to Harvard Square for ice cream. My little girl yearned for more time with me, and I with her. But my apprenticeship was over. I would complete my degree in a year or two. I could already see the shape of my study of Tumulty. And I was now also involved in a major historical project as the junior collaborator of an unorthodox historian, a man whose flair distinguished him, a senior partner in whom I had confidence.

5

In Clio's Active Service

The process of editing the letters of Theodore Roosevelt proved to be as engaging as were the letters themselves. From the beginning that process, in a phrase dear to Elting Morison, who directed it, was a "small-group operation." The staff he first assembled soon changed, to be replaced twice as the young women he employed, recent Radcliffe graduates by and large, married and then moved away or had babies. But the way we worked did not much change after we had completed the first two of eight volumes. From 1948, when I joined Elting, we spent five years editing the letters and therefore living with TR before sending the last volumes to press in 1953. On the title page of each volume Elting listed the names of all those who contributed to the editing, and in the preface briefly described their roles. He could not describe our high spirit of collaboration, a spirit attributable largely to him, which infused the project from start to finish.

The letters of Theodore Roosevelt were safely in the manuscripts division of the Library of Congress, along with other of his papers. We worked from photographic duplicates of the outgoing letters located there, in other collections we examined, and in printed form. Those materials, along with a splendid collection of books by Roosevelt himself and about his era, were then in the Roosevelt Collection in Widener Library at Harvard, to which we had unlimited access. Indeed our whole project rested on a contractual relationship among Harvard, MIT, and the Theodore Roosevelt Association in New York City. The association paid our salaries; MIT housed us and paid us for any teaching we did; Harvard University Press published the edited letters. When we needed to examine incoming letters, one of us would go to the Library of Congress or send an agent hired for that purpose. Periodically we moved batches of photoduplicated copies of the letters to our suite of offices, arranged them chronologically, and began the process of editing. That system was a variant of the way in which Julian Boyd, the dean of editorial projects, had organized his operation at Princeton for editing the papers of Thomas Jefferson. Elting had consulted Boyd but adjusted his operation to suit his own temperament and to allow for the large differences from the Jefferson papers resulting from Roosevelt's access to stenographers, their use of the typewriter, and our intention to publish a generous selection, but not all, of Roosevelt's letters.

Once the editing began, except for the first two volumes, which Elting had started, the initial stages fell to me. I organized the letters into what I thought would constitute a volume. Then I separated the material into large chronological units, for each of which I contrived a working title based on the dominant content of the letters in it, and proceeded to separate the letters I considered suitable for publication from those rejected for that purpose as redundant or trivial. I then made tentative decisions about the identifying and explanatory notes I predicted we would have to add. Each letter was then directed to the editor who was to draft the notes. That division evolved over time, reaching final form in 1950–51 when Hope Williams Wigglesworth was handling the topics of Indian affairs and the Roosevelt family, and Alfred D. Chandler, Jr., had joined us. Al would write about financial matters, the building of the Panama Canal, the membership of the Progressive Party, and other issues. I wrote on politics, most legislative developments, foreign policy, and many legal and intellectual subjects. Elting took on military and naval issues and a melange of matters that happened to catch his interests. When the rest of us had put together what I viewed as a completed volume, we handed the whole thing (with the rejected letters in a separate file) to Elting for his review and critique.

Elting would tear our draft apart. He would insert some letters I had rejected and remove some I had included. He would review the notes, write some of his own, revise a few others, and send many back to their authors with comments about rewriting. His larger revisions then became the subjects of discussion, often at afternoon tea, a ritual we all gladly attended. Only once did he and I fail to work out a difference of opinion about our handling of an issue, and on that occasion we agreed to submit the question to an arbitrator, George Homans, a Harvard sociologist who had been Elting's college roommate. The problem had to do with my note about Roosevelt's criminal libel suit against the *New York World,* a suit I considered an attack on the principle of freedom of the press. On George's recommendation, we kept my note, but slightly softened its tone. Other than that, we settled all our differences over tea, though by the time of publication many of our notes had incorporated so many revisions that no one could remember who had written what.

Once the revisions Elting had suggested were made, copy editors set about making the styling consistent and proofreading the holograph letters. Then both Elting and I reviewed each volume, which would result in more changes. We then decided what to include as appendices, and Elting wrote the front matter. At that stage the volume was at last completed, though the copy editors had a large job ahead, reading galleys as they became available. At full tilt, we had two volumes at press or in galleys, two ready for Elting's first review, and two just underway. Our days were full. The project, so Elting liked to say, was "a modern collaborative job" for which the copy editors were indispensable, most memorably Hope Williams Wigglesworth and Peggy Hinchman Clawson during the first half of the operation, and Sylvia Rice and Eleanor Pearre Abbot during the second. Sylvia became an editor at Harcourt, Brace. Eleanor went on to edit her husband's volumes on the papers of George Washington, and later worked on J. C. Levenson's enlightened edition of the letters of Henry Adams.

No description of our editorial process can convey the personal satisfaction and intellectual stimulation we enjoyed as collaborators. Elting and Al Chandler became two of my dearest friends. My wife and I and our children spent many happy days with the Wigglesworths and some relaxed Thanksgivings with the Chandlers. We also over the years saw Eleanor Abbot whenever the opportunity arose. At afternoon tea Elting revealed a little at a time about himself as he found out more about us. Though born in Milwaukee in 1909, Elting was at heart a Yankee, bound by family ties to the Morison apple orchards in Peterborough, New Hampshire, where he owned a comfortable house. During the Roosevelt editorial years he served as fence viewer for the town, a quintessentially Yankee office. As a boy, the second of three brothers, he had been close to his mother but not to his formidable father. At the Loomis School he had pitched for the baseball team, successfully he said, and in later years he excelled as a horseman and played a serviceable game of tennis, both gentlemanly pursuits at which he was competent but relaxed. At Harvard he was on the editorial board of the college newspaper, he majored in history, and he developed a special interest in the Second Empire of Napoleon III. He taught briefly at St. Marks School and served, also briefly, as an assistant dean of Harvard College before enrolling in the doctoral program in history. His mentor in that program was Fred Merk, and in Fred's seminar he met Richard W. Leopold, whose meticulous professional standards he valued, as did I. Indeed we asked Dick to review the early volumes of the letters for style and content, and we would not have gone to press without Dick's approval. Elting, while unconventional, respected the historical profession, though he was usually bored by professional historians.

Characteristically he avoided teaching history. Instead he taught literature and biography, which allowed him to examine and expostulate upon the human condition. At tea he would give us stunning insights about literature, including several of his favorite texts — the Book of Job, Henry Adams's autobiography, and Edmund Gosse's *Father and Son*. Elting was a patrician with patrician tastes, a man of style in manner and mind. He influenced my approach to history and to life. Though I could not be as insouciant as he, he encouraged me, as he did all his professional friends, to have fun with history and to enjoy the people we met in the past. Elting's biographies of Admiral William S. Sims and of Henry Stimson revealed his own enviable ability to capture the essence of the people he studied, as he did with Theodore Roosevelt most tellingly in his introduction to the fifth volume of the *Letters*.

In 1950, as we moved into volumes 3 and 4, Elting and I found that we needed more help than either of us had anticipated. Elting asked me to locate possible candidates for him to interview for the position of assistant editor. At Yale I talked with five or six graduate students, but I rather resented the chairman's saying that the two ablest were too good for an editorial position or for MIT. Obviously the Yale historians were as conventional as the Harvard historians. But I knew of one Harvard contemporary who had embarked on courses of study at once unusual and significant. Al Chandler had elected to focus on business history as an aspect of economic history. To that study he brought his own trenchant version of the sociology of Talcott Parsons, whose course he had taken. He was at work on a dissertation, later a book, on Henry Varnum Poor, his forebear, who had edited the foremost railway journal of the late nineteenth and early twentieth centuries, a time when railroads were big business in the United States.

When I inquired, Al expressed interest in meeting Elting. I was sure they would get along. Al was the perfect gentleman, a quality Elting would appreciate. Though Al had grown up in Delaware, he had spent summers on Nantucket, where his family owned a home. He was as much a Yankee as Elting was. An Exeter graduate, Al was Harvard College '40, a veteran of the navy, and a student of Fred Merk. A committed scholar, Al worked harder than any other historian I knew; yet he managed to find time for shooting ducks, had a competitive streak that made him a championship sailor, and had also, like Elting, a quick sense of humor and an infectious laugh. Elting offered Al the job and Al took it, to the great advantage of the project and to my personal delight. Like me, he soon began to teach a course for MIT and to take part in afternoon tea.

At tea, politics now and then became a subject of discussion, usually but not always domestic politics. In 1948 Elting, always a Republican at heart, favored Dewey in the presidential election, while I was strongly for Truman. We saw no point in arguing, but we both sympathized with colleagues who were accused of communism just because they supported Henry Wallace, who seemed to me, as did those of his fans whom I knew, to be not dangerous but naïve. In 1952 I was enthusiastic about Adlai Stevenson from the start, whereas Elting, who at first supported Eisenhower, became more and more undecided. On election day he drove up to New Hampshire to vote. At tea that afternoon I asked him for whom he had cast his ballot. In a statement of surpassing ambivalence, he replied, "I voted for Stevenson and I'm glad that I didn't." But neither he nor I were in the least undecided in our common disgust with Joe McCarthy and his outrageous ways. We did disagree, however, about appropriate treatment of former communists who were on the Harvard and MIT faculties. I believed they had suffered enough and should not undergo further penalty. Elting worried, as I did not, about their continued presence on the faculty and its possibly adverse effect on alumni giving and on government contracts. I disapproved of classified contracts in any case. I was also loath to consider recourse to the Fifth Amendment in itself as evidence of proof of guilt or as grounds for dismissal.

Politics entered teatime conversation less often than did developments at MIT. Elting frequently invited academic guests to join us, especially during the first two years, when we were located in an unsightly wartime building that was still being used to house research projects not related to teaching. The intellectual excitement common to the scientists at work in that building probably characterized those engaged in government-sponsored, classified work. It was hard to judge, for those involved could not talk about what they were doing. That restriction seemed to me out of place in any university, where freedom of communication among colleagues was essential to preserve freedom of inquiry. But MIT was not an ordinary university, not actually even a "university polarized around science and technology," as Provost Julius Stratton described it. For the Institute deliberately drew a large proportion of its operating income from classified research. During and after World War II, MIT became, among other things, a research arm of the government, a condition that made me uneasy.

That condition could also lead to amusing misunderstandings. The research organization that was neighbor to our own was listed in the lobby as "Project Meteor." I took that name, as in fact it was, to be a transparent disguise for theoretical work on rockets more advanced than those the United States had developed during World War II. I regularly met the chief of the project as we stood in line awaiting food at the pantry on the building's second floor. I ordinarily had a homemade sandwich for lunch, which I would eat at my desk, but I would rely on the pantry for a half-pint of milk. So did my neighbor, with whom I often chatted while we waited our turn. I knew he was a captain in the United States Navy, for I had once seen him in uniform during a day of inspection of his outfit. But that was all I ever knew about him, and he knew even less about me. One morning when Elting was away the captain walked into our suite and then into my office, closing the door behind him. "John," he said, "you know I have a top security clearance. Tell me, what are you guys doing here?" I told him we were editing the letters of Theodore Roosevelt. "I know," he said. "That's the best cover in the building." I showed him our files and our working manuscript. "I'll be goddamned," he said, shaking his head. " You *are* editing those letters. No one is going to believe me." Strange things were surely going on at MIT, and I missed our old quarters when in 1950 we moved to the new library building.

Our own work was not entirely predictable. Occasionally we would come unexpectedly upon some important Roosevelt letters or records. So it was when I casually asked the registrar of Harvard College whether there was any way we could consult TR's undergraduate transcript. To my surprise and Elting's, he let me have a copy at once. It showed that, contrary to common belief, Roosevelt had not concentrated his academic studies on biology. In his day there were no majors, but the bulk of his courses were in modern languages, some of which he had first learned as a boy visiting Europe. Twenty-five years after graduating, he could and did still read with ease French, German, and Italian. Still more of a surprise was my accidental discovery in the Roosevelt Collection at Harvard of a full file of the *Civil Service Chronicle*. That journal contained many letters, otherwise unavailable, from Roosevelt to its editors about the problems he had had while serving as a U.S. Civil Service Commissioner during the administration of Benjamin Harrison and the second administration of Grover Cleveland. We published quite a few of those letters. Both the journal and the letters opened a window on the politics of the early 1890s, a subject I was happy to explore. So, too, in New York City newspapers I was able to find more Roosevelt letters than we had on hand about his failed campaign for mayor of New York, a telling political episode he chose not to mention in his autobiography.

The most important surprises arose not from our finding new documents but from the contents of the letters themselves. The man we were pursuing had been neither the "bore as big as a buffalo" of Henry Adams's recollection nor the impulsive adolescent of Henry Pringle's biography. Rather, the TR who came to life in our daily experience with his letters had the intellectual qualities of a deeply educated man: he was varied in his interests and knowledgeable about a remarkable range of subjects. He was also as adroit as Abraham Lincoln in politics, not least while he served as governor of New York, and as president he was deliberate, controlled, and informed in making major policy decisions, both domestic and international.

Thus I enjoyed continual intellectual excitement in editing Roosevelt's letters, as I did also in my work with the Tumulty manuscripts. Part of my excitement arose from the challege of organizing intelligently and persuasively the raw empirical data the documents contained. Part arose from the simple satisfaction of handling and reading documents that few, if any, historians had previously seen. I never lost my sense of discovery in doing research in manuscript and archival collections. That kind of research provided the basis for most of the books that I later wrote or edited. As I had expected, writing history provided me with a rewarding intellectual life, and no day ever seemed complete unless I had some time, even just half an hour, to expand or revise a manuscript I had begun.

I could not resist writing about the Theodore Roosevelt I was learning in most ways to admire. Happily Elting encouraged me to work on an essay about Roosevelt as an intellectual, even suggesting that I write it on company time. And after reading it, he decided to include it as an appendix to the second volume of the published letters. By that time I was putting together my notes on the political tactics that Roosevelt used in his first presidential campaign, and as the editing moved on chronologically, I accumulated further notes about his relations with Congress. The latter subject became my focus in appendices I wrote for volumes 4 and 6. Without initially intending to, I was writing a book-length essay about TR.

On my own time I was also of course writing my dissertation and, when the opportunity permitted, reading generally in American history, my special subject for oral examination once my dissertation had been accepted. Those tasks and the editing informed each other. Tumulty, for example, dealt with federal patronage during the early Wilson years, a function Wilson considered beneath him. (For good reason the Irish politicians of New Jersey referred to Wilson as "the Presbyterian priest.") Roosevelt gladly handled federal patronage himself, and when I examined his appointments I found patterns I had first met in writing about Tumulty. Those patterns related federal to local politics, a relationship I learned to look for in reading Roy F. Nichols's *The Disruption of the American Democracy* (1948), a perceptive study of the coming of the Civil War. Indeed Roy Nichols, whom I had yet to meet, in his books taught me more about political history than did anyone at Harvard. History did not strike me as a seamless web, nor did history seem to repeat itself, but American politics, a special form of human relations, involved at all times reciprocal loyalties, ethnic favors, religious prejudices, and other sentimental factors, just as Pareto in my undergraduate years had taught me to expect.

Of course politics, at least as I approached it, also involved social class. Historians of the United States, especially young historians who had experienced the Great Depression and World War II, were turning in the 1940s and 1950s to serious study of those and related episodes, including the progressive period of 1900–1917, a time of social and political reform. Progressivism involved questions of social class that I found permeating my work. Theodore Roosevelt, the most popular of reformers, inspired the many American patricians who, following his example, entered politics as the twentieth century began. Some historians considered those reformers to emanate from the middle class. But Roosevelt, like some of his recruits — for example, the public-spirited New York lawyers analyzed in an appendix to volume 2 of the Roosevelt letters — was not essentially middle class. He and his recruits were patricians. TR came from an old, distinguished family. He inherited what he called a "competence" — enough money to support his own large family comfortably. As a young man he considered himself a gentleman, a category in his view that excluded most of his Harvard classmates. He also despised the ways of the American newly rich, much more typical of the middle class than was he. Those attitudes predated his commitment to social and political reform but conformed to his reformer's discomfort with the giant new industrial and financial corporations. Size did not bother him, but he came to oppose the power and ruthlessness of the industrialists toward their competitors, customers, and employees.

In contrast, Joe Tumulty was a member of the upwardly mobile American middle class. Born into an immigrant Irish family, he received his formal education in parochial schools and his political education in a city machine. As he made his way in the world, his sympathies lay with his neighbors, laborers who were among the exploited in an industrializing society. He identified, too, with his fellow second-generation Americans, who were trying, as he was, to gain what Woodrow Wilson called "a foothold on the ladder of endeavor." Those sympathies persuaded Tumulty and his friends among the Irish politicians of New Jersey of the need to control the exploiters, the railroads and corporations that used their money and power to wield political influence in New Jersey, which Lincoln Steffens called "the tenderloin state." In the New Jersey legislature the rebellious, Democratic Irish met Yankee, Republican suburban reformers, and the two groups came together to launch progressivism in that state before Wilson ran for office. The suburbs voted for Wilson in the gubernatorial race in 1910, and suburbanites and Irish lawyers alike were among the "men on the make" for whom Wilson fashioned the program called the New Freedom in 1912. Both Theodore Roosevelt and Woodrow Wilson, in moving toward reform, served as inspiration for blue-collar and white-collar Americans, for whom they provided not only leadership but also a kind of mediation between and among social classes. Suburban reformers made TR their hero; Wilson caught much of the political enthusiasm Roosevelt had generated.

Successful reform politics joined social classes instead of setting them apart. Indeed any successful politics in the United States in the twentieth century had to achieve a similar joining, a reconciliation of interests. Progressivism, it seemed to me, was a special case of a general political phenomenon. Class was not an insuperable barrier to political cooperation. Neither was national origin (later rendered as "ethnicity") or religion. In progressive politics, as in all politics, a successful national party had to be an inclusive coalition, encompassing all religions, national groups, and ultimately races. These were the kinds of conclusions — based, I felt, on empirical evidence — to which my work was leading me as I studied Joseph Tumulty and Theodore Roosevelt.

Apart from research and writing, maturation in the profession of history required participation in the appropriate learned societies, in my case the American Historical Association (AHA) and the Mississippi Valley Historical Society (later renamed the Organization of American Historians). In December 1949 the AHA was to meet in Boston. In October of that year David Owen, a member of the program committee, and aware of my work on Wilson, asked me to deliver a paper in a panel concerned with episodes of national fright about radicals and foreigners. I was to speak about the Red Scare that had followed World War I. Dumas Malone, a Jefferson scholar a generation older than I, would address the foreign scare of the late eighteenth century. Ray Billington, who had written his first book about the nativism of the mid-nineteenth century, would serve as moderator. The subject of the panel was timely. The Alger Hiss case had become a major public issue, and President Truman was dismissing alleged "security risks" from government. Hearings of the House Un-American Activities Committee, oblivious to the First Amendment, were then trying to find communists in Hollywood and generating the spirit of intolerance of dissent that Senator Joseph McCarthy was about to exploit. As a civil libertarian, I was appalled. I agreed at once to participate in the panel.

My daily labors spoke to the issue I was to address. Theodore Roosevelt in 1915–16 had aroused latent nativist sentiments in his shrill campaign for preparedness. After the United States entered the war against Germany, he became even more strident in his attacks on German sympathizers and domestic radicals, especially members of the Industrial Workers of the World (IWW). After Roosevelt's death in 1919, his friend and disciple General Leonard Wood copied his irresponsible behavior as he pursued the Republican presidential nomination. On the Democratic side, Attorney General A. Mitchell Palmer, a friend of Joseph Tumulty's and a presidential aspirant, was persecuting alleged radicals. Nativism and anti-radicalism had deep roots in American culture. The war and then the advance of communism in Russia and across Eastern Europe revived those sentiments, which ambitious politicians at once exploited and aggravated. With the later rollback of communism in Europe, the reduction of violence at home, and the end of the presidential campaign, the Red Scare receded.

That was the essence of my paper. Elting warned me that the current anti-communist mood of the country, which some historians shared, would open my argument to misunderstanding. But I whistled up my courage and appeared on time at the ballroom of the Boston Statler Hotel to read my essay. Dumas Malone spoke first; I followed. As I finished, a short, stout, middle-aged man stood up to ask for the floor. Ray Billington recognized him. What I heard next is engraved in my memory. "I am Samuel Flagg Bemis of Yale University," said the man from the floor, "and" — pointing to me — "that young man is a communist."

I was too shocked to speak. Bemis, I knew, was a major figure in the profession, an eminent historian of American foreign policy. But smiling, Ray Billington turned to me and asked, "Do you want to answer that question?" I silently shook my head. After a few routine comments from the floor the session ended. Still in shock, I stood with Ray as I awaited Pamela, who had been in the audience. As I stood there, Bernard Mayo, a professor of history at the University of Virginia who had been a visiting professor at Harvard in 1947, came up to reassure me, as did David Owen. Both had the same message. As David put it: "Don't worry, John. Nobody who is anybody in the historical profession has failed to be called a communist by Samuel Flagg Bemis." It was characteristic of David and of Bernard to take the trouble to support a young man, and I have never forgotten their kindness. Still, Bemis's remark had been the quickest and worst review I was ever to receive. Nevertheless, in spite of Elting's continuing doubts, I arranged to have my paper published. David Potter, a Yale historian whom I greatly respected, later complimented me on it; and I later included it, slightly revised, in a volume of my essays published by W. W. Norton, *Liberty, Justice, Order* (1993).

A month after the AHA meeting, in January 1950, I submitted my completed dissertation to the Harvard history department. It was accepted, and in mid-March I passed my final oral examination. In June 1950 I received my Ph.D., four and a half years after leaving the U.S. Navy and only a week after the birth of Ann Shelby Blum, our second healthy and wonderful daughter. (Thomas Tyler Blum arrived to our delight in 1953.) The degree spurred MIT, where I had been teaching for two semesters, to appoint me assistant professor.

Was that the end of the beginning of my professional life? In a sense, but there was no comma, much less a full stop, after I had received my doctorate. I was simply too busy. The first two volumes of Roosevelt letters were almost at press but the next two were only just begun. My dissertation was not yet published, but Elting had taken a crucial step in that direction for me. At his request, I had given him a carbon copy (xerography did not yet exist) of my Tumulty manuscript, no part of which he had previously seen. Without telling me, he had recommended it to Houghton, Mifflin, a distinguished Boston publisher. So it came as a joyful surprise when Elting told me that Houghton wanted to publish my dissertation, slightly revised. Thus the academic year 1950–51 began on a fast track.

At Houghton I met Paul Brooks, a contemporary of Elting's and a splendid example of an elegant Harvard College literary man becoming a force in American publishing. Paul had read my manuscript and offered me a contract. We would work together on other projects in the years to come, but for the Tumulty biography Paul turned me over to Craig Wylie, who became my editor for five books and in the process a good friend. Also a Harvard alumnus, he had taught before the war at the St. Paul's School, a small but intellectually tough redoubt for high Episcopalians, of whom he was one. He was also at that time a solidly conservative Republican editing nonfiction written largely by liberal Democrats with whom he got along famously, both before and after midday martinis. A physically big man, tall and powerful, Craig spoke with the broadest "a" I had ever heard, even in Boston. At the time we met, he was also editing Margaret Coit's biography of Bernard Baruch. I supposed that Houghton, Mifflin could afford to publish a book by John Morton Blum because the Houghton list included best-sellers by Arthur Schlesinger, Jr., and John Kenneth Galbraith. But Craig always treated me as if I were at least minor royalty, and we enjoyed each other's company.

Craig suggested only small revisions in my dissertation, all agreeable to me. But I erred in failing to cut more than I did in the early chapters on New Jersey politics, which retained a fascination for me that no normal reader would share. More important in my view at the time, Houghton's libel lawyer, Charles Curtis, advised me to temper my remarks about a disappointed office seeker who had more or less blackmailed Tumulty. Like any novice historian, I was loath to remove from my account scandalous data that I had uncovered in my research. I had no choice in the matter, however, for I could not prove that the woman was dead, and if she were alive, Curtis feared a libel suit, which my publisher intended to avoid. In retrospect I should have left this figure entirely out of the book. Indeed the work as a whole reflected the youth of its author; as I later put it in a note to myself, it was "still somewhat green — not quite ripe." But I was too excited about the forthcoming publication of my first book to vet the manuscript more objectively. When it went to press late in 1950, I felt proud.

The first two volumes of the Roosevelt letters were at press several months earlier than my Tumulty book. In the early spring of 1951 the Roosevelt Memorial Association gave a prominent party at Roosevelt House in New York to mark their imminent publication. It was a grand affair to which all the editors were invited. What made it particularly memorable for me was the presence of Alice Roosevelt Longworth, TR's only child by his first wife, Alice Lee Roosevelt, who had died in childbirth. Mrs. Longworth had made history on her own. She had been for years the mistress of the late Senator William Borah of Idaho, a stalwart Republican isolationist who fancied himself an expert on foreign affairs. In her Washington parlor had gathered Borah and the other Senate "irreconcilables" who had plotted successfully in 1919–20 to defeat Wilson's Treaty of Versailles and the League of Nations it founded. Over their meetings Alice presided, a diminutive woman with a keen mind and quick wit. "How we did cherish and nourish our hatreds in those days," she remarked in her memoir.

At Roosevelt House in 1951 we had all assembled for cocktails when Mrs. Longworth appeared in the archway leading to the room where we stood. A hush fell as she stood there, a cigarette holder in her mouth, exactly like the holder Franklin Roosevelt had so often used and at exactly the same angle. She had on her head a diamond tiara and she wore a shimmering evening gown of "Alice blue." Mrs. Longworth was about seventy then and I was thirty, but I had never seen a sexier woman. She projected, it seemed to me, the charisma attributed to her father by those who had followed him politically.

The Letters of Theodore Roosevelt, volumes 1 and 2, were published to acclaim. The Sunday book section of the *New York Herald Tribune* greeted them with a front-page review by Richard Hofstadter, a rising Columbia scholar who in my judgment had few peers in our age cohort of historians of the United States. Dick had scoffed at TR in his most recent book, but the letters changed his mind. Getting precisely the reaction we had hoped the letters would inspire, they revealed to him the extraordinary man, warts and all, who Roosevelt had been. The review also praised the editing, a tribute to Elting, who glowed. Dick picked out for separate commendation my appendix on Roosevelt's intellectual life, a subject on which Hofstadter was expert. So I glowed, too. Among the Harvard historians who had scoffed at Elting's undertaking there occurred an instant conversion. Fred Merk, always a believer, now basked in the success of his students, for Elting, Al, and I had all studied under Fred.

But *sic transit gloria mundi.* Later reviews entered some demurrers to the first notices. Howard Mumford Jones, a Harvard literary critic, found the notes "jejune," an adjective that particularly annoyed Elting. Howard Beale, who had been working for decades on a biography of Roosevelt that he never published, criticized Elting for his selection of letters. The selection was also mine, but Beale, openly jealous of Elting, had only praise for my contribution to the volumes and went out of his way to be pleasant to me whenever we met. Elting brushed off all negative assessments until *The New Yorker* published a long review by Edmund Wilson, the prestigious critic and novelist. It seemed to me a triumph that Wilson had chosen to review the volumes at such length, and his reading of Roosevelt's letters was sensitive and insightful. But his review included a devastating critique of the index. That criticism upset Elting.

I said nothing, for the index seemed to me a small matter compared to the success of the volumes in altering for historians the previously dominant evaluation of Roosevelt. Indeed the full eight volumes of letters eventually restored TR to his proper place among the almost great presidents. They also gave Elting a new visibility within the profession, which had earlier underrated him, and they helped Al Chandler and me as well. Dick Hofstadter, for example, continued to review the volumes as they were published, continued to praise my appendices, and drew on Al's appendix to volume 8 — a study of the social background of the leaders of the Progressive Party — to document his contentions about progressivism in general. The *Letters* gave new stature not just to Roosevelt but also to his editors. The previously dominant view of Henry Pringle, a debunking TR biographer, gave way to the balanced interpretation of Roosevelt that the letters documented. For me, working on the letters provided a kind of postdoctoral fellowship on the period of the American past during which Roosevelt had lived. I was later to draw constantly on my learning about those years in my teaching at Yale and in writing my section of *The American Experience,* a textbook published by Harcourt, Brace.

The heady reception of the *Letters* had not yet abated in late June 1951 when Houghton, Mifflin published my *Joe Tumulty and the Wilson Era.* I anxiously awaited the reviews. I had not dreamed that it would appear on the front page of the *New York Times* Sunday book section, so I was elated to find it reviewed there. The reviewer was Henry Steele Commager, a Columbia historian well known for his own work, for his collaboration with Samuel Eliot Morison on an outstanding textbook, and for his involvement as a liberal in issues of national importance. Though the review was on the whole favorable, Commager, an ardent Wilsonian in his youth, found my treatment of Wilson less generous than he deemed appropriate. He was not alone in that view, as later reviews revealed, but the response to the *Letters* had prepared me for a mixed bag of notices, and I was staggered by the space the *Times* had given a book of mine.

Most of the other reviews were also friendly. Arthur S. Link, the leading Wilson scholar, described the biography as warm and sympathetic, Gerald W. Johnson called it "a study in loyalty and . . . a handbook of practical politics," and William V. Shannon praised it as "an excellent example of the newer political history." As time passed, my own retrospective criticism of *Tumulty* meant more to me than did the assessment of reviewers. I found the writing fluent, perhaps, but lazy. As I said in a foreword to a reprint, published by Archon Books in 1968, the biography "reflects some of the transitory identifications and uncertainties of a youthful author." But two letters I received especially pleased me. Andre Siegfried, a French observer of the Wilson years, agreed with me about Tumulty's skill in relating national to local politics. And Edward I. Bernays, probably the first professional in the field of public relations, believed as I did that Tumulty brought an expert's touch to that calling. Without access to the Wilson manuscripts, I had made some errors in dating that Arthur Link gently corrected in his editing of Wilson's papers; but over the years the Tumulty biography proved to be no embarrassment. Indeed I still stand by my major conclusions:

> The defeat of the League no longer shocks, for it is . . . clear that an international organization in itself cannot guarantee peace. Yet . . . the

grand vision of continuing peace through international organization . . .
is precious still to men who would believe . . . that in a good world reasonable human beings can solve amicably . . . the problems of living together. Tumulty should have known that this was doubtful. The mi-
crocosm of experience with which he was so familiar, the processes of
politics, of party structure and partisan propaganda, suggested that
men were wicked and unreasonable, political solutions painful and
ephemeral. Neither he nor Wilson should have expected any League,
or tariff, or antitrust law to end rivalries for power or to overcome the
strong attachments of men to other men and institutions. Yet because
they did expect these things, the premises of Wilsonian liberalism
suffered when his treaty fell. Men were shocked, for they had founded
their hopes on a dream.

I was sure even in 1951 that I could write a more original and important book.
Indeed, with a rising sense of excitement, I devoted the summer that year
to drafting the first five chapters of what became *The Republican Roosevelt*
(1954). Woodrow Wilson had written after publication of his first book: "I
must push on. To linger would be fatal." Was I that compulsive? Perhaps.
Certainly I remained, as I had long been, eager for professional advance-
ment, and I knew that publication provided the surest way to that goal. I
realized that my publications of 1951 were substantial accomplishments. But
I found that these accomplishments gave me only brief and transient satisfaction. Once published, the books became products from which I felt increasingly detached as they began, in a sense, to live a life of their own in reviews and sales. My satisfaction had rested in writing them, in the process
of creation — discovering new approaches to old problems, fashioning fresh
ways to organize empirical data, struggling through a first draft, revising and
revising again until the manuscript seemed at last finished. It was that
process that captured me. That summer and thereafter, I was engaged in the
work I was doing, not the work I had done. When I realized that about myself in the summer of 1951, it marked at last the end of the beginning.

6

Extracurricular

Except for the months Pamela and I spent in Washington, we lived from 1946 until 1957 in the vicinity of Harvard Square in Cambridge, Massachusetts, a community then and since attractive to young adults. During that time I taught for eight years at MIT, an academic community unlike any other I ever knew. The two communities rarely overlapped. It was as if I left daily for a foreign country and returned evenings to a welcoming native shore. Pamela found Cambridge wholly appealing. Her friends and our children's friends lived there. The children attended a good private school, the Buckingham School, of which I became a trustee. Our friends were ambitious young couples. Few wives worked in those years, though many were developing the feelings that modern feminism was soon to express. Indeed in the 1950s Pamela could always create something of a stir among women eager for careers when she said that she enjoyed her children. The men were academicians, architects, lawyers, psychoanalysts, most of them educated at Ivy League colleges. They were successful professionals, and from them, in our many conversations and shared activities, I learned much. In many ways, we grew up together.

After departing Harvard housing, we resided from 1948 to 1952 on the ground floor of a two-family house at 25 Gibson Street. It stood about a block from the old Harvard infirmary and about a mile west along Mt. Auburn Street from Harvard Square. The other half of the house, the upper floors, held Mary and Benjamin Thompson. Our daughters played together. We babysat for each other by using a radio hookup so that we could remain in our own apartment.

Mary, pretty, vivacious, blessed with a catching laugh, continually pregnant, exchanged confidences with Pamela. Ben and I were cordial but never intimate. A founder of the Architects Collaborative, Ben was a disciple of Walter Gropius. He was then working with Gropius on the graduate housing Harvard was building just north of its law school. Gropius, like others in the Bauhaus school, designed furniture for his buildings. Ben quickly discovered that my natural clumsiness made me a useful guinea pig for the furnishings they were planning for Harvard. If a chair could aggravate a vulnerable spine, it aggravated mine. Since inflation was rampant and Harvard was loath to increase the budget for the building, Ben and Gropius had continually to shrink their original plan and economize on their preferred furniture. My back told me and I told Ben when he had economized enough.

While residing on Gibson Street Ben was designing and building a house for his family on Moon Hill, a community in Lexington, Massachusetts, of modern houses planned by various members of the Architects Collaborative. Inside and out, the Thompson house, all mahogany, struck us as at once lovely and practical with its flowing spaces and charming views. I was so impressed with Ben's talent that it came to me as a surprise when he asked me in the mid-1950s to accompany him to Andover to show him the campus. He had decided to bid on some new dormitories near the school's bird sanctuary. As we walked about Phillips Academy I recalled a similar walk two decades earlier with Frank Lloyd Wright. Unlike Wright, Ben said little, though both architects were attracted to Bulfinch Hall, a federal-period classroom building. Several months later Ben asked me to read his intended presentation to the Andover trustees. Though I suggested a few modifications, the statement revealed Ben's understanding of the topography, the traditions, and the meaning of the school. It went far beyond anything I had said during our visit there. He won the contract and went on to design the cluster houses that anchor the northeast end of the campus.

With other neighbors, too, proximity led to friendships from which we derived both joy and edification. Across Gibson Street lived Mary and Ashley Campbell—Polly and Toby—with their growing family. Toby, Harvard '40, was serving then as assistant dean of engineering at Harvard and was the first university administrator willing to tell me the way it really was. From him I learned that deans had to be able to compute budgets, to be sure, but that the far more difficult problems they faced were people. Toby, a man of style and charm, a good listener and easy companion, had a way with people that assured his success. He became dean of engineering at the University of Maine and, after we had moved from Cambridge, at Tufts.

In our first years in the neighborhood, before I signed on at MIT, Mary

Louise and Kingman Brewster, Jr., lived a block and a half away from us, on Foster Street. Constance Buffum, soon Constance B. Cox, was a childhood friend of Mary Louise and a fellow grader at the Harvard Business School with Pamela, whom she had known at Smith. One Sunday in 1946 Connie gave a small sherry party to introduce us to the Brewsters. It was the beginning of what became a long, close, and rewarding friendship. But at first Kingman, then at the Harvard Law School where he became an editor of the law review, seemed distant and formidable to me. A direct descendant of the Elder Brewster of the *Mayflower* and the Plymouth Colony, Kingman was a strikingly handsome young man, tall, dark, and lean, a dedicated sailor who had had no peer racing small boats in his youth on Martha's Vineyard. He had served in navy air during World War II. A founder of the America First Committee in 1940, he had since become a convinced internationalist. I had seen him at organizing meetings of the Americans for Democratic Action and of the Massachusetts Young Democrats, neither of which he joined, and I had observed the deference toward him of many of the others assembled. I was soon to learn of his stature as a Yale undergraduate, when he was chairman of the *Yale Daily News*. Rather in awe of him, I did not yet recognize his innate diffidence, which he sometimes concealed with a seeming certitude.

We did not really get to know each other until 1950 on the beach at his house on Martha's Vineyard. One sunny afternoon, after a lazy picnic, Kingman asked me my opinion about controlling the use of atomic weapons. This led to a long discussion of international affairs, which revealed our strong agreement about the desirability of placing control of atomic energy in the Security Council of the United Nations, without any power of veto. We agreed also about the advantages of creating a military arm for the United Nations, complete with an annual budget, a general staff, and ground, sea, and air forces.

That conversation, which both of us enjoyed, laid our own foundation for the friendship that our wives were developing while they walked their baby daughters together. Though the Brewsters went to Paris for a year so that Kingman could begin his Marshall Plan work under Milton Katz, one of his law school mentors and a deputy to Averill Harriman, after their year abroad they returned to Cambridge. Kingman then spent a year at MIT as an economist before becoming an assistant professor at the Harvard Law School. The Brewsters then bought a house on Craigie Street, their home for as long as they remained in Cambridge, only a few blocks from where we lived.

Gradually we came to know Kingman's family—his sister, Mary Kennedy, a beautiful woman once described as "the Madonna of the Ritz";

his stepfather, the Harvard musicologist Edward Ballantine, a masterful pianist; and his remarkable mother, a loving parent, dedicated gardener, and great and stately lady. Though my duties at MIT allowed met to spend only weekends away, on Martha's Vineyard, where the Brewsters owned a summer house and we rented a cottage, Kingman and I discovered our common interests in antitrust policy, civil liberties, national politics, and higher education.

National politics gave us a subject we never tired of arguing. In 1952 I supported both Adlai Stevenson for president and John F. Kennedy for U.S. senator. Kingman disagreed. He considered Stevenson weak, while I considered his campaign bold. It was said in Cambridge that year that when the Republicans caucused, Kingman met McGeorge Bundy in a telephone booth. Kingman objected even more to Kennedy, whom he considered too permissive toward Senator Joseph McCarthy. I had been loath to support Kennedy until one evening when Pat Jackson recruited me. Jackson, celebrated for his leading role in organizing the defense of Sacco and Vanzetti in the 1920s, assured me that, if elected, Kennedy would work to contain McCarthy. I could not believe that Jackson would misinform me. So I signed a petition of Harvard and MIT faculty members for Kennedy. When the petition was made public, I received many telephone calls asking me if I had been bribed, and for how much. Sheila Gilmore, Myron's uninhibited wife, scolded me for at least half an hour. Kennedy won, but he steered clear of the McCarthy issue. My critics, Kingman particularly, did not let me forget it.

The Brewsters had a way, like my brother and like Mike Ford had earlier in my undergraduate years, of making me forget my writing schedule. They hosted festive pregame luncheons every other year when Yale played football at Harvard. Those parties sent us all, whatever our loyalties, to the stadium in a celebratory mood. The Cambridge dinner dances to which they introduced us proved to be the most enjoyable social events we regularly attended. The Brewsters' cocktail parties before the dances often included McGeorge and Mary Bundy as well as Milton and Vivian Katz and other members of the Harvard Law School faculty and their wives.

At the parties as well as on the Vineyard I came to know Kingman better. He had a deep sense of privacy, and he and Mary Louise enjoyed the closest marriage we ever knew, except perhaps our own. But among friends, when he overcame his shyness he revealed his sense of fun and his zest for living. He was a wonderful mimic, especially of Wendell Willkie, the 1940 Republican presidential candidate, and Franklin D. Roosevelt. He loved good drama and musical comedy. One late evening after a dinner dance, a dozen of us repaired for a brandy to the family room of one of our number. There Kingman tried memorably to sing all the parts in *My Fair Lady*, an effort that at once evoked the competitive zeal of McGeorge Bundy. Mac was then a professor of government and dean of the arts and science faculty at Harvard. He and Kingman, the closest of friends, had a common talent for ribbing each other gently. When the second Brewster son was named Alden, Mac immediately called him "Kingman's chip off the Plymouth Rock."

Every year, two or three days before Christmas, the Brewsters joined us for an expedition to buy Christmas trees. Pamela and Kingman would look for the two tallest trees they could find. They were aggressively tree-proud, a characteristic that clashed with the need to postpone the search to a day so close to Christmas. That need arose from the Brewsters' effort to keep alive the myth of Santa Claus, which their children were unwilling to give up. While our spouses drove about the countryside, sometimes with flagging spirits, Mary Louise and I would sit quietly together at home, consuming a small pitcher of dry martinis and enjoying each other's company. Mary Louise, a small person with red hair, strong views, and a shrewd instinct about people, an avid reader and sharp critic, came to know me better than did any other woman except Pamela. She, Kingman, Pamela, and I were a contented foursome, both when we were alone together and when the children — ultimately their five and our three — surrounded us at the beach or in our Cambridge residences.

In addition to our neighbors, we had other friends, a few at Harvard, but most not in the academy. Of my undergraduate teachers and their wives, Sheila and Myron Gilmore we saw regularly. We occasionally played bridge with Louise and David Owen. Ruth Handlin and our Pammy were classmates, but we only rarely spent time with Mary and Oscar, Ruth's parents. Arthur Schlesinger, Jr., generously asked me to lunch after reviewing my book *The Republican Roosevelt* — on the whole favorably — and soon we were having lunch together three or four times a year, usually with Thomas Reed Powell, a retired law professor who specialized in constitutional interpretation, especially the First Amendment.

I also remained close to some of my undergraduate friends from the track squad. When we could arrange it, we partied with Mimi and Mike Ford, who had moved to the Washington area while he worked as a lawyer for the CIA. Mike wrote our first wills. George W. Goethals, whom I had known since 1935, became a lecturer in psychology at Harvard and included Pammy among the children he was observing in an experiment. Robert B. Kent, a lawyer and law professor then at Boston University Law School, later at Cornell Law School, served as our attorney at two real estate closings. He and his wife, Barbara, were companions at Harvard football games and at track meets in the Boston Garden. Those events also attracted Frederick Phinney and his wife, Eleanor. An Episcopal minister, Fred became pastor of the Church of Our Savior in Brookline, just across the river from Cambridge. He used a low-church liturgy with a family service, qualities that appealed to Pamela, who joined Fred's church. Willard Dalrymple became a house physician in the faculty health plan at MIT, where Dr. Dana Farnsworth, a pioneer in that kind of practice, was in charge and I was one of Bill's patients.

Pamela met her close friend Shirley Carter because of their common concern for the Cambridge Nursery School, a morning home-away-from-home for Pammy and for Shirley's two sons. In organizing and managing the school's annual picnic, a public event designed to raise money, the two women became friends. They continued their collaboration in similar enterprises for the Buckingham School, which the Carter children attended, as did Pammy, with the financial assistance of a generous abatement in tuition. As I became involved in Buckingham affairs I developed an easy comity with Shirley's husband, George Carter, a psychiatrist.

The Buckingham School, an institution for boys and girls through sixth grade and for girls only thereafter, absorbed much of Pamela's and my energies. Indebted as we felt we were for the tuition abatement, without which Pammy could not have attended, we also considered Buckingham excellent academically, with a sound, conservative curriculum and concerned and competent teachers. Pamela helped plan the annual Buckingham circus, a fund-raising event, and I participated on circus day, either in charge of pony rides or as a clown. Kingman was regularly the master of ceremonies. One year when the clowns felt rather put upon because of the burden of their wives' expectations, Vivian Katz, who lived nearby, provided a large pitcher of martinis an hour before lunch. The clowns had a ball that afternoon, and so did the children with whom they played.

It seemed to me that there had to be less labor-intensive ways to earn scholarship funds for the school. About 1953 one of my adult students told me that his wife feared that his continuing education would leave her behind and threaten their marriage. That prompted me to propose a series of Buckingham seminars to be offered to adults in the area, to be taught without remuneration by academic parents of children in the school or by their colleagues. We discussed the idea with the Carters, who urged me to present my idea to the headmistress. The resulting program, which I managed, consisted of four seminars a year, each for six weeks, meeting one evening a week, with assigned reading. The cost for those who wished to enroll was $15, roughly the equivalent of $120 in the year 2000. Enrollment was limited to twelve in each seminar, a number small enough to encourage free discussion. I regularly offered one seminar a year. So at my request did some of my MIT colleagues, most successfully Victor Weisskopf, an eminent theoretical physicist and veteran of the Manhattan Project. He taught a seminar entitled "Scientific Frontiers," which grabbed Pamela's attention. One year I taught a seminar on American biography; another year I focused on American culture in the 1920s. Giorgio de Santillana, an historian of science at MIT, one year offered a seminar on great trials, which began with Socrates, went on to use Giorgio's own book on Galileo, and ended with Sacco and Vanzetti. Teaching adults, I found, provided a special satisfaction, for they had had enough experience in life to understand and discuss questions about which undergraduates were by and large innocents. And they contributed their insights with little reserve.

The program, always oversubscribed, raised a substantial amount of money and enhanced the school's reputation in the community. Doubtless as a result of my instituting the seminars, in 1954 I was elected to the Buckingham board of trustees. When I joined, the other two male trustees were the president of the board and the treasurer. All the other board members were Cambridge women, all of them my seniors. Business on the board remained routine until the president, a Harvard law professor, had a notorious affair with a neighbor's wife. Affairs were not uncommon in Cambridge, then or thereafter, but this one stirred up an unusual amount of gossip. Nevertheless I was surprised when the women of the board called on me one evening to ask me to convince the treasurer to urge the president to resign. No girls' school, they implied, should have a known fornicator as the president of its board. After some discussion, during which I suggested that school business should not be done outside of regular meetings, I said that I would think about their request overnight.

Within an hour of their departure Milton Katz called me. Apart from his teaching at the Harvard Law School, Milton was a kind of éminence grise concerning the professional and community commitments of his fellow faculty members and their friends. He supported the women of the Buckingham board and assumed that I did, too. The school could not afford a scandal, he said; and he and I, he continued, were going to prevent one. He proposed that an emergency meeting of the trustees be called, at which the treasurer would preside and announce the resignation of the president, which Milton would have arranged. Then I would ask for the floor and propose the election as president of Kingman Brewster. I agreed at once, partly because I thought Kingman exactly fit the bill, and partly because I did not know how to say no to Milton. In later years Milton liked to say that he and

I had thrust Kingman into his first administrative job. In fact he had, with me as his willing agent.

In 1952 Pamela found a new rental, the larger part of a commodious Victorian house at 17–17a Arlington Street in Cambridge. (Four years later we bought the building.) Arlington Street, near Porter Square, ran uphill off Massachusetts Avenue about a mile north of Harvard Square. When we first moved in, the other, smaller part of the house was rented to Nancy and Paul Ignatius, who proved to be bright, articulate, and cordial co-tenants. A recent graduate of the Harvard Business School, Paul had founded Harbridge House, a management consulting firm specializing in defense-related enterprises. He went on during the 1960s to hold a number of high positions in the Defense Department and later was president of the *Washington Post*. Like another neighbor, John McNaughton, a Harvard law professor also later in the Defense Department, Paul typified the intelligence and drive of the young professional residents of the Harvard Square enclaves of Cambridge. More and more of the men I knew, academicians included, spent a few days every month consulting for the federal government. Indeed prestige in Cambridge depended increasingly on one's contacts in Washington or one's involvement in national politics. During the 1950s a pattern evolved that accounted for the mass exodus from Cambridge to the District of Columbia during the 1960s.

But many of the area's brightest intellectuals kept at their scholarly pursuits. So it was with Victor Weisskopf, who lived a few houses from ours. He made his scientific enthusiasms contagious, in one instance by setting up an observatory on the flat roof of his house. There, under his perfervid guidance, the neighborhood children received their first lessons in astronomy. Just across the street from us, Betty and Barrington Moore protected each other's privacy during their sacred working hours and in the evenings played an important part in our lives. A studious Japanese American, Betty, who had no children of her own, informally adopted both the Blum and the Ignatius children, on whom she bestowed occasional gifts and loving attention. The Moores frequently invited Pamela and me to cocktails and dinner, where we were often joined by Inge and Herbert Marcuse. As Barry and Herbert paced, slightly bowed at the waist, their hands behind their backs in the style of European intellectuals, they sipped Pernod and discussed their latest adventures in revising Marxism. I would listen as I drank some of Barry's good Scotch.

Their talk revealed the extraordinary range of their learning. Barry, born into a wealthy, socially prominent New York family, had majored in classics at Williams College before engaging in intelligence work during World War II. He then became a senior research fellow at the Russian Research Center at Harvard. During the 1950s he published three incisive books about Soviet politics and the nature of the Soviet dictatorship. In that decade, inspired by Marcuse, he was developing the social theories that imbued his politically radical later work on the causes of human misery and injustice, which in his view stemmed from capitalism. Tall, lean, and ascetic—he hid his wealth except for an expensive sailing yacht he owned—Barrington Moore towered over the short and dumpy Marcuse. Herbert looked exactly like the émigré scholar he was, formerly of the Frankfurt school of German social philosophers and the wartime OSS, currently a professor at Brandeis University, soon to become the pied piper of America's rebellious youth; in 1955 he published *Eros and Civilization,* a Freudian-existentialist tract. In that influential book, he presented the history of civilization as the history of repression. He would later direct his criticism toward the United States. His conversations with Barry foreshadowed his attacks on technological rationality and centralized authority, attacks to which Barry was increasingly sympathetic.

Their heady discourse, by no means easy to follow, proceeded most of the time as if I were not present. Now and then, Barry would pause to ask me some factual question about the historical market behavior of the giant American corporations. Once he liked a metaphor I offered. I suggested that in the late nineteenth century, competitive corporations in heavy industry had moved to consolidation—to surrendering their independence to a large holding company—in the manner of Hobbes's timorous men accepting the Leviathan in preference to the brutality of the theoretical state of nature. But for the most part, Barry and Herbert had little interest in what they considered my conventionally liberal views. Herbert particularly had small regard for the empirical method.

Both men fancied themselves revolutionaries, but I could imagine neither storming any barricades, and Barry's manner of speech and fastidious wardrobe never matched his theories. Indeed when radical students in the late 1960s blocked access to his office, Barry lost much of his revolutionary zeal. During the 1950s I provided an interested audience for the Moore-Marcuse dialogue, but one they did not convince, then or later. Still, their intellectual adventures in social theorizing were just as characteristic of Cambridge mores as were the growing number of Harvard and MIT faculty who took the Eastern Airlines shuttle to Washington twice a week to advise the government about national defense. The two contrasting, even inimical types of intellectual engagement offset each other, but it was hard to hold an intellectual and professional course between them. Yet that was what I tried to do in my own writing and teaching.

For Pamela and me, by the mid-1950s Cambridge had become not just a place to live but also a way of life. Our ties to that city made us loath to consider moving elsewhere even as I came to realize that for professional reasons I had to relocate. For the teaching and writing of history were becoming difficult for me at MIT. In time we did leave. But our youthful affection for Cambridge stayed fresh in our memory for all the years to come, and our Cambridge friends remained friends for life.

7

The Institute

In 1948 I entered the Massachusetts Institute of Technology by a back door, under the wing of Elting Morison, as his associate editor of the Roosevelt letters, and with the rank of research associate. It took me some time to learn that in the freewheeling intellectual world of MIT, a research associate could rank with a lab assistant, a full professor, or any intermediate grade. Prestige little related to title and depended on intelligence or inspiration, and on productivity. MIT was the most meritocratic university I ever knew. There were no women or blacks of whom I was aware on its faculty in 1948, but in contrast to Harvard and Yale, there were many Jews. In the distinguished physics department, among those whom I met soon after I arrived were David Frisch and Francis Friedman, younger members of the department, and its elder statesman, Victor Weisskopf. The economics department, then arguably the best in the world, had hired brilliant, Harvard-trained Jews, among them two future Nobel laureates, Paul Samuelson and Robert Solow. Harvard would not consider them, as John Kenneth Galbraith later complained in his memoir. So, though MIT's humanities department was then weak, the path of opportunity at the Institute, as I was to discover, lay wide open.

But at first I felt distant from both MIT and its possibilities. Elting, by contrast, was successfully exploring both in his idiosyncratic way. Busy with the Roosevelt letters, he taught only one course, an elective for graduate students. It was a study of texts on good and evil, and incidentally of memoirs on Oedipal themes. One afternoon early in my tenure, Elting introduced me to four administrators with whom I would in time have close relations. First I met

Howard Bartlett, permanent head of the humanities department. A tall, sturdy, middle-aged man, his posture always rigidly straight, Bart had no background in the humanities. A specialist in engineering report writing, he claimed no other skill.

Wholly without pretense, reserved, even at times inarticulate, Bart found himself presiding over an odd group of colleagues and was confronted in the climate of postwar higher education with problems he never quite understood. He had no idea of how to convert the department's traditional offerings—a survey of American history, various fragments of literary history, English composition—to a required four-semester humanistic curriculum suitable for undergraduate scientists and engineers. But so long as he could retain command, he willingly delegated educational responsibilities to the best available faculty members, among them Duncan Ballantine, my associate in naval history. But Elting had no interest in any role subordinate to Bart, which became obvious in our brief conversation. It ended without engaging me.

We went on to see the dean of the School of Humanities and Social Studies, John E. Burchard, whose careful wardrobe, gout, and clipped, gray moustache befit his interest in good food and wine. An MIT graduate in architecture, Burchard had served during World War II doing classified research in Princeton, New Jersey. Thereafter he venerated Princeton and attempted at MIT to emulate its Ivy League style and humanistic excellence. Having a versatile intelligence, Burchard at one time worked as music critic for the *Boston Globe*; wrote with charm, as in his *When M. I. T. Was Boston Tech*; and later mounted much admired photomurals, the photographs his own, of the Acropolis and of Notre-Dame de Chartres. His volubility concealed his sense of inferiority, the result of his not having graduated from a Princeton or a Yale. Widely learned, a splendid showman, Burchard presided over one great department—economics—and several second-rate departments or programs that he was beginning to improve—humanities, political science, psychology, music, and foreign languages. In 1948 he was just coming into his own and was rather full of himself. At our first meeting, he talked the whole time about his physical and intellectual plans for the school. Elting and I listened, I impressed by the range of his interests.

We then called on Provost James R. Killian, who was about to succeed Karl T. Compton as president of the Institute. That meeting was brief, little more than a handshake, but we spent at least half an hour with provost-designate Julius Stratton. Jay had graduated from the Institute; but he had also engaged in creative and significant research in electrical engineering. Scientist though he was, his interest in the humanities equaled Burchard's. Unlike Burchard, Jay packaged his ambitions within his vision of MIT as a university "polarized around science and technology." Elting shared that vision, but with less confidence and more reservations than Jay. I could not see, in 1948 or in the years to come, how I, a political and cultural historian, could fit comfortably in that picture. But Jay had a gravitas I felt.

A year later, when I began to teach, I became acquainted with the humanities department, at that time by no means yet a meritocracy. Indeed the department, like a military school, expected its faculty to be either in class or in their offices all day, five days a week. That expectation put a damper on scholarly research and writing unless a professor could buy his way out of the system and its demands, as Elting had with the Roosevelt letters. It was a system that discouraged scholarship and presumably rewarded teaching. But at MIT, as elsewhere, a good young teacher who avoided creative scholarship soon became a banal teacher. Howard Bartlett presided over a group of tenured men, most of them without doctorates or equivalent degrees, and a larger group of younger, nontenured colleagues, most of them, like me, Harvard graduate students, and most of them transients. The tenured contingent included several, like Bart, who had been hired to teach engineering report writing, an assignment they never outgrew.

Now, however, they were expected to offer a core curriculum in the humanities that would be required of all undergraduates for their first four semesters, with a further requirement of four more semesters before graduation of either social science or humanities courses. Most students took at least a year of economics, which gave them half of the electives they needed. Hoping to attract students to humanities electives, the department voted tenure to one teacher whose sole skill was playing folk music on his guitar. Sure enough, his courses on folk music drew large enrollments, which supported the department's budget. Like Elting, the best of the tenured faculty taught only elective courses for upper-class students; the core curriculum was left largely to those of the tenured faculty who had no scholarly credentials or interests. The younger, transient faculty members had little respect for them and little interest in the syllabi they generated. Indeed those syllabi were for the most part no more than reading lists, which were assigned to sections of about twenty students. Teaching was done without supervision and often without much preparatory learning.

Where most colleges used names, MIT used numbers. Indeed numbers stamped the undergraduate regimen at the Institute as baldly as did the universal requirement, regardless of major, of two years of calculus and two of physics. The buildings were numbered. The various major fields were numbered. Civil engineering was Course 1; economics, Course 14; business administration, Course 15. The introductory economics course was 14.01; the second semester was 14.02. The humanities courses for freshmen were 21.01 and 21.02. Grading was supposed to be calculated on a scale, with the highest number 5.0. I was told to submit grades in three "significant" figures. So a 73, for example, in my grade book became a 3.65 when translated to the five-point scale. The fallacy of misplaced concreteness obtruded particularly in grading humanities courses. But MIT liked to look precise.

The organization of the first term of the freshman course fell partly to Duncan Ballantine. To Duncan's seven weeks of cultural anthropology the humanities department added seven weeks on ancient Greece, with a textbook and selected readings in translation. The two halves never meshed well. The second semester focused on Dante and Shakespeare's *King Lear*, at best a difficult tragedy. For the sophomore year students had a choice. One two-term course required only a text written by two members of the department, John Rae and Thomas Mahoney's *The United States in World Affairs*. The younger faculty members called it "Rae and Baloney."

I was eager to teach, but neither that book nor the freshman course. That left the other sophomore course, European Intellectual History, to which I was assigned one section just a week before classes began in the fall of 1949. There was no syllabus, just a reading list of selected passages beginning with Thomas Aquinas and ending with German philosopher Hans Vaihinger. Stops in between included Hobbes, Locke, Burke, Hegel, Darwin, Marx, and Dewey. Some of the readings were mere snippets; others, entire essays or books. Familiar with the work of only half the authors on the list, I had only a week to learn about the rest, and I had to create—if only for myself—a structure for the course.

My ignorance began with St. Thomas Aquinas. I took the subway to Harvard Square and explained my problems to my friend and former tutor, Myron Gilmore, a specialist on the Renaissance (which the reading list ignored—perhaps the students were supposed to remember Shakespeare and Dante from their freshman year). Myron at once recommended one book to me: Theodore Spencer's *Shakespeare and the Nature of Man*. I read it twice with growing admiration. The medieval intellectual synthesis of Aquinas with its endless chain of being, Spencer argued, dissolved under the contradictory work of Copernicus on cosmology, Montaigne on nature, and Machiavelli on the state. The God-centered mind of the Middle Ages became the man-centered mind of the Renaissance. That change opened the way, for the first time since antiquity, to tragedy as Shakespeare wrote it.

Spencer's analysis gave me the beginning of the structure I was seeking. I needed, I decided, to insert remarks of my own about Galileo, who provided proof of Copernican theory, about Galileo's significance for Newton, and about Newton's influence on eighteenth-century assumptions about the "world machine." That would bridge the gap between Aquinas and Locke; and Hobbes could be viewed as attached to the medieval idea of kingship, now stripped of theology in order to fit his own time. My scheme allowed me to follow the reading list and get by without the Renaissance. It also permitted me to move from the eighteenth century to nineteenth-century romanticism as expressed by Burke and Hegel. I found that I could not teach Hegel; I could try only to be Hegel, to immerse myself in Hegel the night before teaching him and then come into class talking as Hegel might have if he had spoken English. But from Hegel to Marx and Darwin the transitions were easy, and Dewey's essay on Hegel opened the door to Vaihinger and his pragmatic philosophy of the "as . . . if."

For several years, using classroom explication of the texts, I taught that sequence. Sometimes the going was tough, for few MIT undergraduates were then interested in ideas and their history. Much depended on the intended major of the students assigned to my classroom. The freshmen and sophomores were organized by class in sections, with each section moving together from subject to subject. I felt blessed when my class was made up of aspiring mathematicians, physicists, or electrical engineers, for by and large these were students with a high tolerance for the humanities. The same could not be said of civil engineering majors. When it came to the humanities—or my course, at least—mechanical and chemical engineers ranged from the involved to the indifferent.

Since I taught at noon, using the midday hour away from the Roosevelt letters, many of the undergraduates ate their lunch during class, for they had no gap in their scheduled courses. One student in a class of physics majors regularly arrived before class began, ate his lunch, and promptly fell asleep. I decided to await the results of the first exam before raising the issue of his inattention. When he came to see me to pick up his blue book and grade, I realized that the sleeper had an A. I told him how surprised I was that he had done so well. "Oh, Mr. Blum," he said, "don't be offended. I sleep through all my classes." This young man apparently worked all night in a lab that was otherwise unavailable to him, and nevertheless earned honors grades. Though the Institute had always been coeducational, in my eight years there I taught only one woman. She had no use at all for the humanities.

Now and then I drew an entire class that felt that way. In one such class, I was trying to get the students to discuss their assigned reading from Edmund Burke's *Reflections on the French Revolution*. I began by referring to the author's writing of the "naked and shivering nature of man." What does that phrase mean? I inquired. No response. Did it remind anyone of Hobbes? No response. Did anyone know the Lord's prayer? One timid hand rose up. Let's write it on the board, I proposed, and he dictated while I used the chalk. He reached "lead us not into temptation, but deliver us from evil" and said: "Oh, I've got it." It was not clear that anyone else had until my lone scholar had related the prayer to Burke's words.

Most MIT undergraduates were bright but lopsided, with high scores on mathematical aptitude and mediocre scores on verbal aptitude. Typically they were sons of successful plumbers or electricians whose fathers wanted them to become engineers or scientists. In turn those sons would send their children to Princeton or Amherst and on to medical or law school. In a sense, the history of MIT mirrored American upward social mobility. Many of the students I knew had ambitions to become corporate executives and to make a lot of money. But the very best hoped for an academic career in science. One of them, Frederic L. Holmes, later a colleague at Yale, completed the requirements for the biology major in his junior year. He spent his senior year reading American history with me and writing a long senior essay with Elting on early approaches to homeostasis. Later he earned a Ph.D. at Harvard in the history of science. But Larry Holmes was exceptional. No other student I met planned to become a historian. To be sure, it was satisfying to teach bright undergraduates, but I missed seeing students with high verbal aptitude and a first interest in my field.

After I received my Ph.D. in 1950, MIT promoted me to the rank of assistant professor. I still taught only one section of the same course, with the rest of my working hours committed to the Roosevelt letters, but the appointment gave me security for five years. I welcomed that security and intended to see the eight volumes of Roosevelt letters through publication, but I was uncertain about remaining at the Institute thereafter. Indeed I hoped that the publication of my Tumulty biography in 1951 would result in some offers from liberal arts colleges or universities. My wishes came true. In 1952 Bowdoin College in Brunswick, Maine, invited me to succeed Edward Kirkland as Munsey Professor of History. Kirk, a leading economic historian, had recommended me. But Bowdoin did not fit my family's needs. The salary of a professor at Bowdoin fell short of my MIT salary. Rentals in the area were few and unattractive, and we were without capital to buy a house. Worse, children from an air base in the Brunswick vicinity crowded the public school, which had to resort to double sessions, and there was no convenient private school for our daughters, then four and one. I was forced to conclude that I could not afford to teach, even as the Munsey Professor, at that excellent liberal arts college.

That was disheartening. I would be able to leave the Institute only if I received a much better offer, probably therefore only if a good university wanted me. To be an attractive prospect for such an institution, I needed to publish. I was already well along in that mission, for my new book, *The Republican Roosevelt*, was nearing completion and we were at work on the final two volumes of the letters. But the prospect of full-time teaching in the humanities department of MIT distressed me. In addition, I knew that Elting was arranging an escape for himself. As a member of the committee that recommended the creation of the Sloan School of Industrial Management, Elting wrote part of the committee's report. As that report noted, the committee had consulted chief executives of the largest American corporations about the qualities they wanted in the junior managers they hired. First on their list was the ability to write clear prose; also on the list was a sense of how the past affected the present and portended the future — a sense of history. Those qualities fit Elting's talents. Further, he was centering his own research on the process of innovation and its consequences. He was planning to move from MIT's School of Humanities to its School of Industrial Management. As he did in starting the Roosevelt project, so in shaping his latest move, Elting was manipulating the Institute to obtain the space he wanted.

If I was to be comfortable at MIT, I needed to follow Elting's example. But he was a tenured professor, and I was only an assistant professor. He helped me out by asking me regularly to offer a course for the Sloan fellows, junior executives with engineering degrees selected from corporations intending soon to promote them. The course was meant to broaden their learning, help them improve their writing, and give them some knowledge of history. These pedagogical aims did not appeal to Elting, even though he considered them important. So he happily enlisted me. I worked out a history of American political economy from about 1890 to 1950, a course that stressed federal public policies as they affected business and industry. When we finished working on the Roosevelt letters, that course, with its able, adult students, became part of my obligations to MIT. I enjoyed teaching it, partly because it meshed with my research interests, partly because the young executives who took it were bright and engaged.

In order to enjoy MIT, I had also to try, with others, to make the core curriculum of the humanities department more structured. That objective would open the way to a more compatible teaching environment, which would in turn increase my desire to remain at MIT. To remain at MIT, however, I would need a promotion. And a promotion would require more published scholarship. So my task ahead was clear: whether I would earn a promotion or attract an offer from outside, I had to write. That conclusion had become obvious by 1952, when Oscar Handlin asked me to write a short biography of Woodrow Wilson for a series he was editing. For several weeks I hesitated. I would have preferred to write a biography of Marcus A. Hanna, for I wanted to explore the conservative mind of the 1890s. But Oscar insisted on Wilson, whom I had come to dislike. A Wilson biography would be my third biography. Would that, I asked, be damaging professionally? Oscar replied in his typical manner. Shrugging his shoulders, he said, "Who writes two books?"

Late in the autumn of 1952 I knew I would soon have done so, though the draft of *The Republican Roosevelt* had not set the publishing world ablaze. Craig Wylie at Houghton, Mifflin rejected the manuscript because, he said, it contained too much history and too little biography. William Miller at Knopf rejected it for just the opposite reason. But Thomas Wilson, then director of Harvard University Press, accepted the manuscript, with publication set for 1954. Elting had told him that the only biographical work coming out of the editing of the letters would be my study of Roosevelt; and Alvin Hansen, an eminent Harvard economist whom Wilson had asked for a review, had praised my manuscript. With some revisions necessary before the book was ready for publication, and with the Wilson biography for Oscar's series pending, my plate was full.

Still, I could not turn my full attention to writing history, for developments at the Institute embroiled me. Perhaps because I turned down Bowdoin, I became more engaged with MIT. Perhaps I had lost patience with deficiencies in the core curriculum and in the staff teaching it. Perhaps I responded to the absence of intellectual leadership in the department occasioned by Duncan Ballantine's resignation to become president of Reed College. I have never understood why I chose to speak out in a department meeting, with the dean presiding, about the core courses. John Burchard realized that the offerings of the humanities department had yet to reach the level of excellence to which he aspired. He also knew that the department had to recruit more able young scholars to revise the core curriculum. So he listened as I delivered a passionate attack on the lack of intellectual coherence in the mix of courses then required in the core curriculum.

We would not need to reinvent the wheel, I argued. We could take our clues from the long-standing required curriculum at Columbia College, with its texts tracking the history of civilization; and from the Harvard "Red Book," James B. Conant's *General Education in a Free Society*. During World War II, Conant had commissioned a study of undergraduate education at Harvard. It resulted in the publication of that book and in a major overhauling of Harvard's undergraduate requirements. Though Conant's book did not apply directly to MIT, it recognized that the conflict between democratic societies and their totalitarian rivals needed to be understood in terms of the great values of the western tradition. I had in mind no specific changes in the department's core curriculum, but I believed that MIT's curriculum needed carefully to be reviewed in the light of the Columbia and Harvard examples.

The next day Burchard called and asked me to take charge of the entire core curriculum, a proposal that Howard Bartlett had approved, but a responsibility I had not contemplated. I was to work with Bart on recruiting faculty, Burchard said, and I was to have the clerical assistance of a full-time secretary. I knew the assignment had its perils. I would need the cooperation of all those who were going to have to teach the core, and I would need the advice of the best tenured scholars, many of whom had long ignored the freshman and sophomore courses. Further, the burdens of my task would impede my writing. But after reflection, I decided that my public criticism of the status quo left me no choice but to accede to Burchard's request. Elting, I suspected, thought I had lost my mind, but he kindly did not say so.

To proceed I formed two committees, one on the freshman year courses, one on the sophomore alternative to the American history survey. I left the survey to John Rae, an informed historian of the automobile industry, who continued to base the course on his text, which was not his best work. John resented what he saw as the declining importance of the text, and I respected his feelings even though I did not share them. I did not want to close him out of a curriculum he had once labored so hard to construct, but I counted on Al Chandler and a new colleague from Yale to enrich the offerings in American history. I asked those teaching to revise all of the core except the seven weeks on the Greeks. For revision of the European intellectual history course, the course I had been teaching, I turned to a reliable colleague who had considerable experience in teaching in the field. He was agreeable to cooperating with the whole staff of the course he undertook to review.

It was necessary, I felt, to involve everyone teaching the core in its revision. Students had long resisted required courses. And faculty resented teaching courses they had not helped to construct. By involving the teachers, I hoped to evoke their intellectual interest and their personal enthusiasm. To some extent, I think, though it was impossible to measure, that hope materialized. Our efforts would have failed, however, without the input of new faculty members, who were hired to help with the historical periods in which they specialized. I did not revise the core; the committees did, and I approved their revisions.

So it was with the freshman-year courses. Lacey Baldwin Smith, recommended to me by Joseph Strayer of Princeton, an outstanding medievalist, provided indispensable assistance in developing a medieval unit of seven weeks to follow the seven weeks on the ancient Greeks. Lacey, a Tudor specialist, also organized the first seven weeks of the second semester on the Renaissance as it unfolded in Tudor England. (He had the good sense to keep *Lear* on the reading list.) After Lacey's departure for Northwestern, we found Charles Gray, then a Harvard doctoral candidate, to replace him. Charles later went on to the University of Chicago. We also hired Theodore Lockwood, another Princeton Ph.D., who later became president of Trinity College in Hartford. At about that time Al Chandler departed for Johns Hopkins to become a professor of history and the editor of the Eisenhower papers. It was I who had recommended Lacey to my old friend Dick Leopold at Northwestern. I valued Lacey as a colleague, but when Dick inquired, I urged him to offer Lacey the job. I did so not because I wanted Lacey to leave, but because I felt that unless the humanities department at MIT could recruit assistant professors able enough to attract invitations to join conventional departments in good universities, we could not obtain the young talent we needed.

As we progressed in our work with the curriculum, we could not avoid the technological imperative of the culture of the Institute. Even before I took on the job of revising the core, the course I had been teaching had been changed to include a unit on the textile mills of Lowell, Massachusetts. There was much to be said for the collection of readings on that subject that a few of the tenured faculty put together. The material, most of it on the Lowell Locks and Canals Company, explained the technology through which waterpower provided the energy the new factories needed. It also described how the mills recruited, used, and abused women operatives. And it caught the interest of most undergraduates studying it. The older faculty were wedded to it, and the politics of revision made it necessary to let them have their way. A strictly coherent structure for the core seemed to me less important than preservation of departmental morale.

Further, technology had a direct relevance to the kind of "heritage" program we hoped to build. History, philosophy, and literature were only part of the western heritage. Science was also a part — and an important part, as the influence of Newton and Darwin demonstrated. So was technology, though we were as yet unskilled in describing the role it played in western culture and intellectuality. Our weeks of instruction on the Lowell mills was a first effort to tie technology to the history of European and American ideas.

Were there then, as C. P. Snow suggested about that time, two cultures, one science and the other the liberal arts? MIT did not afford a good test of that notion, for the Institute then had no culture. It had yet to become strong in science, and it remained spotty and mediocre in the humanities. Physics was excellent, but biology at MIT, as one future Nobel laureate put it, had yet to leave the dark ages, and chemistry was unexciting. Economics at MIT stood out as the only nonscientific field of distinction, though the economists considered themselves scientists, at least in their use of mathematics. Queen of the social sciences, economics also invited imitators in politics and in history, scholars who believed they, too, would find the grail if only they could quantify their monographs. But that fashion had as yet few devotees. A fusion of science with the liberal arts did occur within the fertile minds of several of the MIT faculty — Victor Weisskopf in his search for commonalities among the sciences, Norbert Wiener in his applications of cybernetic theory, Elting Morison in his studies of technological innovation. These thinkers were working to blend fields, to the benefit of scholarship in general. They were the local adventurers in the journey that Crick and Watson took to the double helix and Thomas Kuhn to his paradigms in the history of science. But they did not then represent the culture of the Institute. That culture, such as it was, consisted essentially of engineering, business administration, and research contracts with industry and government. It was a culture of technology, not science, born of the technological demands of World War II on which MIT had flourished. It was a culture more of doing than of thinking, a culture with which, at least at that time, the liberal arts did not comfortably connect.

The core curriculum as it evolved by 1957 was not demonstrably distinguished. It consisted of more or less conventional choices, though the approach to them was innovative in that all units combined materials from history, literature, philosophy, and art or architecture. That mix was, we felt, appropriate for a technological institution that allowed little time for humanistic study.

Later generations of college faculties would take issue with the inattention of the curriculum to questions of race, gender, and nonwestern cultures. The major responsibility for those omissions at MIT in the 1950s was mine, for I could have insisted on a different emphasis. Our revised curriculum, however, reflected the consensus of those teaching it, as I had intended. Further, in the 1950s the western heritage seemed essential to educators who, like average Americans, worried about the barbarians they perceived to be leaders in the Soviet Union and China. Indeed President Killian considered the curriculum weak on Protestant Christianity, which he viewed as a bulwark against "atheistic communism." But he also considered our core curriculum to be genteel, and he wanted to make MIT graduates fit the genteel tradition. In the spirit of the times and in the understanding of my colleagues, we were proceeding exactly as we should have. But we were proceeding also as my own education had shaped my thinking and values. My mother, my teachers at Andover and Harvard, my own reading had determined my sense of a usable past. I had always understood the classical, Judeo-Christian, and English heritage to be my own, as I made the American past mine, and subconsciously, as I later realized, I wanted to pass my heritage along. I still do, but now with attention paid to important issues I had omitted because in the 1950s I simply had not thought about them.

While we were refining the core curriculum John Burchard hosted a series of dinners that brought together the provost, several senior scientists with an interest in humanistic studies, Howard Bartlett, and me. Burchard wanted us to discuss the possibility of creating humanities majors — a "Course 21" — in Science and the Humanities and in Engineering and the Humanities. Within three months we had agreed that without a major of its own, the humanities department would never achieve excellence. We agreed, too, on the desirability of a program on Science and the Humanities, though we were dubious about an alternative in engineering. Without consulting me, the dean and the provost then informed the group that I was to preside over the construction of the new major. As we adjourned that evening, Jay Stratton told me privately that I was to be promoted to the rank of associate professor with an appropriate salary. Despite the promotion, I was depressed by those developments. I did not want any more administrative responsibilities; they would continue to keep me removed from scholarship. No raise in salary could compensate me for this loss. But I could see no way to escape, and I realized that Course 21 would ease our problem of recruiting faculty for teaching the core curriculum. So I went along with Burchard and worked with him in submitting what turned out to be a successful application to the Rockefeller Foundation for the financing we needed.

The prospect of Course 21 lifted the spirits of several senior professors who had rarely participated in teaching freshmen and sophomores. One was Karl Deutsch, a German-Czech émigré who had a Harvard doctorate in political theory, a subject he commanded. But overcome by the technological imperative at MIT, Karl had recently adopted quantification as the source of all truth, and he wanted the department to follow his lead.

In studying the origins of Swiss nationalism, Deutsch counted the increasing number of letters, shipments of goods, and other transactions among the cantons. The growing communication among them, he argued, foreshadowed their union as a single nation. In a graduate seminar, he applied a similar technique to Ireland. He invited me to attend one session as an expert on Ireland, which I was not. (He must have thought a biography of an Irish-American qualified me.) At that session, his students reported on the rising frequency of mail, telegrams, telephone calls, and other communications between Ulster and Eire. So you see, said Karl in summing up, soon there will be a single Irish state. He then asked for my comments. "You haven't taken account of the centuries of division over religion," I said. "Oh, religion," he replied disdainfully. "Religion you cannot quantify." Therein lay the problem: for the committed quantifier, what could not be measured or counted in human affairs did not matter. Clearly, it would have been misguided to build a curriculum on the basis of empiricism alone. Indeed in various ways the technological imperative that prevailed at MIT impeded the development of Course 21 during the months I was involved.

So did the indifference of some of the faculty, most critically Walt W. Rostow. A talented economic historian, also a former Rhodes Scholar, Walt had written his Yale doctoral dissertation on the British economy during the nineteenth century. It was a notable monograph, revealing the kind of intelligence and learning the humanities department needed. For several years after Walt joined us in 1950, he taught skillfully in the core. But his interests lay elsewhere, initially in extrapolating his dissertation into a book, *The Process of Economic Growth* (1953), which adapted modified Keynesian formulations to its subject. The book put forward a provocative thesis based on Walt's argument that propensities (for example, the propensity to bear children) helped to explain economic growth. But as Paul Samuelson observed in a faculty discussion of the book, that propensity, among others, could not be measured. Walt was not necessarily wrong, but in the world of professional economists, what could not be measured could not be included in the calculations significant for proving a hypothesis. The economists rejected their imitators, Rostow as well as Deutsch.

If Walt was discouraged, he never showed it, but he did move away from the department to allot almost all his time to the Center for International Studies (CIS). The center represented in my view a corruption of the academic enterprise. Established by contract between MIT and the CIA, it undertook classified research, much of which could not be discussed with scholars who did not have security clearance. Such secrecy violated my sense of the need for essential openness of scholarship. After World War II, MIT had appointed Richard Bissell a professor of economics, but Bissell never taught a class. He had his friend, Max Millikan, also appointed an economics professor, and Max ran the CIS with Rostow as his deputy. In that role Walt wrote several studies, later declassified and published, on the Soviet

Union, on China, and on the United States Army. The first won some plaudits; the others exposed ideas that forebode Walt's fixed and controversial opinions about Vietnam.

The CIS was located in the same building as the faculty club, but when the elevator stopped at the CIS floor, passengers could not exit without a security clearance. The CIS held conferences in the library, where my office was located. But I could not walk to the men's room without asking permission of the marine corporal who guarded the corridor. I complained bitterly to both the president and the provost. The former told me that I must be coming down with a cold. I had already puzzled him. Around 1953, at the height of the Cold War and near the start of the Eisenhower administration, Killian circulated a form requiring all faculty to indicate their preferred duty in the event of an atomic raid. One could choose air raid warden, firefighter, medical aide, or other jobs that had been useful when cities were bombed during World War II. But as I saw it, those kinds of jobs had become irrelevant in the atomic age. So when it came time for me to complete the form, I wrote that I wanted to be a victim — as indeed I did if an atomic war were actually to begin. Killian sent one of his aides to ask what I meant. He assumed that I was either joking or out of my mind. In fact I felt it was he who was out of his mind. He was encouraging MIT to embrace Eisenhower's policies for the Cold War. He continued to do so until he left MIT to become Eisenhower's scientific adviser. How characteristic of Ike to select a scientific adviser trained in business administration and apparently unaware of the fallout from atomic weapons; and how characteristic of Killian to pass as a scientist. When in the 1970s the relationship between MIT and the CIA became a matter of public knowledge, both institutions had cause for embarrassment that neither felt. But I had objected, alas too quietly, to the CIS from the time I became aware of it, and I was growing increasingly restless at MIT.

Perhaps I had no right to be restless, for the Institute had treated me well. It took me in when I arrived as an editor of the Roosevelt letters. It found teaching for me. It gave me responsibilities beyond my expectations (and probably beyond the effective reach of my limited experience). It promoted me quickly and paid me adequately. In its way the Institute was an important center of learning, but as I repeatedly discovered, its culture was not mine. Not even the attractions of residence in Cambridge offset my yearning to join an arts and sciences faculty, a community of scholars with interests and values I shared.

I tried to fit my wants into the Institute's needs. Following Elting's example, in 1955 I bought a third of my time by arranging a contract through

Arthur Schlesinger, Jr., with Henry Morgenthau, Jr., to write a book based on his so-called "diaries," really the archives of his office as Secretary of the Treasury under Franklin Roosevelt. As an advance on royalties Morgenthau paid me through MIT for a third of my time. Another third went to my administrative tasks. A final third went partly to my old course for the Sloan fellows on American political economy and in 1957 to a new course for humanities majors on the American political process. Since I approached both subjects historically, I was teaching in my field of interest, though not to students who intended to pursue that interest.

I realized how much I missed a liberal arts environment during the summer of 1956. Williams College had contracted with American Telephone and Telegraph to provide a summer program in American Studies for some forty middle executives whose backgrounds were primarily in engineering. A broadening of intellectual experience would presumably make them better executives and better citizens. James Phinney Baxter III, the Williams president, had devised the program but wanted to hire for the first summer someone in American history who had taught business executives. He consulted Elting, who recommended me.

Phinney and I hit it off from the time we met. Then in his sixties, he was an Andover graduate and trustee with a Harvard doctorate, a historian of maritime and naval affairs who had taught at Harvard and served there as master of Adams House. So we had a lot in common. He was a charming and surprising man, short but round, with a large mustache and only one lung—the other had been lost to tuberculosis—who puffed and panted when he played tennis. I gladly joined his summer faculty. My assignment was to teach twentieth-century American political and cultural history, exactly the subject I had hoped to teach. My colleagues for that summer, and the next as events developed, included talented scholars from the Williams faculty who specialized in American literature, the American economy, American architecture, and American government. They were all welcoming and compatible, and so were the executives we taught. I began a love affair with Williams that endured. But accustomed as my family and I were to Cambridge, we found the town too small, so I declined Phinney's informal offer to create a tenured position for me.

My problem was to find just such a position as the one Phinney proposed, but at a liberal arts university in a location we would enjoy. I knew I had to leave MIT when in September 1956 Jay Stratton told me I was to be in charge of a new Master of Arts in Teaching program to be offered jointly by the Institute and the Harvard School of Education. I begged him not to add to my administrative duties. In reply he said, "You don't know your own destiny, John. Be patient and soon we'll make you a dean." But Jay did not know me. I had no intention of becoming a dean or a provost or a president, not at MIT or anywhere else. I intended to be a full-time historian, writing books in my field, teaching undergraduates and doctoral candidates, employed by a university with a strong liberal arts tradition. It was in teaching and writing that I found satisfaction.

During the academic year 1956–57, following publication of my biography of Woodrow Wilson, several offers came my way, the most interesting from the University of California at Berkeley, which wanted me as a visiting professor for one year, with the expectation that during that year a tenured post would materialize. That was an attractive prospect that I began at once to pursue with Kenneth Stampp, who was negotiating for the Berkeley history department. I realized that California was far away from friends and family, but I also recognized that I had to take Berkeley seriously or risk remaining forever at MIT.

Of course academic life for me involved much more than job prospects. I was busy with my responsibilities at both MIT and the Buckingham School. I was caught up in the Morgenthau diaries. I had agreed to participate in a conference on nationalism in Iowa in April 1957 and a meeting in March in Philadelphia with a group of scholars who were writing essays for a book on American culture. For the Philadelphia meeting I had prepared an essay on the contemporary American middle class. It was well received. I was especially pleased that Ralph Gabriel, a distinguished Yale historian of American ideas, invited me to dine with him. We had a fruitful professional discussion over cocktails and seafood.

On the way back to Cambridge, I left the train in Stamford, Connecticut, where I had arranged for my father to meet me and drive me to his home in South Norwalk for a brief visit. I had dedicated the Wilson biography to him but had not seen him for some months. In the interval he had become tense and awkward when driving, and he had aged visibly, beyond his seventy-two years. As we sat down together for tea, I worried about him. But I told him about my negotiations with Berkeley. I would go there, I said, if I could have firm assurances about a tenured contract. "If you go," my father replied, "I'll miss you." It was his way of communicating his love for me. He died just days later, on March 17, 1957. I would miss him.

Father's will left everything he owned to his children and named his lawyer and me as co-executors of his estate, which had larger debts than liquid assets. My responsibilities as executor ruled out a departure for Berkeley until the debts had been paid, the house sold, and various other assets realized. Father's lawyer, a New Yorker he had known for many years, had no knowledge of our family. My brother was alienated from my father, and my sister was financially incompetent. I told Ken Stampp on the telephone that I could not leave the Northeast for the coming academic year. He replied that the California legislature had appropriated funds only for that year, and if I could not accept their offer now, we would have to start all over again. There would be no job and no commitment. I sighed audibly. Cheer up, he said. We'll probably be able to get back to you, and in the meantime something else may turn up. I doubted it. I felt handcuffed to MIT.

One morning early in April as I opened my mail, I was surprised to find a letter from George W. Pierson, chairman of the Yale history department. To my astonishment—I had no idea that Yale knew I existed—Pierson was offering me a professorship. Ralph Gabriel, he wrote, was soon to retire and he hoped I would fill the vacancy Gabriel's retirement would create. But Yale would need me at once to teach while David Potter, a distinguished cultural and political historian, was on leave during 1957–58. I could hardly believe my good fortune. I telephoned Professor Pierson, told him I accepted his offer, and asked his patience while I took care of some pressing obligations, including the Iowa conference. Ralph Gabriel must have known when we dined that I was under consideration at Yale, but he had not so much as hinted at it. My surprise was exceeded only by my delight.

Pamela dreaded the prospect of leaving Cambridge but expressed her happiness for me. MIT tried to meet the Yale offer with a promotion to professor and an increase in salary, both of which Jay Stratton discussed with me during a private lunch. He also promised to make me dean when Burchard retired. Like so many university administrators, he could not believe that any academician would not desire an administrative post. As politely as possible, I explained to Jay why I was going to Yale. He never understood. He repeated his conviction that my future lay in administration. I was decisive, quick, and assiduous, he argued, as well as patient with difficult people, and those qualities would govern my career. I was flattered but not convinced. And in the end, Jay's prediction proved to be wrong.

Just before my family and I left Cambridge that spring, Kingman Brewster and Elting Morison gave a smashing dinner at which many of our old friends gathered. It was a jolly occasion but bittersweet, an evening celebrating our communal bonds. Harvard, the Buckingham School, and the Roosevelt letters were well represented; not so the Institute. The guests at the dinner provided a fair picture of the formative chapter then ending in Pamela's and my maturing lives.

8

Professional Engagements

Scholarship in the 1950s remained what it had always been for most: an exercise in which its practitioners could engage only in their leisure time. On most weekends and evenings, and during most academic holidays, I chose the life of a scholar, largely because I enjoyed writing books and doing the research on which they were based. Indeed apart from teaching history, writing history was the most satisfying activity I knew. I found it just as easy to write two books concurrently as to write them one after the other. That pattern came to me naturally. I was writing about Joseph Tumulty before I began working with Elting Morison on the Roosevelt letters. By the time the biography of Tumulty was published, I had already begun a study of Theodore Roosevelt. Before that book was published, and as the last volumes of the Roosevelt letters were going to press, I agreed to write a biography of Woodrow Wilson. That project was still unfinished when I undertook to put together a book or books from the Morgenthau diaries — and, as an exercise for the left hand, to edit some children's literature on which I had happened. I found it both useful and reassuring to be writing two books at a time. If my interest in one topic flagged temporarily, an alternative task lay at hand. If one book on publication received mixed reviews, the other, so I resolved, would be better.

The larger of the projects on which I was first engaged was, of course, *The Letters of Theodore Roosevelt*. The first set of two volumes, published in 1951, was succeeded by the second set later that year, the third set in 1952, and the last in 1954. Weekdays from nine in the morning until five in the evening TR's letters, especially those on the presidency, wholly absorbed my interest. One series of letters on which I fastened had to do with the way in which Roosevelt manipulated his party to assure himself of the nomination in 1904. A related series focused on his management of his election campaign. In the summer of 1951 I wrote a chapter on each of those political topics.

My editing during the ensuing year focused on Roosevelt's efforts to persuade Congress to pass what became the Hepburn Act of 1906, putting teeth into railroad regulation. The appendices spoke to Roosevelt's approach to executive leadership and to his confidence in the administrative process. Like most of the reformers of his generation, TR did not anticipate the degree to which lawyers would dominate administrative agencies, which he had assumed would reach sound regulatory decisions through the participation of neutral, informed, economic experts. Through the use of such agencies he hoped to reduce the influence of lawyers and courts on issues of political economy, though he also would recommend a jurisprudence less restrictive of regulatory activity than had been the case for the previous several decades. My appendices about the Hepburn Act, slightly revised, appeared in my own book, *The Republican Roosevelt.* Other insights I had learned from editing the letters provided the substance for two more chapters of the book, which examined Roosevelt's thinking about political power in both domestic and foreign affairs. I also discussed his views about the importance of political power as a means to assure order. The last chapter of the book, derived from volumes 7 and 8 of the letters, dealt with Roosevelt's later years, during which he found himself out of power, unable to regain it, moving further to the left and then into his furious bellicosity during World War I. Frustrated, he too often became irresponsible. But until his death in 1919 he remained a much beloved man in the United States and the best-known American in the world. He remained a force.

As I wrote *The Republican Roosevelt,* Elting Morison and Al Chandler made important contributions to my thinking about TR. Like the letters on which it was based, my biography examined a masterful politician and skilled statesman at work. His tactics in dealing with Congress, his sure hand in making foreign policy, and his vision of domestic order provided models for successful presidents to come. The first imperial president, Roosevelt loved power, loved its pursuit and its use, as he said often and unabashedly. As his letters made clear, he also had no peer in managing the process of governing. As a result, I found that the letters, together with the absorbing task of annotating them, provided me with a continuing education about politics and government. To be sure, Roosevelt in his lesser moments sounded and acted like a jingo, and too often he had a smaller regard for civil liberties than I could approve. But he seemed to me overall a near-great president, ranking below only Washington, Lincoln, and FDR. That was the conclusion also of most reviewers of the successive volumes of the letters, which received major space and general commendation in the reviewing media, both popular and learned.

Of all my books, *The Republican Roosevelt* (published in 1954) probably had the most significance in its impact on historical scholarship. Arthur Schlesinger, Jr., and Arthur S. Link reviewed it favorably. Eric Goldman, then an outstanding historian of twentieth-century America, called it "fresh" and "well-written." John D. Hicks, an elder statesman in the profession, described it as "the right kind of book about T.R. Mr. Blum is not one of the 'incense swingers,' but neither is he one of the snide critics of later times who judged Roosevelt by their own era and not his. . . . The book is an interpretation, not a biography. And it is convincing." Citations to it soon appeared in the growing literature on the progressive era. The first paperback edition (published by Atheneum in 1973) and a second edition with a new prologue (published by Harvard University Press in 1977) became something of a staple for undergraduate courses on twentieth-century American history. Indeed, as the twentieth century ended, the book was still in print.

The work was gently revisionistic. Rejecting the tendency of earlier biographies of TR to treat him either as a patriotic paragon or a failed liberal, I defined him as a constructive conservative, not without faults, who fought for change in order to preserve the nation's historic institutions, including the structure of American capitalism. He was not a standpatter like his friends Henry Cabot Lodge and Elihu Root, nor was he an early New Dealer, as Henry Pringle's popular biography wanted him to be. Rather, as his fellow progressives agreed, Roosevelt believed it was necessary to strip capitalism of its undemocratic and antisocial excrescences in order to save it from the populists and socialists of his time. Both radical agitation and the antisocial business practices that provoked it resulted in disorder, a condition Roosevelt feared and detested. So he sought power to keep order by using government to build the influence of labor and agriculture, and thus to balance the excessive influence of big business.

That was his kind of reform, and its design fit the symmetrical contours of his foreign policy, which was aimed at permitting the great powers to keep order in their separate spheres. The United States, in its own national interest, would use its influence to preserve a balance of power compatible with preventing any great nation from dominating the western Pacific or the eastern Atlantic. Accordingly, Roosevelt was apprehensive about German and Japanese visions of glory. He came by his objectives not on impulse or instinct, but after long study of the issues to which he turned. On the whole, the results were commendable.

Historical studies both reflect external forces and exert an influence of their own. So, for example, as I wrote about Roosevelt I found useful the ideas in John Kenneth Galbraith's *American Capitalism* (1952), and my *Republican Roosevelt* in its turn caught the attention of at least two public men. John V. Lindsay, for two terms mayor of New York City, a progressive Republican early in his career, sought the Democratic presidential nomination in 1968. He considered me a likely speechwriter for his campaign, but he withdrew from the race before I had had a chance to consider it. In 1994 President Clinton told the press that he had been reading my account of TR and was embracing Roosevelt's incremental approach to reform. (He should have also read the writings of Charles E. Lindblom, who found the incrementalists' besetting sin to be their failure periodically to reexamine the premises on which they had based their position.) Pleasing though it was to receive recognition from public figures, I much preferred being acknowledged in historical literature about progressivism, the presidency, and of course Roosevelt himself.

Around 1953 Roosevelt had entered my family's lives as well as my own. In many of his early letters, especially those to his children, he referred to stories he had read as a child in *Our Young Folks,* a monthly magazine published from 1865 through 1873 by Ticknor and Fields, later Houghton, Mifflin and Company. *Our Young Folks* regularly included line drawings, the style of which TR copied in illustrating his letters to his children. Before it was absorbed by a rival magazine, *Our Young Folks* reached a national audience of children whose families shared the Victorian values it promoted. It contributed to the acculturation of the American Edwardians who came to positions of authority in the first decade of the twentieth century. So it had some historical significance, and curiosity moved me to borrow the full run of the magazine from the Harvard library. Once I had begun to examine it, I found the verse, essays, and fiction appropriate for reading aloud to my own children and their friends. Consequently Henry Wadsworth Longfellow, Louisa May Alcott, Harriet Beecher Stowe, Edward Lear, and their contemporaries entered my children's lives.

Indeed their enthusiasm for *Our Young Folks* in 1956 persuaded me to suggest to Paul Brooks at Houghton, Mifflin the possibility of publishing an anthology of material from the magazine with an introduction I had begun to contemplate. He asked for a sample, liked it, and we signed a contract for the book. The resulting collection, *Yesterday's Children,* with appropriately decorated endpapers and illustrations, was published in 1959 and failed to find a niche in the market. Houghton promoted it as a book for children, but children at that time were loath to read Victorian literature. I saw it as a book for grandparents to read to their grandchildren, but the few reviews failed to suggest such a possibility. Historians ignored the book. But Mary Ellen Chase, a popular professor of English at Smith College who was old enough to be a grandmother, praised the contents of the anthology in her review in the Sunday *New York Times*. Both Paul Brooks and I took some satisfaction from her assessment. Both of us had been fond of the project and welcomed the volume when it came freshly from the press. Not all happy ideas in publishing achieve commercial success.

Meanwhile I had begun to write the short volume on Woodrow Wilson that I had agreed to contribute to Oscar Handlin's Library of American Biography series. Mrs. Wilson still refused to open either her husband's or her own papers for research, and Charles Seymour had yet to open the papers of Colonel E. M. House. Wilson's widow objected to any scholarly examination of the role she assumed after her husband's stroke in 1919, a role that Arthur S. Link, the eventual editor of Wilson's papers, sharply criticized. So did Phyllis Lee Levin years later, in *Edith and Woodrow* (2001). I had done the same in my biography of Joe Tumulty, as had Thomas A. Bailey in his acclaimed studies of the making and the American rejection of the Treaty of Versailles. Seymour objected to me because I had written about Tumulty, whom he considered beneath scholarly dignity. Further, he knew that once the House manuscripts were open, scholars would discover how shamelessly he had bowdlerized House's "intimate papers" in his four-volume edition of them. I had to rely cautiously on that edition and on Seymour's research notes, which I had already examined. I had also earlier used the papers of several of Wilson's cabinet officers in the Library of Congress, and I was familiar with the newspapers and periodicals of his time, as well as the historical literature about Wilson. In short, my research for the Tumulty book and the Roosevelt letters had prepared me for the Wilson book.

Biographers, it seems to me, profit from either an admiration or an antipathy to their subject. I had begun the Tumulty book admiring Wilson, but what I learned of his snobbish treatment of Tumulty bothered me. Further, I had developed considerable admiration for Theodore Roosevelt, who after 1912 was Wilson's rival. Consequently I came to the Wilson biography with considerable antipathy to my subject, and that attitude surely affected my work. I particularly disliked Wilson's conviction that he was a special agent of the Lord. But my views rested also on a rethinking of the Wilson legend.

I concluded that he functioned best when he took charge of a situation that others had worked to prepare. At Princeton, for example, he succeeded in his efforts to recruit young faculty — "preceptors" — to work closely with undergraduates; Princeton had needed such men for some years. But Wilson failed in his attempted innovations — his attacks on social clubs and his opposition to housing graduate students away from the main campus. The social clubs enjoyed alumni support; the graduate dean raised the money he needed for his housing plans. So it was also with the reforms that Wilson promoted as president in 1913–14. The seeds of those reforms lay in initiatives of the preceding Congress or of Wilson's predecessor, Theodore Roosevelt. Later Wilson's newer ideas frequently faltered, most famously in the Senate's rejection of the League of Nations.

Central to any evaluation of Wilson was his decision in 1917 to ask Congress to declare war on Germany and its allies. That decision flowed from his legalistic and moralistic approach to submarine warfare. I believed that it also reflected his tendency, logical in terms of power politics, to clothe a policy with sanctimonious, though eloquent, rhetoric. I based that interpretation of Wilson on the celebrated interview he had with journalist Frank Cobb. According to Cobb's memoir, the two men had agreed about the illiberal mood that would poison American society if the country went to war, though they could see no alternative. There were some doubts about the validity of Cobb's account, but I took him at his word, as Arthur Link did later, when his editing of the Wilson papers brought him to April 1917. As I saw it, Wilson, aware of the costs of war, nevertheless asked Congress to declare war, as his message put it, for noble ends — to protect the rights of small nations, to make the world safe for democracy, as an end to all wars. The federal propaganda machine repeated that message, and many, if not most, Americans came to believe it. Indeed Wilson unfortunately came to believe it himself. But the war and the negotiations following it did not deliver a New Jerusalem. No war could have done so. Americans had been led to expect too much. There followed the postwar disenchantment that imbued American culture at least until my college years.

Woodrow Wilson and the Politics of Morality, published by Little, Brown in 1956, has become out of date, though as of 2003 it was still in print. The publication of Arthur Link's comprehensive edition of the Wilson papers provided significant data of which I was unaware at the time I wrote the book. But my Wilson manuscript profited from the generous readings and suggestions of both Link and his Northwestern University colleague, Dick Leopold, a good friend but also a strict critic. Like *The Republican Roosevelt,* the Wilson biography attracted little notice at the time of its publication, but it, too, became a staple for undergraduate courses on the United States in the twentieth century, and it found a place in the literature about the U.S. presidency. Indeed critics of Jimmy Carter found the moralism I disliked in Wilson a precursor of Carter's approach to foreign policy. The arrogance inherent in Wilson's certitude about his version of democracy, and the arrogance of his moralism generally, accounted for his bellicose belief that he could teach the Mexicans "to elect good men." That was the case, too, with his demand that the Germans rid their nation of the Kaiser before suing for peace. Those qualities, and the demonizing of foreign leaders that accompanied them, reappeared years later in the rhetoric and, I suspect, the convictions, of both President George H. W. Bush and his son, George W.

During the 1950s I realized that I could not consider myself a true student of twentieth-century American history without researching and writing about the New Deal and World War II. Arthur Schlesinger, Jr., was just beginning to address those subjects in the first volumes of his influential *Age of Franklin D. Roosevelt*. As I read his work, I discovered that very little had been written about the Treasury Department, though its role in monetary and fiscal policy had great significance during a time of depression and war. I decided to ask Arthur whether he thought the Treasury was a suitable subject for me to explore.

Always considerate, Arthur gave me both good news and bad news. The bad news was that there were essentially no Treasury archives for the years 1933–45. Henry Morgenthau, Jr., the Treasury secretary from late 1933 to the early months of Harry S. Truman's presidency, had gathered the material that passed through his office into a collection he called the Morgenthau diaries. With Truman's permission, Morgenthau had removed that enormous collection from the department and deposited it in the Franklin D. Roosevelt Library in Hyde Park, New York. He then kept the collection closed except to scholars he trusted. In 1955 only Arthur Schlesinger, Jr., enjoyed that trust. The good news was that Morgenthau had been looking for a biographer to whom he would give full access to the diaries and related materials. Indeed Arthur had a mandate to locate a biographer of whom he approved, and he was eager to nominate me.

Arthur introduced us one morning in Morgenthau's Manhattan apartment on upper Fifth Avenue. In the several hours we were there I learned that the "diaries" included transcribed tapes of conversations in the secretary's office and of his telephone calls. Those and other documents in the collection contained material that had been classified since their date of origin. Though they remained classified, this was the case only because Congress had appropriated no funds to permit the National Archives to declassify them. I learned also that full access to the diaries would in one way be forbidding. The documents Morgenthau had collected were bound in over 800 large volumes. There were approximately 160,000 documents on more than a million typed pages. Further, I knew that an account of the Treasury under Morgenthau would also have to take into consideration the papers of Franklin D. Roosevelt and those at least of Harry Hopkins and Henry Stimson, powerful men whose relationships with Morgenthau were sometimes difficult. The research would be formidable.

Were I to undertake the task I would also have to find a way to get along with Morgenthau. As I soon discovered, others had begun a biography but soon faltered under the burden of his insecure, gloomy, and sometimes abrasive temperament. He was a naturally suspicious man who needed continual reassurance, who suspected all newcomers of wanting his money, who guarded his career against negative criticism. (Underneath those difficult qualities he was both friendly and rather sweet, but it took me several years to win his trust, which I knew I had done when he asked me to call him Henry.) His vision failing, he expected me to read my manuscript aloud to him so that he could comment on what I had written. In short, after our first meeting I had major reservations about working with Morgenthau. I doubted that we could get along, especially since he had told me that he had no intention of subjecting himself to criticism by a historian of the age of his children.

During the week after our first meeting, I realized that I could disagree with the policies Morgenthau had promoted by quoting those who had opposed him — for example, Marriner Eccles on fiscal policy and Henry Stimson on postwar Germany. As I had hoped, he had no objection to anything "in the records." That attitude gave me some leeway. Still, the thought of having to operate under Morgenthau's constraints troubled me. But Arthur Schlesinger agreed to act as referee in the event that Morgenthau and I could not resolve a disagreement about what to include in the text — and as it turned out, that situation never arose. I also consulted McGeorge Bundy, who had collaborated with Henry Stimson on Stimson's autobiography. "Don't worry, John," Mac said. "It's a great opportunity. Just keep in mind that yours will be the first word on Morgenthau, not the last." It was Mac's statement that persuaded me to sign on.

The wealth of materials in the diaries kept me going. The execution of U.S. monetary policy involved Morgenthau in relations with England, France, Mexico, China, and Japan. The Treasury's role in preparing revenue legislation gave him the opportunity to devise a more redistributive influence for federal taxation than either the president or Congress would approve. As FDR's trusted friend, Morgenthau in 1940 found ways substantially to assist beleaguered England. During World War II his department played a large role in postwar economic planning, though Roosevelt declined to support Morgenthau's plan for federal medical insurance as part of postwar Social Security. In short, the research and writing of the three volumes of *From the Morgenthau Diaries* provided precisely the introduction I was seeking to the years they covered.

One of the reasons that convinced me to agree to a contract with Morgenthau was that it gave me the means to buy out of at least a third of my obligations to MIT, thus allowing me to substitute scholarship for other duties. (Later, Yale expected me to teach full time and to use my leisure to write about Morgenthau.) The contract rested on an advance on royalties from the publisher, Houghton, Mifflin. The advance went to Morgenthau, who sent me a stipend each month. When the advance ran out, Morgenthau continued the monthly payments, deducting the cost on his income tax as a business expense. On that basis we eventually worked through the three volumes, the last published in 1967, ten years after I had left MIT. By that time Henry and I had become friends and I had discovered the gentle side of his nature. But the first few years were tough, especially during my long and frequent visits with him. He also would telephone me early in the morning, just as he had once called his Treasury subordinates. "John," he would begin, "I'm terribly upset. I can't understand why the president did" this or that— denied the U-2 mission, or authorized the Bay of Pigs invasion, or approved an unbalanced budget. He was upset so often that Pamela and I referred to him behind his back as Eeyore, the lugubrious donkey in *Winnie the Pooh*.

When I read him the first chapter I had written, he became seriously upset. The chapter described his growing up, his troubles as a student, and his relationship with his father, "Uncle Henry" Morgenthau, a demanding man who had made a fortune before serving as Wilson's ambassador to Turkey. I had interviewed Morgenthau's sisters to obtain the data on which I based my account. Morgenthau scolded me for talking with them. I had no business prying into his private life, he said. The biography was to treat only his public life, and I was to revise my chapter accordingly. On reflection I did just that. The biography lost a useful introduction to the childhood of its subject, but quotations from the diaries revealed Morgenthau's lifelong dyslexia as well as his uneasiness. He could not wholly exclude me from his private life, because I met his talented and public-spirited children. Henry III, a civil and thoughtful man, later wrote an insightful book about the Morgenthau family. Joan, whom I knew the least, later became a successful physician. Robert, whom I knew best, for many terms seemed to own the public office of district attorney of Manhattan. He enjoyed fighting crime, especially white-collar crime, as much as his father had.

In 1956 Bob Morgenthau and I risked the wrath of the Senate Judiciary Committee. The episode made us friends and won his father's confidence in me, but it also briefly and unjustly made me a security risk, at least in the view of the National Archives. I realized that working with Morgenthau would involve me in research on some of the Soviet agents who had served in the Treasury Department's monetary affairs division under its chief, Harry Dexter White. At a time when congressional committees were still searching for alleged communists who had held government office during the New Deal and World War II, it was perilous to invite association with Harry Dexter White, for the logic of the communist hunters was skewed: White had been a communist, they argued; White had worked for Morgenthau; I was working with and writing about Morgenthau; therefore, I was a communist or a communist sympathizer. At first I could not believe that anyone would suspect me of a communist affiliation. I had opposed communism all my life, opposed even theoretical Marxism. But as it worked out, I was vulnerable.

Harry Dexter White was never a member of the Communist Party, but on occasion he had passed classified information to agents of the Soviet Union. He did not do errands for those agents or their masters. But he operated as a spy when he thought his treachery served what he considered a worthy cause. As the habitués of Washington put it, he operated "outside of channels." White was also a difficult, indeed nasty, man. In the 1950s many Americans considered any communist a son of a bitch. They then tended to reason that any son of a bitch was a communist. By that definition, White qualified. But Morgenthau had known nothing about either the communist cell within his command or about White's subversive activities. Had he known, he would have been aghast, but he was an innocent whom his subordinates easily exploited. He remained incredulous about the charges against White, whom he had trusted, even after those charges were confirmed by the celebrated Pumpkin Papers, classified documents that had been hidden in a pumpkin by Whittaker Chambers, a *Time* magazine journalist who had served as a Soviet agent before turning informer for the FBI. Suspicions about White lingered for years after Chambers famously and correctly accused Alger Hiss, an eminent New Dealer, of spying. White then became an object of the inquiries about alleged communists in government undertaken by the Senate Judiciary Committee under the chairmanship of

James O. Eastland, a Mississippi Democrat. That committee in 1956 issued a subpoena for the Morgenthau diaries, in which Eastland's staff expected to find evidence of White's perfidy and of the espionage ascribed to some of his staff.

The Morgenthau diaries were available in three forms. The original documents were on deposit at the Franklin D. Roosevelt Library. A positive print of a microfilm copy was also deposited there, with the negative in Morgenthau's possession at his apple farm in Hopewell Junction, New York. All three copies were subject to the subpoena. I had the reels of positive microfilm for the years 1933–38, on loan from the Roosevelt Library, in a safe in my office. Robert Morgenthau, advising his father, knew that that library, a branch of the National Archives, would surrender the diaries to the Senate committee. His concern was to protect both his father and me from the negative publicity that might result if a United States marshal were to confront us with a subpoena.

He and I agreed that the best way to avoid publicity was immediately to return the film to the Roosevelt Library. Bob telephoned one afternoon to tell me that he had learned that a marshal had a subpoena for me. I rented a car the next morning, filled it with all the microfilm I had on loan, and drove to Hyde Park. But Herman Kahn, the director of the FDR Library and a personal friend, would not accept the film. "I won't take it, John," he said. "You deal with the problem." I refused. "It's your problem," I said. "I don't own the film. You lent it to me. If it were a book, I'd slip it through your night slot." Herman walked away. I drove my car to the outdoor loading dock of the library, put all the film on the loading dock, and then drove away. Herman, whom I informed by phone, moved the film into the building. Both of us knew the Senate would soon have the diaries, whether the originals or the microfilm.

At the drugstore in Hyde Park I telephoned Bob Morgenthau at his office in New York. He told me his phone was tapped. "Just to report," I said, "that the white cat is back in the kennel, but I'm unsure of the location of the black cat." That rather obvious code provoked Bob, after a moment's hesitation, to ask me to meet him at his father's Hopewell Junction barn, which he called "the cider mill." If any federal agent heard our conversation, I am sure he knew exactly what we meant. But I met Bob as planned, no one approached us, and while I soon started for home, Bob spent the night stamping and addressing some 800 boxes of the negative film of the diaries, and mailing them near dawn to the National Archives in Washington, D.C.

As the staff of the Senate Judiciary Committee went about reading a large portion of the diaries, a task that consumed several years, they found nothing shocking or scandalous. They did select hundreds of pages for publication in the hearings of the committee, pages mostly about American relations with China before and during World War II. It came as no surprise that Harry White in particular, but also his staff and Secretary Morgenthau, too, had disliked and distrusted the corrupt and ineffective Nationalist government. So during the war years had most Americans in Chungking. But the right wing of the Republican Party for propaganda purposes had made heroes of the Nationalists and blamed the veteran American China hands in the State Department for selling them out. Indeed the Eisenhower administration drove those richly informed specialists on Asia out of office, a purge that cost the government essential counsel when the question of American aid to South Vietnam arose. The purge of the China specialists was based on pure myth. The Nationalists fell because they were unpopular with the Chinese people, because the Chinese communists had more capable and less selfish leadership, and because Soviet military aid strengthened Mao's armies. But among deep conservatives, the myths about an alleged Democratic "twenty years of treason" and about the "fall" of China persisted through the rest of the twentieth century.

After a short interval following my return of the microfilm, I applied to use the diaries again. Secretary Morgenthau had expected me to have trouble gaining access, and he was correct. Against that contingency, he had hired Hugh Cox, an outstanding attorney, a former New Dealer, and a partner in the distinguished Covington, Burling law firm in Washington. Cox informed me that the National Archives had declared me a security risk. But not to worry, he said. Senator Eastland's nephew, a senior officer at the National Archives, had so classified me, but no one with any sense paid attention to him. In time, Cox assured me, he would have the classification removed. He asked the U.S. District Court in the District of Columbia for a subpoena to force the Archives to show cause why I was a security risk. At once the National Archives withdrew the classification. But Cox then told me that the diaries remained beyond my reach, for President Eisenhower, for many years a political collaborator of Senator Eastland, had made access to the Morgenthau diaries a matter of executive privilege. There was no chance that the President was going to grant the privilege of access to me.

The situation had become at once ridiculous and outrageous. It was ridiculous because I had a Q clearance — a clearance for the most secret materials — from the Atomic Energy Commission to allow me to read and comment on Richard Hewlett and Oscar E. Anderson's history of the Manhattan Project, the agency that oversaw the making of the atomic bomb.

James Phinney Baxter had made me one of the historians who acted as editorial advisers to Hewlett and Anderson, who later published their work as *The New World* (1962). It was outrageous because the President was still cozy with noxious witch hunters like Senator Eastland, who perpetuated McCarthyism for years after Eisenhower was later said to have destroyed McCarthy by working behind the scenes. Perhaps Republican politics required cooperation with Eastland, but I could never "like Ike."

Ultimately there was a political remedy. In 1960, during the Democratic Convention in Los Angeles, I permitted Ted Sorenson, chief of staff of Senator John F. Kennedy, to alter the text of a letter I had written Kennedy praising a collection of his speeches. The published text omitted a paragraph critical of some of his voting record. The Kennedy team was trying to recruit academic supporters of Adlai Stevenson, of whom I was one. I doubt that my bowdlerized letter assisted that cause, but it did leave Kennedy, as he later indicated, indebted to me. In April 1961 Arthur Schlesinger, Jr., called me from the White House to ask me whether the President could do me a favor. Yes, I replied; he could open the Morgenthau diaries to general use. By executive order, Kennedy did.

Still, from 1956 until 1961 I had had no access to my basic sources. Fortunately for me, I had completed my research on Morgenthau through the period ending in the autumn of 1938. That period included most of the New Deal, not least the recession of 1937–38, and the Treasury's role in foreign policy through the American response to the Munich Agreement. Since President Roosevelt's attention after that agreement moved increasingly toward foreign affairs, and since Morgenthau more and more acted as his special agent in those matters, the period made sound historical sense. I had ample material for a first volume on Morgenthau, a prospect my subject applauded. Indeed that volume, *From the Morgenthau Diaries: Years of Crisis* (1959) was in the end over 600 pages. I had about a third of the volume in draft when I left MIT for Yale.

Since research on the Morgenthau diaries was so time-consuming, it behooved me to devise ways to ease my task. I took notes as I read the material by dictating them for transcription by a typist, with several typists succeeding each other over the years. As I read I categorized the notes by topic — for example, "Taxation" or "Silver Policy: China" — with dates and references by volume and page of the diaries. When I began to write, I also dictated my rough, first draft, which, as we had agreed, I would read aloud to Secretary Morgenthau. Apart from objecting to any discussion of his childhood, Morgenthau asked me to delete nothing significant that I wrote. Also as we had agreed, when I felt the need to express disagreement with his policies, I did so only by quoting from the memoirs or manuscripts of his critical colleagues. Among them were Cordell Hull, Secretary of State, always protective of his turf, on which Morgenthau, at Roosevelt's urging, continually encroached; Marriner Eccles, head of the Federal Reserve system, who frequently took issue with the Treasury Department about both monetary and fiscal policies; and, after 1940, when he was appointed Secretary of War, Henry L. Stimson. I selected quotations opposing Treasury policies from the records those men had left, and Morgenthau never so much as asked about any one of them.

As I proceeded, I became indebted to several economists at MIT who instructed me over many luncheons about issues in which they were expert. They also recommended indispensable scholarly studies I might never have found myself. Of course none of them could prevent me from erring on my own. The first Morgenthau volume, like its two successors, was essentially my doing and my responsibility.

On publication the first volume received much attention but mixed reviews. Morgenthau had kept the diaries closed for so long that some reviewers expected to learn important state secrets from the new book. After all, before the book came out he was quoted as saying, "Let the chips fall where they may." But there were few if any chips, so those reviewers felt disappointed. Eleanor Roosevelt, who had written a blurb for the dust jacket, was correct when she called the volume a "resource book." That it was, for it provided not only a narrative but also in effect an annotated and organized guide to an enormous archival collection. She also wrote that the book told the story of the long and important friendship between the Roosevelts and the Morgenthaus. Oddly most reviewers missed her point. What had accounted for Morgenthau's importance had been that friendship. He and FDR had met not because they were really neighbors — their homes were some twenty miles apart — but because they were Dutchess County Democrats, a rare breed in their day, and they had a common interest in agriculture. After their wives became friends, their own friendship followed. As time went on "Henry the Morgue," as FDR called him, became more and more useful to Roosevelt in New York politics. Roosevelt could count on Morgenthau's unfailing personal loyalty, a quality rarer in politics than journalists normally admit. And in New York Morgenthau had made an excellent record during Roosevelt's terms as governor. I had assumed that reviewers in the popular press would focus on Roosevelt and Morgenthau's service to him. But that approach would have demanded analysis of some relatively complex policies. What resulted in the popular press was many rather trivial but friendly reviews.

The scholarly reviews were also by and large favorable, but bland. Frank Freidel, a major FDR biographer, wrote an eminently fair notice for the *New York Times*. The book, he said, "differs from what Blum might have written entirely independently in that it seems to present Morgenthau's hindsights . . . rather than the writer's. . . . If the result is something less than biography it is also more than autobiography, since the detailed quotations create for the reader vivid images of Secretary Morgenthau, his contemporaries and their policies." Most scholars in 1958 were more interested in Morgenthau's career after 1938 than in the earlier years. Over time, however, *Years of Crisis* came to be referenced in the literature concerning many of the issues that had occupied Morgenthau. No reviewer remarked about the juvenile sense of humor that Morgenthau shared with Roosevelt. None noted that "Henry the Morgue" had little formal education and knew little about economics but functioned nevertheless as a significant figure in a difficult time. He did so during his long tenure because he chose talented subordinates, most importantly Herman Oliphant and Randolph Paul, two of his influential general counselors. He listened to them. And his own instincts were excellent, his honesty and loyalty both steady. Indeed he was a true democrat, courageous in combating injustice, much like Eleanor Roosevelt, who called Morgenthau "Franklin's conscience." Though of course he made some mistakes, Morgenthau demonstrated that even without impressive intelligence, a man of character in high office could and did succeed.

Historians in later years took exception to my handling of two issues in particular in that first volume. I had been taught to measure both the cyclical and redistributive impacts of increased taxation on the basis of what would have been its effect at full employment. Those who found New Deal taxation less redistributive than I did had not made that calculation. They had also slighted the role of both the president and Congress in reducing the tax schedules the treasury had proposed. My most astute critic on the subject of international monetary policy was my former colleague and informal tutor on that subject, Charles Kindelberger, who was then an economist at MIT. He pointed out that Morgenthau and his advisers in 1936 had misinterpreted a Russian monetary initiative, technical in purpose, as political and designed to embarrass the United States, France, and Great Britain. I had reported Morgenthau's view, but had not corrected it. That's what happens, Kindelberger wrote, when financial matters are addressed by a political historian. Technically he was correct; but he failed to recognize that in 1936 international monetary developments were fraught with political implications. Whatever the Russians had intended, the democratic powers saw hostility in their action.

The first volume of the Morgenthau diaries was of great importance to me. The research and writing that went into it allowed me to learn about the Great Depression and the New Deal with the same degree of intimacy I had attained with the progressive period. It was the same with the subsequent volumes, which covered successively the period 1938–41 and the period 1941–45. I could feel entirely comfortable in teaching history only after I had thoroughly learned about my subject by exploring relevant archives and manuscript sources and by reading the available studies based upon them. Only with that kind of background, I felt, could I understand the men and women about whom I was lecturing; could I learn and recall the rich and telling anecdotes that had circulated in the times I was trying to make my own; could I experience Freeman's "fog of history." I would need that grounding when lecturing three times a week at Yale. All of my professional engagements of the 1950s would return large dividends in classrooms to come. The joy and learning I experienced from research convinced me to continue to write books about the subjects I was to teach. Because teaching and scholarship fed each other, a university professor had equal and enduring obligations to both.

9

At Home at Yale

My introduction to Yale began in late April 1957 when I traveled to New Haven to work out with George Wilson Pierson, the chairman of the history department, the details of his offer of a tenured professorship. As I was to discover, George was something of a character. David Owen had described him to me as Yale's Samuel Eliot Morison. Like Sam, George was patrician, initially aloof, physically impressive, expensively dressed, professionally respected, and officially the historian of the university. He had written an important book on Alexis de Tocqueville (still the best on its subject of which I know), an important critique of Frederick Jackson Turner and the frontier thesis in American history, and a history of Yale. As a historian, especially a historian of higher education, he did not reach Sam's heights, but neither did anyone else. George's overriding patriotic purpose was to prove that whatever it was, Yale did it better than Harvard. His immediate purpose was to make the Yale history department the best in the world.

Earlier in 1957, with the concurrence of his tenured colleagues, he had offered professorships to two titans, each a star in his respective field. But Richard Hofstadter of Columbia, a historian of the United States, and Robert R. Palmer of Princeton, a historian of France, chose to remain where they were. But I, only thirty-six at the time, by no means a Hofstadter or a Palmer, and a Jew withal, committed to Yale by virtue of a phone call after I had received Pierson's invitation, I must have seemed pretty small potatoes when I arrived at Pierson's office. There he sat, patrician arms folded across patrician chest, patrician nose in the air, welcoming me with a question: "What business have you at your age looking at a Yale professorship?" Stunned, I replied rather slowly, "Why, Mr. Pierson, you offered me one."

The oral exam continued. Pierson: "Why would a Harvard historian want to come to Yale?" (Pierson always identified me as a Harvard historian. MIT had no standing in his pantheon of academic institutions.)

Blum: "Yours is an outstanding department."

Pierson: "Who, for example?"

Blum: "I've benefited from your work on Tocqueville . . ."

Pierson, interrupting: "Present company excepted."

Blum, trying to continue ". . . and from the works of Samuel Flagg Bemis, David Potter, who is a friend, Edmund Morgan, also a friend . . ."

Just then the door opened and Ed Morgan rushed in with a welcoming greeting. We three went to lunch, at Mory's of course, where the tables themselves, oaken Old Blues, could sing the Wiffenpoof song. After lunch the tenured professors of American history met together to discuss what I would be expected to teach. Sam Bemis, who had clearly forgotten that in 1949 he had called me a communist in public, asked what courses I was offering at MIT. "One on American political economy and one on the American political process," I replied.

"You could call that political history," he said, "but you wouldn't teach foreign policy?" Ed Morgan inconspicuously turned thumbs down. "Oh, no," I said, "I wouldn't teach foreign policy." Later Ed told me that Bemis allowed no one except himself to teach foreign policy. The meeting ended with agreement that I would lecture on twentieth-century American political history to undergraduates, offer a graduate seminar on the same subject, and join several others in a graduate course on historiography that was required of students in the field of American history.

George Pierson and I returned to his office with just about everything settled except for my salary. He raised the subject right away with an offer of less than I was earning. I balked. He eventually met my MIT salary, on which we settled. (Pamela later said I needed an agent, but over the years Yale proved to be generous.) George next took me to visit successively the provost, the dean of the college, and President A. Whitney Griswold, whom I had first met several years earlier with Kingman Brewster on the beach at Martha's Vineyard. We went on to a tea, where I was introduced to a dozen tenured professors, most of them, so it seemed, in English history. (Six of them actually were!) Before Ed Morgan drove me to his home for dinner, George, who had become increasingly cordial, asked me whom I knew who was really Yale. He had to win approval of my appointment from the assembled full professors of Yale College, he said, and they would want recommendations from bona fide college alumni. An odd request, I thought, but I asked whether Kingman Brewster and McGeorge Bundy would do. "Very nicely," George replied. (I later phoned both those agreeable referees to warn them about my use of their names. Mac thought George's request bush league; Kingman thought it hilarious, as did I.)

That evening, after dinner at the Morgans', David Potter arrived for dessert. "Don't mind George," David said as we reviewed my day. "No one takes him seriously. Join us anyway." I assured him I would. Ed and David, as I expected, proved to be splendid colleagues and valued friends — and ultimately, to my surprise, so did George.

But Charles Seymour, the former president of Yale, never overcame his hostility to me. My Tumulty biography had annoyed him because it exposed both the anti-Catholicism and the devious ways of Colonel House, his hero. A few weeks after I arrived at Yale Seymour invited me to lunch at Mory's. After we had ordered drinks, he said, "Before we break bread I want you to know that I did everything possible to prevent your being here." After hesitating, I replied, "I'm so glad you failed." Our relationship went downhill from there. In 1958 the *Yale Review* asked me on short notice to write a review of Herbert Hoover's recently published book and Arthur Walworth's two-volume biography of Woodrow Wilson. Of Hoover's study I wrote, "This is the prose that launched a thousand Democrats." Of Walworth, whose pietistic work later won the Pulitzer Prize, I observed that he had avoided the smell of the lamp but unfortunately put out the light. Furious with me, Seymour, both a friend of Hoover and a sponsor of Walworth, circulated a letter among wealthy alumni urging them to join him in a campaign to rid the history department of the young radical it had hired. Reuben Holden, the cheerful, responsible secretary of the university, advised me to ignore the fuss. Whit Griswold, to whom the complaints about me were addressed, never mentioned them. But George Pierson, who knew Seymour well, summoned me to his office. "What do you mean," he said, "writing a review like that about Herbert Hoover, a former president of the United States?" I asked whether he had read the book. He had not. "When you have read it," I said, "we'll discuss the review." That ended the episode, partly because at just that time William Sloane Coffin, Jr., came to Yale and at once he took my place as the resident dangerous young radical. In any case, I had come to feel too secure at Yale to take Seymour seriously.

Our move to New Haven brought us closer to my brother, who had changed his name to William Darrid and then lived in Westport, only a forty-minute drive away. In December 1956 Bill had married Diana Douglas. I served as best man while Pamela contained the exuberant Douglas boys, Michael and Joel, the sons of Diana's marriage, long since ended, to Kirk Douglas. Like my marriage to Pamela, Bill's marriage to Diana was the best thing that ever happened to him. She was the youngest child of the large Dill family, residents of Bermuda since the sixteenth century. She brought to his life everything he needed for his career on stage and screen — the high style at once of a handsome, successful actress, the support of a loving wife, the literary flair and theatrical smarts of a quiet collaborator. Westport was close enough to New Haven for frequent visits back and forth. Bill and Diana's proximity to us made New Haven begin to feel like home.

So did the unstinting hospitality of friends of former years who now, with their wives, welcomed us to Yale. From my Andover days were Elias Clark, a professor of law, and Delaney Kiphuth, the university's athletic director and a lecturer in American history. Eli Clark and Annie, his attractive and athletic wife, found time to host a dinner at which they introduced Pamela and me to some of the younger members of the law school faculty, of whom several soon became friends, especially Louis and Kathy Pollak. I had known Lou casually as a member of the Signet Society at Harvard. A dedicated champion of civil liberties and civil rights, in 1957 he was working closely with Thurgood Marshall on desegregation cases before the Supreme Court.

It took me less than a semester to feel comfortable in the history department. My colleagues in American history eased the way. The person who did the most to help me feel at home was Edmund S. Morgan. Ed lectured at MIT while I was there, and I lectured at Brown while he was there teaching American colonial history. In addition, he and his wife and collaborator, Helen, would see me at various historical conventions. Over drinks we had become friends, and our friendship spurred me to read Ed's splendid biography of John Winthrop, his equally arresting study of the American revolution, and later his landmark work on slavery in colonial Virginia. His scholarship had extraordinary range.

Without Ed's encouragement, advice, irreverence, and easy humor, I could not have adjusted to Yale ways as readily as I did. Ed had arrived at Yale only two years before I did; almost every unexpected obstacle I met he had already hurdled. And without the shop talk that accompanied our many meals together I would have been a much lesser historian. It was Ed's habit to refer to himself as a good craftsman. He was much more than that. His work, marked by an eloquent simplicity in style and an informed and profound intelligence in content, had an excellence that few historians equaled and none surpassed. The same could be said for Ed's gift for friendship.

David M. Potter left Yale for Stanford less than five years after I arrived

(Vann Woodward succeeded him), but we became friends in those years and remained friends for as long as he lived. With the possible exception of Elting Morison, David had the most creative imagination of any historian I ever knew. Most of his scholarship focused on the onset of the Civil War, but he took on the entire American past in his brilliant book *People of Plenty*. David helped me most significantly in two ways. He had enriched the American Studies program by adding courses in the social sciences, economics especially, to the doctoral electives. A focus on the social sciences suited me better than did the traditional combination of history and literature, and David and I worked as a contented team with graduate students we taught in common. I had no experience in teaching doctoral candidates until I came to Yale, and I was apprehensive about that obligation. But David put me at ease. I asked him how he had achieved such success in directing dissertations. Succinct as ever, and modest, too, he replied, "I just wait." He meant that Yale attracted such talented graduate students that in time many of them would do stunning work no matter with whose guidance they wrote their dissertations. He was correct. The best dissertations I supervised needed little, if any, direction; their authors were naturally gifted.

To my surprise, the most effective introduction to Yale for a newcomer to the history department came from George W. Pierson himself, assisted by his extraordinary, earthy, artistic, and adoring wife, Letitia. Formidable with strangers, George showed his other side as soon as those strangers became colleagues. That other side, his fun side, enjoyed Letty's deliberate naughtiness, loved ballroom dancing and golf, and served the best Scotch whiskey and the best French wines available in the area. Letty and Pamela became fast friends almost at once, while George arranged for me, as he once put it, "to suffer for Yale." He was doing the same for Ed Morgan. Only by suffering for Yale, as he explained at a faculty meeting, could a new faculty member learn to love Yale and never wish to leave. So we suffered in the committees George arranged for us to join, with compensation provided in the charm, good fellowship, and good taste of the Piersons' hospitality. George exemplified the qualities so often listed as necessary for tenure: substantial and excellent scholarship, dedicated and successful teaching, and unselfish and intelligent citizenship. He was so caught up in the importance of citizenship that his other talents sometimes languished, but he could succeed in all the pursuits for which he had time.

The other American historians in the department I knew less well until some years later. Howard Lamar in 1957 was an assistant professor, about to receive tenure; only several years later did we become friends. The other assistant professors found my arrival threatening, for I filled the only tenure appointment on the horizon for American historians. One of them never forgave me for coming to Yale. Another had the good sense to accept a tenured appointment elsewhere. A third persevered and was eventually given tenure when Bemis retired, though after receiving it he departed for a college presidency almost at once.

I was to benefit from the collegiality of my peers in fields other than American history in later years, but in that first year, apart from the senior American historians, it was the president of Yale who made us feel most welcome. A. Whitney Griswold, a historian himself, brought to his office sensitivity as well as devotion to the university. In 1957 he was a healthy, vibrant, entertaining, and stylish man in his fifties who seemed much younger, though just six years later he died of cancer. Walking to the hall where I lectured, I passed him three times a week on his way to his office. He knew who I was and he knew I was a friend of his friend, Kingman Brewster, but he was uncertain about how to address me. As we worked it out, the greeting became, "Good morning perfesser," in the manner of Casey Stengel, and my reply was, "Good morning, Mr. President." But Whit soon consulted me privately, and thereafter I was "John," and was invited now and then to join the company he assembled for trips to visit groups of alumni and to discuss "Yale Today."

Yale was then small enough to permit the Griswolds annually to invite all the new professors and their wives, several couples at a time, to a formal dinner. It was understood that whenever the invitation arrived, the recipient would accept it no matter what previous commitment had to be canceled. With a conventional host, the affair might have been stuffy, but Whit made it joyous. He introduced his guests to each other with some apt comment, he joked about Yale, he made everyone feel comfortable. He had come to dislike the Christmas season, he told us, because the newspapers so often included "Yule" in a headline and he at first glance thought Yale was about to receive adverse publicity. At the dinner table his immediate neighbors found him a delight. Pamela enjoyed that proximity, seated as she was at Whit's right with Louis Kahn, the eminent architect, on his left. Whit told the story of how he had met Kahn. Always adorned in stylish clothes, Whit had gone into J. Press to pick up a suit he had ordered. He then searched for a new necktie to go with the new suit. Just as he selected one, a stranger snatched it from his hands, gave him another, and said, "Not that one. This one." "You're right, but who the hell are you?" Whit asked. "I'm Louis Kahn," the stranger replied, "and I've just submitted a bid on your new art gallery." Kahn had devised a glorious design. He won the contract, and the two became fast friends. That story revealed Whit as he really was. Unfettered by tradition and a shrewd judge of architects, Whit during his presidency commissioned buildings that made Yale a showcase of modern American architecture. Kingman Brewster continued in that mode.

I embraced Yale at once primarily because of the sheer delight I felt at teaching at last almost exactly what I wanted to teach and what the students wanted to learn. I had been working toward that satisfying combination for nearly two decades. I even took pleasure in the graduate course on the literature of American history, where I was joined by Ed Morgan, Sam Bemis, and David Potter. One week of that course had long been devoted to the history of Native Americans. I substituted a week on African Americans, taking advantage of the Yale library's James Weldon Johnson Collection. Indeed I directed graduate work on African American history until Vann Woodward joined the department. I also devoted a week of the course to the history of immigration, a week to intellectual history, a week to economic history, and two or three weeks to political history after 1876. Both Ed Morgan and I found the course awkward because by its nature it demanded instruction in ideas about ideas — our and the students' ideas about the history others had written. We both preferred to instruct students about the raw materials and the writing of history. But we realized that graduate students found the historiography course useful, and we kept at it until in 1965 the university decreased teaching loads.

I learned every year from the work of the doctoral candidates who enrolled in the seminar I offered. Since I had never before taught a graduate seminar, I reached back to my own experience at Harvard in planning my course. I took Fred Merk's seminar as my model. I started the students at once on research topics. For those just beginning, I drew up a list of some thirty possible topics, all of them potentially worthy of a dissertation. At our first session, I spoke briefly about each topic and asked each student to choose one topic or to define one of his or her own. (The Yale Graduate School of Arts and Sciences had long admitted women.) Each student was to report two weeks later on a beginning bibliography and a tentative definition of the dimensions of the topic. During the intervening week each student would meet privately with me to work toward those goals. Then each succeeding seminar, two hours in length, would be devoted to reports from three students about what they had done, with all members of the seminar expected to comment about each of the reports. Later during the year we had a round of progress reports and still later of final reports. For the weeks in which we scheduled no reports I assigned reading — monographs or public documents or sections of a manuscript collection — which we then discussed. I wanted those enrolled to become familiar with the variety of re-sources available for historical scholarship. I also closely edited the drafts of their research papers, for clear, organized, grammatical, and lively prose seemed to me essential for good historical writing. And I hoped the students would exchange their drafts, for I was eager for them to learn from each other. The system worked best when the students' topics were clustered around a common set of issues.

In the initial year my seminar included two recent Yale College gradu-ates, Robert Bannister and Henry Chauncey, Jr., who was known as "Sam." Bob selected a topic from a group pertaining to aspects of American pro-gressivism. His was "Ray Stannard Baker as David Grayson." (Baker, a pro-gressive journalist and the first significant biographer of Woodrow Wilson, had later written books under the pen name of David Grayson.) Bannister went on to write his dissertation on that subject, which in turn became a book—a fulfillment of his work in my seminar such as I had hoped. Ban-nister went on to teach American history, especially intellectual history, for many years at Swarthmore College.

Sam Chauncey, the second son of Henry Chauncey, who had admitted me to Harvard College, chose to address a difficult subject, the problem of planning occupation currency for defeated Germany, one of the topics I had listed on World War II. About a month after the term began, Sam came to see me during my regular office hours. He had been offered, he said, a po-sition as assistant dean of Yale College. What did I advise? I told him that ac-ademic administration was obviously in his genes, and that I considered deans to be important college officers. I suggested he accept the offer. He then told me that he already had. Sam always made his own decisions. He went on to become an assistant to Yale President Kingman Brewster, and was later the secretary of Yale University, still later the CEO of an indus-trial park and then the Gaylord rehabilitation hospital in Wallingford, Con-necticut, and then became a lecturer on the delivery of health care. Sam eventually also became a neighbor of mine in Vermont, and of all the grad-uate students I ever knew, the closest friend.

Sam's career seemed to me, like Bannister's, a desirable fulfillment of graduate education (even if, in Sam's case, that education was brief). It was just as important to train administrators as to train teachers, and academic administrators profited from exposure to education beyond the college level. I took great pride over the years in my association with men like Sam and women like Ellen Gluck Ryerson, whose dissertation—later a book—on the children's court movement I directed before she went on to law school. Later she became a dean at the Yale Law School, the New York Law School, and the Yale Graduate School. In time another personal friend, William Lilley III, who matriculated in 1960, wrote his dissertation on Francis Newlands, the progressive Nevada senator and conservationist, but found teaching not to his taste. He moved into journalism, then to a subcabinet position in the Nixon administration, then to a vice presidency at CBS, and later to the publication of dazzling books of computer-generated maps on the political, ethnic, and economic geography of all the assembly districts in the United States. A decade or so after Bill Lilley, Jonathan Fanton became another veteran of my seminar and a personal friend. He was successively an assistant to Kingman Brewster, president of the New School University, and head of the MacArthur Foundation.

But the central task of graduate teaching at Yale was to prepare Ph.D. candidates to write and teach history. To that end, by 1963 I was directing about a dozen dissertations, all that I could manage. What field of history the students entered was a matter of indifference to me. Indeed the most talented student I ever encountered, Jonathan Spence, a graduate of Cambridge University, arrived at Yale intending to study some American history before launching his career, probably in the foreign service. I urged him to venture more boldly, to work with two new colleagues in Chinese history, Mary and Arthur Wright. He did, learning Chinese in record time, and succeeded Mary after her untimely death. In his first year at Yale, he wrote a stunning research paper for me about the legislative record of Robert LaFollette as governor of Wisconsin. Absorbed in modern Chinese history, a field in which he excelled, Jon never bothered to have that paper published. He wrote a dozen or more splendid books instead.

The ablest American historian to work with me during my early years at Yale, Robert F. Dalzell, Jr., came from Amherst College, where he had begun a study of Daniel Webster under Henry Commager. His mentor had given Yale a special fellowship for an Amherst graduate who intended to make a career of American history, a fellowship Bob won. At Yale he continued his work on Webster with David Potter, but when David left for Stanford, Bob switched to me. I applauded as he finished his *Daniel Webster and the Trial of American Nationalism,* which I recommended to Houghton, Mifflin and which they published in 1973. Bob went on to Williams College, where he taught in the American Studies program for many years and wrote two more stunning books, one about the Lowell textile manufacturers and the other about Mount Vernon. In his study of Lowell, Bob made a connection between Scottish moral philosophy and the Lowell entrepreneurs that had eluded us at MIT. The Lowell adventurers, he wrote, resolved to prosper in order to support worthy cultural institutions, such as Harvard College and the Boston Museum of Fine Arts.

One of Bob's contemporaries, Cynthia Eagle Russett, wrote her dissertation on a subject she first addressed in my seminar. The resulting book, *The Concept of Equilibrium in American Social Thought,* was published by Yale University Press in 1966. Her reflective mind and crisp prose characterized her later writing and teaching as a professor of history at Yale. Students like Bob Bannister, Bob Dalzell, Cynthia Russett, and their successors did not need me to succeed as historians, but their careers provided me with a degree of professional satisfaction deriving, as Dean Acheson put it in a different context, from having been present at the creation.

My greatest satisfaction, however, came from lecturing to undergraduates, as I did in my year-long course on the United States in the twentieth century, at first entitled "Politics and American Culture," later retitled "American Politics and Public Policy" so as better to describe its changing content. Apart from reading monographs at learned conventions, before reaching Yale I had lectured only a few times, in the Williams summer program. I meant to write a dozen or more lectures during the summer of 1957, but teaching Bell executives and drafting the early chapters of the first Morgenthau volume left me time for only two, and those two seemed wooden to me. So out of necessity I lectured from notes, especially notes on names and dates, which I was prone to forget. The decision to lecture from notes proved to be fortuitous. I discovered during my first lectures that I lectured in two selves, much, perhaps, as actors act — one a performing self and the other an observing self. The observing self told the performing self when and how to alter a lecture in order to hold the attention of the audience. Working from notes rather than a written text, I found it easier to make adjustments. Further, as I lectured from notes I could make occasional comments, as they occurred to me, about the foibles of the actors in the drama of history or about other aspects of the content of the lectures or the current relevance of whatever we were examining. Also unlike a text, notes did not tie me to the lectern, so I could move around (I had a tendency to pace). I rarely used a microphone. Indeed instead of altering my voice as I lectured, I simply talked as I would have to a few students in my office. In short, I found myself able to deliver informal lectures — structured and timed, to be sure, but unpredictable, even for me. Each lecture required an extemporized creativity; each consumed much adrenaline; each, if successful, provided a quick and transient reward.

To my delight, the students liked my lectures. Enrollment in my course rose in three weeks from 40 to 120, where I held it until the next year, when we moved to a large hall and some 300 students took the course. It grew to about 400 in 1962–63, leveled off, and then dropped back to about 300. It was never an easy course. The required reading averaged about 250 pages a week. Some of the assignments at one time or another were in volumes in the Harper and Row's New American Nation series as those books became available — one such example was William Leuchtenburg's *Franklin D. Roosevelt and the New Deal,* published in 1963. Other assignments were taken from biographies, including my own of Theodore Roosevelt and Woodrow Wilson, or from monographs, like Ellis Hawley's on New Deal economic policies. I wanted the reading to supplement the lectures, not repeat them, and I intended the examinations to test both. The median grade, no matter what the grading system (which often changed), remained about the equivalent of B. Still, some students failed and some received Ds, even during the grade inflation of the Vietnam war years. Many others deserved their As.

Until the late 1960s the departmental budget allowed only for course graders, about one for each one hundred students. The graders helped evaluate papers but did not teach sections (later they did). I tried to read at least a hundred exams myself to give myself ample feedback and take it into account as I revised the course. I made small revisions every year, and every seven years I tried to reconstruct the course entirely. In doing so I could keep up with the aging twentieth century. In 1957–58 I divided the semesters at 1919; by 1986–87, it was up to 1945. (My lecture notes also provided the basis for the six chapters I wrote on the period 1901–32 for the first edition of *The National Experience,* a textbook published by Harcourt, Brace in 1963.)

A course as large as mine called not for lectures, some critics said, but for a performance. Perhaps that is so. It was surely true when a given topic called for a special effort. So it was with a lecture I gave annually to introduce Theodore Roosevelt. I began by explaining the disposition of American forces at the base of the San Juan ridge outside of Santiago, Cuba, in 1898. I then described TR's order to his troops, delivered in his patrician falsetto: "Gentlemen, the Almighty God and the Just Cause are with you. Gentlemen, *charge!*" Eventually they did, of course, and they conquered, but at first Roosevelt's troops did not hear him, and he had to shout the order again. We spent much time deconstructing Roosevelt's use of the term "gentlemen" to address the Rough Riders, which was a collection of cowboys, Indians, Ivy League jocks, and hangers-on. TR was a well-born Republican, as I tried to make obvious, but also a democrat. Some years after first delivering that lecture I realized that students were coming to the class for the precise purpose of hearing it again, or came to hear it with no intention of enrolling in the course. So for a few years I suspended the lecture, and when I brought it back I made it less of a performance. I saw it as a tribute to Fred Merk that I always followed the outline I wrote on the blackboard, always finished a lecture on time, always began a lecture by reminding the class of what we had done "at the last hour." Entertainment was secondary. My first purpose was to teach American history.

But an attentive student could quickly realize that an ancillary purpose of mine was to interest Yale students in public life. Theodore Roosevelt provided a great example by accepting the responsibility of educated, comfortable, moral men and women to their communities. He performed community services, and he preached the importance of those services from his bully pulpit. So did his niece, Eleanor Roosevelt, and so did others on whom the course focused, John Lindsay and Jonathan Bingham, Yale alumni, two examples among my contemporaries. Further, like Wilson at Princeton, Presidents Griswold and Brewster believed, as I did, in "Yale in the nation's service." Indirectly I urged undergraduates to assist the campaigns of worthy local candidates for office, or to run themselves, as several did, or to accept appointments to national office. Senator Joseph Lieberman of Connecticut, Governor George Pataki of New York, and President George W. Bush enrolled during their undergraduate years in my lecture course. They did not need my urging to enter public life, and ironically on most issues all three stood well to the right of my own political position. Governor Howard Dean and Senator John Kerry, also students of mine, took positions in their 2004 presidential campaigns with which I was sympathetic. I was closer to former students who became political journalists, most of them liberals. Seven of the most influential have been Bob Kaiser and Bob Woodward of the *Washington Post,* Steve Weisman and Alison Silver of the *New York Times,* Tom Anderson of CBS-TV, Jane Mayer of *The New Yorker,* and David Greenberg of *The New Republic.* Any effort to interest Yale students in public affairs became redundant when the civil rights movement began to sweep through American colleges. But I deemed it worth continuing to praise reformers in the American past who had strengthened democratic institutions and thus democracy itself. Corny? Perhaps, but more my style than storming the barricades, as some of my peers tried to do.

Did I bring a bias to my course on politics and public policy? Yes, as I warned the students in my first lecture and intermittently thereafter. No history can be wholly objective. Historians, even beginners, should keep in mind the uncertainty principle, which applies as much to their work as to high-energy physics. In order to examine subatomic particles, the physicist must energize them, a process that changes the way in which they would otherwise behave. So, too, with the historian examining the past, who "energizes" his or her subject by bringing to the resulting account of the past —to history—his or her particular, but often unacknowledged, biases. So Herbert Butterfield famously argued in 1931 in his attack on the then dominant "Whig" interpretation of eighteenth- and nineteenth-century English history. But Butterfield by no means was innocent of bias himself: he went on to write a Tory account of George III.

I told my students to examine what I said with the foreknowledge that I was an independent Democrat, leaning left from a centrist base. When I was moved to speak on some current issue, I did so in an aside, telling the class that I was about to make a parenthetical remark, which was not part of the course. I intended the class to know what I thought. I did not expect the students necessarily to agree with me. Indeed some came by during office hours in order to disagree.

I also required good manners during lectures. Winter and summer, until I retired in 1991 I always wore a jacket and tie. I permitted no smoking, though I was then a smoker myself, no sleeping, no reading of newspapers, and, after Yale became coeducational, no necking or knitting. If I observed violations of those rules, I asked the offending students to leave the hall. If they did not, I stopped lecturing until they did. It never took more than two minutes for the culprit to depart.

Since the size of the course made it impersonal, I tried to make myself available to undergraduates by posting and holding ample office hours, at least eight a week. Those hours were always filled with students who had questions, or wanted recommendations, or were eager simply to chat. But shy students would not come by. So after several years of experience, I came up with an easier way for undergraduates to meet with me. I reserved a table in the dining hall at Branford College, the residential college to which I had been assigned as a fellow, from noon until two o'clock every Thursday. I announced to the class that I would be there to see anyone who wanted to join me for an informal lunch. Each week there gathered at the table some eighteen students, not all at once, half of them regular in attendance, most of them interested in talking about sports, national politics, or goings-on at Yale. I had a good time with them, and I think they enjoyed our palaver. More important, I came to know some of them quite well, particularly those who began also coming to office hours for counsel about their career plans or to discuss academic matters.

In April 1958 I was gratified to receive an invitation to become an honorary member of Book and Snake, one of Yale's secret senior societies. I took it as a vote of confidence in me and in my teaching, but I also wondered about the propriety of joining. I knew that Kingman Brewster, while chairman of the *Yale Daily News* in 1940–41, had attacked the senior societies for their exclusiveness and had refused to become a member even of the most prestigious of the "tombs." So informed, the members of Book and Snake urged me to consult Franklin Baumer, a historian of European ideas, who was already an honorary member. Assuring me that the routines were entirely innocent, he urged me to accept the invitation. I did and found nothing objectionable in the way the group conducted its affairs. On the contrary, at the occasional Thursday dinner I attended I met interesting students every year. A few were interested in an academic career, others were absorbed in athletics or other undergraduate activities, all on their best behavior. I continued to attend sporadically except during the period when the active members tolerated smoking pot. As an officer of the university I could not endorse that illegal habit by failing to report it to Yale and the public authorities.

Just as in 1958 the invitation to join Book and Snake had seemed a tribute to my teaching, so did the positive report in the undergraduate annual guide to Yale courses. The polls that guide took and the comments of the editors gave my lectures a high rating. After a year or two one of the editorial comments was: "Blum — biased about everything." I felt the students and I understood each other.

Two episodes revealed how quickly and fully I embraced Yale. In 1959 Delaney Kiphuth invited me to become a member of the Board of Athletic Control, a faculty body that advised the director of athletics. It tickled Kip's fancy to add to that group a Harvard alumnus who lacked the ability to earn a varsity letter. He knew, too, that I had volunteered as a judge at track meets and had attended swimming and other intercollegiate competitions with Pamela and our children. At that time he also invited Eli Clark, an Andover classmate no more athletic than I, to become a member of the board. Kip's belief in amateurism gave him strange but enthusiastic bedfellows — and produced unexpected results. In 1957 I rooted for Harvard in the football game against Yale. In 1958 I saw no football games. In 1959 I saw them all as a member of Kip's board. Further, through my lectures I had come to know a large number of the Yale squad. As we entered the Yale Bowl for the Harvard game, Pamela asked for whom I was cheering. I told her I did not know. Then on the kickoff the Yale receiver fumbled and Harvard recovered. I jumped to my feet and said, "God damn it!" Sitting in front of me, Harold Whiteman, a Yale dean and former football captain, turned around and said, "That's the first time I've ever seen anyone cross the Rubicon." Unable to abandon my students, I remained a Yale booster for many years. Especially in 1960 when the Yale football team beat Harvard in Cambridge to complete an undefeated and untied season, I rejoiced in Yale's victories. I held a special affection for the "undefeated class of 1961," whose reunions I often joined at their request. After all, we had all arrived at Yale in 1957.

At the meeting of the American Historical Association in December 1961, in the bar over drinks, Jerome Blum, no relative but then chair of the Princeton history department, told me that Princeton wanted me to become a professor there with some of my assignment in the Woodrow Wilson School of Public Affairs. He asked me to come to Princeton to see the university and discuss the offer. I would have jumped at the chance to go to Princeton in 1956. Now I had no wish to leave Yale. Further, Princeton already had two first-rate historians of the United States in the twentieth century — Eric Goldman, who taught a famous class, and Arthur Link, just arriving as editor in chief of the Wilson Papers. Both were professional friends. And Princeton was a great university with a distinguished department of history. I saw no way to refuse to visit; but as I told George Pierson, who was still chairman of my department, I was going to visit only. I had already decided to remain at Yale. George nevertheless informed President Griswold. The night before I took the train to Princeton, Whit called. "Stay with us," he said, "and we'll give you an athletic scholarship."

The reception at Princeton was warm, but peculiar. It became clear that I was wanted largely to teach the history of American public policy to the graduate students at the Wilson School. I would also be expected to serve as a preceptor, a kind of teaching assistant, in Eric Goldman's course, an assignment that I resisted. The day's events merely strengthened my intention to stay where I was. I so reported to George Pierson, and at the end of the academic year Whit came through with the "athletic scholarship." More important, the Princeton initiative and my response to it revealed the strong sinews, grown in only a few years, that held me to Yale. The university and I had bonded. Though opportunities continually arose thereafter, I never seriously considered going elsewhere.

Companionable for more than sixty years: Jack Walsh, George Wagoner, the author, Gordon Tuttle. Y2K.

Bill Darrid, my perceptive brother.

Aboard the USS PC 616.

Bride and groom, June 28, 1944.

Elting E. Morison, ca. 1970: unconventional master of his craft.

Alfred D. Chandler, Jr., ca. 1992: premier historian of American business.

Our three, 1955: Ann, Pamela, Thomas.

George Wilson Pierson, "Father Yale," ca. 1989. (Courtesy of Michael Marsland)

Edmund S. Morgan, ca. 1971: a profound and informed intelligence.

With Sam Chauncey, ca. 1991: friend, Vermont neighbor, model citizen.

Lecturing in the Yale Law School Auditorium, 1962.

C. Vann Woodward, ca. 1965: preeminent historian of the South. (Courtesy of Pach Bros.)

The Lodge, Queens' College, Cambridge University.

Kingman Brewster, Jr., ca. 1970: President of Yale.

With Chester Kerr, 1985: an elegant party. (Courtesy of David Orrenstein)

The President and Fellows of Harvard College, 1970–71.

Stumping for McGovern, 1972.

With Dr. Pamela Z. Blum, Fellow of the Society of Antiquaries.

With Howard Lamar, President of Yale 1992.

Tory Democrat.

10

Undertakings

Apart from teaching and writing, I quickly became involved in various undertakings on campus and off. George Pierson choreographed my introduction to Yale by carefully selecting and limiting the number of committees, departmental and otherwise, to which I was assigned. Because he started me slowly I had more time during my first several years for off-campus commitments than I would have thereafter, though from the first either a faculty or a department meeting absorbed two hours every Tuesday and Thursday afternoon. Good citizenship mattered at Yale. Presidents Griswold and Brewster expanded the concept to include engaging in education at every level, as well as to assisting the troubled city of New Haven. But in the beginning I had some free time in my schedule.

John Burchard, the Dean of Humanities at MIT, arranged for Pamela and me to join him for two weeks in the summer of 1958 at the Aspen Institute in Colorado. He and I were to serve as moderators of a seminar for senior business executives. Mortimer Adler, the Great Books guru of the college curriculum at the University of Chicago, had prescribed the assigned reading. It was not to my taste, but I could manage it. All went well until the penultimate session, for which the assignment was *The Communist Manifesto*. In the view of the executives, that work was so subversive that they would not read it. Consequently discussion languished until I proposed to pretend to be Karl Marx and to respond as he might have to their questions and comments. As we proceeded for about an hour the tension grew. Then one executive accused communists of practicing free love. On the contrary, I said as Marx, free love was a capitalistic fashion, most visible in the serial monogamy of Hollywood but endemic, as divorce statistics demonstrated, in the serial monogamy through-out the United States. "That's enough!" he shouted. "Be yourself or we'll all leave." Burchard took over for the balance of the session, but the executives at our farewell dinner presented me with a hammer and sickle.

For cocktails before that dinner we were all invited to the grand residence of Mrs. Walter Pepke, "Pussy" to her friends, the first lady of Aspen and a major sponsor of both the institute and the much celebrated annual music festival. As we stood in the living room, drinks in hand, the executives ex-pressed their amazement at the great paintings on the walls. "That's noth-ing," I said, joking. "You should see the Picasso upstairs." Burchard took me by the arm and, leading me out of the room, whispered, "Be quiet! Pussy doesn't want them going up. But you and Pamela may if you're discreet." We found to our delighted edification a superb cartoon for *Guernica,* drawn by the master.

We gladly accepted invitations to return to the institute in 1960 and, with the whole family, in 1962 and 1968. In 1962 one of the public intellectuals at-tached to the seminars was Eric Sevareid, the celebrated newscaster, seem-ingly dour on the air but in person a friendly, cooperative companion. With his foreknowledge, I told the executives without warning that instead of dis-cussing Plato's account of the trial of Socrates we would improvise a drama-tization of the text. To that end I made a few alterations — for example, cre-ating a jury to render a verdict. Our jury found Socrates not guilty. Eric had contrived a role for himself as the anchorman for Radio Athens on a news program sponsored by Togawhite ("To be sure of a bright, white Toga, use Togawhite in every laundry"). We had such a good time and scored such a pedagogical success that thereafter I continued to treat the trial the same way, though with different public intellectuals, of whom Erwin Canham of the *Christian Science Monitor* especially shone. No jury ever found Socrates guilty.

While the Aspen Institute prolonged my experience with continuing ed-ucation, Elting Morison persuaded me to become involved in issues in pri-mary education. Elting was spending much time with Jerome Bruner, a daz-zling Harvard psychologist who had studied public opinion during World War II but since had switched his interests to cognition. In 1959, in prepara-tion for establishing an institute to promote new approaches to teaching the sciences in primary and secondary schools, Jerry organized a conference of interested college professors and administrators at Woods Hole, Massachu-setts. He and Elting decided to include a delegation of historians, for which Elting recruited me, but in the end he did not attend. Donald Cole of Ex-eter, who had to leave early, was the sole historian other than myself. Un-deterred, Jerry simply classified me as a psychologist and assigned me to a group of biologists who were discussing the question of sequencing in the teaching of Mendelian theory. Other groups were pondering related questions in proposed new approaches to teaching math and physics.

Much concerned with algorithms and heuristics, we all spent some time in plenary sessions that persuaded me of the virtues of what then was called the "new math" and the "new physics," both developed by MIT faculty members. (A Johns Hopkins professor was about to add the "new biology.") The new math utilized wooden rods of various lengths and colors to introduce children to mathematical theory while they were also taught arithmetic. The new physics, focusing on wave theory, substituted a ripple tank —a baking pan filled with water and agitated by an electric motor—for a standard laboratory. Local schoolchildren responded with excitement to classroom demonstrations of those subjects. Our group on Mendelian theory remained divided over which of two sequences to adopt. Some favored just telling ninth graders what the offspring of a white and a black fruit fly would look like over several generations. Others, of whom I was one, preferred to teach probability first by having the children flip coins and count the resulting heads and tails. Then we proposed to move on to fruit flies bred in the classroom. That "discovery" method had the support of Elting's brother, Dr. Robert Morison, an astute officer of the Rockefeller Foundation, and of Henry Chauncey, then the head of the Educational Testing Service. But the innovative approaches to teaching the sciences ultimately failed, largely because the teachers in most schools could neither understand nor instruct their charges in the new methods.

President Griswold promoted faculty cooperation with the mayor of New Haven, Richard Lee, a prominent urban reformer and friend of John F. Kennedy. The new city charter Lee had promoted called for a bipartisan board of ethics, with its primary duty to review city contracts for evidence of influence peddling. To that board, the mayor appointed Russell Atwater, a Republican real estate lawyer; Monsignor Francis Donnelly; and me. Monsignor Donnelly happened to be the mayor's confessor and a Democrat in his sympathies, so when there was a split vote, Russ was usually the dissenter. But it was he who made a convincing case for proceeding on the basis of stare decisis. Our first cases indicated how difficult it was to prevent conflicts of interest in a city as small as New Haven. For example, the city let a contract for roofing all the firehouses to the low bidder, who was the largest roofer in the area and arguably the most reliable. But that firm had also contributed to the mayor's most recent campaign. Russ Atwater, who would like to have made an issue of the contract, had to admit that no other interested roofer had the personnel to do the job. While Russ abstained, Monsignor Donnelly and I voted to approve the contract, since we found no evidence of an intention to bribe or even of political favoritism. I remained on the ethics board for several years, during which most cases we decided resembled the roofer's.

With some exceptions, Yale historians had generally made little effort to participate in their profession's learned associations during the years before George Pierson's chairmanship. Shortly before the annual meeting of the American Historical Association in 1957 George urged his colleagues to attend. He had planned an elaborate Yale smoker for alumni and friends, he wanted us to be there, and he expected us to use the occasion to find academic appointments for our graduate students. In that search we were to take care, he said, not to cultivate what he called "fresh water colleges," presumably because they were unworthy of Yale graduates. Of course it was precisely this attitude that had made midwestern American colleges uninterested in Yale candidates. Ed Morgan and I, both regulars at historical conventions, were determined to change the impression that George and others had inadvertently made. We had growing numbers of graduate students to place in a market then just beginning to boom.

My efforts fell short of Ed's, but for a decade I did go almost always to meetings of both the American Historical Association, where historians of all fields gathered, and—as it came to be named—the Organization of American Historians, a society of historians of the Americas. Those conventions gave me the chance to catch up with old friends, especially Barney Keeney and Dick Leopold. Dick knew so many historians that he was constantly surrounded in the lobbies of the hotels where we met. "There stands the ancient mariner," it was said of Dick. "He stoppeth one in three." John K. Fairbank, the distinguished Harvard historian of China, organized a group within the AHA to promote the study of Chinese-American relations, which during the 1950s and 1960s were at a disturbing impasse. I had come to know John well when I approached him for help in understanding Morgenthau's policies toward China. He sent me to his friend Dorothy Borg, a strikingly beautiful expert in China policy during World War II. Soon John and Dorothy were arranging special meetings of their own. In those years I also accompanied my older colleague, eminent German émigré historian Hajo Holborn, to meetings of officers, which he had to attend while he was vice president and then president of the AHA. But after 1968 I became so burdened with Yale responsibilities that I just about abandoned my ties to the learned associations.

The affairs of the history department consumed more and more of my energy as the years passed. George Pierson broke me in by naming me at once to the department's publication committee, charged with allocating its limited funds for historical publications of the Yale University Press. The budget was so small that we could afford to publish only two or three books annually, too few to assure all worthy dissertations of reaching print. But the new head of the press, Chester Kerr, made some of his own budget available, to our common gratification. A stylish, even flamboyant personality, Chester married four women, divorced three, lived graciously and strenuously, gave some of the best parties Pamela and I ever attended, and brought a new distinction to the Yale press, not least to its history list. Nevertheless my publisher remained Houghton, Mifflin, though I later moved to Harcourt, Brace and then to W. W. Norton. Still, for some thirty years I worked with Chester's editors to improve the books of history he sent me for advice. Serving on the publications committee also allowed me to meet Yale colleagues in distant fields of history who were promoting manuscripts by their graduate students for departmental publication.

The hardest-working and most important department committee was the one that recommended appointments—both promotions of junior colleagues, who had to leave if they failed to earn tenure within nine years, and invitations to scholars from outside of Yale, some at the start of their career, others well established and available only as tenured professors. George Pierson, eager to expand and improve the department, considered those objectives achievable only by recruiting from without and therefore by allowing fewer promotions from within. He was especially eager to build strength in areas where Yale had long been weak, most urgently in Russian and Far Eastern history. But Whit Griswold wisely demanded scholarly excellence as an essential requirement for tenure, and after a long search in Chinese history rejected the department's recommendation of a candidate with shaky qualifications. The following September George asked me to be chairman of the appointments committee for the ensuing year. Recognizing the request as burdensome but flattering, I also had great respect for the rest of the committee: Ed Morgan, already an influential counselor to George; and Bill Dunham, a particular friend of Whit Griswold, and a respected specialist on British constitutional history. At once I accepted the position.

George had more on his mind, however. "Leonard Krieger is coming up for promotion to full professor," he said, "and I do not want to see this department go the way of the law school." I was stunned. Krieger was a deeply learned historian of ideas, most comfortable in the early modern period, and a talented teacher. He was also Jewish. I made a quick decision to play dumb.

I knew the law professors described the rules of their special culture as "dress British; think Yiddish." But I said, "What do you mean about the law school?"

"All its recent appointments," George replied, "have been Jews." I paused before saying, "But I'm a Jew."

George answered at once, "So you are. You stay on the committee, but we had better make Dunham chairman." He did, but Krieger was promoted, as he deserved to be. The next year he accepted a professorship at the University of Chicago.

George's comment demonstrated that some measure of anti-Semitism continued to affect academia. But by 1960 I had made peace with that problem. I had no interest in Judaism but I saw no need to apologize for that, nor for my doubts about Zionism. The Holocaust, and the indifference of the United States government and almost all other governments to the plight of the European Jews during World War II, made necessary an asylum like Israel. But I believed, as I still do, that Jerusalem, a city sacred to three faiths, should be dominated by none of them, with the United Nations the appropriate governing body. Nevertheless I defined myself as a Jew, for the world so defined me, and I had learned to get along very well without fraternizing with anti-Semitic people and without bowing to their prejudice. Further, despite George's remark anti-Semitism did not much affect appointments at Yale at that time, except among the old guard, who were already losing control. After all, I had been appointed, Krieger was promoted, and the history department included Robert Lopez, a distinguished medievalist, and Rollin Osterweiss, a historian of New Haven, both Jews. More important, President Griswold, responding to a faculty consensus, was about to name Georges May, a professor of French born in Paris of a Jewish family, to the position of Dean of Yale College, an appointment, as it turned out, of paramount importance and prestige.

Now and then, as in my conversation with George Pierson, unfortunate and outmoded attitudes broke through. At a meeting of the Board of Permanent Officers of Yale College — the full professors — one crotchety classicist objected to Judah Golden, the eminent first appointment to the new Religious Studies Department. "I do not mean to criticize Golden," he said. "But if you appoint a Jew, first thing you know you'll appoint a Catholic." He was correct. Golden won approval with ease, and the next year the board, by a thumping majority, endorsed the appointment of a leading authority on St. Thomas Aquinas, Stephan Kuttner, who had been born a Jew in Germany but had long since converted to Catholicism.

In the case of George Pierson, as I suspect in many others, anti-Semitism was a conditioned response of little more than rhetorical significance.

George had every known prejudice of his generation of proper patrician male WASPs. He dropped those prejudices as soon as he met someone he initially suspected but found he liked. So it was that by 1960 he had come to treat me as a valued friend. More telling, he said to the Board of Permanent Officers, "Over my dead body will a woman join this faculty," but just a year later he recommended the appointment of Mary C. Wright, a historian of modern China; without serious objection, she won approval, the first woman to do so. By 1961 religious prejudice had ceased to be a significant factor in Yale appointments, and other prejudices went the same way within a decade. Yale was abreast of the national culture, and after 1963, under President Kingman Brewster, Jr., was well ahead of it.

By 1963 five senior appointments in history had enhanced the reputation of the department. The first two, Mary and Arthur Wright, gave Yale an unmatched team in Chinese history. Arthur, an elegant man, specialized in Buddhism. Energetic and ambitious for Yale, he recruited John W. Hall, another admirable colleague, in Japanese history. Arthur and George Pierson also persuaded Whit Griswold to approve their plan for a program in area studies, which the Ford Foundation agreed to finance. The Ford grant led in time to positions in African, Latin American, Russian, and Eastern European history. When Yale lost David Potter to Stanford, Ed Morgan and I immediately told George Pierson there was only one way to replace David. That was to appoint C. Vann Woodward, then at Johns Hopkins and already the premier historian of the American South. George reflected only a minute before telephoning Vann and offering him a Sterling professorship, the most remunerative and prestigious chair Yale had. The courtship that followed involved us all, Ed and I as collaborators with Vann on a textbook then underway, George as an effective suitor who succeeded in convincing Glenn Woodward, Vann's wife, of the merits of Yale and New Haven. Vann and Ed also soon teamed up to recruit another Hopkins professor, Hans Gatzke, a historian of Germany and of European diplomacy, who relieved Hajo Holborn of a growing burden of teaching. And George recruited Gaddis Smith, a former doctoral student of Sam Bemis and a former chairman of the *Yale Daily News,* to succeed his mentor.

Those appointments, all of them but Vann and Gaddis recipients of a Harvard Ph.D., completed George Pierson's program for improving the department. Before his term as chairman expired, he had made the department a great one, a company of major scholars, all of them dedicated teachers, all devoted to the university. To be sure, selection of our new colleagues had moved through "the old boys' network." That is, professional friends turned to each other during the process of recruitment. In later years appointments had to conform to rules created to assure affirmative action. To give equal rights to women and minority candidates, those rules had obvious merit. But no system of appointments could have improved on the department's decisions to invite to Yale the Wrights, Jack Hall, and Vann Woodward, all truly outstanding scholars. Indeed the quest for diversity in later years tended at times to allow race or gender to trump scholarly excellence.

The new appointments affected our social lives. Academic friendships grow only if spouses nurture them, and Pamela and my colleagues' wives liked each other, a boon to our professorial relationships. From the mid-1960s until several of the principals died, many dinner parties and weekend gatherings included all or some of our group — Robin and Jack Hall, Helen and Ed Morgan, Letty and George Pierson, Glenn and Vann Woodward, Mary and Arthur Wright, and Pamela and me. Never exclusive, our friendship expedited departmental affairs, but we did not always agree about Yale policies.

Whit Griswold made the appointment that proved most important for Pamela and me and most crucial for Yale. He called me at home one morning, teased me about working there instead of in my office, and told me, as he gently put it, "to get your ass down here right away." When I arrived, he said, "I want you to talk to me as if we were sitting behind Kingman's shithouse on the Vineyard." Having thus established the seriousness of the occasion, he said that he was dissatisfied with the candidates from within the Yale faculty who had been recommended to succeed the outgoing provost. He had in mind instead two Yale alumni who were then teaching at Harvard: Zeph Stewart, an elegant professor of classics, and Kingman Brewster, Jr., a professor of law. He wanted me to evaluate them. I said that I thought either would be excellent, that I knew Kingman much better than I knew Zeph, but that, discounting bias, I considered Kingman potentially the more capable administrator, largely because of his skill with people. The provost's job, seemingly a budgetary post, powerfully affected the educational programs of all Yale schools and required close relations with many faculty members. It was a people job, requiring tact and humor as well as insight, qualities Kingman had in abundance. Unbeknownst to me, Whit first offered the position to Zeph, who declined. He then appointed Kingman, whose enterprising educational spirit was to infuse Yale for the next fifteen years.

Pamela and I had become friends of the Brewsters in Cambridge, and we remained good friends after they moved to New Haven while Kingman was provost, while he was president, and after he left Yale and turned to the practice of law. Our children knew each other. Pamela and Mary Louise often had lunch or shopped together. We four frequently, usually on the spur of the moment, had cocktails together. Occasionally Kingman asked me to undertake an administrative or committee chore. But he did not lean on me, or I on him, and he understood my strengths and my limitations. We both knew that when it came to administrative tasks, I was a sprinter, not a long-distance runner. I could pour energy into a brief, time-limited assignment, but I tended to tire under the pressure of a long-term responsibility, for I was always eager to get back to my teaching and scholarship.

Kingman, of course, preferred to have me agree to his requests, though he accepted disagreement, usually with a friendly barb. So it was one evening while he was provost. At cocktails, he announced that he was going to take a walk and wanted me to accompany him. He had never before in our experience felt the need for a walk. But I went along, wondering what he wanted our wives not to hear. After strolling for a block or so, Kingman said that Whit wanted me to become the master of one of the residential colleges. I declined. "Is that no for now or no forever?" he asked. "No forever," I replied. "I value my privacy too much to share it." Silent but obviously annoyed, Kingman walked another twenty strides. "What a shame," he then said. "Pamela would have been so good at it." And she would have. But Kingman was grateful when I suggested somebody else, who seized the chance to become a college master. We had found a formula to which we returned. Years later, declining his request that I become provost, I recommended someone else, who accepted.

Many of my colleagues assumed that I had special influence. Charles E. Lindblom, deep into a study of power at Yale, told me that because of my friendship with Kingman and Mary Louise, I must be the most powerful professor on the Yale College faculty. "What would you say," I asked him, "were I to tell you that I almost always see Kingman when our wives are present. And mostly we talk about our children or national politics or Yale athletics." Ed reflected only briefly. "If that's the case," he said, "you have no power at all." And so it was. Even presidents need friends. But the arrival of the Brewsters in New Haven lifted Pamela's and my spirits and bound us even more strongly to the Yale community.

Before Kingman joined him, Whit Griswold had drafted several Yale historians to assist in a scheme he had devised to attract annually to the Yale graduate program young British aspirants to the Ph.D. in U.S. history. The historians of England in the Yale department had all profited from years of study at Oxford or Cambridge, and Whit proposed to return the favor. To prepare a formal plan to that end, he created a committee that included four Yale professors and several English scholars with demonstrated interests in American studies. From Yale, along with me, he selected Ed Morgan, David

Potter, and Archibald Foord, whose field was eighteenth-century English politics. The two foremost English representatives were Harry Allen, then a professor at University College, London, and Herbert Nicholas, a reader (more or less an associate professor) at New College, Oxford. We met as a group only twice before Whit's health failed, but his initiative had introduced me to Harry and Herbert, who in later years invited me to teach at their universities.

Whit had large ambitions for Yale. He authorized a major study of admissions policies that led to significant changes. He pushed the biology department into modernity. He appointed an energetic dean, John Perry Miller, to inspirit the Graduate School. He also wanted to enhance Yale's international reputation. To that end, he planned to make Yale in 1961 the guest for a week at the University of Munich, which annually acted as host to a delegation of foreign scholars from a single campus. He expected to lead the Yale group, but instead had to undergo emergency surgery for cancer of the colon. Hajo Holborn became the group's leader, and it was Hajo who formally asked me to come along, an invitation I had to accept. To Pamela's outspoken dismay, I had been declining opportunities for European lecturing for a decade. I had promised Pamela that I would embrace the next invitation I received just days before Hajo approached me.

Early in June 1961 we departed on the first trip to Europe either of us had undertaken. It was a wonderful trip, a delayed and abbreviated grand tour. We spent two glorious days in London, just enough time to know we had soon to arrange a longer visit. In France we drove south, stopped en route to inspect the cathedral at Sens, and went on the next day to the beautiful abbey church at Vezelay. In Dijon we had a luncheon omelet I have never forgotten. In Strasbourg we crossed the Rhine. When the German border guard asked to see my passport, I could not find it until Pamela extracted it from the inner pocket of my jacket. "What did you think," she asked when I stopped for gasoline, "that they were going to put you in a concentration camp?" "Exactly," I answered.

Munich was beautiful, our German hosts generous, and the assembled Yale group compatible. We admired the Nymphenburg palace and heard Mozart's *Abduction from the Seraglio* in the theater for which it was written. But my lectures did not please the German historians who attended them. I had three related topics: one on American character, then a fashionable subject; another on political and cultural changes accompanying the growth of big business in the late nineteenth century; and a third on the nature of the American middle class. The Germans dismissed them all as "sociology."

Alex Bickel, whose sinewy lectures on the Supreme Court had failed to excite his academic audience, suggested only partly in jest that we get even by visiting Dachau, in 1961 a site so fashioned as to suggest nothing about the Holocaust.

With the Eichmann trial then underway in Jerusalem, the Germans were busy trying to forget the past. But some of them retained its spirit. The rector's wife told me as we drove along together that she and her husband, while in the United States a year earlier, had devised a solution for the race problem. "Just put all the black people in Alabama and Mississippi," she suggested. "As you did with the Jews," I replied. For the rest of our drive we were silent.

Returning westward, Pamela and I spent several lovely days in Paris, where we swooned over the paintings in the Louvre and Jeu de Paume, and strolled in the sunshine through the gardens and along the Left Bank. One evening with Helen and Ed Morgan we partied as typical tourists, with a grand dinner at Le Pied de Couchon in Les Halles, champagne at the Lido, and onion soup back in the market. Another day I bought Pamela a slinky, becoming cocktail dress at the Dior boutique. Paris was for us, as it was for so many, the city of love. We knew we would return. Whit had arranged the Yale week in Munich to make his university more visible in Europe. Though it was not his purpose, he gave western Europe to Pamela and me. So it remained, an exciting, incomparable gift, treasured then and for the rest of our lives.

But Whit's surgery, though its findings were kept secret at the time, had revealed a growing, inoperable cancer. Increasingly frail, he persevered for almost two years. When he died, the Yale Corporation began its search for his successor almost at once. But without serious dissent, the tenured faculty of Yale College agreed that Kingman Brewster should become president. He had proved himself as provost and was continuing to do so as acting president. He understood Whit's educational objectives and intended to pursue them. He had won the admiration of everyone with whom he worked. A stylish man, he had revealed constantly his stylish mind. A member of the corporation asked me at a luncheon he had arranged whether I, or any colleague of whom I knew, had an interest in the presidency. Only Kingman, I replied, should be considered for that position. He agreed, he said. The corporation, he added, was only going through the necessary motions. But the Senior Fellow believed a Yale president should have earned a Ph.D., which Kingman had not, so the days went by with no decision.

In that season of uncertainty in 1963 I had a full plate. With Ed Morgan on leave, I was filling in on some of his committees while Howard Lamar served as acting department chairman. I was eligible for leave in 1963–64, but Yale paid only the base salary for professors on leave, so I was applying for grants to cover the rest of our family expenses. Besides my normal teaching, I had four books underway — the second volume on Morgenthau was partly drafted, research was proceeding on the third, I was developing a plan to do something with the lectures I had given in Munich, and I had agreed to write part of a textbook for Harcourt, Brace. My grant applications requested funds to defray living costs in 1964 while I wrote a book based on the lectures, but the other projects needed attention at once.

William Pullin, who had scored great successes in putting together two textbooks, each with three authors, for Prentice Hall had moved to Harcourt, Brace, where he hoped to duplicate his feat. A restless bundle of entrepreneurship, breathless as he hurried through his days, on entering our house Bill would always call a taxi to take him to his next appointment. In 1959 he had persuaded me to write one sixth of a textbook on American history, though at first he was unsure about the other contributors. But I brought Ed Morgan and Arthur Schlesinger, Jr., into the project, and Bill signed Vann Woodward, Kenneth Stampp, and Bruce Catton. At a meeting in New York Arthur volunteered a brilliant mode of organization to which we all agreed, with the further understanding that the emphasis throughout the text would be on political history and public policy interpreted through a liberal lens.

At first no one wrote much. Bruce Catton, who was designated editor, put no pressure on anyone because he did not want to write his own section on the period 1853–77. Formerly a journalist, an expert on the Civil War, and by 1959 an editor of *American Heritage*, Bruce was needlessly tense about collaborating with a group of academic historians. But Pullin brought to Harcourt a tough, talented, in-house editor from Prentice Hall, Everett Sims, who began immediately to demand manuscript from the authors. They had, after all, accepted advances against future royalties. Bruce then dropped out, though he had written only one chapter and edited nothing. For the Civil War and Reconstruction, either Ken Stampp or Vann Woodward could have produced authoritative text. Both refused. So Bruce's job, including his editorial responsibilities, fell to me as the youngest and therefore most vulnerable author. By 1961 I had completed my six chapters on the period 1901–32. By no means expert, I then turned to the coming of the Civil War and to the war's aftermath, for Bruce had managed to complete enough on the war itself. I also during 1961–62 worked closely with Ev Sims on other aspects of producing the textbook. We had bound copies ready for academic adoptions in 1963, and we had agreed on a title, *The National Experience*.

None of us really expected much from the textbook. We were wrong. By the year 2002 it had sold some two million copies. Harcourt pushed sales, but the success of the text owed much to the popularity in the 1960s and 1970s of political history. In those decades politics dominated the news, as the "imperial presidents" and their policies stirred the nation, as the civil rights movement gained momentum, as the war in Vietnam escalated, and as Nixon revised American foreign policy and threatened democratic government. Arthur Schlesinger, Jr., found Carter's a "failed presidency," but the office and the politics of its incumbents retained their power through the reign of Ronald Reagan.

No text matched ours for our beginning and ending chapters. Ed Morgan's sections on the colonial and federal periods encapsulated his deep learning and glowed from his simple eloquence. Similarly outstanding were Arthur Schlesinger's sections on the era of Franklin Roosevelt, about which he was the acknowledged master, and on the Kennedy administration, of which he was a significant member. What other text had an author in the White House? Those of us who wrote chapters that made up the filling in the sandwich were good cooks whose contributions were enhanced by incomparable wrapping. But we were all surprised in the spring of 1964 when we received our first, large royalty checks. We were then also committed to revisions every four or five years, with Arthur Schlesinger later deeding his section to me, and Willie Lee Rose and eventually William McFeely redoing the section Bruce Catton had begun.

The financial boon I would enjoy from sales of the textbook lay in the future in the winter of 1963 when I received the grant for which I had applied to the American Council of Learned Societies. I had not begun to plan my work on that grant when in April Cambridge University asked me to serve in 1963–64 as Pitt Professor of American History and Institutions. The invitation arrived late because Perry Miller, the great Harvard interpreter of Puritanism, had just canceled his agreement to take the position. He had a hunch, correctly as it developed, that he would not survive the year. Henry Commager, who had been on the ACLS grant committee, knew I had a leave. Always generous to me, he recommended me to the Cambridge committee that was looking for a substitute Pitt Professor.

Pamela and I decided instantly that we wanted to accept the invitation, and with it, a year in England. But Yale regulations forbade faculty members from teaching during a sabbatical. In addition, Cambridge was proposing a salary of several thousand dollars below my Yale salary, and we had no way to make up the difference. So I consulted Kingman, who as provost had the authority to rule on the matter. It was much more important for Yale, he said, to have me serve as Pitt Professor than it was for me to take the ACLS grant. Further, Yale would make up the difference in salary. Pamela and I rejoiced, hoping that Kingman's decision would have been the same had we not been friends.

During the late summer of 1963, just before we sailed for England, at a party for the Brewsters, I joined Kingman in the garden. I was sorry, I said, that he had not yet been named president. I was also sure that eventually he would be. Before Pamela and I left, I wanted him to know that he was entitled as a friend, not as a president, to ask me to do anything that would help his administration. "Is that a blank check?" Kingman asked. "Yes," I said. "Not a bank account but a blank check." Neither of us ever forgot that conversation. But it was far from my mind as Pamela, the children, and I sailed for Southampton. We were embarking on what proved to be our most memorable year as a family.

II

In King Arthur's Court

We received a royal welcome when we arrived at Cambridge. Peter Mathias, then a lecturer on English economic history there, had met me through Al Chandler some years earlier. (Peter later became a professor at Oxford and then the master of Downing College, Cambridge.) When he learned we were coming to Cambridge, he arranged for me to become a fellow in his college, Queens' College, of which Arthur Armitage was president. Queens' at that time was an old, small, relatively poor, absolutely beautiful college with a stunning fellows' garden across the River Cam from the main buildings. (The gardener's name was Twigg.) Peter and Arthur and their wives represented the warm, embracing spirit of the place. That spirit seemed palpable in the striking sixteenth-century lodge.

The University of Cambridge had purchased a residence for the Pitt Professor, which we rented for the odd amount of a guinea (one pound, one shilling) a day. Commodious and conveniently located, it was ten minutes by bicycle from Queens'. With a view of the river, my study looked out across a field where a horse grazed peacefully — except on the regular, daily occasions when an aggressive swan attacked him and he galloped frantically away, the swan in hot pursuit. The children attended the Perse Schools, to which they had mixed reactions, as they did also to the touring we arranged. We went to the great sites in London, to the theater in London, to fancy teas in nearby Trumpington (to which we traveled by bicycle), to the continent on holidays, to Wales for hiking.

Pamela had more freedom than she had enjoyed since our wedding. She developed an alert interest in English medieval art, particularly as that art was manifested in the churches of East Anglia, an area she thoroughly explored. Her skill in rubbing English memorial brasses triggered her explorations. She learned more as she audited the lectures delivered that year by Nicholas Pevsner, a Polish refugee from Hitler and the leading authority on English medieval art. That year in Cambridge provided the most intellectual stimulation of any in Pamela's life. Her enthusiasm for her new interest derived in part from our travels together, but it arose primarily from Pevsner's instructive course. As she later said, she "rushed to see the monuments on which he lectured." On returning to New Haven, she enrolled in the doctoral program in art history at Yale, which led to an exemplary professional career in medieval art history. Her experience in Cambridge gave significant scholarly momentum to her life and work.

I had ample time to write. My obligations to the university were light, just two lectures weekly on my usual subjects during the fall and winter terms, with no exams to set or grades to submit. The undergraduates who attended were prepared by their tutors and tested by the university in examinations given at the year's end. But I did keep office hours, during which now and then I provided an informal tutorial on American history to Judith Herrin, then in her second year, as assiduous and intelligent a student as I have ever known. She wrote the prize essay on American history the following year and went on to a doctorate and a career as a Byzantinist, with several years as a professor at Princeton.

In the spring I gave a series of six public lectures, which were open to all members of the university. Those I wrote as chapters in the book for which the ACLS had given me a grant, though with my salary continuing, I never accepted the money. (That book, *The Promise of America*, was published by Houghton, Mifflin in 1965.) I used most of my nonteaching time writing the six lectures, seeing the second Morgenthau volume through galley proof, and writing the third volume, for which I had taken with me a trunk full of notes.

I also enjoyed my routines as a fellow of Queens' College, the companionable lunches, occasional dinners at high table, conversation after dinner with port or claret, and most of all the fellows' meetings, which revealed the folkways of Cambridge college life. Friends and acquaintances of earlier years invited me to dine with them and their scholarly colleagues at colleges in which they were fellows. So it was that I first dined at Trinity, the most famous of the Cambridge colleges, with Peter Laslett, a historian I had met at conventions in the United States and a friend of Henry Commager. I dined more often at Peterhouse, where I knew the visiting Marshall Professor, the brilliant economic theorist and incidental humorist Robert Solow. Bob, Harvard '44, had taught at MIT while I did, but he remained there for his entire career, in time becoming a Nobel laureate and a star even in his peerless department. In the spring he gave a series of lectures about an imaginary economy that he manipulated with differential equations in order to demonstrate some principles he was introducing. Peter Mathias and I, attending together, admitted to each other that we understood little of what Bob said. Another celebrated Peterhouse fellow, Sir Denis Brogan, had spent a year teaching at MIT. Expert on American politics and culture, he wrote more incisively about things American than had any foreigner since Lord Bryce. Denis introduced me to the Master of Peterhouse, Herbert Butterfield, who taught me how to manage a college feast, normally a prolonged and festive dinner with nine or ten courses and as many wines. To prevent dyspepsia, so directed lean and careful Herbert, "One spoon of each course, one sip of each wine." Another frequent host, J. H. Plumb, an eminent historian of eighteenth-century England, published in the United States with Alfred A. Knopf, his admiring advocate. As successful a teacher as he was a scholar, he later recommended to Yale one of his gifted students, Linda Colley, who, with her talented husband, David Cannadine, became close friends of ours.

Predictably there were moments of unexpected misunderstanding. One evening at St. John's College I was introduced to the elderly Lord Tedder, the famous British air marshal of World War II. "Professor Blum," said my host, "was in the American navy during the war." "Really!" Teddy replied. "Did you know Ike?" I explained that I had served only as a junior officer in the Pacific theater. At Trinity, Lord and Lady Adrian, because of my professorship and his office as vice chancellor, gave a private dinner in our honor. Pamela and I reckoned we were the youngest by several decades of the guests at the table. I was seated at the right of Lady Adrian, a woman revered for her social work. She said she had been observing me at cocktails. "You don't know how to address my husband, do you?" she asked. "I call him Master," I said. "But I call him Adrian," she replied. Later, after the women returned to join the men, who had had their port separately, we got ready to depart. When I thanked Lord Adrian, I again addressed him as "Master." Moving on to thank Lady Adrian, I was greeted by her teasing glance and pointed comment: "I say, Yank, no guts!"

While in Cambridge we read the Paris *Herald-Tribune* daily for its American news, and our mail kept us abreast of news from Yale. I valued particularly the weekly letters from Ed Morgan, acting chairman of the history department for the year. Very early one Sunday morning in October, about 2:00 a.m. London time, Letty Pierson called from the Brewsters, where a great party was celebrating the announcement of Kingman's elevation to the Yale presidency.

When Kingman and Mary Louise came to London later that season, we had lunch with them in London at the Connaught. Kingman asked me what I considered the most outstanding aspects of Cambridge. I was most impressed, I replied, by the high quality of the college masters. Assisted as they were by bursars to attend to financial matters and head tutors to see to undergraduate academic schedules, the masters could continue with their own important work. At Corpus Christi Sir Frank Lee had been a senior civil servant, at Queens' Arthur Armitage sat occasionally on the Queen's Bench, at Kings Noel Annan, a Labor Party intellectual, carried on in the tradition of John Maynard Keynes, at Trinity Lord Adrian continued with his medicine, at Peterhouse Herbert Butterfield wrote history, at Christ Lord Todd was a distinguished chemist, at Gonville and Gaius Sir Neville Mott was an equally distinguished physicist (thus the ditty "Todd thinks he's God; Mott knows he's not"). The Yale college masters could not match those men.

Kingman mused about recruiting similar talents for Yale, about finding educational functions for the colleges, about the college system in general. He had been thinking about those matters before I answered his question, but I believe my remarks confirmed his decision to appoint as masters at Yale outstanding scholars like Elting E. Morison, John W. Hall, and Robert Triffin, author John Hersey, and musician Phyllis Curtin. It was characteristic of Kingman to interrogate his faculty about their experience and its possible significance for Yale. He did not want for ideas; but, a careful listener, he also assiduously collected thoughts from others. And he was born and trained an adversary. He would pick up an idea in conversation and then try it out on an unsuspecting friend, who would disagree. Then he would try out the disagreer's point of view in a third conversation. In that manner he honed his own thoughts. Our talk about the colleges probably represented only one stage in his deliberations.

Later that October of 1963 Arthur Schlesinger, Jr., wrote that President Kennedy wanted me to lecture in Germany the following May about Franklin D. Roosevelt's foreign policy. The Germans had never understood Roosevelt, Arthur held, and the president expected me to begin properly to inform them. I strongly suspected that Arthur was attributing his own views to his boss, but I could not say so politely. I wrote him to ask whether he was sure that the president really had me in mind. I seemed the wrong ambassador, I suggested, for I was writing about Henry Morgenthau, Jr., whom the Germans detested because of his plan to convert postwar Germany into a country "pastoral" in nature. And, like Morgenthau, so I reminded Arthur,

I was Jewish. Arthur kept me on the hook. He agreed to my requests to limit my itinerary to the Rhineland and to have Pamela accompany me, but he repeated his claim that the president wanted me to make the trip. So I said I would.

A few weeks later we set out to attend a dinner party for Dick Hofstadter, who was then visiting in England. As we started the car, our elder daughter came running out with the unbelievable news that President Kennedy had been shot. Minutes later, our host reported that he was dead. Though we went on with the party, it became a shocked discussion of the implications of the assassination. Dick, avoiding any request to appear on television to assess Kennedy's death, left for France the next day. The day after Jack Ruby shot Lee Harvey Oswald, BBC-TV called to ask me to appear that evening on a discussion program about the two murders. As an American, I mourned Kennedy and was saddened and embarrassed by a second, seemingly political shooting. I felt as if my country were a banana republic. So I tried to beg off, but the American embassy phoned to say I had to go.

At the studio I found awaiting me Lord Gladwyn, formerly ambassador to the United States and a friend of John F. Kennedy, and Max Beloff, an Oxford don. We sat in a row at a wooden table while a monitor displayed a French journalist who was to join the discussion from Paris. The program began at 11:00 p.m. with a question for all of us to answer in sequence: "How do you explain the assassinations?" Beloff spoke first. Though by reputation anti-American, he now took care to provide a calm answer that suggested that the Soviet Union had been in no way involved. Gladwyn agreed, adding that he saw no reason for alarm about American policy in the next weeks. I expressed confidence in President Johnson and in a continuity of Kennedy policies. Then I went on to point out that political assassinations in the American past had been the work of individuals, some of them crazed, but not of members of a political conspiracy, domestic or foreign. At once the Frenchman broke in. He was sure the assassinations had been planned by a communist conspiracy. Oswald, he argued, had been a Soviet agent and Ruby a Soviet hit man employed to keep Oswald silent about his masters. Lord Gladwyn joined me in a rather prolonged dispute with the journalist, to no clear end. Talk turned then to Lyndon Johnson, about whom I was asked many questions. I predicted, only partly accurately, that he would champion civil rights legislation and other reforms, but that he would give as little attention as possible to foreign affairs.

Kennedy's death threw a pall over our family, as it did to most Americans. We would like to have been home at the time, but our hosts were supportive. Pamela received letters of commiseration from parents of the children's schoolmates. Queens' College allowed me to postpone a Thanksgiving dinner we were planning there. After the BBC broadcast I was invited periodically during the next months to join other television and radio programs on matters American, with Max Beloff often also so engaged. In the wake of the assassinations I felt depressed about my country. Speaking about Kennedy to the local Elks in Cambridge, I broke up. I nearly did again during a talk to a Quaker group in London. John F. Kennedy had displayed such great promise as president that his violent and untimely death was an American tragedy.

Despite our sadness over the Kennedy assassination, we proceeded with our plans to spend Christmas in Italy with some friends from Yale — and afterward we all agreed that that Christmas in Rome was the best we ever had. We stayed in a suite in the YMCA, but we spent much of every day with Reuben and Betty Holden, on leave that year from Ben's duties as Secretary of Yale University. With their children and ours, we went as a group on excursions Betty had arranged to the ancient and medieval ruins of the city. Ben had procured seats only ten yards from the pope for his Christmas morning devotionals and the ensuing mass. On that bright, crisp morning, we walked back from the mass along the Tiber to the Holdens', where others from Yale awaited us for a wonderful Christmas dinner. A few days earlier we had been enjoying the Vatican museum when we ran into Myron and Sheila Gilmore, old friends from Harvard, and accepted their invitation for an evening Christmas dinner. It, too, was a delight, the culmination of a totally satisfying day. And the wonders continued, especially in Florence and Sienna.

With the coming of spring in April, with the ducklings newly on the Cam, Pamela and I resumed our travels by taking the younger children to France. We visited Mont Saint Michel and Chartres, my favorite sites in Europe, memorably introduced to me in 1940 by Henry Adams in his beautifully written history. In May, without the children, Pamela and I set out for my lectures in Germany on Franklin Roosevelt's foreign policy. In Frankfurt I spoke after dinner to a dozen Germans who were informed about American history but dubious about American assistance to Great Britain and the Soviet Union in the months before Pearl Harbor. The atmosphere was tense, in large part because of the Fritz Fischer controversy about which Hajo Holborn had warned me by mail. Fischer's recent biography of Bethmann Holweg, German chancellor in 1914, argued that the guilt for World War I, as the Treaty of Versailles had asserted, was indeed Germany's. The Germans, willing to admit guilt for World War II, remained convinced that their forebears were not the only ones guilty for World War I. They attacked Fischer, but in my opinion they did not refute his new evidence. Though I carefully avoided the controversy, I could not escape the defensive mood it had generated among German academicians. The discussion at Frankfurt, polite but not amicable, forebode trouble to come. It came at Cologne the next day, and again at Heidelberg, a beautiful university city.

Cologne set the pattern. The German audience, again polite, took issue with my support of Roosevelt's antagonistic policies toward Nazi Germany. (An abbreviated version of my remarks can be found on pages 152–61 of my book *The Promise of America*.) Their mood imbued their response. I pretended to know no German, which gave me a chance to think while the interpreter translated their questions, which I answered in English. Why, they inquired, had we made an alliance with the Soviet Union? I replied indirectly, observing that Germany had done so first. But why, they insisted. I reminded them that Churchill, a fervent anticommunist, had said in the House of Commons that he would make league with the devil if that would help to defeat the Nazis. "Next time," said one of my German interrogators, "we have strong, not weak, allies." The questions continued. Why did the United States support China? Because Roosevelt opposed Japanese aggression, I said. But why not support the stronger party? I was asked. I suggested they had learned nothing from their defeat in World War II. Silence. Then the questions took another track. One German historian, the offspring of a noted family of historians, asked, "Why did you bomb our cities?" Trying not to offend, I said, "Sherman was right. War is hell." "But *our* cities?" he persisted. "When were you last in Coventry?" I replied. *"But our cities!"* "Shall we discuss war crimes?" I retorted. The questioning went on for a little longer, to no satisfactory resolution. The same kind of reception met us at Heidelberg and Freiberg. I have not been back to Germany. I believe that I was correct in assuming that a Jewish American historian, writing about Henry Morgenthau, Jr., and lecturing about Franklin D. Roosevelt, would not be entirely welcome in the Rhineland, not in 1964, not ever in the twentieth century.

Traveling without Pamela, I next lectured at Queen's University in Belfast. Northern Ireland was peaceful in 1964, the countryside was charming, and my host, Michael Roberts, an accomplished historian who had devoted his career to studying Charles XII of Sweden, saw to my every need. He even drew me a bath every morning — a cold bath, which he followed by offering me a shot of Irish whiskey before breakfast, his preferred remedy for chills. My lectures there focused on aspects of the New Deal, about which I had a neutral audience.

In late June Pamela accompanied me to the European American Studies meeting in Oslo, where Vann and Glenn Woodward met us. I had known Vann since 1945 in the navy, but Pamela had barely met the Woodwards until our time in Norway, which proved the start of a valued friendship. The Nazi invasion and occupation still a recent memory, the Norwegians hated the Germans. On midsummer night the delegates to the American Studies meeting joined our hosts on a boat that took us into the fjords near Oslo where resistance fighters had killed Germans, and where each German death was now marked by a bonfire. After our return to Britain, and a week in Wales during which the whole family climbed hills in the Snowdon region, our year abroad was nearing its end.

The professional discourse Vann and I had begun in Oslo continued for years back in New Haven. We had both read papers at the Oslo meeting, Vann's on the burgeoning civil rights movement, mine on twentieth-century American foreign policy, with an emphasis on the years since 1945. My paper had evoked hot dissent from the Europeans at the conference, who took the same position that was spreading through the New Left in the United States. As they saw it, not Soviet expansionism, but American imperialism brought on the Cold War. Further, they attributed American imperialism, early and late, to corporate influences, to "corporatism" (their preferred word). I disagreed about corporatism, and I still do. But Vann, a loyal disciple of Charles Beard in his view of nineteenth-century imperialism, had considerable sympathy for my critics at Oslo. Indeed there were many historical issues about which Vann and I disagreed. Vann loved controversy. His deep friendship with Dick Hofstadter floated on their profound disagreements about Populism.

My differences with Vann were more marginal, but he cherished them for the stage they provided for argument. Almost all of our many lunches together were punctuated by friendly debates about historical causation, with Vann ordinarily taking Beardian positions. Like Beard, Vann rejected socialism and communism, but he had a deep distrust of American business leaders and their political influence. He was, as he said, a Populist at heart. I was not. We both considered ourselves latter-day New Dealers, but I found the origins of my liberalism in the Progressive movement, not in Populism. Vann was schooled by Henry Demarest Lloyd and Tom Watson; I went to Herbert Croly and Walter Lippmann. In short, I was basically more conservative than Vann, more inclined to attribute causation to ideas and sentiments, less inclined to be satisfied with economic explanations, though I never excluded them. So in analyzing foreign policy I attributed greater importance than did Vann to the influence in the 1890s of Admiral Alfred

Thayer Mahan and in the Cold War period to George Kennan's doctrine of containment and its elaborations by Walter Lippmann.

Further, Vann was proudly Southern in his approach to history, as I was not. He referred often in conversation, as in his writing, to the importance of the experience of defeat, which no Yankee had had. By nature a pessimist, he resisted my instinctive optimism. By nature a pragmatist, I resisted his absolutism about the causes he nurtured. He believed fervently in the rights of individuals; I believed those rights had at times to yield to the needs of community. But nurtured by argument, our friendship grew over the years. We enjoyed each other's company, we were both democrats with a small and a capital D, and neither of us was comfortable with either the rigid conservatism of Barry Goldwater or the tactics and doctrines of the New Left, still in its strident infancy in 1964.

But in 1964 I failed to realize how polarized American culture was becoming. My sojourn in England contributed to that failure. As Vann pointed out, so did the experience of almost every professor visiting abroad, for the strong antipathy to the United States of some of the English and Europeans provoked a defensive response. That defensiveness, he argued, influenced my book *The Promise of America*, which he first read in manuscript. "You're suggesting everything is all right," Vann complained, "but everything's all wrong." At the time I disagreed, partly because I was focusing on some of the noblest American ventures and ideals, including lend-lease and the Four Freedoms. But I was wrong. The book should have been more openly critical of American politics and culture than it was. It sold well, especially in its Penguin paperback edition, but the scholarly reviews tended to be critical. William Ward noted my praise for energy, which he compared to the ideas of Herbert Croly; but he observed that energy could flow to unworthy causes. Eric Goldman thought I overrated the idealism of the middle class. By 1968 I had come to consider my optimism of 1964 embarrassingly misplaced. Still, the book had some merit. It spoke intelligently about the symbols of American middle-class striving, about the nature of the middle class itself, and about the ingredients — both ideational and concrete, that imbued American foreign policy. Yet, as Vann tried gently to warn me, it was not my most trenchant effort.

Before we went to Oslo I had received a portentous letter from Kingman. He asked me to become chairman of the history department on my return. He was not, he continued, "cashing his blank check." Rather, he had polled the members of the department and they had expressed their belief that it was my turn to serve. I knew I had no choice but to agree, but I bargained before I surrendered. Relations between the tenured and the nontenured members of the department, I wrote Kingman, needed improvement. To that end, I asked for a new budgetary item to allow Pamela and me to give a series of dinner parties, one every few weeks, at each of which we would mix senior and junior colleagues. Kingman provided enough funds for assistance in serving dinner and cleaning up afterwards, with the food and drink our contribution. Neither Pamela nor I fully understood how much those dinners would weigh on our schedules, or how insistent my duties as chairman would be in Brewster's newly energized Yale. Neither of us predicted how contentious the country and the university would become in the late 1960s, or how deeply I would find myself embroiled in administration. The last, sweet weeks in Cambridge sped by, soon only a treasured memory.

12

Chairman

The first person I encountered after returning to New Haven was William Sloane Coffin, Jr., Yale's chaplain, who had made a significant contribution to the movement for civil rights. He had led dozens of Yale students on Freedom Rides and in other demonstrations. I applauded his purpose, as I did his candid and stirring ministry to Yale students, but he considered me stodgy and I sometimes found his methods questionable. That morning he gave me a bear hug and said: "John, I'm looking for a cause." He found one within the week—the agitation against the war in Vietnam. I signed a petition against American involvement in Vietnam at about the same time. But as ever I wanted to work within the system, within the political process, while Bill believed, as did the radical student movement, that the system was corrupt, that the influence of corporations in American politics and government was widespread. He and I remained far apart in our separate views of appropriate tactics for effecting change, and far apart in our responses to other campus causes embraced by undergraduates in the next six years. During that time there would be few bear hugs. Instead the "student revolution," to which Bill contributed, characterized and complicated the life of the university.

For the pastor of a university community, Bill Coffin had curiously little patience with serious discussion of ideas. He tended to dismiss academic discourse as "intellectual ping-pong." A committed activist, he organized various forms of civil disobedience in an attempt to advance the movement for civil rights. His temperament and convictions accorded with those of Martin Luther King, Jr. Segregation struck him as primarily immoral, contrary to the teachings of Jesus. It struck me as primarily illegal, contrary to the Fourteenth Amendment of the Constitution. My temperament and convictions accorded with those of Thurgood Marshall of the NAACP, who would soon be appointed to the U.S. Supreme Court. Like Marshall, I preferred litigation to confrontation. Like Marshall, I considered it expensive to have to bail out those whose protests against segregation had predictably landed them in jail.

Similarly, in 1964 and thereafter, Bill viewed the American war in Vietnam as immoral, whereas I viewed it, in a phrase of General Omar Bradley, as "the wrong war against the wrong enemy in the wrong place." By the end of the 1960s, Bill had begun to advise young men who opposed the war and the draft to burn their draft cards. I could not bring myself deliberately to break the law or to advise others to do so. Instead I suggested that students opposed to the war enlist in the presidential campaigns successively of Eugene McCarthy, Bobby Kennedy, and later George McGovern. Bill sided with the campus radicals, I with the campus liberals, a group the radicals wrote off as ineffective.

At Yale, as at other college campuses, the radicals received much more attention from the media than did the liberals, but at Yale the liberals had a sympathetic president and in the end enjoyed crucial student support. No one could have predicted that outcome in 1965 when radical students first made the war their central issue. For the balance of the decade, in one episode after another student agitation challenged university policy. But until the spring of 1969 the normal course of the educational enterprise at Yale continued to hold the attention of faculty and students alike. Departments still needed budgets and new recruits. Junior faculty members still expected promotions. Department chairmen, of whom I was one, had a full agenda of responsibilities.

My chief concern in 1964 as my chairmanship began lay with the Yale budget, which could not support all the new ventures that I, other department chairmen, and particularly President Kingman Brewster hoped to launch. Ambitious for Yale, Kingman intended to make both its faculty and its student body the best in the world. He wisely appointed a provost, Charles Taylor, who shared his purpose but pursued it with prudence. While Kingman stomped on the accelerator, Charlie kept his foot on the brake. Like other chairmen, I was caught between Kingman's expansive temperament and Charlie's budgetary caution. When I submitted my first departmental budget, which called for increased funding to pay for two of several possible and desirable new appointments, Charles summoned me to his office. "What do you mean," he asked, "sending me a Harry Truman budget?" I replied, "I'm a Harry Truman Democrat." "Not at Yale, you're not," Charlie said, and not at Yale did I ever again submit a budget one dollar above his guidelines. I maneuvered instead between Coffin on my political left and Taylor on my budgetary right, with annual appeals to Kingman for more money. (Charlie prevailed, so much so that he soon removed the funds Kingman had granted for dinners to bring junior and senior colleagues together. That economy left us with the dinners to give but without hired help.)

On assuming the chairmanship, I was determined to keep up my teaching and scholarship as if I were still only a professor. It was a punishing determination, for I had far too much to do, but my professional satisfaction still derived from teaching and writing, so I felt it essential to make time for them. My first graduate seminar after our return from England included several of the ablest doctoral candidates I ever taught, of whom the most outstanding was David M. Kennedy, later the author of three prize-winning books, most notably his *Freedom from Fear*, deservedly a Pulitzer Prize winner. David in our seminar pursued a topic I could not have handled myself, a study of Italian-Americans' response to the outbreak of World War II. He could read Italian-language newspapers, as I could not, though I was at the time considering a book about the home front during the war. For his dissertation David wrote a biography of Margaret Sanger. As with his seminar paper, I for the most part just stood aside and applauded his work.

While chairman I also sustained a full publishing agenda. During 1965 *The Promise of America* came out and so did *From the Morgenthau Diaries: Years of Urgency*. The latter showed Morgenthau at his best, acting directly as Roosevelt's agent in organizing aid to England between the outbreak of war in Europe in 1939 and the enactment of lend-lease in the spring of 1941. Indeed in 1940 the Treasury found a legal way to send surplus American war materials to the British and in 1941 played a central role in drafting the lend-lease bill. Concurrently Morgenthau joined Harold Ickes and Henry Stimson as the leading interventionists in the president's cabinet. The *New York Times* kept the Morgenthau book on its recommended list for several weeks. In *The New Republic* Andrew Kopkind wrote perceptively, "The Secretary . . . comes off as a somewhat stiff, basically humanitarian, thoroughly humorless and half-believed prophet of gloom, not doom. Despite his murky manner, he had a greatness of spirit." Morgenthau liked that review.

I was still chairman when Houghton, Mifflin published *From the Morgenthau Diaries: Years of War* in 1967. It was the most controversial of the three Morgenthau volumes. On the plus side, R. H. Miller in *America* described the book as "first-rate history" and called the trilogy "well-deserving of the sobriquet 'indispensable' for those who want to know what F.D.R. and the

New Deal were really all about." But Louis Hacker, a Columbia historian and former communist who was a generation older than I, attacked the book for being too soft on Harry Dexter White and other communists in the wartime Treasury Department. Yet he offered no proof that any one of them had significantly influenced policy. Further, I had discovered no hard evidence to indicate that White was ever a member of the Communist Party, though later revelations did identify him as an occasional Soviet spy. To be sure, White made waves at the Bretton Woods Conference, where the International Monetary Fund was created as he had planned it, but the IMF was the conservative, capitalistic alternative to a more innovative proposal put forward by John Maynard Keynes. It offered no advantage to the Soviet Union.

More important, neither Hacker nor any other reviewer seemed to me to give Morgenthau the credit he deserved for persuading Roosevelt to create the War Refugee Board, the late but only effective initiative the President took to rescue European Jews from the Holocaust. In describing Morgenthau's efforts in behalf of the Jews, I was unaware of the blatant anti-Semitism of Breckenridge Long, the assistant secretary of state, who kept a diary not available for research until after I had published my work. But I said enough about Long to reveal his obduracy in the face of Morgenthau's continual attempts to save as many potential victims of the Nazis as possible. In that objective, as in his earlier support for the British and in his wartime advocacy of social and economic reform, Morgenthau earned accolades that historians have too rarely given him. He was a brave and honorable man, and an effective public servant.

With the publication in 1972 of *Roosevelt and Morgenthau,* a revision and condensation of the three earlier volumes, I hoped that Morgenthau's significance as a responsible cabinet officer in a trying period became more obvious. It was not reviewed. John Kenneth Galbraith suggested that I should have published only the condensation instead of the other books. That course was never a possibility, for Henry Morgenthau, Jr., was impatient to have his career fully described. In doing so, I learned much about the problems he confronted and therefore about the New Deal and World War II, and I was inspired to further work on the war. Indeed by 1967, when I left the chairmanship, I had become as involved in the history of that war as once I had been involved in the history of progressivism.

During my term as chairman, then, teaching and writing absorbed almost as much of my time as ever, and so did my responsibilities outside of Yale, as a trustee of the Hotchkiss School. The head of that school, A. William Olsen, Jr., Yale '43, asked me to join the board after he solicited and adopted my recommendation to offer to selected, inner-city, black junior high school boys a summer of study at Hotchkiss. The Greater Opportunity (GO) program went forward under excellent leadership, but Bill Olsen persuaded me that I should observe its progress for several years. Bill struck me as the ablest headmaster I had ever known. He understood boys, recruited an able faculty, and got along famously with the alumni. When his only Greek master went on leave one year, he asked me to suggest a substitute. I recommended Frank Benton, my Andover Latin instructor, who had just retired for the second time after five years at Groton. Frank took the Hotchkiss position and won Bill's heart with his private analysis at the year's end of the school's strengths and weaknesses.

The Hotchkiss board during my tenure included, among others, Henry Ford II; Joe Cullman of Philip Morris; John Murchison, who held with his brother Clint joint ownership of the Dallas Cowboys and of oceans of oil; Dick Watson of IBM; a member of the Du Pont family; and the general counsel of General Electric. At the end of the 1964–65 school year, the trustees passed the hat in order to make up a small deficit. Though they had done so regularly, I objected. "Don't worry," Watson said, "we'll take care of it without you." That was exactly the problem, I said: the school needed an endowment sufficient to support itself. Instituting a fund drive would permit each board member to contribute a substantial sum. That had been the objective of a minority of trustees for some time, but as the new kid on the block I tipped the balance, and we persuaded my wealthy colleagues that a major fund drive should begin as soon as possible. By the time I left the board in 1971, I was convinced that Hotchkiss provided a first-rate academic experience and believed that the school was enriched when Bill Olsen led the board to adopt coeducation. The school, renowned for its excellent teaching, made mathematics, languages, and the basic sciences the core of its curriculum, just as Andover had in my time there, and just as I thought appropriate for secondary education.

But for three years my responsibilities as chairman of the Yale History Department dominated my academic life. At the start I addressed my concern that communication within the department should be freer and fuller than it had been. To that end, and with the support of my tenured colleagues, I appointed an advisory committee of three, of whom the most senior was Howard R. Lamar. An experienced hand who had been acting chairman and was now director of graduate studies, Howard brought his balanced judgment, reasonable temperament, and personal devotion to Yale to the department's affairs. Those qualities later also characterized his terms as department chairman, dean of Yale College, and briefly president of the university. There was no major issue about which I failed to consult the advisory group. But privately I relied as much, as always, on the guidance of Ed Morgan, who knew me better than did any other historian at Yale.

I left decisions on the departmental major to Henry A. Turner, Jr., then director of undergraduate studies. With the assistance of Howard Lamar, who had previously held the same position, Henry revised the requirements. Like a majority of our colleagues, he had concluded that the departmental examination demanded of all majors tested nothing significant other than the memory of those taking it. With nearly unanimous consent, he proposed to abolish the exam and substitute a required essay to be written during the senior year. Previously only candidates for honors had submitted senior essays. Now two semesters of seminars for majors during the junior year were to help students prepare for undertaking a research essay as seniors, with a faculty member directing the essay. Over the years the essays varied widely in quality, as did the abilities of the students submitting them. Each year a few were worthy of publication, while a few others revealed the laxity of their authors. But for the rest of the century the major as Turner and Lamar had structured it remained unchanged.

Departmental deliberations focused more often on appointments and promotions. Because George Pierson while chairman had brought to Yale so many historians trained or teaching at other institutions, I was eager to promote junior colleagues to tenured positions whenever possible. Departmental morale demanded it. But was tenure — the granting of assured employment for life to its senior professors — necessary? Yes, for two commanding reasons. First and more important, tenure protected the faculty's freedom of belief and expression, which otherwise would be susceptible to threats from alumni or administrators. Second, since all major universities offered tenure to their qualified faculty, Yale could not compete without also doing so.

Because tenure involved a sizable and continuing commitment, we required for promotions to tenure evidence of dedicated and effective teaching, as well as certain scholarly credentials. At that time, following the standards Pierson had established, as prerequisites for tenure we required European and American historians to have published at least two books, favorably reviewed. Howard Lamar had met that standard, and so had Henry Turner in German history, Robin Winks in British imperial history, and Gaddis Smith in the history of American foreign policy. By far the ablest candidate we promoted was Jonathan Spence in modern Chinese history. He had learned Mandarin in record time and proceeded forthwith to write his dissertation, which was published by Yale University Press. When Mary Wright became ill, I asked Jonathan to take over her courses. He did so brilliantly. Arthur Wright, Ed Morgan, and I agreed that we should advance Jonathan as quickly as possible so that no other institution would attract him. Scholars in fields requiring difficult languages, Arthur argued, needed more time for publication than did American and European historians. One good book, he proposed, should be enough.

The tenured professors agreed, and Jonathan went on to write voluminously and incisively, indeed without peer in his field. But the adoption in later years of reduced standards for the promotion to tenure of European and American historians let down barriers that should have been maintained. One distinguished colleague insisted that a former student of his, then an assistant professor, should receive tenure on the basis of a single book that rested on research in economic statistics. The resulting appointment proved to be a mistake, as did several others based on permissive criteria. George Pierson had lifted the quality of the department. His prescription for doing so should have continued to prevail. When it did not, the quality of the department's promotions began to decline.

Student agitation on behalf of popular junior faculty members foreshadowed that decline. The issue was joined in 1965 when the philosophy department failed to promote one of its members, a teacher with a substantial undergraduate following. Beneath the surface of the protest lay the influence of Chaplain Coffin and of a professor of English, both friends of the young philosopher. Indeed almost always student protest reflected in part the leadership of one or more faculty members. In this instance the department's decision prevailed. But the agitation persuaded Kingman to appoint a committee to review Yale's qualifications for tenure, and the review concluded that departments should give more weight to teaching than they had been doing. That conclusion was in error. Departments had always taken teaching into account. Indeed at Yale no department to my knowledge had ever recommended tenure for a reputedly bad teacher. Further, students were notoriously poor judges of teaching. When polled about their teachers, they almost invariably responded favorably. In contrast, published scholarship was judged by other scholars, at Yale and elsewhere. Given sufficient evidence, the judgment of scholars normally proved sound. The review of qualifications for tenure did at least have the desirable effect of formalizing and strengthening the procedures departments had to follow.

George Pierson's standards figured strongly in the department's recruiting professors from other universities. So in looking for a junior medievalist, a search to which the advisory committee and I gave priority, we took into account both the department's needs and the candidates' credentials.

We sought a young scholar whose learning and research covered both England and western Europe. After some months we found a candidate, who was teaching at an excellent small college. But we offered him a salary that proved to be less than he was receiving. To improve the offer, I asked the provost to raise the proposed salary by $2,000. He refused. "Then you are telling me," I said, "to find the second best young medievalist." He was annoyed but relentless. Consequently we offered the position to a less versatile and incisive young man whose scholarship proved negligible and whose teaching became dazzling but irresponsible. His salary for six years wasted our resources, a calculation that neither the provost nor I had made when my preferred candidate seemed too expensive.

Budgetary restrictions thus limited the department's opportunities. But in one case Kingman Brewster overcame that obstacle by persuading a donor to move the professorship he was endowing from engineering to history, specifically Russian history, in which the department was weak. There then began a frustrating search. We needed a historian of nineteenth- or twentieth-century Russia to build up our inadequate Russian Studies program. But the troubles of that program dissuaded first-rate Russian historians from coming to Yale. The position was thrice offered with no takers. The donor withdrew his professorship, which reverted to engineering. That outcome dismayed Kingman as much as it did me.

Nevertheless we succeeded in hiring some commanding historians. Jointly with classics, we identified Ramsey MacMullen as the leading historian of the Roman Empire, and he accepted our invitation to join the department. By the mid-1970s he had become the most distinguished scholar in his field in the entire world. I also tried to persuade Peter Gay to join us. Renowned for his scholarship on the Enlightenment, he was about to embark on his celebrated study of Freud and middle-class culture in the western world. Reluctant to leave Columbia in its troubled time, he asked us to invite him again later. When Howard Lamar, then chairman, did so the next year, Peter came to Yale. The appointment that gave me the most personal pleasure originated with Kingman. He invited Elting Morison to become the master of Timothy Dwight College, one of Yale's residential colleges. That position belonged on the budget for the residential colleges. But Elting would not leave MIT without an assurance of tenure, which was possible only through an academic appointment. With Kingman's approval, I invented a new line item on our budget, a professorship of American history without salary. Then I won a unanimous vote of consent from my colleagues, and Elting agreed to join us. While at Yale he managed several undergraduate programs and, as a college master with his wife, played an important role during the troubles on campus between 1965 and 1971, when he returned to MIT. His presence at Yale meant a great deal to me.

We also attracted some promising junior scholars, among them Michael Holt, who became the foremost historian of the American Whig Party. By 1967 I had come to hope that Michael might eventually succeed Vann Woodward when Woodward retired, but when the time arrived my colleagues turned to a social rather than a political historian. Most of the junior faculty in American history developed rewarding careers. Several others, political radicals, consumed much of my time and concern. Two of them allowed their muse to recommend to them outrageous behavior in lectures for the introductory course in American history. One of the two accepted a desirable offer from a distinguished university. The other agitated for tenure. When it was not forthcoming, he threatened to resign to accept a professorship at a less than outstanding campus. We did not promote him and he left.

Yale's most controversial radical then was Staughton Lynd, whom Ed Morgan had hired in 1964. The son of the authors of *Middletown*, the celebrated and trenchant sociological analysis of Muncie, Indiana, in the 1920s, Lynd grew up in a dissident tradition. He honored that legacy in his leadership, with Tom Haydn and others, of Students for a Democratic Society (SDS), an organization that attracted radicals on every campus. By 1965 SDS had made the war in Vietnam the major target of its organized protests. Supported at Yale by Bill Coffin, Lynd was the most stirring speaker on the antiwar circuit. I, too, opposed the war, but I had no sympathy for the radicals' rhetoric or methods. Still, Lynd commanded respect. His students praised his seminars, and his study of the American Revolution in New York State had won Ed's endorsement. About 1965, when Lynd told me he was looking for a lawyer, I sent him to Lou Pollak, then dean of the law school, who in turn recommended a New Haven attorney. Lynd would not have come to me, and I would not have involved Lou, had we not then trusted each other. Lynd later assumed that his visit to Hanoi during the 1965 Christmas bombing of that city antagonized me. He was wrong. I considered his trip foolish and exhibitionistic, but within the boundaries of peaceful protest. It was months later that I learned that Lynd scheduled his two seminars and his individual meetings with students on two successive days, leaving him free to travel for speeches or demonstrations the rest of the week. In my view, that arrangement shortchanged Yale. I expected the history faculty to be available to students on most weekdays. But I had no opportunity to discuss the matter with Lynd before a more exigent issue arose.

Early in 1967 Lynd gave one of his rousing antiwar lectures in Ottawa,

Canada. His peroration included an angry attack on the Unites States government. Distressed by that speech, the U.S. ambassador to Canada, a Yale alumnus, sent Kingman Brewster the text as it was reported in a local newspaper. Kingman asked Ed Morgan and me to meet him privately. His assistant, Howard Weaver, was also present at the meeting. Kingman described the episode to us and asked us how we thought he should proceed. "Well," I said, "you have to remember that Staughton is paranoid." Kingman pounced. "You're no psychoanalyst," he said, "and you've no right to use that word." Ed suggested that in a nonclinical sense I was probably correct, but Kingman did not retreat. Instead he told me to ask Lynd to edit the reported version of his speech so that it would accurately represent what he had said. To that end, I asked Lynd to my office, where he read the text and made some small alterations. (He may later have added further small changes.) I vividly recall his irritation at what he considered censorship, though I had threatened no penalty for his remarks, and no Yale officer had asked to see the text of his remarks before they were made. Lynd allowed that the text as reported was essentially correct.

The following day Kingman asked Lynd to see him. Again Howard Weaver was present. Before Kingman could properly examine the subject of the Ottawa speech, Staughton said, "First of all, Kingman, you've got to remember that I'm paranoid." Brewster and Weaver, their session with Ed Morgan and me fresh in their memories, exploded with laughter. During the rest of the meeting they learned no more than I had.

Meanwhile a wholly separate issue had arisen. Charles Taylor had decided to ask all department chairmen to submit detailed projections of their budgets for the next five years. After consultation with the advisory committee and a meeting with the tenured professors, I submitted a recommendation to the provost. We had decided that the department's urgent needs were for tenured positions in modern European history, Latin American history, ancient Greek history, and modern Russian history. Since American history was strong, the department foresaw at most one new tenured position in that field. Consequently even our wish list boded ill for the junior historians in the American field. Similar situations characterized the economics and philosophy departments. At lunch together, the chairmen of those departments and I discussed ways in which to transmit the bad news to affected assistant professors. The wise chairman of economics planned to have a meeting of all junior faculty at which he intended to explain the budgetary restrictions. I should have done exactly that, as I later realized, but instead I hoped to soften the blow by talking individually to each young Americanist. One was

Lynd, who apparently believed that the department's budgetary projections and priorities were designed specifically to block his promotion. As a colleague suggested at the time, it took a vaulting ego to reach that conclusion.

Depressed by the news I conveyed, several assistant professors in the American field began, with my support, to search for appointments elsewhere. Lynd requested permission for a one-year leave to teach at Roosevelt University in Chicago. After consulting Kingman, I approved the request but warned Lynd that a decision about his possible promotion was due that year, and the chances of a favorable outcome would be reduced to miniscule if he were absent and unobservable. Interpreting that warning as politically inspired, he published an article to that effect. I would not dignify his charge by answering it, but Ed Morgan and Vann Woodward did. I was on leave the next year when the department decided against promoting Lynd, who had gone to Chicago.

As Jack Hexter, my colleague in Renaissance history remarked, I had erred by standing between a martyr and his way to the cross. Lynd's supporters rallied to his side. Bill Coffin started one day to lecture me about how to run a department, but I told him he knew nothing about the subject and asked him to leave my office. Some of the graduate students in history believed I should have consulted them about Lynd. The thought of doing so never entered my mind, but they presumed I was about to involve them when I called an evening meeting of all graduate students. Many of them were surprised to discover that I had brought them together for the sole purpose of warning them that the theft of books from the Yale Cooperative Store was illegal and, if discovered, as in one case just terminated, would be punished by instant dismissal.

The next year a group of graduate students looked into the whole Lynd saga. They found me not guilty of any harassment. But they also concluded that the decision to deny Lynd tenure had no basis in budgetary stringency. In that they were correct, for just after I left the chairmanship, Yale subjected the budget to a new calculus. In keeping with a recommendation of the Ford Foundation, Kingman and the Yale Corporation agreed to spend annually a portion of the endowment's unrealized capital gains. That risky adventure in academic finance eased the budgets of all departments. Indeed the new calculations gave Howard Lamar scope for a series of grand appointments from outside Yale, including, among others, Peter Gay, Charles Boxer, Leonard Thompson, David Brion Davis, and Robert R. Palmer. Given the chance, Howard proved to be a builder at least as successful as George Pierson. Before Howard departed as chairman, the Yale history department had become arguably the most distinguished in the world. And it had the largest number of majors at Yale, evidence of the compatibility between teaching and scholarship.

Questions relating to appointments and promotions consumed a large portion of my time as chairman, but they shrank in comparison to the poignant personal problems of some of the department's members. One, an émigré, suffered a nervous collapse, two others took leaves to enter institutions combating alcoholism, and Hajo Holborn, our most eminent colleague in European history, developed a circulatory disease that soon led to his death. Here, as chairman I had to play a pastoral role. Indeed I found that role the toughest part of the job, though my colleagues' personal problems were not often as sad or severe as Hajo's. As Ed Morgan had told me, Fridays were easy, for our colleagues, eager to begin their weekend, rarely asked for Friday appointments with the chairman. But Mondays were hell, for an itch on Friday had become a rash by Monday, and seemingly dozens of problems demanded instant attention, not least the anguish of those who constantly felt underappreciated, a disease not easily cured. As a pastor, I'm sure I had grave limitations, but not for want of trying.

The chairmanship of a department as large as history made the incumbent quite visible to Yale officers, who appointed the university's many committees. Those committees became as irksome as departmental demands. At one time I was on fourteen, most of them trivial but all of them time-consuming. The Yale College Executive Committee, indisputably important, considered penalties for academic and parietal failings of undergraduates. I served on it for years with mixed reactions. While Dean Richard Carroll was in charge, the committee made disciplined and sensible decisions. It wandered off track after losing his guiding hand. Most important was the Yale College Steering Committee, an advisory body for Dean Georges May and his successors. Georges brought to his office his exquisite sense of situation, his wit as a presiding presence, his fairness, and his wisdom about academic affairs and all other things human. He was a major figure at Yale, a significant supporter of Kingman, and an admired personal friend. In general, however, my responsibilities as committee member palled, as did my job as chairman. Three years of administrative tasks confirmed my belief that I was not cut out to be an academic dean or provost or president. I yearned to resume life primarily as a teacher and scholar.

The provost allowed me to take a week off in the winter of 1967 in order to accept an invitation to give that year's Commonwealth lectures at University College, London. One of the lectures was to take place at the annual meeting of the British American Studies Association. For that occasion I used an essay I had written for a book Vann Woodward was editing on the comparative approach to American history. Herbert Nicholas of Oxford, a good friend, presented an informed and incisive critique of my remarks, a critique so significant that it fundamentally altered my thinking about my plans for a book on the American home front during World War II. That alone would have made the trip worthwhile, but Pamela and I received the additional bonus of several evenings of London theater, visits to London's magnificent museums, and dinners at London's incomparable seafood restaurants.

Kingman eased my transition out of the chairmanship by recommending me for a fellowship from the National Endowment for the Humanities, which I received. (In later years individuals applied directly for NEH grants, but in 1967 institutions took the initiative.) My project called for archival research during my fellowship year on American politics and culture during World War II. I had completed my work at the Franklin D. Roosevelt Library and begun my labors at the National Archives and in newspapers and periodicals by the spring of 1968. I had also become involved in national politics.

For several years Yale undergraduates had been soliciting my advice about the proper response to conscription for service in the Vietnam War. I could not in conscience suggest that they burn their draft cards or otherwise break the law. Neither could I recommend application for status as a conscientious objector unless the student had a plausible record of principled opposition to the war. Usually therefore I suggested enrolling in the National Guard. The students knew that I considered American involvement in the war a tragic mistake. The escalations in 1964 and 1965, contrary to the president's promise, had made American soldiers substitutes for the South Vietnamese.

As I saw it, we had no national interest in South Vietnam, an American client state with an arbitrary border. The war was in fact a civil war. Moreover, the government we were supporting was corrupt, ineffective, and authoritarian. There was no longer a Sino-Soviet bloc plotting to take over Southeast Asia, if there ever had been. Indeed the Soviet Union and China were competing for dominance in Vietnam, and we should have let them battle it out. Instead we sacrificed thousands of American soldiers, we bombed North Vietnam, and we burned the forests of the entire country. I bitterly opposed the war, but I also believed that opposition should flow through available political channels. I was resolved to work through those channels to unseat President Lyndon B. Johnson in the Democratic primary. Success in that endeavor seemed unlikely, but the effort would at least set an example for my students, an example that would contrast with the demonstrations of the SDS on other campuses, where agitators of the New Left had trashed libraries or seized buildings and destroyed academic records.

I had come to my decision in stages. In the summer of 1966 Bill Moyers, President Johnson's assistant, asked me to write an introduction to a book of essays about Johnson's domestic achievements and their place in the history of American reform movements. Vann Woodward had already agreed to contribute an essay about Johnson's support for legislation on civil rights and voting rights. I was willing to write the introduction, I replied, but only if the president knew that I openly opposed his policy on Vietnam. Moyers reported the next day that Johnson did not "give a damn" about what I or anyone else thought about Vietnam. Before I finished the essay, Moyers had resigned. That resignation persuaded me of the difficulty of convincing Johnson to negotiate an end to American involvement.

In the spring of 1967 the White House called again. This time it was Douglass Cater, formerly an editor of a liberal, anticommunist magazine called *The Reporter,* now an assistant to Johnson. The president had to see me at once, he said, about a confidential matter. Would I please take the next Eastern Airlines shuttle from LaGuardia to the National Airport in Washington? I did, and Doug met me in a White House limo and drove me to his home in Virginia. When we arrived, he refused to explain what the president wanted until the next morning, but he and his wife, Libby, served me a delicious lobster dinner.

On the way to the White House early the next day, Doug finally admitted that the confidential mission to which he had summoned me was essentially political. Moyers's book of essays had never been published. Instead Johnson wanted a competent scholar to prepare a one-volume edition of his selected state papers for use in the 1968 campaign. I immediately refused, but Doug persuaded me at least to look over the material. For six hours I skimmed a four-foot stack of the president's speeches. The exercise reminded me of his continual deceitfulness about the war in Vietnam and American policy there. I told Doug how I thought a book could be put together, I recommended Eugene V. Rostow, then undersecretary of state, to do the job, and I went home, furious that I had been used, just as Doug was furious with me.

My eagerness to unseat Johnson received practical direction in August 1967 at an open-air, antiwar meeting at the ski lodge on Mt. Ascutney, Vermont, which I later described in the prologue to my book *The Progressive Presidents,* published in 1980. Ken Galbraith opened that meeting with a militant speech, after which several of us held discussion sessions, all of them involving a hundred or more people. The size of the crowd and its enthusiasm, common attributes of the meetings Ken had been addressing all summer, suggested the strength of antiwar sentiment. Galbraith wanted to harness that energy behind a movement to nominate as president Senator Eugene McCarthy of Minnesota, an eloquent Democrat with a commendable antiwar and liberal record. Like many of his associates, Ken would have liked to support Robert F. Kennedy, but Kennedy had declined to run. It was at best a quixotic crusade for members of his own party to oppose a sitting president. Even McCarthy was hesitant. So informed, I wrote a short historical piece, signed "Americus," for *The New Republic*, in hopes of convincing McCarthy to run. Gilbert Harrison, the editor of that journal, was a neighbor and friend of McCarthy. Alex Bickel, a regular contributor, sent Harrison my article, which he agreed to publish. Often attributed in error to Arthur Schlesinger, Jr., my article discussed the presidential campaign of 1911–12. Robert LaFollette's decision then openly to oppose President Taft on a progressive platform drew Theodore Roosevelt into the race; TR's subsequent campaign and his founding of the Progressive Party influenced the Democrats to nominate Woodrow Wilson as a progressive candidate of their own. I argued that, by analogy, a McCarthy candidacy, worthy in itself, might also draw Kennedy into the race, and either man, if nominated, would push the Republicans toward an antiwar standard bearer.

By that time McCarthy had just about decided to run, and when he announced, I enlisted in the McCarthy campaign in Connecticut. In the ensuing months I devoted evenings and weekends to assisting the leaders of that campaign, Joe Duffey and Ann Wechsler, and, within New Haven, Chester Kerr. He and his wife, Joan, organized a McCarthy rally that the senator considered a high moment in his candidacy. I endeavored to prepare my ward for the primary battle in March 1968. My daughter Ann recruited some of her schoolmates to accompany Yale students, then still all male, in canvassing the area. A couple ringing doorbells had a much better chance of gaining admission than did a young man alone. Good manners and a conservative wardrobe marked the McCarthy canvassers as the middle-class young people they were. That image was politically useful. Our ward was "Clean for Gene" for months, and at the polls we beat the Democratic party machine. Suburban women were even more important to the McCarthy campaign than were students, as I commented in a *New Republic* article later that spring.

I even took to the stump myself. Late in April the McCarthy headquarters in Washington called me with the unlikely request that I campaign for the senator in Maine. He had planned to do it himself but had decided instead to spend his time in Indiana, where Robert Kennedy, by then a candidate, was campaigning and where Vice President Hubert Humphrey was also at the hustings for the administration. When Kennedy at last declared his candidacy after McCarthy's strong showing in the New Hampshire primary, I had spoken with both Arthur Schlesinger, Jr., and, at his suggestion, Steve Smith, Kennedy's brother-in-law. Both had urged me to stay with McCarthy, for the Kennedy supporters would need friends, they said, to bring together the Kennedy and the McCarthy delegates at the nominating convention in Chicago. I was being asked to campaign against Senator Ed Muskie, Maine's favorite son, in the imminent election of delegates from that state. Surprised, I asked the woman who had called why McCarthy wanted to enlist me, a person unknown to Mainers. "To be frank, Professor Blum," she said, "eleven other possible speakers have turned us down." That seemed to me such an honest and pathetic answer that I agreed to do it.

On May 6 I flew to Portland, Maine, where I was met by two college students in a VW van painted in surrealistic colors. They drove me to several colleges and on to a dinner of Maine Democrats. There Muskie's representative came up to me and said: "Professor, what the hell do you think you're doing campaigning on this turf?" I told him that I was McCarthy's twelfth choice for the role. He enjoyed a long laugh and bought me a drink.

Back in New Haven on May 7, to our surprise Mary Louise and Kingman Brewster stopped by after dinner to wish Pamela a happy birthday. Kingman had an ulterior motive. At one point while we were alone, he said, "I've come to cash my blank check." He went on to report that the faculty library committee and the provost had persuaded him immediately to discharge the university librarian whom Kingman had hired only a few years earlier. The library budget was out of control, and library services had become unsatisfactory. He wanted me to take over the library at once. With a sinking heart, I said I needed a night to think it over; but a promise was a promise, and I could not let down an old and valued friend. Though I intended to bargain with Kingman about several matters relating to the position, early the next morning I told him I would serve. I also resigned from the balance of my NEH fellowship. I knew that for months to come there would be no time for antiwar politics and, worse, no time for teaching or for scholarship. With brooding recollections of the chairmanship, I realized that managing the library posed an even more formidable task.

13

Double Trouble

Kingman and I needed only a few minutes to agree about the issues that worried me as I contemplated a year in command of the library. I was not and did not intend to become a librarian, so I wanted a title that said as much. Borrowing from Harvard practice, Kingman suggested Director of Libraries. I preferred Acting Director of Libraries, which implied the finite nature of my commitment. To be sure of a timely successor, I asked Kingman to make me chairman of the search committee to find a new University Librarian. He was to accept our candidate, he agreed, unless he found him or her truly obnoxious. Instead of reporting to Kingman, who had little interest in the library except as a problem to be solved, I asked to work with Charles Taylor, who as provost had a learned and continuing interest in the library and its budget. Kingman found that request convenient, but he told me to keep away from the Beinecke Rare Books and Manuscripts Library, for the Beinecke family, major Yale donors, were content with the incumbent associate librarian there. It was no problem for me to leave the Beinecke Library alone, for I had no interest in rare books except as instruments for scholarly research. Indeed I thought that bibliophiles had long had too much influence on general library policy. Finally, there was the question of Aspen. I had agreed to spend eight weeks of the summer at the Aspen Institute, with part of that time serving as moderator of the annual executive seminars. I was willing to cancel the engagement, but Kingman thought it was too late to renege. He urged me to go but to keep in touch by telephone with the library staff.

Then it was time to meet the professional librarians, who had assembled at Kingman's invitation. He spoke with his characteristic generosity and sense of accountability. If anyone was responsible for the departure of the University Librarian, he said, he was, for he had hired James Tanis and he had fired James Tanis. He expected me to work with the librarians, expected them to work with me, and expected us to get along. Then it was my turn. I said I knew nothing about libraries but meant to learn. I would need their help. I also said my first administrative post had been as executive officer of my ship, and I ran a taut ship. There were no questions.

At Kingman's request I next called upon Albert Van Sinderen, the CEO of the Southern New England Telephone Company, who was chairman of the Associated Yale Alumni committee on the library. A collector of rare books, he had been supportive of James Tanis. When I arrived at his office, I could feel his hostility. "What makes you think you can run a library?" he asked. "I will learn to run a library for a year," I answered, "and I'll find a new University Librarian while I'm learning." I had no ambition, I said, to remain in the library beyond the current academic year. He was relieved. I also told him that my main interest was not in rare books. Yale needed a library addressed primarily to the service of scholarship, and I intended to start moving in that direction at once. He did not argue. On the contrary, he and his committee became staunch allies.

I then visited Charles Taylor to review library problems with him. He explained his dissatisfaction with James Tanis, who had already overdrawn the library budget for 1967–68 and refused to submit a budget for 1968–69, the fiscal year beginning July 1. He had unfilled vacancies on his staff, books and serials recommended by faculty still unordered, and correspondence with the provost's office yet to be answered. Kingman had hired Tanis without a professional search. Instead he had accepted the advice of the retiring University Librarian, James Babb, a rare-book specialist, and Fritz Liebert, Babb's subordinate in Beinecke, who had known Tanis since Tanis's undergraduate years at Yale. Tanis had become librarian at the Harvard Divinity School, from which he left to succeed Babb, the last "gentleman librarian" Yale was to have. As Charles Taylor saw it, Tanis, experienced only in small libraries, was simply overwhelmed by the Yale library. Like Babb before him, he left administration of the library to the associate university librarian, John Ottemiller. When Ottemiller had become ill and died, Tanis, alone in his responsibilities, more or less gave up.

Charles Taylor knew that a great university needed a great library. It was a crucial resource for all humanists, most social scientists, and some scientists. The Yale library had the third largest collection in the western world, exceeded only by the Library of Congress and Harvard. Charlie intended to keep it so. But Yale needed a University Librarian committed to making the library a reliable support for scholarship of all kinds. Indeed service to scholars had to be the librarian's first objective, though almost equal concern had to be given to the efficiency and morale of the library staff. Only with their ready help and the advice of the faculty could the University Librarian sustain the excellence of the collections — an expensive objective, especially at a time of rising prices for books and serials. In 1968 the University Librarian had also to be alert to enormous changes in technology, which were then at the brink of revolutionizing traditional library practices in cataloging, circulation, and the processing of information. The computer, the Internet, and even the fax machine had yet to find their appropriate places at Yale. Indeed at that time I was barely aware of their existence, though I realized we needed a University Librarian prepared to explore them all.

Yale did have a great library building, the Sterling Memorial Library, constructed as a neo-Gothic skyscraper with a ground floor that resembled the nave and transept of a cathedral, with the delivery desk in place of a high altar. There were also branch libraries, some departmental, others attached to professional schools. But space was inadequate, as I was to learn. Faculty had hundreds of borrowed books in their offices scattered over the campus, but the books could not be recalled because there was no room for them in the stacks. Also, especially during examination periods, students had trouble finding space to study.

Charlie expected me to act as client for the new construction already planned. I knew better than to agree. The plans for a cross-campus library, running underground east of Sterling toward College Street, had provoked student controversy. The proposed building was to house the bibliographers and collections for the various councils Arthur Wright had gathered under his international program — councils on East Asian, Latin American, African, and Russian and Eastern European studies. The roof of the new building was to protrude aboveground, with skylights providing daylight. But that protuberance would intrude upon the grassy area where undergraduates played frisbee. At that time, with every college campus close to the turmoil that had escalated into riots at the University of California at Berkeley and at Columbia, Yale students seized on the local issue of freedom for frisbee. It served as their way of demanding a student voice in university decisions affecting student life. That issue had become part of the mixed bag of questions provoking agitation by college students, especially those in the

New Left—civil rights, the war in Vietnam, students' role in university governance. Frisbee and its place on the cross-campus provided that spring a Yale surrogate for the nationwide student revolution.

The new library would interfere with their traditional privileges, and they had not been consulted, so argued the protesting undergraduates, with architectural students leading the chorus. Surprised by the controversy, the administration had postponed groundbreaking. As I told the provost, I had not been involved at all in plans for the cross-campus library or for its use. In contrast, as chairman of the university's buildings and grounds committee, the provost had been deeply involved. I saw no reason to replace him, certainly not until I had studied the matter. Reluctantly Charlie agreed. He would defer any building until autumn, and in the interim I would direct the associate librarians to report about their priorities for the cross-campus structure.

We could not defer the budget. With that as my first priority, I went at once to the office of the University Librarian. Situated within Sterling Library, it was arguably the most handsome office at Yale, with a wall of French windows looking out onto a garden court. Tanis was there, his secretary told me, but not available. I decided not yet to make an issue of the office. But the secretary, after consulting him, also denied me copies of the 1967–68 and 1968–69 budgets. I would return after lunch, I told her. I would then want an office of my own, copies of the budgets, and a stenographer. All were ready when I returned. Both budgets were a mess, and the budget for the coming year, 1968–69, was incomplete. As accompanying documents revealed, the library had simply ignored the 1967–68 budget, overdrawing it. Either Tanis or Ottemiller, his associate, or both of them had acted irresponsibly. I had as yet few clues about what the budget for 1968–69 should include, so I suggested to the provost that the library live month to month, using one twelfth of the 1967–68 budget each month, until I could submit a more carefully considered budget of my own. On that basis we would proceed until November.

I also needed to consult more widely. I arranged a luncheon with Louis Martz, a professor of English and chairman of the faculty library committee, whom I had come to know while he and I had been chairmen of our respective departments. Louis, eloquent with horror stories about Tanis's unwillingness to cooperate with his committee, could add nothing useful about the library's budget. Neither could Jim Babb. At my request he examined the budgets I had obtained, but in response he only threw up his hands in despair. He had known nothing about the sorry state of affairs since his retirement. (That summer he died.) I turned next to the associate librarians. One of them, about to retire and so obviously resentful of my presence, I saw no problem in leaving undisturbed. Another, J. Gordon Kenefik, a Yale graduate only a few years from retirement, made every effort to assist me in any way he could. But his responsibilities lay primarily with school and department libraries, which were in relatively good shape. Further, he was preoccupied with defending his own turf from incursions by David Sparks, the ambitious, energetic associate librarian for public services. As I was to discover, Sparks's professionalism and the range of his information about libraries were welcome, and his ambition was easy enough to contain.

The associate librarian for technical services, Bernice Field, then about sixty years old, was the gem of the staff. A small woman, alert, professional, and cooperative, she had a temporary office next to mine alongside the outer wall of the exhibition room, which had been desecrated by Tanis's construction of temporary offices within its broad and handsome space. Unlike most of her colleagues, Bernice welcomed me. To my delight she began by educating me about cataloging and about the economies that might result from the application of computer technology to both the cataloging and the circulation of books. I knew from the first that I would learn from her and could rely on her. Bernice privately supported my growing conviction that as a chief deputy I needed not another librarian but a business manager skilled in budgeting and personnel. Charles Taylor also endorsed that prospect. After a brief search, during which I failed to persuade a young member of the Defense Department to take the job, I offered the position to Radley Daley, a vice president of Pepperidge Farm. Rad, a perfervid Yale alumnus, proved perfect for the job, eager and quick to learn, companionable with staff, and experienced with number crunching.

I needed more talent like Bernice and Rad to join the regular Monday morning policy meetings I intended to hold with the associate librarians. So I recruited for those meetings Fritz Liebert from the Beinecke Library to represent the interests of the rare-book people. As a group, they tended to take a superior attitude toward librarians who were concerned with artifacts of no intrinsic value except for their content. But Fritz was a realist about money and management. I also asked the law librarian, Arthur Charpentier, whom I had met at luncheons with friends, to join us. In my judgment he was the wisest and most effective librarian at Yale. Arthur agreed with me on the need for still more first-rate help. So with the permission of the provost, I invited Herman Kahn to become head of the division of manuscripts and archives. I had known Herman for years, first in his role as director of the Franklin D. Roosevelt Library, later when he moved to Washington to supervise all presidential libraries. Bored in retirement, he was happy to return to work, and Yale needed him. The young woman in charge of the division had latent talents as an archivist but lacked the self-confidence to manage all of her responsibilities. Herman had just the right manner and experience to teach her. Further, he knew libraries well — so well that after their first conversation, Charles Taylor suggested, not to my surprise, that we give him the rank and salary of an associate librarian. Bemused though he was to find such an amateur as I in charge, Herman joined the Monday morning group, to which both he and Arthur Charpentier contributed wisdom and stability.

By the end of June 1968, with the new fiscal year almost underway, most of those changes were in place. I had also begun to consult a few senior librarians at other universities. Robert Vosper, the chief librarian at the University of California at Los Angeles, who knew Kingman, warned me that Kingman had offended the profession by failing to consult its leaders about the Yale vacancy when Babb had retired. I would be wise, Vosper suggested, as soon as possible to see the Librarian of Congress and the head of the Association of Research Libraries (ARL). I called both and made appointments to meet them in the early autumn. Vosper also recommended as Yale's next University Librarian the former second-in-command at the Library of Congress, Rutherford D. Rogers, who was now in charge at Stanford. Charlie Taylor was planning to accompany his daughter to Stanford when she matriculated in September, so he and I agreed that he would arrange to consult Rogers about libraries while also unofficially looking him over as a candidate for Yale. I had yet to throw Tanis out of his office, but I saw no harm in postponing that unpleasant task until I returned from Aspen.

That summer in Aspen gave me an interlude away from Yale during an otherwise hectic academic year, but life there presented problems of its own. Though I was busy — I used most of my time to condense and revise the three Morgenthau volumes — I could not ignore the troubles that visited the town. Aspen had become a mecca for young people immersed in the counterculture, and some of them were addicted to hard drugs. The Diggers, reformed drug users, did their best to help the transient addicts avoid arrest, give up their habit, and get out of town, often to a camp at some hot springs in the mountains about twenty miles away. But as often as he could, the local sheriff arrested hitchhiking youngsters, whether or not they carried drugs, charging them as vagrants. Without trial, he would temporarily incarcerate them and then see them out of the county. Those actions suited the preferences of the owners of expensive properties in Aspen. But the violation of civil liberties provoked the editor of the Aspen newspaper to hire a lawyer, and the two revived a local chapter of the American Civil Liberties Union.

I became involved with the work of that chapter as soon as my daughters told me about it and a neighbor introduced me to some members, many of them physicists visiting the Aspen Institute for the summer.

The neighbor was William James, a grandson of the philosopher, now defending principles his grandfather had valued. A gifted professional artist, Bill and his wife, Julie, typified the humane and creative spirit of the town, a spirit by no means universal there. Indeed the administrative head of the Aspen Institute, a retired diplomat, objected to the Diggers, to the ACLU, and to a rally for Gene McCarthy that Julie James and I organized. He suggested that I either let the locals protect their turf from outsiders or take my leave. I was a visiting professor, I replied. If I were visiting Yale and its president spoke to me the way the Aspen administrator just had, I would inform the American Association of University Professors about the threat to my academic freedom, my freedom to believe as I chose and to express my beliefs. I had done nothing illegal, I said, and I did not intend to leave. Angry, he walked away but took no action. For the rest of the summer we avoided each other. But in those weeks the ACLU continued to protect innocent transients, and the Diggers removed most addicts before they could be arrested.

Aspen that summer provided my first significant experience with the counterculture, an expression of youthful rebellion contemporary with, but wholly different from, the New Left, though the two often overlapped. Both were foreign to my temperament, but I felt that it was important for me to try to understand them, for both groups were growing stronger in colleges all over the country. As I saw it, the New Left fell into the tradition of American radicalism. Its adherents pressured liberals (as I considered myself to be), who in the absence of such pressure tended to drift toward a bland, conformist centrism. But just as I disagreed with the tactics of the New Left, so did I disdain the behavior of the counterculture. The young in the 1960s, as always, thought they were immortal. So convinced, many of them ignored the dangers of using hard drugs and the risks of sexual promiscuity, disregarding the fact that the likely consequences of their behavior were addiction and venereal disease.

I was too "square" to hold the attention of cultural rebels in Aspen in 1968 or in New Haven during the next years of "the greening of America." In contrast, conventional liberals, of whom I was one, were seen as enemies of the New Left and as such were open to argumentation and attack. I respected the New Left, however, even when we disagreed. In contrast, for the children of the counterculture, including the many Yale students who later became followers of Charles Reich, I felt sad, for I believed they would one day discover that they could not in the end escape the realities they tried so hard to deny.

The wealthy burghers of Aspen wanted no part of either group in their resort. But they were learning that scientists and humanists visiting the Institute took seriously the ideas in the great books assigned in the executive seminars. Those ideas influenced the best educated of the young rebels on the left, and influenced their defenders, too, who did not need to agree with them in order to protect their right to be wrong.

At the end of August I left Aspen for my return to New Haven and the Yale library. James Tanis was still camped in the office of the University Librarian. The time had now come for him to leave. At nine o'clock the first morning after my return, I told him to be gone within the hour. He was, but for months to come I had to cope with his careless legacy. The associate librarians who met with me on Monday mornings responded constructively to my regular consultations with them and to the independence I gave them in their various domains. They proved wholly capable of handling the routine work for which they were responsible. They also contributed effectively to solving the major problems on my desk. I was resolved before Christmas to identify a candidate for Kingman to appoint as University Librarian. I was committed, too, by November to submit to Charles Taylor an acceptable budget for 1968–69. And I had immediately to present Charles with a plan for the cross-campus library. During the summer, the associate librarians had studied the library's needs for space. They had ready for me an oral report about the waste of space within the Sterling Library, and their written report redefined the purpose of the cross-campus library. The most pressing need for space, the associate librarians agreed, was for undergraduate use, for easy access to books assigned or recommended in their courses and necessary for their research for course papers. But accessibility was not enough. Students also needed space just to sit and read. Redesigned, the cross-campus project would provide convenient and ample space for an undergraduate library, and the various international councils could remain operative within Sterling, where they already were. I found that reasoning persuasive, and so did Charles Taylor. Further, Edward Barnes, the architect for the building, proposed for its revised use a two-story, rectangular-shaped structure that would not protrude aboveground. The students' frisbee playing could resume as soon as construction had been completed.

I was ready to support such an undergraduate library, and Charles, glad to have me do so, was delighted with the savings that the new design would permit. Barnes built the cross-campus library with two large stairwells as entrances from the street level. Handsome structures, they allowed daylight to reach the main delivery desk and foyer at the upper level of the structure.

But one winter morning I found three future architects camping in my office. They were having a sit-in, they explained, until I set up a committee of their fellows to review plans for the cross-campus library and to recommend desirable changes. Their sit-in would not move me, I replied. They retorted that they had no intention of departing. So be it, I said. They could remain, but under my rules. They could sleep on the furniture, but only if they removed their shoes. They could use the private lavatory attached to the office. They were also to be quiet while I held conferences or spoke on the telephone. And they would have to go out to eat.

To my surprise they agreed to those conditions and then remained in my office for about eight days. I had not consulted either Kingman or Charles Taylor about the arrangement but neither complained, nor did the dean of the school of architecture. Every weekday a reporter from the *Yale Daily News* looked in to see if the sit-in was continuing. It was, but it soon ceased to be newsworthy. While it lasted I visited my designated successor, with whom I discussed plans for the cross-campus library. He found them satisfactory except for the design of the carrels for private study, which he considered too small. Yale would soon be coeducational, he said, and then men and women would want larger carrels, where they could hold hands. That prediction seemed sound to me. Back in my office, I told my three sitters-in, as well as an undergraduate reporter who had wandered by, what I had in mind. "I hope you don't object to interdigitation," I said. One of the architectural students looked puzzled. He asked what I meant. "Holding hands," I explained. He and the others then agreed that they had been consulted and the sit-in ended. "Blum Plans Interdigitation for New Library," the reporter suggested as a headline for the next day's paper. "That's O.K.," I said, "as long as no one thinks it's salacious."

Meanwhile I had been mulling over ways to retrieve the space in Sterling Library being used by tenants with no need to be there. The various projects within Sterling to edit manuscript collections — the Papers of Benjamin Franklin, for example — had to be located next to the library's stacks. But several operations were less defensible, and none proved easy to evict. The likeliest candidate for eviction was the Theater Collection, of which most records reposed in boxes. Three of them were labeled imaginatively "Big Blue Box," "Bigger Blue Box," and "Biggest Blue Box." It was two years after I left the library before that collection was relocated.

Historical Sound Recordings presented a different problem. That collection consisted of rare and valuable recordings of classical, operatic, and popular music, some on rolls dating from the era before the phonograph. A rare-book dealer, Larry Whitten, was giving the collection to Yale, donating it little by little while it remained in Sterling, accessible to him and open to other users. But as curator, whose salary the library paid, Whitten had appointed a particularly difficult and uncooperative person. After a few futile efforts to bring the curator into line, I warned Whitten that he was dealing with an unreliable subordinate. Whitten would not listen. He insisted on retaining the curator, who a year or two later fled to London with some of the collection's choicest items in his possession.

Whitten was one of many rare-book enthusiasts who had developed special ties to the Yale library. It had been he who sold Yale the Vineyard Map, reputedly a Norse map of the North Atlantic and its shores dating — so it was said — from decades before Columbus and providing evidence of the Norse "discovery" of North America. Funds for the purchase came from Paul Mellon, a generous donor to Yale. With consummate tactlessness, Yale University Press had published the map and supporting documents on Columbus Day 1964. Their publication raised a storm in the large Italian-American community in New Haven. It also offended every member of the history department specializing in aspects of the history of the map's supposed period: none of them had been consulted. Instead the Press had turned to British scholars. As the Yale scholars saw it, the British experts had erred. The Yale historians found the map a forgery, a clever hoax. Whitten always refused to provide a provenance, and because the ink on the map kept fading — in itself a suspicious development — the map was soon withdrawn from exhibition. Some years later friends of Mellon commissioned a new review of the map, which alleged to authenticate it. The Yale historians remained unconvinced. So did I, for I was confident of the analyses my colleagues had made.

The numismatic collection had a right to space in Sterling, but its budget was sufficient to keep it open only several mornings a week. Records indicated that almost all requests for access emanated from classical scholars. I suggested therefore that Yale sell all but the classical coins. We could then put the return from the sale in a special endowment and use the income from that fund both to acquire other classical coins and to defer the annual cost of caring for the collection and making it available during regular library hours. Charles Taylor, laughing, told me to try that proposal on the faculty library committee. At our next meeting I did. As Charles had predicted, every member of the committee objected to selling any coins even remotely related to his field of interest. Few faculty members ever endorsed deaccessioning for any purpose.

Meanwhile, substantial progress was being made on the budget. We had found few employees who were redundant and little evidence of the need for more. Accordingly we neither added nor subtracted from the roster of personnel listed in the 1967–68 budget; we simply repeated it, allowing for some flexibility in allocation to departments, for 1968–69. We allowed, too, for some increases in salaries to be offset by the lower cost of new recruits. With personnel costs constant, we could submit a reduced budget, because expenditures for equipment had been much too high. In purchasing shelving, paper, typewriters, and just about everything else, the library, operating apart from the university's purchasing office, had relied on only one vendor. Indeed Ottemiller, the late deputy librarian, had allowed no other vendor in the building. Just by moving to competitive bidding we could effect substantial savings. The provost received the proposed budget before the beginning of November and approved it almost at once.

Through all of those developments my priority remained the search for a new University Librarian. The head of the Association of Research Libraries gave me an hour or more of useful advice, including a strong recommendation that Yale hire Rutherford Rogers if he could be moved from Stanford. Rogers had favorably impressed Charles Taylor when they had conversed earlier that month, so his name went right to the top of my list. That choice drew additional support from Douglas Bryant, the senior Harvard librarian, whom I had called to ask for advice. To satisfy the leaders of the profession, however, it was important to conduct a search, so I met with the special faculty committee Kingman had appointed to work with me, and I consulted the librarians at Princeton and the University of Chicago, the former at one time a professor of literature, the latter a library professional. At their suggestion and with their help, I drew up a list of possible candidates, a few of whom I interviewed, and circulated it among a dozen leading librarians. They were just about unanimous in rating Rogers at the top. That was the view also of Fred Adams, the head of the Morgan Library in New York and a member of the Yale Corporation.

Early in November Rudy Rogers and his wife visited Yale. Pamela and I wined and dined them, and Rudy and I spent hours together talking about the library and inspecting Sterling and Beinecke from top to bottom. The following Monday Rudy and I went to Columbia, where we attended a meeting of the Gnomes, the head librarians of Harvard, Yale, Princeton, Columbia, Cornell, Stanford, and the University of Chicago. Discussion that day indicated that all research libraries faced common problems, most urgently the growing cost of books and serials, and the still uncertain future applications of computer technology to library management. Rudy and I returned to those subjects the next day, at lunch with Kingman.

But just a week later Rudy called to report that his wife had decided they could not leave Stanford, where their daughter and only child was an undergraduate. Charlie Taylor and I could not persuade Rudy to change that decision. I resumed the search, but when I proposed an alternative candidate, Kingman telephoned Rudy. Whatever he said proved convincing, for early in December Rudy agreed to leave Stanford for Yale. Charles Taylor and I reported that good news to the library staff at their annual Christmas party. They rejoiced, but none of them rejoiced as much as I did. In another semester I would be free of administrative responsibilities.

Even in my absence from teaching in my library year, during the spring of 1969 I was aware, as were all faculty members, of rising student unrest. Since 1964 the civil rights movement had been moving to a radical peak, with the Black Panthers now receiving the attention previously accorded to moderate reformers. The moderates had spurred Lyndon Johnson to support and sign the Civil Rights Act of 1964 and the Voting Rights Act of 1965. Martin Luther King, Jr., the prophet of civil disobedience as the tactic of the movement, had come out against American involvement in Vietnam, as had Robert Kennedy, and both of those courageous men had been assassinated. On college campuses all over America students, not just those in SDS, were demanding a larger voice in decisions about their affairs, protesting the continuing social and economic injustice of the nation's treatment of African Americans, and condemning the "obscenity," as they put it, of the war. The protesters identified the armed forces with the supporters of the war in Vietnam, though many soldiers, both regulars and conscripts, chafed at their mission there. That identification carried over to the reserve officers training corps. Student critics of the war almost invariably demanded abolition of ROTC on campus. That issue and the issue of justice for black Americans sparked the confrontations that led in April 1969 to the "bust" at Harvard.

There was much to be said against the army and navy ROTC programs. The Yale College faculty, expressing grave doubts about them, withdrew the academic credit their courses had been afforded. In my personal opinion, ROTC was a waste of students' time. My experience as a midshipman had persuaded me forever that instruction in such things as seamanship, gunnery, navigation, and fire control had little intellectual content. Close-order drill offended adult sensibilities. Worse, a student who elected to continue in ROTC beyond his sophomore year could not withdraw if he changed his mind later. Forcing young men to make such a serious decision at such a young age seemed to me unfair. So many professors held similar views that the Yale College faculty had appointed a committee to study the future of ROTC on campus.

But Yale student protesters against ROTC, which for them was a surrogate of the war, were agitating for immediate action, and the imbroglio at Harvard suggested how disruptive that agitation could become if the university did not respond with sensitivity. The faculty therefore asked Kingman to hold a meeting on ROTC open to all members of the Yale community. As Kingman announced on April 27, 1969, Charles Taylor would call and chair two meetings, one on governance, the other on ROTC, with the latter being held in the hockey rink, with its ample seating. The ROTC meeting began ominously. Charles was unable to maintain order as student activists shouted resolutions from the floor. It was probably a mistake to select Charles as chair, for the students did not know him and he did not know them. Once proceedings were underway, Robert Dahl, a prominent and distinguished professor of political science, was set to preside, but the tumult continued. An SDS representative introduced a motion about procedure. Kingman had intended speakers only previously selected to get the floor, but the SDS motion called for speeches from the floor and for a resolution about ROTC to be submitted to a vote before the meeting adjourned.

As I saw it, the immediate need was to establish order. I raised my hand for recognition, was recognized, and started for the podium at the north end of the rink. On the way I noticed members of the Yale Corporation seated to one side of the platform. The crowd had subsided by the time I reached the microphone. There I introduced an amendment to the SDS resolution. It had two parts: one called for the adoption of Robert's *Rules of Order* for the rest of the meeting; the other called upon those present to recognize that no resolution adopted could be binding on the corporation. As I learned the next day, at that point Stewart Alsop, the conservative newspaper columnist sitting with the members of the corporation, turned to Tracy Barnes, one of Kingman's assistants, and asked, "Who's the little man with the confident voice?" He meant me, but I felt no confidence. On the contrary, I feared my amendment might set off a demonstration. But Daniel Yergin, an undergraduate leader of the movement against ROTC and later a national authority on the oil industry, speaking from a floor mike, called out: "Mr. Blum, we accept that as a friendly amendment." There was immediate, murmured agreement.

Kingman, seated at the podium, leaned to his left and, whispering, suggested I take over. I replied that Bob Dahl should continue while I would serve as parliamentarian. After Kingman announced that arrangement, I asked whether any SDS student in the rink had a copy of Robert's *Rules* and would be willing to serve as joint parliamentarian. A young Harvard College graduate who was enrolled in the Yale School of Public Health volunteered. While an orderly debate began, he and I asked for student and faculty volunteers to act as counters, with one faculty member and one student to tally each section of the rink when the time came to vote. We organized the counters while debate went on about an SDS motion to abolish ROTC. Kingman, opposing the motion, said he saw nothing wrong with military service. About half an hour before midnight the motion came to a vote. The counters for each section brought their totals to me. The student from Public Health and I added the results from each section to calculate the total vote in the rink. We agreed on the tally, but we could not believe it. I asked Kingman and Bob Dahl to check our arithmetic. They did. Kingman then announced the astonishing result: the vote was a tie: 1,286 for the motion, 1,286 against. The rink broke out in mirth.

The vote meant nothing. Further, any brace of counters could have made a mistake. But the tie, and the jovial response to it, gave the Yale College faculty time for consideration the next day of a resolution proposed by the committee on the ROTC. That resolution asked the president and corporation to renegotiate Yale's contract with the armed services on new terms: ROTC, army or navy, was no longer to have the authority to ban cadets from any major, as it had previously been allowed to do with anthropology; students in ROTC were to be allowed to resign at any time before they graduated; and ROTC was to pay all of its own instructional and administrative costs. That resolution passed by more than a two-thirds vote. A second resolution, introduced by a radical professor of philosophy, demanded that Yale immediately sever all connections with ROTC. It failed by about a three-to-one vote. Predictably, as several professors had said during the debate, Yale's terms did not suit the armed services, which rejected them. Only then did ROTC leave Yale. The process for terminating it had fit Kingman's sense of appropriate procedure. Indeed the evening at the rink had ended on a note of civility, a quality important to him, his administration, and his friends and admirers.

Though the next stages in student unrest would be less agreeable, Kingman had accomplished a great deal for Yale and had succeeded largely in neutralizing the issues about which students were agitating. The college was about to become coeducational, which was long Kingman's objective as well as that of most undergraduates and faculty. He had reformed the standards for admission to increase minority enrollment. And he had managed a graceful exit from ROTC. The Yale record contrasted favorably with the record at Harvard, Columbia, and Cornell. For most undergraduates and the Yale faculty, two of his constituencies, Kingman was a hero. But many of the alumni, his third constituency, were restless. Many of them disapproved of democratizing admissions; many of them, especially among those of my generation, opposed coeducation and the end of ROTC. The future was uncertain.

The resolution of the ROTC issue marked the effective end of my academic year. I handled routine matters in the library until early June when, with Rudy Rogers soon to arrive, Pamela and I departed for the summer in Vermont. Because of my part in the meeting in the rink, I had gained an undeserved reputation as a parliamentarian. In fact I knew little about Robert's rules, though I did care deeply about keeping order. This newfound reputation was soon to make me a convenient parliamentarian for Yale College faculty meetings, a role I did not cherish. But my spirits were high. I had spent two years away from teaching, one on leave, the other in Sterling. Now eager to resume my usual duties, I revised my lecture notes during the summer and organized my thoughts for a graduate seminar to be focused on aspects of World War II. I was even able to give some time to writing an early chapter of my book in progress about the home front. By September I was ready to return to normality. But I was about to learn that the prevailing student mood had made normality at least temporarily obsolete.

14

Yale Students and Harvard Fellows

Sheer exuberance describes my mood as I returned to writing and teaching in the fall of 1969. Kingman had brought coeducation to the college, and the small, first groups of women proved academically excellent. Eventually women would constitute half the student body. The arrival of coeducation improved Yale College. By doubling the number of students eligible for admission, Yale raised the standards for matriculation and the median level of academic performance. I could see the results in the work of women in my lecture course and, even more impressively, in their senior essays, many of which I directed. Though at first some of the undergraduate men resented the tougher competition, from my perspective, coeducation was a great success.

I was equally impressed with the minority students who chose to work with me, especially Henry Louis Gates, Jr., a bright, eager, articulate African American undergraduate with the ambition I encouraged to become at once a scholar and a journalist. His senior essay, which I directed, helped him win a Mellon grant to Cambridge University, where he earned his D.Phil. in literature while working as a stringer for *Time*. Skip went on during the 1990s at Harvard to build the foremost African American program in the country.

The graduate program at Yale thrived, too. My seminar in 1969–70 was larger than ever before. That large but unusually cohesive group focused on topics relating to World War II. Their research papers aided the progress of my manuscript about the home front. In *V Was for Victory* (1976) I cited their helpful work in my notes.

The autumn of 1969, at Yale as elsewhere, was notable for the tensions roiling the campus. Students in every Yale school were impatient to gain a voice in the governance of the university, a subject the faculty debated and Kingman studied with sympathy. Kingman approved the October 15 Moratorium Day on the Vietnam War, when he addressed a crowd of some 50,000 gathered on the New Haven Green, denouncing the war. He also testified before a Senate committee in favor of altering the conscription law to make it fairer to young men who could not afford or did not wish to pursue higher education. Also in October, the Black Student Alliance at Yale (BSAY) charged both the city and the campus police with harassment of blacks. Chanting "Stop the cops," some of them disrupted classes at the law school. My friend Lou Pollak, then dean of that school, responded with moderation. Kingman had wanted a more punitive response, but Lou was teaching him a lesson he quickly learned, as did many professors — that patience, sympathy, trust, and respect were indispensable in dealing with students.

Still, the conservatives on the law school faculty attacked Lou. The Yale College faculty, too, was beginning to divide into three groups — radicals, conservatives, and moderates, the last a majority with Kingman ordinarily its leader. Those divisions echoed student attitudes, which were often passionate. Passion also attended the increasing arrest of Yale students for possession or use of drugs, particularly marijuana. Proponents of the drug culture rejoiced when Allen Ginsberg visited Yale to read his own and Jack Kerouac's poetry. The times were changing, and Yale was both feeling and expressing the change. The burden on Kingman was intensified because of "stagflation" — the combination of inflation and a stagnant economy — which hampered the financing of higher education. Indeed the administration had to announce budget cuts for 1970–71, especially for faculty.

In that charged atmosphere a relatively trivial episode escalated into a disturbing crisis. A waitress, Colia Williams, a black woman employed in the dining hall of Jonathan Edwards College, was fired for allegedly participating in a slowdown. A hearing on the case was scheduled, but BSAY and SDS at once attributed her discharge to racism. On November 3, 1969, a group of at least forty-seven students, some of them members of the SDS, broke through the campus police guard to enter Wright Hall. Located there were the offices of the manager of the dining halls and of the person he reported to, the business manager of the university, former Yale football great Jack Embersits. The students demanded the immediate reinstatement of the waitress, which Embersits properly refused to consider until after the hearing. (Unbeknownst to both him and the students, Williams had already been rehired.) The students then held Embersits and the dining hall manager captive for three hours. Embersits, a physically powerful man, had the good sense not to try to break out. But the students' occupation of Wright Hall violated the university's long-standing regulations against the use of force to prohibit free access and egress.

About half past six that evening, Provost Charles Taylor arrived at the building and warned the students that they would be suspended if they did not leave Wright Hall. He was following a scenario for dealing with student takeovers that Kingman had outlined to the faculty the previous spring. When the students did not depart, the residential college deans, who had also been summoned to the scene, identified them, and Taylor announced their suspension from Yale. Once again, it was probably an error for Charles Taylor to stand in the eye of the storm. He was a skilled provost, probably the best Yale had in the twentieth century, a man of reason and understanding. But he did not know the undergraduates — he had not taught them, he had not had meals or conversations with them — and they did not know him, nor did they understand his status in the university. A more familiar officer, one closer to the students, might have been more persuasive in enlisting their cooperation.

As it was, the issue of the suspension was joined. At Yale, as elsewhere, student activists and their leaders resented being held accountable for the methods of their protests. At Yale, moreover, the episode at Wright Hall had no precedent, so the punishment of suspension came to those it affected as an unpleasant surprise. Indeed their suspension had the effect of further polarizing the campus. To mitigate the resentment the executive committee of Yale College voted to permit the suspended students to use their dormitory rooms and to eat in their college dining halls until after their hearing. That hearing fell to the executive committee itself. It was the traditional body for examining allegations of undergraduate academic and parietal misbehavior, and its procedures were essentially informal, designed to give accused students every chance to explain their actions but without quasi-legal, adversary regulations. More important, the executive committee reflected the spirit of community represented then by the Dean of Yale College, Georges May, and his Dean of Students, the committee's presiding officer, John Wilkinson. Georges May, a man of unmatched wit and an exquisite sense of proportion and a popular and successful teacher of French literature, stood for rationality, urbanity, and civility. He had approved the modification of the suspensions, a decision his critics viewed as undermining the authority exercised by the provost. But Georges was determined to ease the tension.

Dean May's civilized sense governed his approach to the episode at Wright Hall. After reflection, the executive committee on November 10 readmitted the suspended students but placed them on disciplinary probation for the rest of the academic year. That status would result in separation from the university in the event of another malefaction during that time. The unprecedented nature of the event, Dean Wilkinson announced, accounted for the diminution in punishment, but in the future similar actions would result in suspension. At the meeting the next day of the Yale College faculty the hard-liners, a minority, spoke out for harsher treatment of the offending students. Two and a half hours of debate resulted in no conclusion. Another debate two days later again left the controversy about the executive committee's decision unsettled. A third meeting was scheduled for November 20, the following Thursday. "The faculty," as Georges May put it, "is strongly united in its revulsion for the events which went on in Wright Hall and is determined to do everything in its power to avoid this in the future; the problem is the means. There are strongly divergent ideas about what should be done."

On the Sunday before the third meeting I telephoned Georges to suggest that an unofficial, informal committee might be able to work out in private a resolution that the faculty would endorse. I proposed that Ed Morgan, Alvin Kernan (a professor of English who was to be acting provost the next semester), and I make up the committee. Georges suggested adding Jim Tobin, a Yale statesman as well as a future winner of the Nobel Prize in economics, and Bill Kessen, a psychologist whom the undergraduates particularly trusted. We five first met that afternoon in my office, to which I had brought a bottle of Canadian whiskey and six glasses. The sixth glass proved handy, for Lloyd Reynolds, another economist, joined us later in the week, when we shared a second bottle. In our discussions we tried to take into account the opinions of both the majority of moderates and the minority of conservatives. We wanted to frame a resolution acceptable to all. We wanted to restore and reinforce the sense of community that distinguished Yale College during the Brewster years.

On Monday afternoon we completed a draft. It contained phrases or sentences each of us had suggested, though Ed Morgan, as I recall, drafted most of what became the first paragraph of the final resolution. On Tuesday we each took a copy of the draft to the offices of several departments, at each of which we discussed our phrasing with as many faculty members as we could find. Late that afternoon and again on Wednesday we altered our draft to include suggestions we had received. Kessen continually protested that, as the youngest and most permissive of us, he was the "house liberal," but in fact we had no serious differences among us. Wednesday evening Ed and I, as our committee had agreed we should, visited Georges at his home, where we presented him with our resolution and a scenario for its submission to the faculty. I told him that as soon as the meeting began he should recognize Kessen, who would introduce the resolution. One of us would then immediately second it. After some discussion, but not much, one of us would call for the question. We promised Georges that the motion would carry, as would the resolution itself. Georges, who properly prided himself as a presiding officer, at first balked at my scenario. "John," he said, "this is blackmail!" But after Ed and I explained how we had consulted many members of many departments with our draft, he relented. When the faculty met on Thursday things went just as we had planned. After the resolution was put to a vote, the hall rang with affirmatives, with only one voice registering a nay.

The meeting, Georges told the *Yale Daily News,* had agreed on "what we held in common." The text of our resolution became a part of the introduction to the annual pamphlet, "Undergraduate Regulations." It read: "The Yale College Faculty: reaffirms its commitment to protect free expression and peaceful dissent and to preserve mutual respect and charitable relations among all members of the Yale community. Believes that physical restriction, coercion, or intimidation of any member of that community is contrary to the basic principles of the University. Expects that such action will ordinarily result in temporary or permanent separation from the College."

The peaceable settlement of the Wright Hall confrontation revealed the spirit the faculty resolution commended, a spirit of respect and civility toward students. SDS had been counting on a triumph of the faculty hardliners. Instead the faculty proved reasonable. That outcome cost the SDS credibility at Yale then and later. After the faculty meeting our committee met informally again in my office for a brief celebration at which we consumed the last of the Canadian whiskey. As we departed, Kessen delivered a valedictory. "This is the last time," he said, "that six mandarins are going to settle matters at Yale." He was correct.

Several weeks later, in December 1969, to my complete surprise, I learned as I left my graduate seminar that President Nathan Marsh Pusey of Harvard was trying to reach me. When I called him, he asked if I could meet him in New York the next afternoon. I could not, I explained, because I had office hours during which several students expected to see me. I suggested that he stop over that evening for dinner with me. He agreed. The evening of the telephone call, by previous arrangement Pamela and I got together for a drink with the Brewsters. I told Kingman that Nate Pusey had called and that we were dining the next day, though I could not imagine why. Kingman said that Pusey was probably going to ask me to join the Harvard Corporation. Pusey had asked him to compare two Yale professors under consideration for that role, and Kingman had designated me as the preferable candidate. At his request, I promised to let him know after our dinner what Pusey's mission was.

I had met Nate Pusey twice, both times at dinners Kingman had given after Harvard-Yale football games. We barely knew each other. I was aware, of course, of the student troubles that had disrupted Harvard the previous spring, though I knew only what the *New York Times* had reported, including the decision of the Harvard administration to call in the city police. At dinner at the New Haven Lawn Club President Pusey came right to the point. He asked me to become a Fellow of Harvard College. The five fellows, with the president and treasurer, constituted "the President and Fellows of Harvard College," commonly known as the Harvard Corporation. It was the junior but more powerful of Harvard's two governing boards, of which the senior body was the Board of Overseers. The overseers were elected by the alumni for limited terms. The fellows, with no fixed terms, were a self-perpetuating board with controlling authority over the budget and at that time over the selection of the president as well. One former fellow had put it well: the role of a fellow, he had said, was to choose the president of Harvard, to advise and support the president of Harvard, and if necessary to discharge the president of Harvard.

President Pusey told me confidentially that he would soon announce his resignation, effective June 30, 1971. Before a search began for a new president, two fellows also intended to resign. The senior fellow, William Marbury, a Baltimore lawyer, would leave at the start of the new term, in February 1970. His successor as senior fellow, Keith Kane, a New York lawyer, would depart after the June commencement. Then Francis H. Burr, a Boston lawyer, would become senior fellow and, if all went as planned, Charles Slichter, a professor of physics at the University of Illinois, would join the corporation. The fellows — the others were Albert Nickerson, former CEO of Mobil, and Hugh Calkins, a Cleveland lawyer — wanted Slichter and me to be active in the selection of the next president.

Pusey was candid about the duties of a fellow. The corporation met at least two Mondays each month, often with a committee of some kind on the preceding Sunday evening. In the months to come there would be still more meetings in order to choose a new president. The commitment of a fellow to Harvard, he said, outweighed any honor in receiving the appointment. He knew I had attended Harvard on a scholarship, but he said that no feelings of gratitude should move me to join the corporation. The role of a fellow would take most of my leisure time. Indeed he recommended that, if I signed on, I give up any other obligations I had beyond those to Yale. I would want to meet the fellows before making up my mind, he predicted, and they had arranged to see me a few days later at the Century Association in New York.

I thanked Pusey for his explanation, agreed to the rendezvous at the Century, and said that I would have to discuss the whole question with Kingman. Of course, Pusey replied. Then, as I had been planning to, I asked him whether he and the fellows were aware that I was a Jew, though not a believer. "Just now," he replied, "that will be very convenient." That statement suggested to me that the Harvard Corporation had been looking for a Jewish fellow. Pusey urged me to give him an answer as soon as possible after I had left the Century. Kingman made exactly the same request. "Go see them," he said when I reported my conversation with Pusey, "and call me as soon as you've decided what to do."

Pamela and I had an inconclusive discussion about Harvard the night before I met the fellows in New York. They were all there except for Francis H. Burr, who was detained in Boston. With them was George Bennett, president of the State Street Investment Corporation and the Harvard treasurer. He, William Marbury, and Keith Kane dominated the discussion, all of them coming back again and again to the budgetary squeeze that Harvard, like all universities, was feeling. For my part I tried to assure them that my instincts had always been prudential. Hugh Calkins, the youngest of the fellows, exuded cordiality but said very little, as did Albert Nickerson. But Hugh did indicate that he was deeply concerned about the alienation of so many Harvard undergraduates and impressed by Yale's contrasting record. Still, I went away with the impression that the Harvard Corporation needed a financier or economist, not me. On the train back to New Haven I decided to decline to serve.

As promised, I called Kingman as soon as I reached home. "I'm not going to do it," I said. "You get down here right away," he replied. "Not the office; the house." Charles Taylor was with him in Kingman's living room when I arrived. "What do you mean," Kingman said as I entered, "you're not going to do it?"

"I've thought about it. I don't like administration. I'm not fit for it."

Kingman: "It's not administration. You go up there and listen and advise and then you come on back here for two weeks. That's not administration. And we'll give you administrative immunity here."

"There are better people."

Kingman: "Of course there are better people, but you're the one who was asked."

"I've a book to write and things to do for Yale."

Kingman: "Write the book during the summer. Charlie and I have talked it over. When Harvard sneezes, we all catch cold. Joining the Harvard Corporation is the most important thing you can do for Yale."

"Kingman, you bastard!" I said. "O.K., I'll do it," I continued, "but on two conditions. You let me tell Nate that you made me sign on. And I intend to serve not for life but only for seven to eleven years."

Kingman: "That's long enough, and you can tell Nate anything you want to."

I then went home, called Nate Pusey, and told him about Kingman's role in my decision and my desire for a seven- to eleven-year term. He had no objection. Instead he responded by welcoming me warmly. Pamela said it was the only decision I ever made that surprised her.

I had yet to be appointed officially by the Board of Overseers, Pusey had said, so the matter should remain confidential until they voted in January. But confidentiality was impossible with so many people in the loop. At first I knew of no leaks. Indeed there were no comments when Hugh Calkins spent a night with Pamela and me, during which he and I had a long and useful talk about conditions at Harvard. He told me that the fellows had asked Nate to resign after the student troubles of the previous spring. They had then decided that Marbury and Kane should also resign, that their successors would take part in choosing the next president, and that they needed at least one academic fellow. Hugh was eager to have a colleague who had been involved in student issues. Equally concerned about Harvard finances, he intended to develop a formula to restrict expenses.

Only a few days after he left, the seeming confidentiality expired. I received a call from Theodore H. White, the journalist celebrated for his books about presidential election campaigns. I had met White years earlier through our common concern about students who commuted to Harvard. Now a member of the Board of Overseers, White was calling, he said, on behalf of the Harvard history department. Some of its members, in particular Oscar Handlin and Robert Lee Wolff, thought I should decline to become a fellow. I had never been offered a tenured appointment at Harvard and therefore, in their view, lacked the qualifications for a fellow. Furthermore, the corporation had not consulted the American historians. White, who agreed with Handlin and Wolff, urged me to withdraw. I told him that I would think about it. After a few days of rumination I decided to put the question to

Nate. I called him, reported my conversation with White, explained that I did not want my status to become an issue that increased tensions at Harvard, and asked for his opinion. "Don't you withdraw," Nate said. "We want you. Pay no attention to those historians or to White. They're just jealous." I decided to do as Nate advised.

There was more to come. In January the editor of the Harvard alumni magazine came to New Haven to interview me. He expressed his surprise that I was, as I told him, an "independent Democrat." It had never occurred to me that that political stance would be newsworthy. Then at the Board of Overseers opposition to my appointment arose, as I was later told, from an African American overseer who believed that the time was past due for the selection as a fellow of a black man. But after a prolonged discussion I was appointed.

The announcement of the appointment prompted a heartening response. A *New York Times* editorial expressed approval of Harvard's selection of an academician and, for the first time, of a Jew as member of the corporation. Milton Katz called me and reminded me of the weight of responsibility of a Harvard fellow. The mail brought warm letters from many old friends, including Fred Merk, who was "especially pleased by the favorable reception by the press to the new idea of having teachers and their point of view present in the Corporation." Among others who wrote were Florence Ballantine, Kingman Brewster's mother; Barbara Tuchman, a notable historian on the Radcliffe board; and Arthur Schlesinger, Jr., a distinguished professional friend and formerly a Harvard professor. I was especially gratified to receive letters of welcome from other Harvard faculty I knew — from Paul Freund and Ben Kaplan at the law school; from historians Myron Gilmore, John Fairbank, Paul Buck, William Langer, and Stuart Hughes; and from other scholars, including Gerald Holton, a physicist, and Zeph Stewart, a classicist and the master of Lowell House. They obviously disagreed with Handlin and Wolff. Elting Morison in his letter asked me to "accept the fact that what all of us believe to be this great office has found the right man." Elting was my professional mentor, and I appreciated but discounted his version of "facts." I also valued the words of Felicia Lamport, Ben Kaplan's wife and a talented writer of witty verse:

How splendidly exuberant the landscape has become
Since the Corporation flowered in a burst of brilliant Blum.

It was all heady stuff, a moment in the sun. But I had to get to work and to get to know my colleagues. The first Monday in February 1970 I took my seat at the corporation's table. I had attended tea at the Puseys' the previous afternoon, spent the night at the Dana Palmer House, the corporation's guest house, studied the long docket, and had an early breakfast at the faculty club. That was to become a regular schedule, though Sunday night sometimes involved a committee or dinner with one of my daughters, both of whom lived in greater Boston. Mondays on occasion I remained until ten in the evening for dinner with students or for a committee assignment. The drive to or from New Haven took about two hours and a half, so some Mondays seemed long.

Both Hooks Burr and I tended to arrive at the table ten minutes early. Hooks, as I was to learn, was distinguished for his character in the manner of a proper Bostonian. He exuded rectitude without being in the least stuffy. Bright, efficient, dedicated to Harvard, he was also a towering moral figure. My seat at the table was next to his, and soon we became friends. Knowing Hooks was in itself sufficient reward for assuming the duties of a Harvard fellow. Al Nickerson also impressed me. Tough-minded but gentle in manner, a model of good taste and proper behavior, he had a quiet sense of humor and a winning modesty. Al liked to eat an apple as he walked across Harvard Yard, and he bought me one the first time we took that stroll together. Hugh Calkins, intelligent, tense, impatient, reminded Ben Kaplan of a musical saw — bent steel trembling for release with great kinetic energy. Hugh's self-imposed mission at the table was to keep business moving, particularly any business pertaining to finances. Keith Kane, in the months we served together, impressed me with his cordiality. Charles Slichter, who replaced Kane, brought to the table his good humor, the academic expertness of an experienced physicist, and a steady educational conservatism. George Bennett struck me as a decent, stolid Boston banker, conservative and timid about change. Presiding, Nate made his own preferences clear, tended to be impatient with dissent, which he nevertheless allowed, and commanded the details of every matter discussed.

I learned a lot about Harvard and about my colleagues during the first months I served. Hooks Burr struck me as the ideal fellow of Harvard College. He did his homework, rarely missed a meeting and then only if he was ill, quickly identified latent problems that needed attention, supported the president but never hesitated to disagree politely if he felt the need, wasted no time, brought humor and a sense of proportion to deliberations, and never sought center stage. He cherished Harvard College. Charles Slichter and I, as it was hoped we would do, provided outside academic points of view that may have been of some value to the others, and we sometimes disagreed, a reminder that there was no academic party line. In my experience, academicians served no more wisely or effectively in such a position than did lawyers and businessmen. Indeed Bob Stone, the successful businessman who succeeded Al Nickerson, served Harvard with distinction for several decades.

The proceedings of the Harvard Corporation were confidential, including the proceedings of the search for a new president. As Hooks Burr once told me, a fellow had to be discreet about the issues we discussed. Most of them had to do with investments, expenditures, the budget, and its ramifications. We authorized a small fund drive before Nate left office, an effort to finish the job Nate had begun. Al Nickerson led that effort, which proved successful. Nate asked me to give special attention to the library and its problems, which were largely budgetary. Douglas Bryant, the Harvard librarian, was wholly cooperative, particularly in our objective of persuading a wealthy donor to make a substantial benefaction. Nate also arranged for me to succeed him as chairman of the board of the Hellenic Center, a Harvard scholarly facility in Washington, D.C., endowed by Paul Mellon and managed by Bernard Knox, a distinguished classicist.

I had few disagreements with Nate. Except for Hugh Calkins, the fellows had not mentioned the student problems of 1969 in my presence. Hugh had described his own failed efforts to pacify the campus. From newspaper accounts I knew that radical students had taken over University Hall in 1969, that the administration had then called in the city police, and that the intervention of the police had — predictably — further polarized the Harvard community. Neither the radicals nor the administration, as I saw it, had recognized the fragility of the academic enterprise, a fragility that made negotiation and compromise essential. The issue of ROTC, one of the major issues of the Harvard troubles, could have been negotiated and compromised, as the Yale experience showed. At Harvard in 1969, furthermore, the commanding officer of the naval ROTC program, Captain Thomas J. Moriarty, USN (by coincidence my regular golf partner in later years), had urged Nate to permit the abolition of military training on campus rather than risk a confrontation. The debate over governance at Harvard in 1970 reflected the still raw emotions of undergraduates and faculty alike. Indeed the liberal and conservative caucuses, spawned by the crisis in 1969, still divided the faculty. Because the mood remained fragile, the governing boards and the administration had to proceed with sensitivity in addressing controversial issues.

One such issue arose when we received a recommendation from one of the deans for the renewal of a nontenured appointment of an assistant professor who had been actively engaged in the protests. Because of the person's record, Nate wanted to deny the reappointment. I disagreed. The president and fellows, I argued, should ordinarily accept any dean's recommendations for junior appointments unless there was strong cause not to do so. The young man in question had had no disciplinary hearing at the time of his alleged protest. Now he should not be subjected to termination against his dean's advice. Nate began to reply, but Hooks interrupted him by saying, "John's right." We turned to another subject.

Later Nate asked Hugh and me to investigate the antagonisms within the faculty and between faculty and students at the School of Design. Conflicts over appointments and educational policies had erupted during the troubles of 1969, and they had not yet wholly subsided. I considered that assignment improper for a fellow. It required intervention in the daily affairs of a school, an intrusion into academic matters that were properly the business of the faculty. But Hugh urged me to join him. If we declined, he argued, the administration would act without adequate information. I agreed to the investigation under two conditions: first, this would be the last such task any fellow undertook; and second, we would proceed through confidential hearings under rules set and enforced by a master. Hugh suggested Paul Freund as master, but Paul declined. I suggested Ben Kaplan, who took on the task. Ben managed the hearings with tact and skill and assisted us in preparing our report to the president. In the final draft I inserted, with his consent and Hugh's, a slightly revised version of the first paragraph of the resolution we had adopted at Yale after the episode at Wright Hall. I was not surprised to find that many Harvard faculty members, still nursing grudges from 1969, considered it quaint to commend "mutual respect and charitable relations."

By that time Ben had become the "wise man" whom Kingman had advised me to identify. Kingman believed that I would profit from finding a Harvard citizen of good judgment and experience with whom I could talk confidentially about issues of current importance as they had developed before 1970. I would gain, too, from informed and disinterested counsel about the issues of governance then much mooted at Harvard. I had every reason to trust the other fellows, but their views and the views of the wisest faculty members might diverge. Hooks Burr obviously thought I needed to meet the faculty leaders who could rise above the hostilities of 1969, and to that end he scheduled interviews for me as we began to ask faculty for opinions about the major issues the next president would confront. By the end of May I had spent an hour or so with Edward Mason of the government department, John Finley in classics, Robert Ebert of the medical school, and Derek Bok of the law school. All of them were impressive and engaging; but of all the wise men I met, I was most comfortable with Ben Kaplan, an old friend from our postwar Cambridge days, a quiet, reflective, judicious law professor with a noble spirit and incisive mind. During my years as a fellow, I ate many Sunday suppers with Ben and his wife, Felicia, and I received only sound advice from Ben about the questions I raised with him.

The first of those questions pertained to the search for a new president, which began under Hooks Burr's guidance as soon as Nate officially announced his resignation. I did not discuss candidates with Ben except for those from the law school, particularly Derek Bok, a young dean whom Ben deeply admired. Indeed Ben confirmed my own enthusiasm for Derek, who struck me from the first as the foremost person we could appoint, though he did not want the job. But I had to try to withhold judgment while the search gathered momentum. At its start I made my only important contribution to it. Hooks had asked faculty and alumni to send their suggestions for president to the corporation. The early responses put forward more than a hundred names. Perhaps a dozen letters suggested one or another of the fellows; and two letters of which I knew, one from a classmate and the other from a historian, named me. While Hooks and I were walking together to lunch, he asked me if I wanted to be president of Harvard. "Goodness, no!" I replied. "I have never wanted to be president, provost, or dean of any university." Then I continued. If the fellows, conducting what they described as a global search, selected one of their own small company, they would lose their credibility. I was right, Hooks said, and he would make it a rule to exclude the fellows, two of whom, he sensed, yearned for the appointment, though he did not want them chosen. I went on to observe that many of the recommendations we had received were for public figures, John Gardner or Elliot Richardson, for example. But with campuses in turmoil, if Harvard appointed other than an academician, it would send the wrong message. It would suggest that the academy was bankrupt, lacking in men and women who could handle the presidency of a great university. Again Hooks agreed, accepting my point as a condition of the search, as he told the other fellows.

But we had months to go before we could produce even a short list of candidates. As a preliminary task Hooks assigned each of us an area of the country to explore for promising possibilities. At that time Slichter had yet to join us, so I was still the junior fellow. Because of that fact, Hooks assigned me the South. Where did the South begin, I asked. After a brief pause, Hooks answered, "Princeton, New Jersey." Perhaps only a Bostonian would think so, but having New Jersey in my region gave me the chance to talk with Princeton's able president, Robert Goheen, about the responsibilities of a university president. The first thing he told me, in confidence, was that his talented young provost, William Bowen, had been elected his successor, though that decision was still unannounced. We had had Bowen high on our list for Harvard, but clearly he was already engaged.

One Monday in April 1970 I remained in Cambridge to have dinner with the Society of Fellows, a group of advanced students selected to be junior fellows, each working on an important project of his own definition. Many of them went on to become Harvard professors. Of my generation several of the most eminent had been McGeorge Bundy, Arthur Schlesinger, Jr., and Thomas Kuhn. The junior fellows dined on Monday evenings with the senior fellows, advisers to the program. Among the senior fellows on the occasion when I visited was Charles Wyzanski, a federal district judge known for his innovative antitrust decision in the case of the American Shoe Machinery Company. I was chatting with Judge Wyzanski during cocktails when we first heard the news from New Haven: Kingman Brewster had announced his regret that he doubted that a black radical could receive a fair trial in the United States. Wyzanski, for many years a friend of Kingman's, was appalled, as were many others on the bench. But he knew little of the background to Kingman's statement, with which I concurred. And he overlooked the importance of two of Kingman's words: "regret" and "doubt."

New Haven had been in turmoil over the murder of Alex Rackley, a Black Panther alleged to be a police informer, who had been found dead along the banks of the West River. Bobby Seale, a Panther leader who had been in Chicago at the time of the killing, was alleged to have ordered it. Seale was indicted, with others, for conspiracy to murder Rackley. The resulting trial of Seale shook the city and occasioned Kingman's controversial remark. Across the whole country extremists had been using the rising agitation about civil rights and the war in Vietnam to advance their own agendas. So it was with the Weathermen, young white radicals who preached and practiced revolutionary violence. And so it was with the Black Panthers, champions of constructive social reforms but also paramilitary radicals. Murder and the threat of murder had become tools in their internecine warfare. On that account Eldridge Cleaver, another Panther leader, fled the country with his family. When he returned, his wife, Kathleen, became a Yale undergraduate, one of the most eloquent students whom I ever advised.

The murder in New Haven had no direct connection to Yale, but Yale was situated in the city, and many Yale students, particularly but not exclusively black students, were caught up in agitation to free Seale. With the campus seething, with the threat growing of a strike by black students, the university had become the proximate target of radical black anger, just as ROTC had been the proximate target of antiwar fervor. Kingman had made his statement in that context, issued out of conviction and timed for its placatory message.

By April 1970 black radicals on campus had developed plans to organize a strike in order to force the university to shut down. Yale's shutting down was supposed to indicate support for Seale. Some students, some parents, and some faculty believed the university should shut down of its own accord before a strike and the expected attending violence could begin. But Kingman, with the support of the Yale Corporation, defined a middle way. It was no easy task. Radicals, black and white, had been organizing in the residential colleges. In my college, Branford, the master, J. P. Trinkaus, a Marxist biologist, followed the lead of Kenneth Mills, an assistant professor of philosophy, West Indian by birth and Oxford trained. Mills, a doctrinaire Marxist, liked to play the part of the noble savage and preached revenge on the white bourgeoisie, particularly those at Yale. He and some local Panthers dominated a meeting at the rink, which they had organized as a testament to student support for a strike. They would permit no parliamentary order. On the contrary, they used physical coercion to still dissent, just as they had at prior meetings in the residential colleges, where they had prevented dissenters from gaining the floor. They were latter-day fascists. Coercion was central to their method of agitation, and the threat of coercion frightened a minority of students and faculty.

At an ensuing meeting of the Yale College faculty, with Georges May presiding, Kingman sat in the front row. He spoke briefly about the tension on campus and urged the faculty to listen to an undergraduate's version of the trouble. Dean May then allowed a student to address the group. Kurt Schmoke, a black student leader who later became the mayor of Baltimore and a Yale trustee, rose to the occasion. He explained that Yale students who were black were forced to deal with competing pressures — the pressure to conform to the position of the black protesters, and the contrary pressure to protect their university. Conservatives on the Yale faculty resented having to listen to an undergraduate. Even more vigorously they opposed Kingman's response. He had no intention either to close Yale down or physically to resist a student strike. But he asked for support for a motion to "suspend ordinary academic expectations" until both the strike and the demonstration planned for the weekend of May 1 were over.

The majority of a divided faculty supported Kingman. The suspension allowed students to go home, if they wanted to, and to postpone their final examinations until September. Or they could remain at Yale, where classes were to continue to meet, and help protect their residential colleges from the outsiders who were expected to gather, among them practiced, violent agitators who traveled from campus to campus.

The division within the faculty affected me. Two of my friends, Alex Bickel and C. Vann Woodward, disagreed with Kingman, whom I strongly supported. Alex considered Kingman the naïve captive of misbehaving undergraduates and dangerous black revolutionaries, a view common among the conservative faculty and alumni. Vann, as ever more concerned with individual rights than with the preservation of community, thought Kingman conceded too much to the radical blacks. There is a corpse, Vann argued, and there is a killer, and he's probably Bobby Seale. Kingman should keep out of it and let the court decide. (In the end the court found Seale innocent.) But Yale and Kingman had been drawn into the issue. And the Panthers were not interested in preserving free speech, Vann's preferred issue. Indeed they had been preventing it, whereas Kingman had promoted it. But in Vann's case and others, emotion had come to warp the debate, especially the emotion of recent recruits to the faculty who had come from institutions earlier visited by radical violence. Nevertheless I was able to remain on friendly terms with both Alex and Vann.

In the end, the so-called strike at Yale involved only some undergraduates, a minority in my lecture course, though most black students in that course. The morning it began I found several black students, all large young men, barring the entrance to my class at the law school auditorium. Why not let me in, I asked, and let me begin my lecture. Then, if I said something offensive, they could raise a hand as a signal of dissent, I would thereupon consider the lecture disrupted, and I would dismiss the class. They thought my suggestion over and then allowed me and my students to enter the room. Only one black student took a seat. I told him privately that he could depart with my permission if he wished to do so, and later I would share my lecture notes with him. He decided to stay. Most of the students enrolled in the course were in their seats when it was time to begin. I started by commenting on the fragility of a classroom. There would be no need for demonstrations in my class, I said again, for anyone could stop the lecture by raising a hand to signal disagreement. Several black students who had been standing at the doors then entered.

I began to lecture, but not on the topic scheduled for that morning. Instead, while driving to the university, in my head I had composed a special lecture for that day. I delivered it without interruption. In the lecture I described three styles of recent American politics—the bland, the cool, and the passionate. The Nixon Republicans, I suggested, represented the conventional, the bland, in their addiction to the Cold War and the war in Vietnam, which they could have ended on the terms the Democrats had negotiated in 1968. So also, effective affirmative action could not be expected from Nixon's southern policies and his conventional attitudes toward race. Before his assassination, I contended, Bobby Kennedy had been the spokesman of the cool, of rational approaches to ending the war and advancing equal social and economic rights. Martin Luther King, Jr., had brought passion to the cause of those rights, a desirable passion in a cause since usurped by advocates of violence like the Weathermen and the Panthers. I knew that I was creating at best a loose typology, but I did so to address the occasion. I concluded by urging the students to adopt passionate but nonviolent means to achieve cool ends. No one left the lecture. No one raised a hand in protest. Most applauded. My brave wife, who had attended without my knowledge in order if necessary to protect me, slipped away. In the days before the examination period, days I devoted to my usual lectures, attendance remained at about two thirds of normal, and that ratio obtained at the final exam. In my case and all others of which I knew, the "strike" did not halt education at Yale.

But the threat of an invasion of radicals during the weekend of May 1 was genuine, and the Brewster administration took steps to prepare for it. At the time I knew nothing of those preparations, but months later I began to hear about some of them. Kingman consulted with his former colleague, Archibald Cox of the Harvard Law School, a wise man committed to peaceful resolutions of student troubles and a veteran of the troubles at Columbia in 1968 and Harvard in 1969. Archie in 1970 was also advising the Harvard Corporation about potential disturbances in his own university, and he was able to identify the traveling agitators who had invaded and intensified student protests he had observed. With that information, Yale officials, with Kingman and Sam Chauncey in the lead, took steps to divert the invaders from New Haven. With his Yale assistants, Kingman and the New Haven chief of police worked out a joint scenario for responding to any dangerous developments in the city. Cyrus Vance, a member of the Yale Corporation and a former Secretary of the Army, in effect took command of the city police. Perhaps most important for the morale of students choosing to remain at Yale through the weekend, Kingman mobilized the masters of the residential colleges. Each master planned to help house strangers in the city, and each would join with his students in some service — for example, setting up an infirmary at Pierson College and a nursery at Davenport College. But at Branford College Master J. P. Trinkaus did nothing, while one of the honorary fellows, with the undergraduates' help, set up a dispensary, while other undergraduates planned to serve granola to all comers. Rudy Rogers recruited a dozen or more faculty to protect the library from fire or vandalism. I, like most of the involved faculty, decided to spend my time with undergraduate members of my college—students I knew, students who chose to remain at Yale, students who might need a friend or adviser as the weekend unfolded.

After lunch the Friday of that weekend I, a foot soldier in Kingman's army, began to check all rest rooms in the Hall of Graduate Studies in order to be sure that no one was hiding in them. Then I walked down to Branford College, where two students I knew were worried about the platoon of National Guardsmen standing at parade rest outside the college's York Street gate. I led the students across the street to the entrance of Davenport College, where we sat down. Pointing to the guardsmen, I directed attention to the ammunition belts they were wearing. I pointed out that the belts had no bullets in them. Further, the students could see that the guardsmen were mostly teenagers, who looked more apprehensive in their uniforms than did the Branford students in their jeans. As the students returned to their college, I asked a campus policeman to call headquarters and request the authorities to station the guard at the southern end of the street, away from the colleges. Within ten minutes the guard had moved. For the rest of the day nothing of note transpired, and I went home in the early evening. But that night a bomb exploded in the hockey rink, fortunately with no injuries and only reparable damage. As tensions rose that night, the New Haven police chief, with Kingman's foreknowledge, dispersed the crowd along Elm Street and on the green by releasing tear gas. I learned of those developments only the next morning.

On Saturday morning I arrived by design at the great court in Branford College at about six o'clock. A haze of pot smoke overhung the area where couples were stretched out on the grass. Recognizing none of them, I assumed they were outsiders. On impulse I walked over to Pierson College to ask John Hersey, the master there, to have a look at Branford. He accompanied me back to the great court, looked around, and said: "I'm getting out of here. This place has gone mad." Before he left he promised to summon some campus police. Several of them arrived, wearing suits and fedoras, and stood in the entryways with their arms akimbo. The word got around. The couples on the grass arose and disappeared. The haze of pot smoke lifted. Half an hour later the senior fellow of the Yale Corporation, Ted Blair, entered the court in company with the secretary of the university, Ben Holden. Ben had timed their appearance well. Blair glanced at the peaceful court, exchanged greetings with me, and walked out. Where had the radical Trinkaus been? The master was huddled with his wife in their quarters, where he stayed most of the day. During the previous night, while he had remained hidden, strangers had entered the basement and broken into a supply of emergency rations left over from the days of bomb shelters.

As other fellows of the college began to arrive, I walked into neighboring Saybrook College, where the master, Basil Henning, a historian of seventeenth-century England, and his wife, Alison, had been holding an open house for their students all night. They had known nothing about the goings-on in Branford, but while I informed them, they served me a cup of coffee and a martini, the first and last I ever consumed before eight in the morning.

The situation grew even more tense that afternoon, as we learned about Nixon's "incursion" into Cambodia. The issue of justice for African Americans, the issue attached to the Bobby Seale case, receded at once as the issue of the war in Vietnam seized the attention of everyone around the campus. By twilight crowds had gathered on the green and in the Old Campus across College Street from the green. As darkness fell, Jack Embersits asked me to join him while he walked east from Branford College to the Old Campus. We walked right into a wave of tear gas, for the police chief had used it again to disperse a crowd before it could turn violent. I soaked my handkerchief at the dispensary at the college, left Embersits, and started in the other direction, away from the gas and toward my parking lot. But just then along came George Pierson, "Father Yale." He was determined to experience tear gas, as he never before had, and was unwilling to take the precaution I had of breathing through a wet handkerchief. Worried about him, I accompanied him eastward until, a few steps from the Old Campus, he decided to give in to the gas. I then led him, gasping and crying from the exposure, to his car. We both went home.

In crossing the great court in Branford earlier I had stopped when I observed a student I knew, Peggy Buttenheim, quietly crying at the table where, now exhausted, she had been serving granola all day. I asked her if I could do anything for her. "Oh, Mr. Blum," she replied, referring to Cambodia, "I feel so helpless." She was speaking for thousands of Americans. We were all helpless when the nation's president expanded a war that the nation had never declared. The deaths at Kent State soon drove that lesson home. Peggy's reaction that evening struck right at my feelings about the weekend, my feeling that the Yale students defending their colleges were also bearing witness for social justice and against the war in Vietnam. As I later told Peggy when she began graduate work in psychology, I hoped she would never feel helpless again.

She could take as an example Kingman Brewster. Concerned but controlled, Kingman had brought wisdom and courage to the crisis at Yale, the university he loved. He had proved himself the ablest crisis manager in higher education. In listing the qualities I thought essential for the next Harvard president, I had put first "Someone Kingman Brewster will learn to respect." Derek Bok had been a student of Kingman's, and the two men respected each other. I believed that the two universities were informing each other. In times of danger and stress, however, developments at Harvard and Yale had contrasted vividly. To my mind, Kingman had made the difference.

15

The Busy Hum of Academe

As the events of the spring of 1970 suggested, normality, and with it productive contemplation, lay in the future. Every campus felt the tremors of the deaths at Kent State and Jackson State. Every campus remained tense with student skepticism about the war in Vietnam and about the slow and timid pace of governmental action for racial integration. May Day at Yale proved to be only a way station to further tribulations.

During the previous winter Theodore Lockwood, a former MIT colleague who was now president of Trinity College in Hartford, had asked me if I would accept an honorary degree, a doctor of humane letters (DHL). I was delighted. He warned me that in return I would have to deliver the commencement address, to which I casually agreed. I soon learned that it would not be so easy. Ted informed me in April that the graduating seniors had demanded to select their own speaker. Further, they had chosen Kenneth Mills, Yale's best-known New Left agitator. I could cancel if I wished, but Ted hoped I would not. I assured him that I intended to speak. So on the appointed day Mills and I were both to appear.

As the Trinity commencement began, outdoors on a bright morning, Pamela was sitting in the midst of the group of trustees with Ted's wife, Betty, and I was on a platform with the other honorands and Ted. After opening the ceremonies, Ted said that he supposed that everyone was wondering why Trinity was awarding me a degree. Years earlier, he explained, at MIT I had offered him his very first job. He added a brief citation and draped a purple hood across my shoulders. Surprised and amused by his remarks, I was also anxious about the reception of my speech. I had written a fifteen-minute version of the lecture about political styles that I had delivered to my class on the day the so-called strike at Yale had begun. Now, at Trinity, again I compared the bland, the cool, and the passionate. As I went on, so I later learned, a trustee's wife sitting near Pamela said, sotto voce, to Betty Lockwood, "Who is that awful young man up there saying those terrible things?" But the graduating seniors applauded. Then Mills spoke. He had prepared no text, a great mistake, and his ramblings continued for more than thirty minutes. Capable of a much better performance, he had misjudged the significance of the occasion for the students and their parents. The graduating seniors were embarrassed that their chosen speaker had laid an egg.

At the invitation of Nate Pusey I had also agreed to address the Harvard chapter of Phi Beta Kappa at its meeting two days before commencement. As that day approached, I became more and more uneasy about the prospect of speaking on the occasion Ralph Waldo Emerson had used to deliver his famous address, "The American Scholar." I felt totally inadequate as a distant successor. Casting about for a subject, I seized upon a draft I had written for a section of my intended book on the home front. I had been thinking about the soldiers whom the media selected as heroes during World War II. They were brave men, but they were presented not only as courageous but also almost invariably as exemplary of American values, as the media interpreted those values. The heroes typically loved their mothers, delivered newspapers door to door in their youth, wrote letters to pretty high school sweethearts, played baseball, and hated the Japanese. Even John Hersey, a talented reporter who knew better, described General Douglas MacArthur with similar banalities. But in 1970 the media selected no such heroes in Vietnam. There were many brave Americans there, too, but the war was so hated that the media would not attribute to bravery the qualities of character that American culture had made common for heroic status. The capacity for heroism had not changed; the popularity of the war had. Pursuing that idea, I delivered an antiwar speech entitled "Where Have All the Heroes Gone?"

As I spoke, I could see the dismay in the face of Barbara Solomon, once my neighbor and fellow doctoral candidate, now a dean and a marshal that day of Phi Beta Kappa. And I could feel the disapproval of President Pusey, sitting behind me, and of much of the audience. To my surprise, when the ceremony had ended and the Phi Beta Kappa members were filing out, another of the marshals, law professor Milton Katz, took me by the arm and led me quickly into the Harvard Yard. He was taking me home for lunch, Milton said, his pace increasing. He avoided conversation until we arrived and then busied himself making drinks. I assumed that he, an old friend, was kindly protecting me from adverse responses to my speech, but we talked only of other matters. Many years later I asked him about his purpose and he confirmed my assumption. The faculty and administrators who had been present, he said, with a few exceptions like himself, were shocked to hear a Harvard fellow criticize the war at a university affair. He was sparing me predictable arguments that would have sprung up and that would delay luncheon when I was surely hungry and thirsty. I had not expected such an adverse response, and I had considered my remarks, later published in the alumni bulletin, only gentle criticism of the war. But apparently I underestimated their impact. "Uncle Sid" Lovett, the beloved retired chaplain of Yale College, wrote me that my essay in the Harvard alumni bulletin was the best antiwar sermon he had read—high praise from a dedicated democrat.

As at Trinity, controversy over the war had not ceased at Harvard, nor had controversy over local issues involving race. At Harvard the latter had centered on the housing the university owned in the area along the Charles River and east and south of the Yard. The aging, frame buildings that had been occupied by Irish Americans in my undergraduate years were now rented largely by African Americans. The tenants had formed an association, headed by Sandra Graham, a black woman, to demand lower rents and various improvements. Their demands had become a part of the SDS indictment of the university. Harvard made a reasonable profit from the real estate it owned, but the tenants' association and the SDS considered the university infinitely rich and the tenants infinitely deserving. There was a case to be made for moderate improvements. But the accusative mood that had characterized the issue at the time of the problems in 1969 continued to fester in 1970.

The housing controversy almost disrupted the 1970 commencement. A characteristically Harvard commencement, full of pageantry and ceremony, the day began with a parade. Led by degree recipients, followed by the president and the governing boards, attending faculty in their robes, and alumni in ranks with the eldest classes first—each with a marshal dressed in morning coats, striped trousers, and top hats (the uniform also of the governing boards)—the parade wove through the Yard and passed the steps of Widener Library. There it turned left into Tercentenary Theater, a rectangular space between the library and the chapel. At the north end of that rectangle stood the platform where the dignitaries sat, among them the honorands, the president in a special chair, the governing boards, and the faculty. In 1970 television cameras, observing it all, honed in on the platform as the parade ended. Participating in my first commencement since becoming a fellow, I had lined up behind President Pusey. The fellows were paired by height, which put me next to Hooks Burr. We climbed the platform to our seats together and sat down next to each other. The president opened the ceremony. Perhaps fifteen minutes into the proceedings Sandra Graham, demanding use of the microphone, suddenly appeared on the platform. Archie Cox, Harvard's troubleshooter, who was seated near the president, crawled up the stairs of the platform and said to Hooks, "He wants to call the police!" In almost a single voice, Hooks and I replied, "Oh, no! Tell him to let her speak." Hooks suggested in a whisper that George Bennett and Al Nickerson would talk with representatives of the tenants' association in University Hall while Sandra Graham addressed the audience for ten minutes. Nate reluctantly accepted that plan.

The alternative would have been a disaster. I could only imagine the police racing into the commencement, in full view of the television cameras, in order to evict a black woman trying to address the assembled crowd. Harvard Yard was no place for the city police. Nate had learned at least to consult Archie before summoning them. As it was, Nate became restless when Sandra Graham exceeded her allowed time by a couple of minutes, but she stepped down of her own accord after trying to make her case.

Meanwhile Al Nickerson and George Bennett had agreed to some of the tenants' association's modified "demands." But Nate, angry, on resuming the podium declared that all those qualified for a degree in any of the schools were rendered that degree, and abruptly terminated the ceremony half an hour early. He could have conducted the proceedings as planned and it would have run no more than a quarter hour late. Instead there was time to kill before luncheon, time spent imbibing extra drinks, which no one needed.

Yale also had its problems with local African American protest groups who blamed the university for allegedly high rents and decrepit housing, even when Yale was not the owner of the real estate, partly because Yale was viewed as a very rich institution in a very poor city. I could not imagine Kingman calling the city police to interfere in an interrupted commencement. Indeed Tracy Barnes, Kingman's assistant in dealing with African American protest groups, strove for peace. Tracy was a Yale College graduate, a Harvard LL.B., and a retired senior official of the CIA. He and his team cooperated with local church and civic groups on joint ventures, including the development of better housing, to improve the conditions of the poor in the city. But many town-gown tensions remained. On one occasion Tracy met with a group of black activists who were angry with Yale, and listened to their demands. In the course of the meeting, one woman picked up a large, cut-glass ashtray and hurled it at him. It whizzed past his ear. Tracy told me that he comforted himself with the thought that she had intended to miss him. But the situation was not relaxed.

Tracy related this story as a prelude to inviting me to join him and his wife, Janet, at a luncheon they were giving that day in their house for half a dozen black leaders from the city's protest organizations. Janet served drinks in a hostile environment she chose to treat as friendly. Conversation remained cordial until, announcing that lunch was about to be served, she requested that at the table we all refrain from the "m–f" word. Her guests at once proceeded to use "m–f" as their only adjective until they departed. But only the activists' language challenged Yale that afternoon, and it was as predictable as it was rude. As I sat there at lunch, I recalled the Harvard commencement of 1970. The next Harvard president, I thought, would have to know how to deal with an emergency without losing his cool.

During the summer of 1970 the Harvard fellows met at Al Nickerson's lovely island off the coast of central Maine where, joined by Nate Pusey, we narrowed the list of those recommended for the presidency from almost two hundred to fewer than one hundred. With much work still to do, by October we had developed a relatively small list with several candidates from Harvard ranks. One of the Harvard professors who was thought to be high on the list struck some of the members of the liberal faculty caucus as too close to Nate and his policies. Though that assessment may have been unfair, it troubled them. One Wednesday afternoon a physicist in the liberal caucus telephoned me with an urgent plea that I drive up to Cambridge at once to attend a dinner of that caucus to which he had also invited Hugh Calkins. The faculty liberals were worried about our search. Hugh and I both reached Cambridge in time for the dinner. Of the ten or twelve faculty there, I knew only one, an undergraduate contemporary, formerly in publishing, now teaching English. He and the others reminded us that the liberal caucus had objected to the president's way of handling the troubles in 1969. Now they objected to the probability, as they saw it, that a faculty member close to Nate might be selected to succeed him.

They wanted us to know the sources of their concern. For one thing, they contended, Nate had never appointed a Jewish faculty member to a major committee of the Faculty of Arts and Sciences. Neither Hugh nor I knew enough to confirm or to challenge that contention, but I found even the sense of discrimination unfortunate. So, I thought, did Hugh, though there was no way for us to communicate. As the meal drew close to its end, the leader of the group asked us what we intended to do about their concerns. I had been thinking about just that. Among possible candidates to succeed

Nate, I had never had a high opinion of the faculty member to whom they objected. I could not believe he was anti-Semitic, but I knew that for my taste he was too conservative about the issues dividing Harvard. I also wanted to keep the liberals quiet at least until after we had made a decision about the presidency, which I still privately hoped would be offered to Derek Bok. So I spoke up. I could not tell them, I said, who was going to be the next Harvard president. But I could say that I opposed the man they were worried about, that I considered his chances very slim, that I could not comfortably work with him, and that therefore if he were elected I would have to resign from the corporation. Satisfied by those assurances, the liberal caucus adjourned the meeting.

Hooks deliberately postponed any decision about the outcome of the search until December 1970. Late in November, after the Yale football game in Cambridge, which I did not attend, McGeorge Bundy telephoned me. He had heard many rumors about the search during the weekend of the game. He hoped we would select someone identified with JFK's New Frontier. But, he had concluded, no Kennedy associate was on our short list. He had also concluded (accurately, though I did not know how) that I had said that my friend Robert Solow, an outstanding MIT economist and a Harvard graduate, would not be interested in becoming president of Harvard. Bob had been on the staff of Kennedy's Council of Economic Advisers. Mac argued that I had no right to speak for Bob. So the following Monday I told the other fellows that I thought we should concede to Mac at least an interview with Bob, who was after all both a product of Harvard and a leader in his field. Al Nickerson and I had a long talk with Bob soon thereafter. We found him so impressive that we asked him to return to meet the other fellows the following week. But a few days later, Bob called to tell me he had been thinking things over and decided that he did not want to become president of Harvard. He wanted to continue as an economist, with the hope that his work would one day win him a Nobel Prize. (It did.)

I had not altered my personal preference for Derek Bok. As I discovered when in December Hooks called for a vote, the others had come to the same conclusion. At first Derek declined, but when Hooks pressed him, he agreed to reconsider if he could in confidence consult three people. The first was John Dunlop, the labor economist and Dean of the Faculty of Arts and Sciences, a friend of Derek's with whom he had collaborated on a book. The second was Kingman Brewster, a former teacher of Derek's who had helped persuade him to accept his post as Dean of the Law School. The third, to my great surprise, was I. Why, Derek asked when we met, had I agreed to be a fellow of Harvard College? The position struck him as incongruent with my usual academic and scholarly interests. I replied by telling him about my conversation with Kingman and Charles Taylor just before I had signed on. "Kingman made me do it," I concluded. Derek and Sissela, his talented wife, spent a weekend in New York with Kingman and Mary Louise Brewster. Soon thereafter Derek agreed to be president. In part at least, Kingman had persuaded him to do it. On Christmas Day 1970, truly a day of rejoicing, Hooks telephoned to tell me the news.

For commencement 1971 the fellows of Harvard College invited former President James B. Conant to be their guest. I considered him one of the great university presidents of the twentieth century. Indeed he had led Harvard to much the same goals that Kingman later pursued at Yale, particularly a more diversified and more accomplished student body and faculty. But Conant, president during the depression and war years, had not been able to raise enough money to permit many new educational ventures or even to sustain the physical plant. Pusey resented the condition of the physical plant as he found it, and he blamed Conant for the rehabilitative spending over which he had to preside. So during the Pusey years Conant avoided commencements. But now, with president-elect Bok scheduled to be present (and to receive a surprise honorary AB degree — Derek had attended Stanford as an undergraduate and would be the first president without an earned Harvard AB), it seemed timely to have Conant also on the platform — a prospect that excited me because I had never met James Conant.

The meeting I had looked forward to occurred really by chance. Returning from a luncheon the day before commencement, I reached the gate in the Yard across from the Dana Palmer House, where both the Conants and Pamela and I were staying. President Conant was standing there, looking around.

"Why, Mr. Conant," I asked, "what are you doing here?"

"I thought," he replied, "that you fellows invited me."

I blushed. "Of course," I said. "I meant why are you standing at this gate?"

Conant pointed to two large bags and explained that his wife had gone to find a porter. I volunteered to take the bags to their room. We arrived just as Mrs. Conant did. After introductions I began to depart. "Just a minute, Blum," Mr. Conant said. "Before you go I want you to know that you have just done the most important thing you will ever do as a fellow of Harvard College." He was teasing, to be sure, but he had never had much use for the corporation. And in some ways he was quite right in his assessment of my errand. We became friends, a joy for me except when we would meet for breakfast at the faculty club, where Jim, increasingly deaf, would discuss confidential matters in a voice audible all around the room.

During the 1970s the Harvard Corporation became my most time-consuming and significant administrative responsibility. Most of those years I served as chairman of the committee on honorary degrees. Every year at least one overseer and a couple of faculty members were appointed to that group. I was especially eager for Harvard to honor, as we did, men and women in the literary and creative arts and men and women in the forefront of the civil rights movement. Among the latter group were Helen Susman, the liberal South African spokeswoman against apartheid; my friend and colleague, C. Vann Woodward, a leading opponent of Jim Crow; and A. Philip Randolph, the renowned organizer of the wartime March on Washington movement for civil rights.

Since the honorands were in Cambridge for only a couple of days, there was no time to get to know them. But one, Father Ted Hesburgh, the president of Notre Dame, spent enough time with me, first having a drink and then volunteering as my temporary valet while I dressed for dinner, to make me feel that we had been pals for life. It rained while Ted spoke to the alumni meeting the afternoon of commencement. "Don't blame me," he said, using a well-rehearsed line, "I'm in sales, not production." I also proposed for an honorary degree Olaf Palme, the eminent Swedish prime minister, a leading social democrat whose reforms made Sweden the foremost welfare state in Europe. He had also welcomed Americans fleeing from the Vietnam draft. The corporation approved my recommendation, but Elliot Richardson persuaded his fellow overseers to vote it down. That vote prevailed, for as Hooks Burr and I agreed, honorary degrees were too unimportant to provoke a fight between the two governing boards. Indeed in the 1980s the overseers were given responsibility for those degrees.

Hugh Calkins chaired a much more important committee, concerned with corporate responsibility. It included both students and faculty members. The continuing issue they faced arose from the need for Harvard to vote its stock in American corporations doing business in South Africa. Some, like IBM, hired, trained, and promoted black workers and executives. Many others, however, accepting apartheid, employed black South Africans largely in menial jobs. Could an ethical investor properly own their stock? With Hugh in the lead, sometimes pushed by the students, the committee regularly recommended that Harvard support stockholder initiatives to influence corporations to desegregate their South African operations, or else abandon its investment in those companies. The President and Fellows regularly followed the committee's recommendations, but the treasurer, whose first interest was in the yield of the endowment, sold stock in offending corporations only reluctantly.

The treasurer's grudging retreats irritated President Bok, who tolerated them until the question of owning stock in tobacco companies arose. With all the fellows, Derek had come to believe that a university with a medical school should not own tobacco stock, not even shares of Philip Morris, an especially profitable company that the treasurer was loath to sell. Outvoted, he sold Harvard's shares, but the episode seemed to exhaust Derek's patience. He soon recommended a new treasurer, George Putnam, head of the Putnam funds, a Bostonian whose family had long been involved in Harvard affairs. I liked and respected George, who played a major role in persuading Derek and the fellows to set up the Harvard Investment Company, which thereafter managed the endowment with great success. In promoting that development George was joined importantly by Robert Stone, an affable and successful New York entrepreneur who replaced Al Nickerson as a fellow when Al's failing hearing forced him to resign. (George once asked me why I was the most prudent of the fellows. "That's easily explained," I replied. "I work for Yale.")

Derek gave focus to the corporation's activities. He ordinarily opened meetings with a description of his most pressing problems or priorities. He and his vice presidents reported at length about their activities, as also from time to time did the deans of the major schools. Only rarely did any fellow express disagreement with the reports or recommendations brought to us. In one matter especially did the president need the fellows' support. That was the plan, originated by the senior vice president, for a multipurpose disposal facility and power plant for the medical school, its neighboring, affiliated hospitals, and nearby Harvard-owned real estate. The technology involved was innovative; the politics of gaining support from the Commonwealth of Massachusetts and the city of Boston, complicated; the projected cost overruns, at first alarming. But Derek, alerted especially by Hooks Burr, put an able vice president, Joe Billy Wyatt, in charge of the project, and Wyatt, reporting directly to him, had the project under control within two years. During that time the corporation learned about the continuing progress of the power plant at almost all its meetings. Wyatt for his part later became Chancellor of Vanderbilt University.

As President of Harvard, Derek Bok, during the years I was a fellow, led the university with exemplary skill. Like James B. Conant and Kingman Brewster, he became one of the eminent university presidents of the twentieth century. In office, with the encouragement of the fellows, he appointed four vice presidents, managers all, under whom he reorganized the noneducational affairs of the university. Before he retired after twenty years in office, he had also managed a major fund drive. After he retired he wrote several books infused with the liberal spirit that marked his thinking about social as well as academic issues. But of all his accomplishments, the most significant in my opinion were the annual reports he composed in his first decade in office, reports that included his reflections about education in the major Harvard schools, notably arts and sciences, law, business, and medicine. Those reports constituted an incisive, but much overlooked, charter for the future not only of Harvard but also of higher education in the United States more generally. They were the work of an outstanding academic statesman. The fellows' role was only to admire them, as I did, and to endorse any expenditure attendant on their implementation.

In 1972 Jim Tobin introduced Senator George McGovern to a group of Yale professors eager to assist his campaign for the Democratic presidential nomination. A leading opponent of the war in Vietnam, McGovern had a liberal voting record. Much of his support came from former Kennedy Democrats who stood to the left of Hubert Humphrey and Ed Muskie, also potential party candidates. Most of the professors Tobin assembled were economists or political scientists who had skills useful for the McGovern campaign, the economists as instructors in their field, about which the candidate was relatively unschooled; the political scientists for their expertness about public opinion. Since McGovern was a trained historian himself with a Ph.D. from Northwestern, I felt that my only use to him might be as a cheerleader, but he asked me whether I would be willing to deliver speeches for him when he was unable to fit the occasions into his crowded schedule. Though I promised I would, no such occasion arose until after his nomination. Then in October I received a telephone call from his Connecticut headquarters asking me to speak for him briefly at a Democratic rally on the last Sunday of the month in Lakeville, Connecticut. There the main attraction was to be Ella Grasso, who was running for reelection to her seat in the U.S. House of Representatives. Grasso was considered a sure thing, but McGovern was trailing Nixon badly in all the polls. My topic, I was told, was to be "Why McGovern?"

The rally took place on the shores of the lake in Lakeville, a small town in northwest Connecticut where perhaps 150 folk had gathered, most with picnic lunches and barbecues, most with children, many of whom were playing on seesaws and slides. Some of the adults were still preoccupied with their barbecues when we arrived. The scene seemed to resemble a camp meeting of the 1896 William Jennings Bryan campaign. The Grasso people were in charge, however, and were reluctant to allow any time for McGovern, whom they had dismissed as a loser. Eager to get the McGovern business out of their way, they scheduled me first while the small crowd was finishing lunch. I had been following the national campaign in the *New York Times,* the *Washington Post,* and *The New Republic.* Those publications, especially the *Post,* had reported fully on the scandalous maneuvering of the Nixon camp, not least the emerging news about the break-in at the Democratic headquarters at Watergate. Indeed the *Post* articles by Bob Woodward, one of my former students, and his collaborator, Carl Bernstein, had revealed much of the data that later became the basis for the impeachment of Nixon, though in October not many Americans were paying attention. So in explaining "why McGovern" I concentrated on listing the Nixon scandals. Inside of ten minutes I concluded: "Why McGovern? Because the dirtiest five-letter word in the English language is N–I–X–O–N."

Though McGovern was losing and I was small fry, we learned two days later that the Nixon campaign was planning a suit against me for libeling the president. The *Hartford Courant* reported that story, followed by the *Yale Daily News* and then, using the Yale report, the *Harvard Crimson.* I was not worried because I knew that in political speeches there was very little that could be judged libelous. No suit was ever pressed, and (to my great disappointment) I never made Nixon's enemies list. But the report of my speech provoked Hooks Burr to telephone me. As soon as I answered the phone he said, "John, how could you?" Months later Senate hearings revealed that American Airlines, of which Hooks was a director, had illegally contributed a million dollars to the Nixon campaign. I called him and when he answered I said, "Hooks, how could you?"

On only one other occasion did politics affect my relations with my colleagues on the corporation. At a dinner party Al Nickerson and his wife gave, Pamela and I were guests, along with Paul Brooks of Houghton, Mifflin and David and Peggy Rockefeller. Over brandy after dinner David Rockefeller began to praise Nixon's policy in Vietnam. As he went on, I became increasingly restless until I could no longer resist disagreeing with him. We argued for about ten minutes, with Brooks now and then taking my side, until our host suggested joining the ladies. It was probably indiscreet of me to argue with a major Harvard donor, but surely Rockefeller knew that many historians dissented from his views. If he did not, I figured it was time that he learned.

During the early 1970s I continued whenever I could to proceed with my research and writing on the home front during World War II. I intended to end my book on the subject by showing the relation between American culture and national politics in the 1944 election and in the international tensions of 1945, the first year of Harry Truman's presidency. A central figure in those developments was Roosevelt's wartime vice president, Henry A. Wallace of Iowa, who in the period 1933–40 had been a controversial secretary of agriculture. I had read the available biographical literature about Wallace but had gained no sure impression of him when I had the good luck to be introduced to his widow, Ilo Wallace, a wise and gracious lady, and her talented and equally gracious daughter, Jean Wallace Douglas. Paul Brooks introduced us. He was a friend of Jean Douglas, who shared Brooks's concern about the nation's growing ecological problems, and Jean had asked him to find a biographer for her father. She was looking for a historian the family could trust with the Wallace diary, then still unopened to scholars. With my curiosity piqued, Paul took me to lunch at Ilo Wallace's residence in South Salem, New York. I found the Wallaces welcoming and encouraging, but still undecided about their disposition of the diary. I volunteered to read it and then to suggest a plan for publication, a proposal that both Mrs. Wallace and Paul Brooks would review.

The diary, almost all of it about the war years, fascinated me. It also spoke directly to my intended book on the home front. But I could not write both that book and a biography of Wallace. So I suggested to Paul Brooks and Ilo Wallace that I edit the diary for publication, with notes and an introduction. That project would remind the interested public of Henry Wallace's glowing liberal record during the years of the war. It would also enhance my own work, though it would not preclude the family from continuing their search for a biographer. In 1973 Houghton, Mifflin published my edition of the Wallace wartime diary, entitled *The Price of Vision*. It made no waves, for public interest in Wallace was minimal. Indeed he had almost been forgotten.

But the book did assist scholars with an interest in Wallace and his wartime activities, especially as head of the Board of Economic Warfare, as author of the liberal tract "The Century of the Common Man," and as FDR's rejected candidate for renomination as vice president. The diary also spoke to Wallace's involvement with the secret development of the atomic bomb and his agreement with Secretary of War Stimson on the advantages of sharing scientific but not technological information about atomic energy with the Soviet Union. McGeorge Bundy told me later that he found my edition of the diary helpful in writing his own book, *Danger and Survival* (1988), an unequaled study, in the words of his subtitle, of "choices about the bomb in the first fifty years." Through 1945, Wallace had not made the political error of accepting communist support, as he did in his quixotic bid for the presidency in 1948. Rather, through the war years he had tried to promote liberal causes, among them equal rights for people of color and for women and government commitment to full employment. He also insisted on decent wages and living conditions for foreign workers who were producing raw materials that he was buying for American use and to preempt German purchases. All in all, Henry Wallace deserved a major place he never received in the pantheon of American reformers.

At Yale the administrative immunity that Kingman had promised me soon expired. I could not in conscience decline to help the new Dean of Yale College, Horace Taft, a respected physicist and the youngest son of Senator Robert Taft, the "Mr. Republican" of my parents' generation. Horace, a friend and frequent golf companion who gave me a stroke a hole and still always won lunch, brought to his new task his good judgment, his powerful loyalty to Yale, his deep concern for both creative scholarship and excellent teaching, his compassion, and his ready humor. I served on his steering committee until I had been a member for so long that I began to seem too much a company man at faculty meetings. In addition Kingman, probably overrating my Harvard experience with budgetary issues, appointed me chairman of an emergency committee on Yale's financial problems, which had become severe by 1974. Indeed that spring the treasurer forecast a deficit for the fiscal year of more than $1 million, at that time still a considerable sum, enough to worry Kingman and his new provost, economist Richard Cooper. (Charles Taylor had resigned in order to complete his training as a Jungian analyst and to embark on a career in psychiatry.)

I could see that the financial committee's meetings and eventual report would consume most of the summer. In order to complete my manuscript of the Wallace diaries, I needed at least three quiet weeks in Vermont, so I asked Kingman to appoint a co-chairman. He and I and the other committee members agreed that the logical candidate was Jaroslav Pelikan, a distinguished scholar of the early church fathers and of the Reformation. Jary also had a learned interest in higher education, particularly as Cardinal Newman had promoted it. The committee became known, as Yale committees often did, by the names of its chairmen: "the Blum-Pelikan committee." But its deliberations profited especially from the contributions of Horace Taft and Dick Cooper, both members ex officio, and Bill Brainard, a gentle and trenchant economist with unfailing common sense. Their realistic analyses of Yale's finances contrasted with Pelikan's quasi-philosophical exposition of educational purposes. The committee also included three current or former college masters, who tended to resist any recommendations that would alter the traditional workings of the residential colleges; but a majority of the committee was more adventurous.

As a start, the committee exposed the treasurer's inadequacies. A pleasant but stubborn fellow, the treasurer testified that the university budget included a large sum for "miscellany." Questioning that category, the economists and I asked him to disaggregate it. A week or two later he brought in a table that again showed a large, unexplained sum, now labeled "sundries." That unsatisfactory report proved to be the best he could do. It left us, as Kingman had already become, without confidence in the treasurer. In September he admitted ruefully that his projection of a $1 million deficit had been wrong; in fact, the fiscal year would end with a small surplus. But the committee's projections for the next few years indicated that a deficit would soon develop and grow.

To prevent that projection from materializing, after much study the committee recommended increasing the undergraduate "throughput," in the phrase of that time. It meant simply the number of bachelors' degrees we could grant in any four years, and thus the total amount of tuition, less financial aid, the university would collect. We intended to achieve that result by making mandatory for every undergraduate at least one summer semester, to be taught by Yale faculty. Participating faculty members would receive in return a semester on leave in the spring or fall. The regular semesters would have to be shortened by a week each to make room for a summer term long enough to allow for full-credit courses. We circulated our report and recommendations in the fall term of 1973. The plan we proposed encountered several objections. Some traditionalists argued that the loss of a week a term would compromise undergraduate education. The varsity coaches worried that undergraduates might lose a season of participation, though in fact students could arrange their schedules to avoid that possibility. College masters noted that, under our plan, students would attend Yale in irregular patterns, which they worried would disrupt normal college elections and other affairs. They were correct in believing that the colleges would have to adapt, but it did not necessarily follow that such adaptation would be destructive of college life. The alumni office expressed concern that a mandatory summer term would weaken class loyalty; but the graduation timetables of the wartime classes, who had proved notably loyal to Yale and generous in their contributions, had been interrupted by military service.

The faculty was to meet and consider the report in the Strathcona Hall auditorium, an unusual place, but big enough to seat all comers. Dean Horace Taft would preside; I was to explain the committee's recommendations. On the appointed afternoon, Horace, who had participated fully in the committee's deliberations, stood with me at the entrance of the building while we awaited Kingman's arrival. Five minutes before the meeting was to begin,

Kingman appeared and told us that, after reflection, he had decided he could not support our report. The mandatory summer term, he said, would in his view discourage applications from too many students of the kind he most wanted as matriculants. Horace was furious that Kingman had given us so little notice. I saw no choice but to defer to Kingman's preference, though I told him that I could not propose a voluntary summer term without holding further meetings of the committee. Horace then informed the faculty that the scheduled session would be deferred for two weeks and that they would in the interim receive a revised report.

Our revised report did recommend a voluntary summer term, which we hoped would draw enough attendance to erase the projected deficit. After a tough debate the faculty approved the proposed plan for a trial of three years, beginning in 1975. Kingman appointed his young assistant, Jonathan Fanton, to organize and manage the summer term. While an undergraduate, Jon had been one of my students. Now he was working with me toward a Ph.D. in history, a bold objective for anyone as loaded with responsibility as he was. Jon had a track record that demonstrated his ability to make things happen; like Kingman, I respected him; and Pamela and I enjoyed his company. So I gladly agreed to represent the humanities on his planning committee, which also included Keith Thomson, a biologist who was representing the sciences, and Bill Kessen, a psychologist who represented the social sciences. We were a compatible group.

Without dissent we believed that a summer semester represented a splendid opportunity for constructive experimentation with the curriculum. I was especially interested in creating interdisciplinary combinations of several courses that would permit students to immerse themselves in a field of learning for a whole semester. The others were agreeable. In the humanities curriculum for the summer of 1975 we planned three interrelated courses on the Renaissance: one on art history, a second on English literature in the same period, and a third on Machiavelli and Dante, with an optional fourth course, a seminar, designed to integrate and enhance the other three. A similar combination related to American participation in World War II, with courses in history, economics, and political science.

The summer semesters failed as a solution to Yale's financial problems. Although they were taught largely by Yale faculty, the courses did not attract a substantial number of Yale undergraduates, who found the humid heat of New Haven in the summer and the absence of normal extracurricular activities unappealing. The relatively small enrollments were largely from other colleges. In addition, Yale undergraduates complained that faculty members with whom they wanted to work in the fall or the spring terms were often away on leaves they had earned by summer teaching. (If we had paid faculty otherwise for summer instruction, we would not have made any money.) So the Yale College faculty canceled the summer semester in 1978, replacing it with a summer program in languages and sciences. No effort was made to preserve the intellectually exciting interdisciplinary combinations. Those combinations required more interdepartmental cooperation than was forthcoming. Still, for the students and faculty involved in them, the summer semesters had been educational experiences stimulating in both purpose and execution.

From September 1974 through June 1976 I taught continually while also serving as a Harvard fellow and completing my work on the Wallace diary and on *V Was for Victory*, which was scheduled for publication in September 1976. I saved my leave gained from summer teaching for use in the academic year 1976–77, when I was to be Harmsworth Professor of American History at Oxford University. During the preceding summer I devoted my leisure time to an essay suitable, so I hoped, for the bicentennial celebration of American independence at Peterborough, New Hampshire, where Robert Morison, Elting's older brother and then the provost for health sciences at Cornell, had invited me to speak. I had difficulty drafting "The Burden of American Equality," an essay about the social and economic inequalities that for two centuries had contradicted the promise of the Declaration of Independence. The text of the speech I eventually delivered served as an introduction for *Liberty, Justice, Order*, a book of essays I published in 1993 with W. W. Norton. But in 1976 my accumulated fatigue probably impeded my early drafts. Certainly I was dissatisfied with them when the summer ended.

I had then spent a decade working intermittently on *V Was for Victory*. It was the most satisfying task I undertook during that period. In addition to revisiting the diaries of Henry Morgenthau, Jr., and Henry A. Wallace, I read five years' worth of two newspapers and several magazines, examined the archives of various federal agencies for the war years, searched through the holdings at the Franklin D. Roosevelt Library, and read relevant historical literature as well as wartime reportage and fiction. I also researched the wartime civil rights movement and race riots, the incarceration of the Japanese Americans, the cruel delay in American efforts to provide sanctuaries for the threatened Jews of Europe, and other manifestations of enduring ethnic prejudices. I focused, too, on wartime consumerism, as revealed in the pages of the *Wall Street Journal*. As my notes grew, so did my conviction that the war years at home raised the curtain on postwar American culture. I concluded that the cultural and ethnic developments of the war years shaped politics in that period. As I proceeded, so did my excitement about interpreting the material I was accumulating. That mood persisted through the many months I spent writing the book, months in which I also lectured in class about my subject and directed my graduate students to issues my research exposed. So I had lived the book for a long time before it was published, and I felt that it represented the best work I was capable of doing.

William B. Goodman, the book's first editor at Harcourt Brace Jovanovich, had made several insightful suggestions that improved the scope and tone of the book. But just as I had submitted my completed manuscript, Bill Jovanovich discharged Goodman. Thereafter my book was something of an orphan. Nevertheless *V Was for Victory*, a study of the home front and national politics during a necessary war, received generally favorable reviews. Henry Fairlie, a British journalist long interested in American politics, complained in *The New Republic* that I should have devoted more space directly to FDR rather than to lesser men like Henry Wallace and Wendell Willkie. But Roosevelt, whether on stage or off, was always near the center of my attention. An analysis by P. D. Zimmerman in a review in *Newsweek* exactly caught my purpose: "Blum argues persuasively," he wrote, "that the contours of American society after World War II were shaped in large part by the Roosevelt Administration's deliberate decision to subordinate all initiatives for social change to the quest for victory. . . . Our failure to debate and determine what we were fighting to preserve contributed to our inward-looking, militaristic, and materialistic postwar society."

The reception of *V Was for Victory* heartened me. Over time the book, its sales continuing, remained in print. Even New Left historians found it "mildly revisionist." Along with *The Republican Roosevelt* it remained my favorite of the books I wrote, and in my view also the most important in its professional impact. But in 1976, as ever after I had published, I was ready to turn to a new project—though now, for the first time in my career, I had not yet defined one. I would give that matter some thought during my year at Oxford.

16

Changes Large and Small

From October 1976 until early June 1977 I served as Harmsworth Professor of American History at Oxford. Where Pamela and I lived was an easy walk to Queen's College, the designated college for holders of the professorship. It was also an easy drive to the chapter house of the Salisbury Cathedral, about which Pamela was writing her doctoral dissertation. Her technique for examining bas reliefs permitted her to differentiate between original and restored reliefs and thus to provide accurate interpretations of the original iconography. The same technique produced similar, significant advances in understanding the abbey church of Saint-Denis, the monument to which in time she devoted many months. In Oxford she enjoyed a most productive year, enhanced by her deserved election as the Miriam Sacher Visiting Fellow at St. Hilda's College.

For my part, I found the Queen's fellowship compatible but never as comfortable and embracing as Queens' Cambridge had been. The fault was mine, for I was away much of the time with my monthly trips to Harvard Corporation meetings; our occasional travel to lecture in England, Belgium, and Norway; and our holidays, Christmas in Paris and April in Egypt. Our trip down the Nile depressed me. The great pyramids and the Sphinx were indeed wonders, but the poverty of the villages along the river, the unintended agricultural disaster produced by the effects of the Aswan dam, and the primitive way of life that still prevailed were perhaps quaint but surely tragic.

We were by no means lonesome. Herbert Nicholas, the Rhodes Professor of American History, an old friend, resided only a few blocks away with his three sisters. Always good company, witty and urbane, Herbert entertained us royally, sometimes at New College, long his beloved site of work, a beautiful place. Apart from Denis Brogan, Herbert seemed to me the Englishman of his era best informed about American politics and culture. Also now at Oxford were our generous friends from Cambridge University, Anne and Peter Mathias. Peter, an economic historian, held a professorship attached to All Souls College. During the spring months Nancy Pollak, the oldest daughter of Lou and Kathy Pollak, lived with us while she recuperated from meningitis and pursued her study of Russian literature. William Cronon, son of David Cronon, a former Yale colleague, was a Rhodes scholar working with Peter Mathias and auditing my lectures. We came to know Bill quite well. After Oxford he intended to study western history at Harvard for his American doctorate, but I persuaded him that since the retirement of Fred Merk, he would be better off studying with Howard Lamar at Yale. Bill proved to be a major talent.

My efforts at scholarship faltered. In October I began research in the Public Records Office (PRO), then still in central London. I became engrossed in the minutes of the British War Cabinet pertaining to food. Before leaving New Haven, I had read enough in American public documents to conclude that food and the politics related to food constituted a significant subject for scholarly study. While thousands had starved during the Great Depression, governments had responded to the political influence of farmers by regulating the growth and trading of food, for which there nevertheless remained a glut on commercial markets, since people could not afford to buy it. During World War II thousands of acres of agriculture were destroyed, food shortages plagued Europe and parts of Asia and Africa, and American farmers, assisted by federal subsidies, prospered as they rarely had. The United Nations organization for food and agriculture, reflecting prewar attitudes, was created to deal with overabundance — despite the fact that the postwar world for at least a decade was faced with continuing food shortages. A study of the politics of food from the 1930s through the 1950s seemed to me a ripe topic.

I started to make weekly visits to the PRO and almost daily ventures in the American public documents available in Oxford at the library at Rhodes House, the center for American studies at the university. Before Christmas I realized that I was accumulating a surfeit of research notes for 1939–40 alone, and there remained much of that year still to explore. Obviously my intended topic was too big for me to complete in a year of work in England. Indeed records of the British War Cabinet would in themselves require several years of research. That commitment, I had to admit to myself, exceeded my intellectual interest. So I abandoned the subject while hoping some Yale graduate student would later make part of it the basis for a dissertation. But none did.

During the winter term I concentrated on revising my July Fourth essay, "The Burden of American Equality," so as to make it suitable for the inaugural lecture I was to give at Oxford in the spring. Herbert Nicholas praised the resulting text, and one of my predecessors found it the most radical Harmsworth lecture he had read. But after writing it I ran out of intellectual energy, and it seemed to me that the essay was little to show for a year's work. My failure to use the Oxford year more creatively rankled me. So did my realization during that year that in general I had to learn to be more efficient in my scholarly efforts. My energy level was bound to decrease, partly because of age (at fifty-six, I was no longer young), but largely because of hypertension, which worsened while we were at Oxford and required the use of enervating medications. Before we returned home I began to think about ways in which to reduce my nonscholarly obligations. Since in 1976–77 my frequent absences from meetings of the Harvard Corporation in no way impeded the work of that body, I suspected that I was no longer much needed, if I ever had been. But I decided to continue for several more years.

The most important event of our year at Oxford came in the spring of 1977, when Kingman Brewster resigned as Yale's president and accepted appointment as United States Ambassador to the Court of St. James's. It was a position he and Mary Louise had coveted. Further, he had never had much enthusiasm for raising money, which was then a priority for Yale. As president, Kingman had deservedly won the loyalty of most students and most faculty members, but his conservative critics, especially those among the comfortable alumni, resisted his efforts to open their purses for Yale. His new post would allow him to escape a trying situation while promising him, as he liked to tell his friends, a job with substantive responsibilities within and beyond the "special relationship" that existed between Great Britain and the United States. Pamela and I rejoiced for the Brewsters as we tried to bury our anxieties about Yale without them. On our last visit to London before we returned to New Haven we had lunch with Kingman and Mary Louise at their official residence. As ever, seeing them was a joyous occasion. Obviously life for the Brewsters was about to undergo major changes. But just as obviously, they were looking forward avidly to the experience.

Just a week or so earlier, while on a visit home, I had driven from Cambridge to New Haven in order to advise several graduate students about their dissertations. My timing fortuitously put me in New Haven on the day a group of faculty members were giving a luncheon to celebrate Kingman and bid him farewell. Two of the organizers of the event, Jim Tobin and Bill

Lichten, a physicist, invited me to attend. It was a remarkable occasion—
perhaps 150 were in attendance, and there was no room for more—an out-
pouring of affection and gratitude from an admiring faculty for a departing
president. Among the speakers, Lichten stressed Kingman's determination
to improve the facilities for and the faculty in the sciences. Others observed
Kingman's similar efforts for the social sciences and humanities. Tobin
praised Kingman for his admissions policies, for promoting diversity within
the college. Those long-term achievements had changed Yale from "a New
England academy," in a phrase of Elting Morison's, to a great university.
Kingman's extraordinary crisis management added to his luster. A bittersweet aura swept through the room as Kingman responded, for we all knew
that we would deeply miss a great president, the greatest Yale president of
the twentieth century. His personal friends would particularly miss his sense
of fun, his humor, his sense of proportion, his exquisite manners, his zest
for living, his humanity.

While returning home from our year in Oxford aboard the *Queen Elizabeth II* I used the library every day as a peaceful place in which to write a pro-
file of Kingman for the London *Vogue*. But I had no chance to talk with Kingman until after Mary Louise had departed for London and Pamela had gone
to Vermont to open our cottage there. I stopped by at the president's residence on Kingman's last night there to ask him to dine with me at a nearby
Italian restaurant we enjoyed. He was alone, busy sorting memorabilia—
too busy, he said, to go out to dinner. But while we had a drink together, he
asked me who in my opinion should be the next Yale president. I said I supposed the provost. "Can't you be more imaginative than that?" Kingman
asked, rather impatiently. "I really haven't given the matter any thought," I
replied. "You see, you are my president." He was—and still is.

Mary Louise Brewster was Pamela's close friend, and Kingman was
Pamela's great fan. But they had to leave for London a year before Pamela
in 1978 received her Ph.D. in art history, which she would have enjoyed receiving from Kingman. Even in his absence, it was a grand achievement for
a student of fifty-five who had earlier raised a family of three children. While
earning the degree she had engaged in part-time teaching at Wesleyan University and at Yale. Now she received a full-time assistant professorship at
Columbia, a position she held until she retired. She remained in that time
one of the most gracious hostesses in New Haven. Both of us were busy, but
we were never too busy to miss the Brewsters.

During the academic year 1977–78 Hanna Holborn Gray served as both
provost and acting president of Yale—a heavy load. The daughter of Hajo

Holborn, Hanna had a Ph.D. from Harvard in Renaissance history, which she had studied under the direction of Myron Gilmore. I had first known her casually while her husband, Charles Gray, a historian of the British constitution, was teaching, as I was, at MIT. Hanna had been dean of the arts and sciences faculty at Northwestern University and a member of the Yale Corporation before Kingman appointed her provost. She brought to that position a broad knowledge of the academy, her sure intelligence, her wit — often wicked — and a manner at times authoritarian. She seemed to me also academically more conservative than Kingman, though I knew her too superficially to be sure. During most of her tenure as acting president, Hanna had the Yale Corporation looking over her shoulder as the search went on for a successor to Kingman, a position for which she was an obvious possibility. That continual inspection must have been trying, especially because in the end she was not selected for the Yale presidency. She could take solace, however, in her appointment as president of the University of Chicago.

My only official relations with Hanna had to do with affirmative action, a subject we never actually discussed but about which we appeared to disagree. The issue arose with the *Bakke* case. Allan Bakke, a white applicant, had twice been denied admission to the medical school at the Davis campus of the University of California. That school reserved 16 of 100 places in its entering class for minority students. Bakke, claiming that the minority quota had excluded him in violation of state and federal law, sued the Regents of the California system. After the California Supreme Court ruled in Bakke's favor, his case on appeal reached the United States Supreme Court. It was a divisive case, closely watched across the whole nation.

At the simplest level, Bakke's supporters considered the Davis quota a flagrant and unjustifiable example of "reverse discrimination," while many of his opponents viewed it as a necessary application of "compensatory justice." At the Supreme Court, fifty-eight briefs were filed by parties interested in the outcome of the case. Among those speaking for the Davis medical school in one way or another were the American Bar Association, the NAACP Legal Defense Fund, the American Civil Liberties Union, Americans for Democratic Action, and several outstanding private universities: Columbia, Harvard, Stanford, and Pennsylvania. Briefs supporting Bakke came largely from white ethnic groups believing that admission policies favoring blacks would penalize them. Alex Bickel, whose jurisprudential views had been moving right for a decade, stood up for Bakke by insisting that the only moral basis for admission — or for success of any kind — was meritocratic. That was a characteristic belief of those who, like Bickel, a Jewish immigrant, had fought their way up in their profession by virtue of superior effort and intelligence. I respected Alex, long a friend, but I respected equally Lou Pollak, also an old friend, who stood with Derek Bok and the Harvard brief, my own preferred position.

Archie Cox was to argue the case for Davis at the Supreme Court. He and Derek Bok in the Harvard brief made their case on educational grounds, and in supporting them, the Harvard Corporation endorsed their educational argument, which I deemed commanding. The brief rejected quotas but commended race as one criterion of an admission policy designed to assure diversity in a student body, for diversity had significant educational value, not the least for white males. Harvard under Conant in earlier years had slanted admission to favor students from west of Albany so as to promote geographical diversity when the college was still a redoubt of Bostonians. Now racial diversity had a similar, salubrious effect at a time when the college was dominantly white. The chief beneficiaries were white students, who learned to understand the outlook of contemporaries they would never otherwise have met. Affirmative action brought to Harvard talented young men and women who later made important contributions to American society, a boon dependent in large part upon the excellent collegiate education they received.

So Derek Bok believed; so he later demonstrated in his book, written with William Bowen, *The Shape of the River* (1998), a study of race in college admissions. Though in 1977, when the Bakke case was pending, I had only theory on which to rely, I privately urged Hanna Gray to have Yale join Harvard's brief. She did not commit herself, and Yale did not join the brief. I have no way of knowing whether that was her decision or the decision of the Yale Corporation. I am, however, confident that Kingman would have enlisted with his like-minded friends, Archie Cox and Derek Bok. But of course Kingman was no longer president. In the end Archie prevailed. The four conservative justices then on the Supreme Court found for Bakke; the four liberals, for Davis. Justice Lewis Powell in a compromise opinion ruled against numerical quotas but for race as one acceptable criterion of admissions. He cited Harvard practice and the Harvard brief as exemplifying his definition of appropriate policy. Yale's policy was much the same. Of course Harvard and Yale were keeping implicit a policy Davis had made explicit.

With Yale admitting more and more minorities and women, the questions of race and gender naturally arose with respect to faculty recruitment. Women undergraduates wanted more women on the arts and sciences faculty, in which there were very few in 1977–78. There were even fewer blacks. Referring the issue to committees in each of the four academic divisions, Hanna asked me to chair the committee for the humanities. It included another tenured professor, Martin Price, a wise and fastidious literary critic, and several women, but no blacks. We decided to select English, French, and history as fields for examination and to inquire of a group of eminent universities in each field about the number of women and of minorities on their faculties and among their graduate students. Their information would give us a rough idea of the prospects for Yale in attempting to attract new faculty at both the tenured and nontenured ranks. The responses to our questions indicated that many women were then pursuing doctoral programs. In four or five years there would be a cadre of women in each of the fields we were studying. But there were very few women already qualified for Yale tenure appointments. And there were virtually no minority candidates available in those fields, for so few existed that Yale in trying to hire one would at best move a teacher from an established institution to New Haven without increasing the pool. There were also few minority candidates in doctoral programs. Bright undergraduates from minority groups were heading not for higher education but for law or business or other more remunerative careers.

The report we submitted made two general recommendations. In order quickly to recruit more tenured women, we proposed temporarily to reduce the publication standard for tenure for women to one well-reviewed book and one promising manuscript close to completion. That standard would apply to women already at Yale, and to women candidates for assistant professorships. We also recommended establishing a program at ten elite universities, including Yale, to recruit blacks for higher education. For ten years each institution would designate eligible black undergraduates, to each of whom the consortium of universities would offer a five-year fellowship covering all expenses, including living expenses, for a doctoral program in one of the fields of the humanities. Upon completion of the degree, each recipient of a fellowship would become a junior faculty member at one of the universities in the group. There would be sizable expenses involved, but we were confident that some foundation would agree to meet them.

The provost's office acknowledged receipt of our report, but we heard nothing more about it. Hanna tabled it, which was her prerogative, but she never told us why. If Kingman had rejected it, he would have explained his reasoning, partly to be polite, partly for the fruits of an instructive argument. But again, Kingman was no longer president. Twenty years after our report Yale had a growing contingent of tenured women in the humanities but few tenured minority professors. In addition, by the late 1990s the publication standard for all tenured appointments had fallen below the reduced level we had recommended be temporary. Once a university lowers its standards for any reason, the revised standards tend to become permanent. Hanna may have feared exactly that result. Further, by the time we submitted our report, she knew that she would not succeed Kingman. She may have decided to leave the report for the next provost, who was to be a law professor unlikely to promote our purpose.

During the summer of 1977 an accident of my friendship with Ed Morgan had involved me in the Yale Corporation's search for a new president. Ed and Helen Morgan enjoyed occasional scholarly visits to the Huntington Library in Pasadena, California. In 1978 rumors, though false, circulated among the graduate students in history that Ed was about to move permanently to the Huntington. Worried about that possibility, a woman doctoral candidate who was working with Ed, stole some letterhead from the office of the president. She wrote Ed a letter on the stationery and forged my name as the signature. I knew nothing about the forgery until, in Vermont, I received a letter from Ed in which he expressed his surprise that I had accepted the Yale presidency but promised to stay close while I assumed the duties of the office. Stunned, I telephoned him at once at his New Hampshire summer home. Together we realized that the letter he had received on official stationery, a letter in which I supposedly asked for his help, was a forgery, and Ed guessed its source. While he looked into the matter, I called William Bundy, the Yale trustee in charge of the presidential search, to explain to him what had occurred. I was afraid the forger might have reached him, too. But it was news to Bill. After I had explained the episode, I volunteered that I had no interest in becoming president of Yale or of any other university. "Are you sure?" Bill asked. "Absolutely certain," I replied. In that case, he continued, I could be of assistance to him if I would meet with his committee and review with them the candidates they had listed, of whom some might have been on the Harvard list seven years earlier. I agreed to his request, and he set a date for the coming September. Meanwhile Ed had identified the forger, who had confessed. He asked me as a personal favor to initiate no action against her, to which I agreed, though I had been ready to report her to the dean of the graduate school.

The list of possible candidates Bill Bundy showed me for comment in September did contain the names of several men whom Harvard had thought about in 1970, but neither university considered any of them seriously. Hanna Gray's name was not on the list. When I asked why, a member of the Yale search committee replied with a question: "Have you ever heard her say anything interesting about education?" Taking the question as rhetorical, I said no more. But her name did appear on a short list about which the search committee later solicited the opinions of some twenty tenured faculty members. Half of them met one night with Bill Bundy and me, the other half the next night with Bill and Georges May. Bill had asked Georges and me to join him as silent co-chairs of those confidential, informal gatherings. At the dinner I attended the candidate who aroused the most enthusiasm was the dean of the Harvard Faculty of Arts and Sciences, Henry Rosovsky, an economic historian. Of the Yale candidates on the list we were shown, A. Bartlett Giamatti, a young professor of English, seemed to have the most support, with a few voices for a medical professor I did not know. No one supported Hanna's name when Bundy introduced it. Georges's experience the next night was identical. Soon thereafter the Yale Corporation offered the presidency to Rosovsky — an offer that became public knowledge. But he declined. Yale then turned to Giamatti, who eagerly accepted.

Bart Giamatti, a graduate of Andover and Yale, the son of a Mt. Holyoke professor, in 1978 a slim scholar of much charm, at once voluble and eloquent, superficially outgoing, had many friendly acquaintances at Yale, very few of whom really knew him well. As I quickly discovered, I neither knew him well nor understood how his mind worked. But we were friendly neighbors in the Hall of Graduate Studies, neighbors brought together by our common love of baseball, a bond Bart shared with others, too. I expected him to become a successful Yale president, a persuasive enthusiast for liberal education, and an object of student affection. To my sorrow, things did not work out that way.

Bart's start was uneven. His first appointments in Yale College won deserved applause. To succeed Sam Chauncey, who had resigned as Secretary of the University, Bart named his friend and Yale classmate, John Wilkinson, who had been a thoughtful assistant dean of the college. As Dean of Yale College Bart chose Howard R. Lamar, an exemplary teacher and scholar with a constructive loyalty to the university and the winning manner of a southern gentleman. Bart also found a talented vice president for finance, Jerry Stevens, who was professionally prepared to bring order to Yale's budget and investments. But Bart and his first provost proved to be incompatible, and the provost was forced to resign after less than two semesters in his post. Then a strike by workers in the dining halls, departmental offices, the hospital, and the library complicated life on campus and lingered while Bart resisted negotiations, in my view for too long. Student protests about apartheid in South Africa, and the construction outside of his office of a model of a typical black worker's shack, bothered him much more than they should have. He retreated behind a shield of inaccessibility that his personal assistant held between the president and the undergraduates, who in turn resented his anxious distance from them. That shield also kept faculty at an impersonal remove from the president.

My relations with Bart remained cordial but never close. He tested them in his first year in office by suggesting that I resign from the Harvard Corporation. He had plenty to keep me busy at Yale, he said, and he did not want me involved in raising money for Harvard. I promised to think about it. I had signed on at Harvard for only seven to eleven years, and I was in my tenth year in 1979. I had joined the corporation only under pressure from Yale's president, but now a new president had different priorities. I knew, too, that my scholarship had been less vigorous than in earlier years, and that I was not essential to Derek Bok, for whom I had only admiration. But I did not want Bart's parochial Yale views made public. Like so many Old Blues (but unlike Kingman) Bart had an obtrusive "Avis complex": like the car rental company that was second to Hertz, Bart wanted Yale and its people to try harder. I decided that I should resign — in Derek's kind word, "retire" — and I wrote him and the other fellows a letter expressing my confidence and affection for Harvard and its president but asking for personal reasons to be replaced as soon as it was convenient. In October 1979 I attended my last corporation meeting, followed by my colleagues' thoughtful departing dinner and gift, and in 1980 by the traditional honorary degree for a retiring Fellow of Harvard College. Privately I was wistful.

As he had said, Bart Giamatti intended to keep me busy. My teaching kept me busy as well. Enrollments in my courses remained high, as did the number of undergraduates who joined me for lunch on Thursdays. I reorganized my lectures and brought my undergraduate course up to date. I also changed my graduate seminar. With the war in Vietnam over, and with the market for graduate students shrinking, enrollment in the graduate program had been dropping since the mid-1970s. The ablest undergraduate men, no longer worried about conscription, and the ablest women, too, were setting their sights on law, business, and medicine. At the time, I was avidly studying the Warren Court, its controversial decisions, and their political impact. So I changed the content and title of my graduate seminar to "The Supreme Court in American Politics" and invited law students as well as graduate students in history, American Studies, and political science to apply.

The resulting seminars were a joy, the students assiduous and bright, the mix of disciplines rewarding. Indeed one of the very brightest students I ever met, Emily Buss, graced one seminar with her extraordinary talent in textual exegesis. She had majored in English as a Yale undergraduate, won her degree summa cum laude, and carried her skills to law school. At her request

I recommended her as a clerk to Lou Pollak, then a federal district judge, who found her as impressive as I did. I also recommended her, again at her request, to all the justices of the Supreme Court. Justice Harry A. Blackmun appointed her his clerk and later wrote to thank me. Justice Sandra Day O'Connor later told me that she had made a major mistake in not appointing Emily. And to my good fortune, though Emily was the most talented of the law students who took my seminar, there were others every year who were almost as good.

Committees continued to require time and deliberation. Ellen Ryerson, now an associate provost, had asked me to join her committee on phased retirement, an issue the university was just beginning to study. Ellen had assembled a first-rate group of faculty, among them Rosabeth Kantor, then in the early stages of her distinguished career as an expert on business, and Rick Levin, a bright young economics professor who later became president of Yale. Prodded by Ellen, Rosabeth made a compelling case for a phased retirement program. Business experience showed, she said, that men and women about sixty years old who elected partial retirement almost always found their new leisure so satisfactory that they soon retired fully. Yale's mandatory retirement age was then seventy, but encouraging partial retirement before that age would create new openings for hiring younger faculty, especially women and minority scholars, then still underrepresented. And partial retirement, as Rosabeth suggested, might lead some to early retirement. Without dissent, we moved on to develop a plan for phased retirement that the provost endorsed and the several faculties approved.

At that time I was just about sixty, and I had myself in mind during the committee's deliberations. Within five years I expected phased retirement to appeal to me if I had found a commanding scholarly project to undertake. For the while I had begun a book based on my earlier work on three strong American presidents, TR, Wilson, and FDR. My editor at W. W. Norton suggested adding Lyndon Johnson. The four, each the subject of a separate essay, with a prologue and epilogue made up the substance of *The Progressive Presidents,* published in 1980. Dedicated to Mary Louise and Kingman Brewster, the book spoke to presidential accountability, a favorite subject of Kingman's. Robert F. Drinan, a distinguished Jesuit priest, lawyer, and member of Congress, writing in *America* called the work "a sensitive and wise study." In the *New York Times* Godfrey Hodgson, a British historian of American politics, described it as "a notable meditation." "Professor Blum," Hodgson wrote, "has a historian's sense of time and context, and of the elusive way one generation's dilemma goes underground, only to emerge subtly transformed in the different circumstances of another time." I could not have been more pleased, and the book's brisk and continuing sales also re-warded me. Even more did the exploration I had begun of LBJ, for it inspired me to plan a new book, related to my teaching, on the presidencies of Kennedy, Johnson, and Nixon and the political culture of their time. But the relevant research in presidential libraries had to await either my completion of my administrative tasks or a term's leave of absence.

I had also begun to examine the large collection at the Sterling Library of the papers of Walter Lippmann. Ronald Steele had published an authorita-tive biography of Lippmann, which at his request I had read in manuscript. Doing so whetted my interest in Lippmann, whose many incisive books of political thought had been for decades on the list of required readings I gave my students. I had been reading Lippmann's newspaper columns since my years at Andover. Now, in the library, I found his letters engaging. Encour-aged by Chester Kerr, then director of Yale University Press, I planned to se-lect and edit the most interesting Lippmann letters for publication. That ven-ture would take some years, but with two projects again in hand, I felt like my old self for the first time in more than a year.

Further, Lippmann provided a life and a corpus of writing with which I could identify. Like Theodore Roosevelt, whom he had admired, Lippmann had an informed concern for social and international order. So did I. He re-jected both Judaism and Jewish ethnicity. So did I. He had found Wilson's moralism empty. He had praised the important Keynesian policies of the New Deal. In editing his letters I was living with a sympathetic intelligence, a commentator whose thinking had influenced me for decades. I could not share, but I could understand, the conservatism of Lippmann's later years. While I edited, the project afforded continual satisfaction.

Nevertheless my first obligations remained to my students and to the committees to which Bart Giamatti appointed me. From the first days of his administration the steadily rising costs of energy had strained the univer-sity's budget. The president consequently created a special committee, with me as chairman, to study the energy problem. Fortunately Horace Taft, a member of that committee, provided indispensable assistance by introduc-ing me to several experts whose advice shaped our report. Our recommen-dations, all of which were adopted, called for an academic calendar that min-imized cold days. We would begin the fall semester about Labor Day and end it before Christmas, making much of the month of January a holiday for the students. Our "spring" break would be a fortnight in early March, and commencement would be in May, before air conditioning would be needed. During winter holidays thermostats would be set low. To reduce the cost of heat, which Yale supplied for itself, we recommended supplementing our oil generators with gas generators. Then on any day the university engineers could choose the cheaper fuel. We also called for widespread substitution of neon for incandescent lighting, and for weatherproofing of windows and doors. The cost of those changes, while considerable, seemed small compared to the resulting and continuing savings.

Bart next assigned me to a committee overseeing the writing of a contract with Miles Laboratory, an American affiliate of A. G. Bayer, the German pharmaceutical conglomerate. Yale wanted the income from that contract, which would permit Miles to use Yale facilities for research on calcium blocks, a form of medicine for high blood pressure. Bart was wisely insisting on preventing Yale personnel from any involvement in research that they could not discuss with any of their students or colleagues. The contract suited his purpose, but I contributed little to a negotiation best understood by scientists. I concluded that Bart appointed me to the committee partly because he believed erroneously that either my Harvard or my MIT experience had prepared me for its mission and partly because he wanted a humanist keeping an eye on scientists, for whom he had limited understanding. The committee continued for several years to review the work of Miles Laboratory, which was invariably innocent of any conflict with Yale policy.

During Bart's administration I also served for three years on the divisional committee for the humanities. The four divisional committees had a loose sovereignty over the departments they represented. If a department needed strengthening or reorientation, its divisional committee sometimes initiated and ordinarily oversaw the process. The divisional committee also reviewed all departmental recommendations for tenure and had the authority to endorse or reject them. In my term, Peter Brooks of the French department chaired our committee. A young scholar close to Bart, he brought to his task a sophisticated ease of manner and the insights of an experienced literary critic. We spent too much time refereeing a conflict among departments about control of the growing but unsystematic university film collection, an issue we failed to resolve. But we used most of our time reading the works and discussing the merits of the deconstructionists, who were then in fashion and who were being recruited by the English department. Reading their criticism left me cold, but I tried to adjust to the new fashion well enough at least to discuss their work with my colleagues. I never was happy with the controversial mode of thought the deconstructionists embraced. But Paul DeMan, at one time a Nazi collaborator, now the most controversial of the Yale deconstructionists, in his relations with me was always the soul of consideration. Indeed I found myself agreeing with him most of the time during discussions in a faculty seminar on modernism.

In spite of my committees and various departmental obligations, including a seemingly endless term as acting chairman of the history department, I was pleased by the scholarly progress I was making. During a term's leave I completed my planned research in the John F. Kennedy Library at Columbia Point in Boston, a beautiful building on a gorgeous site. In 1981 I also completed my explorations in the Lippmann papers and photoduplicated the letters I had chosen for editing. I had received a one-month fellowship from the Rockefeller Foundation for study at its glorious conference center, a villa in Bellagio on Lake Como, that summer, and Pamela would be joining me. There I intended to begin editing the Lippmann letters. We thoroughly enjoyed our month at the villa and the company of the other fellows. Though on many afternoons we explored the Lake Como region, I was able to complete the editing of some one hundred pages of letters.

Not long after our return Bart made me a Sterling Professor, a rank unsurpassed at Yale and a local scholarly honor. I recognized that at least in part he was rewarding me for services rendered, but I was no less pleased on that account. But Bart had further plans for me. In September 1983 he named me chair of the university-wide Council on Priorities and Planning. Made up of faculty and students from many of the schools, the council focused its attention on Yale's relationship with New Haven, a complex subject. Frequently as meetings began I experienced episodes of angina. My body and my temperament were informing each other. Just as the term ended, in December, I developed unstable angina, which led to a triple bypass in January 1984.

A fussy patient, I recovered enough to do a little work in April. An advantage of working on the Lippmann letters was that I could write just a few notes at a sitting and then rest before resuming my task. Assisted by Anne Bittker, who helped with my research in the Yale library as well as typed for me, I completed the notes and wrote an introduction by summer's end. By that time, however, Chester Kerr, who had encouraged me to undertake the Lippmann project, had retired from Yale and had become publisher at Ticknor and Fields, which was owned by Houghton, Mifflin, named for Houghton's nineteenth-century predecessor, with offices in New York. I moved with him. In 1985 Ticknor and Fields published *Public Philosopher: Selected Letters of Walter Lippmann*. Joseph Harsch in the *Christian Science Monitor* wrote one of the many generous reviews: "Not until I read this new volume of letters . . . did I realize that Lippmann not only helped to shape history from outside the government but he also influenced history from the inside." In the *New York Times* Warren F. Kimball, a historian of the twentieth century and an experienced editor, wrote, "Almost all the selections seem important. . . . The significance of the letters is a tribute to Walter Lippmann's mind and to . . . Blum's hard work." Chester and I were pleased by the book's reception. Sales, however, were unimpressive, even for a volume of letters.

About that time I was finding that teaching was becoming more taxing. In the autumn of 1984, for the first time ever I had found my adrenaline regularly spent after fifty minutes, some twenty minutes before the scheduled end of my lectures. I also found that my lectures no longer regularly met my standards, though the students seemed content. Further, it seemed increasingly difficult for me to find time for research and writing, though I had a fruitful week in Austin working in the Lyndon B. Johnson papers. In 1984 I told Bill Brainard, an especially decent and caring man who was then Yale's provost, that I had decided to elect the option of phased retirement. As I saw it, I could no longer carry a full load. Bill generously suggested that most faculty did less than I did and said he would gladly endorse a diminution in my obligations. But my conscience would not allow me to accept full pay for what I deemed a partial workload.

Beginning in 1986 I taught only the one-quarter time then prescribed for those on phased retirement. I gave up graduate teaching, for graduate students needed mentors who would see them through the doctoral program and help them find their first jobs. They deserved someone who could assist them longer than I planned to be available. I also gave up my lecture course, though I did lecture once again, for fifty minutes at a time, in my last semester of teaching in 1991. Because I knew that soon I would no longer be an active member of the department, I did my best to give up participation in tenure decisions, for I would not have to live with their results. Indeed one of the reasons why I had opted for phased retirement was that my friends in the department had retired. There was some compensation for the loss of my closest colleagues in the arrival of John Merriman, a historian of France, and Linda Colley, a splendid historian of modern England. But George Pierson had retired long since, Vann Woodward not long thereafter, then Jack Hall, and Ed Morgan in 1986. Ed had been for me an indispensable colleague. As I told him, I had little interest in continuing in his absence. In 1985 Bart Giamatti, who had been unhappy as Yale's president, also departed to become head of the National League and later commissioner of baseball. Privately he told me that the presidency had bored him. How different he was from Kingman!

Bart's successor, Benno Schmidt, soon made a series of deeply conservative administrative appointments. Two of them, one as Dean of Yale College, the other as provost, were announced after inadequate consultation with faculty. Both appointees proved to be as autocratic as the manner of their choice. The provost set out to reduce the academic budget by 15 percent with little consultation of the divisional committees or departments. The dean publicly attacked the faculty as irresponsibly liberal. Both men complained continually about what they called the "feminization" of the university. As Benno realized too late, his subordinates' actions cost him the confidence and support of the faculty. Like most of Kingman's admirers, I found Benno's tenure distinctly uncomfortable.

In the fall semester of 1986 Pamela and I both taught at Yale in London in a program in British Studies open only to Yale undergraduates. It stressed art history. Pamela offered a course on British medieval art; I, a course on Anglo-American relations, 1921–63. Teaching that subject took me back to my undergraduate essay about the interbella diplomacy of naval disarmament. The semester closed a major chapter in our lives, for it was the last time we saw Kingman Brewster. After his four years as ambassador, he had practiced law with Winthrop, Stimson, a distinguished New York firm, before becoming in 1984 the Master of University College, Oxford. By that time he had begun to have serious coronary problems. When in 1986 we visited the Brewsters in Oxford, Kingman was already in only marginal shape for performing his many duties. But, ever resolute, he slighted no obligation. He and I attended a Harvard dinner in London in the late fall. When I picked him up at his hotel that night I was shocked by his drawn appearance and uneven gait. But we still planned to spend Christmas with him and Mary Louise until she reported that, sadly, Kingman was ill. He died the next year, following a stroke. Yale had never been the same without the Brewsters, nor was it ever again. Indeed after the memorial service for Kingman, I felt more and more like a relic from ages past.

I continued for several years to teach one undergraduate seminar a year. In 1986, to my complete surprise, my former dissertation students had arranged a dinner for me at which they presented me with a festschrift. Edited by David M. Kennedy and Michael E. Parrish, the volume was entitled *Power and Responsibility: Case Studies in American Leadership,* and was published by Harcourt, Brace in 1986. I was overcome by the attendance of students from years long past as well as from the decade then ending. Bob Bannister and Bob Dalzell stood out as scholars among the older contingent, David Kennedy and Laura Kalman among the younger. The assembled company reminded me that I had been teaching a long time. Obviously the day was close for my retiring fully; I did so in 1991.

Epilogue: The Great Adventure

Retirement, I was to discover, involved a series of retreats from the familiar obligations of a tenured professor. Some of those retreats occurred naturally with the entropy of the aging body, but some were planned. Upon retiring I decided on my own to follow two rules of two words each that seemed to me appropriate for an emeritus professor: 1. Shut up. 2. Look away. The first rule supposed that active faculty would ask if they wanted my opinion; the second would serve to subdue any impulse to speak up without being asked. There was life after Yale, and it was up to me to live it. At first some of my active colleagues, perhaps out of politeness or habit, now and then consulted me. But like other emeriti, I soon lost touch with departmental matters. Appropriately a younger generation took control.

The ascendancy of that generation coincided with the cycle of fashion that marked historical scholarship. Social history had dominated the profession during my undergraduate years. But my generation of historians, coming to maturity during the New Deal and World War II, turned naturally, though not exclusively, to political history, to the history of the state and its role in governing the economy, making foreign policy, and waging war. As political historians, we also of necessity examined the various social and intellectual forces that shaped politics and voting behavior, including slavery, immigration, and class, and the conflicts they underlay. Our children, growing up with the civil rights movement, with feminism and skepticism, had interests of their own. The history they wanted to write did not ignore politics or the state but stressed race, class, gender, and family, often in nonpolitical contexts. That change in emphasis especially characterized monographic literature, the stuff of learned journals, in the years after 1980.

In retirement I could see, on reflection, the ways in which my own interests had changed. At MIT I had taught the history of political economy, a subject I had encountered while editing the letters of Theodore Roosevelt. Like many progressive statesmen of his era, Roosevelt had turned for advice to institutional economists such as William C. Ripley and Jeremiah W. Jenks. Parting company with the laissez-faire theorists of the nineteenth century, the institutionalists examined economic history to gain an understanding of the growth and characteristics of trusts and the economics of railroad competition and consolidation. They concluded that the federal government had to intercede in the market by regulating corporate behavior in order to protect the public interest, and they instructed the progressives of the early twentieth century who moved to that end. Their scholarship brought economics and politics together, and their resulting political economy bore on public policy.

The political economists fell out of favor by the 1930s, partly because their work did not provide useful clues to moderating the business cycle, a preoccupation of policy makers during the Great Depression. But I believed that they were succeeded in their public role by the disciples of John Maynard Keynes. Keynes did focus on the business cycle and what to do about it, and after 1937 his scholarship gradually came to influence and instruct New Deal fiscal policy, including the Employment Act of 1946 and its successor legislation, which aimed at full employment. Like the institutionalists, the American Keynesians melded economics and politics.

In the academy, however, economists after World War II returned to mathematical formulae and to a focus on theory — at first Keynesian theory, which they modified. Most political scientists did little with economics as they sought to understand politics and government. The study of political economy fell largely to political historians such as I, who examined the origins and development of public economic policies. But of course those historians looked also at other subjects integral to the political culture. Two decades before the twenty-first century, political history, and especially the history of political economy, interested fewer and fewer historians. But political economy, though not the phrase, continued to receive significant academic attention, now from political scientists who were rediscovering history as a useful approach for explaining the past politics of public policy. It could be said that in the academy political economy migrated during the twentieth century from economics to history to political science. It did not vanish; it only changed departments. Further, political history, still a popular subject with general readers, held the interest of many nonacademic historians, some of them outstanding authors. And narrative history, too, a natural vehicle for exploring the past, continued to capture a popular audience. Within the academy, then, a revival of political history, including some focus on issues of political economy, is likely to occur in a not-distant future.

Meanwhile, like political history, other subjects that the Yale history department had stressed in the 1950s had ceased to receive much attention by the 1990s. In the earlier decade English history had dominated departmental offerings. As one retirement in that field succeeded another, English history almost disappeared. American history saw a marked decline in the volume of instruction in many traditional subjects — the Revolution, the Civil War, the Great Depression, the New Deal. Changing personnel brought changes to the curriculum. That development naturally reflected changing interests within the historical profession and, more important, within the student body.

Both teachers and students, in my experience, are at their best when they share a common and vibrant interest in the subject they are addressing. The subjects that ought to be taught are those about which students most want to learn and instructors most want to teach. When the two coincide, learning and teaching flourish. Whatever the subject, the successful professor of history conveys both the methods of understanding and writing history and the context, complexity, and fascination of the subject.

During the decade after World War II, I thought I knew what should be taught to college students, particularly to those planning careers in engineering or science. Out of that certitude, which my fellow humanists at MIT shared, came the core curriculum we constructed and required of undergraduates. But by the late 1960s I had come to question all requirements. Undergraduates tended to resist them, and that resistance impeded education. Accordingly I supported the proposal adopted by the Yale College faculty to drop requirements and substitute recommendations. Most students continued to satisfy the old requirements, for the recommendations made sense to them. Undergraduates majoring in fields of the humanities and social sciences, however, had often balked at the science requirement — two terms of any natural or physical science. Indeed the undergraduate culture at Yale seemed antiscientific to me, especially in contrast to MIT and Harvard, where science engaged many more students. But in advising sophomores at Yale, as I regularly did, I recommended that students take science courses remote from those they had taken in high school — for example, courses in paleontology that I knew to be well taught. Most of my advisees enrolled in such courses and enjoyed them, as others did in newly constructed courses on geology or biology "for poets."

After I left MIT the humanities department separated into several departments, of which history was one; and the school abandoned the core curriculum in favor of a broad offering of courses in both the humanities and the social sciences. From that menu students could select what most interested them. That seemed to me a substantial improvement. But when Bart Giamatti became president, the Yale College faculty restored both the science and the language requirements, the latter intended to make undergraduates fluent in some language other than English, an objective only rarely achieved. A small minority, of which I was one, voted against that regression. I considered fluency commendable but just as likely to develop when language courses were recommended but not required.

Requirements had less pedagogical importance in a university, I believed, than did youth, for in my experience, students learned most eagerly from young teachers, especially teachers only half a generation older than the undergraduates themselves, teachers who might have been their older cousins or their young uncles or aunts. In my first years at Yale I fell into that category, and among the undergraduates I met in my lecture course, many in later years remained friends. But like any other teacher, I found as I grew older that the nature of my relationship to my students changed. By the late 1960s I had become the age of the undergraduates' parents, as had many others on the Yale faculty, including Kingman Brewster. The parental role is not an easy one during the years of a child's adolescence. Yet living as we faculty members did with children in their late adolescence, children who felt and expressed the tensions of that time, we were, it seemed to me, on the whole more sympathetic toward student protest and rebellion than were most of our older, and some of our younger, colleagues. The older group usually had little understanding of adolescent attitudes; the younger group had too recently been adolescents themselves, but in an age not shaped by countercultural fashion. On approaching retirement, my contemporaries and I reached the age of our students' grandparents, with the accompanying combination of affection and remoteness characteristic in that relationship.

Relative age played a less discernible role in graduate teaching, for doctoral candidates were at once students and future professional colleagues. Some of those whose dissertations I directed taught for a time at Yale. Many more became professors or administrators elsewhere. But without regard to place or age, in the 1980s as in the 1950s those I knew well while they were apprentices became and remained valued friends as they forged their careers.

Because youthfulness enhances teaching, when gerontological lobbies persuaded Congress to end mandatory retirement, students suffered, for old men hung on too long before surrendering their tenured positions. Most of them had few fresh ideas, were no longer engaged in research on new topics, and had lost rapport with undergraduates and graduate students, whose intellectual interests accorded with those of young scholars. The old men who taught on and on blocked the appointment of younger women and of people of color. Those were the scholars who looked like and thought like an increasingly large percentage of undergraduates. Some of the oldsters were still able to teach vigorously, but they need not have continued in tenured posts. If retirement had remained mandatory at age seventy, they could have accepted temporary appointments at universities other than the one they had left. Time and the market would have led them soon enough to full retirement. Of course tenure could have been abolished, but its real importance — to protect freedom of academic belief and expression — remained good reason for its continued existence. Further, the abolition of tenure would make a university noncompetitive with its tenure-granting rivals. For all these reasons, most faculties continued to include too many old white men.

As an emeritus professor, I happily continued to write, but I did not miss teaching. I had lost the necessary energy for it. I did miss seeing young people, though not enough to grade any more papers. But my love affair with Clio went on. During my last two years of phased retirement, I completed my research and finished writing *Years of Discord: American Politics and Society, 1961–1974*, which was published by W. W. Norton in 1991. I had begun the book, as I had begun work on Morgenthau years earlier, in order to immerse myself in the history of a period I was teaching. In that I succeeded. But James T. Patterson of Brown University, who read the manuscript, said the book was really about presidents and American culture — a fair comment, for as the text and notes revealed, I had done much of my archival research in presidential libraries. William O'Neill in the *New York Times* published a friendly review to that effect. The liveliest part of the book, he wrote, in a comment with which I agreed, was "devoted to the Nixon era. Constrained by his own liberal politics where Kennedy and Johnson are concerned, Mr. Blum opens up on Mr. Nixon with his heavy guns, even while he acknowledges the man's achievements." (I had also, however, fired those guns at LBJ.) All in all, O'Neill concluded, *Years of Discord* was "a readable work and a trustworthy introduction to the Presidential politics of this critical era." After a slow start, the book sold well enough for several printings. It remained in print as the new century began.

I had, however, approached my subjects too soon for access to some crucial materials not yet declassified and unavailable at the presidential libraries I visited. Robert Dallek in his excellent biographies of Johnson and Kennedy made splendid use of materials I had not been allowed to examine. I would have been wise to pull back from writing on the basis of only partial learning. Where the record was open to research, as was the case with the Nixon Materials Project, a branch of the National Archives in Alexandria, my account benefited. I was "constrained" less by a liberal bias than by incomplete information.

On returning from London and Paris in the spring of 1993, I learned from Arthur Schlesinger, Jr., that he and Carl Schorske had arranged for me to serve as chairman of a conference of historians that autumn at the Franklin D. Roosevelt Library about recent scholarship on the Holocaust. Because I had done little research on the Holocaust since completing *V Was for Victory* in 1975, I would have preferred to avoid that conference had I had a choice. But I could not refuse two old and valued friends who meant at once to use and to flatter me. Consequently I had a shelf of reading to do that summer, for the Holocaust had received continual and controversial historical attention since the mid-1970s. There had begun to appear an absurd and dangerous literature of denial, contending that the Holocaust had never happened. The scholars invited to the conference had no truck with that mythology. But there was also a considerable and growing body of scholarly work contending that FDR had only too late and too cautiously made an effort to save the threatened Jewish population of Europe. He was criticized particularly for providing no American asylum earlier than January 1944.

Both in reading the large and often angry literature about the Holocaust and later in listening to the conferees at Hyde Park, I began to modify my previous conclusions about the subject. I had decided during the 1960s that Roosevelt had held back from assisting the persecuted Jews partly for political reasons. He was eager in a time of widespread anti-Semitism to prevent Americans from viewing the war as a war to protect the Jews. He was also influenced by Americans' antagonism to all immigrants, refugees especially, an antagonism Congress shared. Also sensitive to British concerns about the Arabs, during the war Roosevelt opposed enlarging a Zionist homeland for Jews fleeing Europe. Above all, as I argued in *V Was for Victory*, he subordinated all issues to military considerations, to his effort to win the war as quickly as possible. Only after that was accomplished, he believed, could effective rescue begin. Consequently, about the Holocaust, a matter requiring boldness, he temporized too long, with awful consequences for the victims of Nazi terror. He was not alone. No nation, with the possible exception of Denmark, had demonstrated the courage to rescue a significant proportion of European Jews. That the failing was common in no way excused the cruel evasiveness of American policies. In spite of these shortcomings, however, Franklin D. Roosevelt remained the historical figure who inspired my greatest enthusiasm, remained long after World War II my commander-in chief.

Preparations for the conference had reawakened my interest in the influence on American foreign policy of powerful United States senators, whether Democrats like William Fulbright or Republicans like Arthur Vandenberg or Jesse Helms. I wrote an outline with a bibliography for a book on that subject for the period after World War II. It was obvious from the number of archival sources I listed that I would have to travel extensively and spend considerable time at remote sites in order to do the research necessary for my project. But the prospect of travel and of life in motels and second-class hotels palled. On reflection, I concluded that archival work no longer suited my taste. In my twenties and thirties I had enjoyed doing research in archives and manuscript collections. In my forties and fifties I found that research tolerable but taxing. In my seventies I decided to give it up.

From archival research I had gathered the material essential to most of my books. Now I continued to write, but no longer from manuscript sources. Instead during my first decade of retirement I tried my hand at various biographical essays. One was on Archibald MacLeish, a liberal poet I had known and admired. Another focused on the intellectual bases of the writings of Arthur Schlesinger, Jr., a generous and like-minded friend whom I classified as a "Tory Democrat," an appellation I would give myself, an American in the reform tradition of English Tory Radicals like Benjamin Disraeli and Winston Churchill. The *Yale Review* published both of those pieces, as it did an essay-review I wrote comparing the several books on war by Paul Fussell to several by other authors. For the *Washington Monthly* I wrote a critical review of Henry Kissinger's memoir. Only the MacLeish essay was completed in time to be included in my 1993 book *Liberty, Justice, Order,* which also reprinted some earlier writings of mine, including the introductions to my editions of Walter Lippmann's letters and Henry Wallace's diary. Like most books of essays, mine did not sell well. The *Library Journal* prescribed it for readers "fascinated by political history." *Booklist* recommended it for "progressives." Harvey Mansfield, a staunch conservative, in the *Times Literary Supplement* dismissed it as unrealistic liberalism. I could have lined my study walls with unsold copies. Except for Mansfield's, the reviews were valid. I did not have to be told that my kind of history and my kind of politics were out of fashion. My dear friend Edmund Morgan was surely correct in saying that historians normally did their best work before their sixties; but his short biography of Benjamin Franklin, published when he was eighty-seven, demonstrated that even a wise generalization had to allow for exceptions.

Advancing age did not break my company with history. Now and then I served as a "talking head" in biographical documentaries, including studies of Theodore Roosevelt and Woodrow Wilson. National Video Resources hired me as a consultant for a new venture in adult education — courses for use in public libraries, with the courses consisting of available documentary films. My task was to structure several coherent six-week units, each based on available documentaries. I also wrote part or all of a teachers' guide, with bibliographies, for each course, and on several occasions demonstrated in person how to go about teaching a typical unit. In that unusual way, my involvement in teaching continued until my eightieth year, when I thought the time had come for my employers to find younger consultants.

I still found joy in reading new works of history on topics that appealed to me. That reading allowed me to conduct a private, silent, but absorbing dialogue with the authors whose books I read. An actual conversation often followed with Vann Woodward or Ed Morgan or, less frequently, Arthur Schlesinger, Jr. Arthur's evocative and engaging memoir enlivened the last weeks of the year 2000. I, too, found myself increasingly caught up in the past, a characteristic leaning for a historian past eighty.

More and more I realized how much I owed to the elite institutions in which I had spent most of my life. My brother was correct: Andover did turn my life around. Without Andover there would have been no Harvard; and as one of my younger friends put it, I became "captured by the crimson web," though I was more deeply involved at Yale. Between 1935, when I matriculated at Andover, and 1991, when I retired from teaching, elite educational institutions had changed profoundly. In my class at Andover there was only one black student and not a single Asian American or woman. A similar lack of diversity existed during my years as a student at Harvard, and it was not significantly different in the first classes I taught at Yale. By 1991 all three institutions had come to admit appropriate numbers of those previously excluded groups. Andover, Harvard, and Yale, now eager for diversity, tried also to preserve meritocratic standards in student admissions as well as in faculty appointments. They remained elite in the quality of the instruction they offered, and their graduates continued disproportionately to play important roles in American life. Never a populist, I was enough of an old-fashioned progressive to believe that meritocracy helped make democracy function.

Looking back, I considered myself especially fortunate in my colleagues, particularly Elting Morison and Al Chandler at MIT, and Ed Morgan and Vann Woodward at Yale. Who could have worked on a textbook with more talented contemporaries than Ed and Vann, Arthur Schlesinger, Jr., Ken Stampp, and Bill McFeely? I was just as fortunate in teaching so long at Yale, where so many undergraduate and graduate students approached learning with high spirit and high talent and where members of the administration included generous and effective friends. The commitments they discharged to Yale made my administrative chores seem meager. More important, the academic environment they built and preserved made Yale an ideal university in which to teach.

The great adventure of my generation, I and most of my contemporaries believed, was World War II. My personal great adventure came at the end of that terrible war under the gentle command of Elting E. Morison, a discerning analyst of the human condition and an irreverent companion in Clio's service. My experience with him in writing the history of naval logistics provided the beginning of my adventure as a professional historian. Because of our Harvard connections, it was no accident that I fell in with an old boys' crimson network that included such figures as Wilbur Bender, Henry Chauncey, Richard Leopold, and Myron Gilmore. Those older friends of mine had no connections at Yale. But, like those older friends, the company I found at Yale was professionally stimulating. And teaching at Yale constantly exposed me to vibrant, young minds in the making. Research continually rewarded me with the delights of discovery; only love exceeds my pleasure in coming upon a new, original, and persuasive way of explaining the past. History from the time I met it through the rest of my life has been for me the most answering calling. Life in the academy has been equally rewarding. That is where Clio pitches her tent, where most professional historians live, and—if they are engaged teachers, scholars, and citizens— where they live fully in the alternative reality they nurture and embrace.

Index

Abbot, Eleanor Pearre, 80
Academic life, x–xi
Academic salaries, x
Adams, Fred, 201
Adams, Henry, 84, 170
Addison Gallery of American Art, Andover, 13–14
Adler, Mortimer, 151
Admiral of the Ocean Sea (Morison), 69
Adrian, Lord and Lady, 167, 168
Adult education. *See* Continuing education
Affirmative action, 158, 222, 247–48
African Americans, 202, 266; Black Panther murder case, 219–21; Harvard housing controversy, 228–29; Harvard overseer, 214; New Haven protest groups, 229–30; students at Yale, 206, 207; on Yale faculty, 248, 249
African American studies: Gates's program at Harvard, 206; at Yale, 142
Age of Franklin D. Roosevelt (Schlesinger), 70, 126
Age of Jackson (Schlesinger), 69
Ahlstrom, Sydney, 72
Allen, Harry, 160
Alsop, Stewart, 203
Alumni, Yale, 205
America (magazine), 177, 253

America First Committee, 95
American Capitalism (Galbraith), 123
American Civil Liberties Union (ACLU): at Aspen, 196–97
American Council of Learned Societies, 163
American Defense: Harvard Group, 32–33
American Experience, The (textbook), 91
American Historical Association (AHA), 86, 150, 154; Blum's talk on Red Scare at meeting of, 86–88
"American Scholar, The" (Emerson), 227
Americans for Democratic Action, 95
"Americus," 189
Anderson, Oscar E., 131–32
Anderson, Tom, 147
Andover. *See* Phillips Academy, Andover, Mass.
Annan, Noel, 168
Anti-Americanism, 173
Anti-communism, 87, 129–31, 151–52
Anti-radicalism, 87
Anti-Semitism: at Andover, 8; at Harvard, 22–23, 103; in Roosevelt's administration, 178; at Yale, 155–56. *See also* Jews
Anti-submarine warfare, 41–42, 46
Architects Collaborative, 94
Armitage, Arthur, 165, 168

Art history, 13–14

"Aspects of Logistic Planning" (Gilmore and Blum), 70

Aspen, Colo., counterculture in, 196–98

Aspen Institute, 151–52, 191, 196–98

Athletics and sports: at Andover, 4, 10, 11; at Harvard, 21–22, 26; at Midshipman School, 39; at Yale, 149–50

Atomic bomb, development of, 237

Atwater, Russell, 153–54

Australia Star (ship), 51–52

Babb, James, 192, 194

Bailey, Thomas A., 124

Baker, Ray Stannard, 143

Bakke case, 247–48

Baldwin, A. Graham, 12–13, 16

Ballantine, Duncan, 64, 66, 67, 68, 104, 106, 110

Ballantine, Edward, 96

Ballantine, Florence, 214

Baltimore (ship), 58

Bannister, Robert, 143, 145, 258

Barnes, Edward, 198

Barnes, Janet, 230

Barnes, Tracy, 203, 229–30

Bartlett, Howard, 104, 105, 111, 114

Barton, Bruce, Jr., 22

Baumer, Franklin, 149

Baxter, James Phinney, III, 117, 132

Beale, Howard, 90

Beard, Charles, 172

Beer, Thomas, 70

Beinecke Library, Yale, 191

Bellagio, Italy, 256

Beloff, Max, 169, 170

Bemis, Samuel Flagg, 87–88, 137, 142

Bender, Wilbur, 16–18, 25, 34, 64, 267

Bennett, George, 212, 215, 229

Benton, Frank, 13, 179

Bernays, Edward I., 91

Bernstein, Carl, 236

Bickel, Alex, 161, 189, 221, 247, 248

Billington, Ray, 86, 87

Bingham, Jonathan, 147

Bissell, Richard, 115

Bittker, Anne, 256

Blackmer, Alan, 14–15, 16

Blackmer, Josephine, 16

Blackmun, Harry A., 253

Black Panthers, 202, 219-21, 222

Blacks. *See* African Americans

Black Student Alliance at Yale (BSAY), 207

Blair, Ted, 223

Blum, Ann Shelby (daughter), 88, 189

Blum, Edna L. (mother), 2, 4-6, 21, 41

Blum, Jerome, 150

Blum, John Morton: administrative responsibilities of, at Yale, 238–40; AHA speech on Red Scare, 86–88; American foreign policy, analysis of, 172–73; as "Americus," 189; at Andover, 4–19; and archival research, 265; at Aspen Institute, 151–52, 191, 196–98; at Bellagio, Italy, 256; and Bemis's name calling, 87–88; boyhood ambitions of, x; Buckingham seminars, Cambridge, 98–99; Cambridge, Mass., friends of, 93–98, 102; at Cambridge University, 163, 165–70; as chairman of history department, Yale, 173–80, 186, 187; childhood of, 1; college friends of, 22, 35; and Commonwealth lectures, London, 186–87; on Council on Priorities and Planning, 256; as director of Yale libraries, 190–96, 198–202; doctoral dissertation of, 70, 76, 84, 88, 89; at European American Studies meeting, 171–72; and European intellectual history course, 106–7; family of, 1–2, 4, 5, 6, 118; festschrift presented to, 258; financial concerns of, at Andover, 4–6, 61; and forged letter to Morgan, 250; and graduate students, 140, 142–45, 206, 252; at Harvard, 18, 20–37, 71–77; Harvard honorary degree awarded to, 252; health problems of, 245, 256, 257; and Holocaust conference, 264–65; and Kennedy's assassination, 169–70; and McCarthy campaign, 189–90; as member of Harvard Corporation, 211–19, 230–36, 243, 245,

252; at MIT, 88, 93, 102, 103, 106–19;
naval training and service of, 33, 36,
38–61; and NEH fellowship, 187, 190;
on New Haven ethics board, 153–54;
off-campus commitments of, at Yale,
151–54, 178–79; at Oxford University,
241, 243–45; as parliamentarian, 203,
205; phased retirement of, 257, 258;
Ph.D. awarded to, 88; Phi Beta Kappa
chapter, Harvard, address to, 227–28;
Phi Beta Kappa induction, 36;
political views and activities of, 82,
96, 132, 147, 148, 187–90, 221–22, 235–36;
pragmatism of, 173; and primary and
secondary education, 152–53; prizes,
awards, and scholarships, 5–6, 18, 36;
religious beliefs of, 12–13, 56;
religious services at sea held by, 50,
55–56; in retirement, 259–60, 263–67;
Rockefeller Foundation grant to, 256;
and ROTC controversy, 203, 204, 205;
schoolboy friends of, 9–10; schoolboy
pranks of, 9; social life, at Yale, 158; as
Sterling Professor, at Yale, 256;
student jobs held by, 5–7, 21, 32–33, 35;
and student unrest, 199, 221–24;
teaching experience of, in navy, 53;
travels of, 160–61, 168–71, 243; Trinity
College honorary degree and
commencement address, 226–27;
tutoring by, at Andover, 6; and
undergraduate regulations, at Yale,
209, 210; and undergraduate students,
145–49, 252; at Williams College, 117;
Yale, introduction to, 136–40, 136–42,
151; and Yale committees, 155–56, 186,
248–49, 253, 254, 255; and Yale in
London program, 258; Yale
president, search for, 250–51
Blum, John Morton, works of, 120;
biographical essays of, 265; "Burden
of American Equality, The," 241, 245;
From the Morgenthau Diaries, 128,
132–35, 177; history of naval logistics,
63–70; *Joe Tumulty and the Wilson Era*,
88, 91–92; *Liberty, Justice, Order*, 88,
241, 265–66; *National Experience, The*

(textbook), contribution to, 162–63;
Price of Vision, The (Wallace diary),
237; *Progressive Presidents, The*, 188,
253–54; *Promise of America, The*, 166,
171, 173, 177; *Public Philosopher: Selected
Letters of Walter Lippmann*, 254, 256–57;
Republican Roosevelt, The, 92, 97, 109,
110, 121, 122, 123, 242; *Roosevelt and
Morgenthau*, 178; Roosevelt letters,
editing of, 75–76, 78–91, 120–22; *V Was
for Victory*, 206, 241–42, 264–65;
*Woodrow Wilson and the Politics of
Morality*, 124–26; *Years of Discord:
American Politics and Society, 1961–1974*,
263–64; *Yesterday's Children*
(anthology), 123–24
Blum, Morton G. (father), 2–6, 21, 39,
118–19
Blum, Pamela Powell "Pammy"
(daughter), 74–77, 97, 98
Blum, Pamela Zink (wife), 36–37, 56, 60,
61, 62, 119, 190, 236; and Blum as
Harvard fellow, 210, 212, 213; with
Blum at Aspen Institute, 151, 152;
with Blum at Harvard, 73, 74; with
Blum at MIT, 76; with Blum at Yale,
137, 139, 140, 141, 149, 158, 174, 201, 205;
with Blum in Europe, 160, 161, 165–66,
167, 169, 170, 171–72, 187, 243, 256; and
Blum's address at Trinity College,
226–27; Blum's courtship of and
marriage to, 39, 41, 42, 50–51; and
Blum's lecture during student "strike,"
222; in Cambridge, Mass., 93, 94,
97–100, 102; at Columbia, 246; doctoral
dissertation of, 243; Ph.D. awarded to,
246; at St. Hilda's College, Oxford,
243; in Washington, 70, 75; and Yale
in London program, 258
Blum, Thomas Tyler (son), 88
Blum, William (brother). *See* Darrid,
William
Bok, Derek, 217, 218, 225, 231–32, 234, 235,
248, 252
Bok, Sissela, 232
Book and Snake, 148–49
Booklist, 265–66

Borah, William, 89
Borg, Dorothy, 154
Bowdoin College, Maine, 108
Bowen, William, 219, 248
Boxer, Charles, 185
Boyd, Julian, 79
Bradlee, Ben, 22
Bradley, Omar, 176
Brainard, Bill, 238, 257
Branford College, Yale, 222–24
Bretton Woods Conference, 178
Brewster, Kingman, Jr., 95–100, 119, 138,
    142, 147, 149, 151, 157, 204–5, 238, 253; as
    ambassador to England, 245; and
    Black Panther murder case, 219–20;
    and Blum as member of Harvard
    Corporation, 210–13, 217; and Blum's
    NEH fellowship, 187; Blum's profile
    of, 246; and Derek Bok, 231–32;
    illness and death of, 258; and Lynd's
    antiwar lecture in Canada, 184; and
    mandatory summer semester, 240; as
    president of Yale, 161, 163–64, 168, 173,
    174, 176, 177; as provost of Yale, 158–59;
    and recruiting of professors, 182;
    resignation as president of Yale,
    245–46; and ROTC program, 203, 204;
    and student unrest, 204, 207, 221, 222,
    225; and tenure decisions, 181; and
    university libraries, 190, 191, 192, 196,
    202; and Yale alumni, 205
Brewster, Mary Louise, 95–97, 158, 168,
    190, 232, 245, 246, 253
Brinton, Crane, 31–32
British American Studies Association, 186
Brogan, Denis, 167, 244
Brooks, Paul, 88, 123–24, 236, 237
Brooks, Peter, 255
Bruner, Jerome, 152
Bryant, Douglas, 201, 216
Buck, Paul, 214
Buckingham School, Cambridge, Mass.,
    93, 98, 99
Bulfinch Hall, Phillips Academy, 94
Bundy, Mary, 96
Bundy, McGeorge, 96, 97, 127, 138, 219,
    231, 237

Bundy, William, 250, 251
Burchard, John E., 104, 110, 111, 114,
    151, 152
"Burden of American Equality, The"
    (Blum), 241, 245
Burr, Francis H. "Hooks," 215–18, 229,
    231, 233, 234, 236
Bush, George H. W., 126
Bush, George W., 126, 147
Business cycles, 260
Buss, Emily, 252–53
Buttenheim, Peggy, 224
Butterfield, Herbert, 148, 167, 168

Caine Mutiny, The (Wouk), 59
California, University of, 118; Bakke case,
    247–48
Calkins, Hugh, 211–17, 230, 233
Cambodia, 224
Cambridge, Mass., 93–102
Cambridge Nursery School, 98
Cambridge University, England, 163,
    165–70
Campbell, Ashley and Mary, 94
Canada, Lynd's antiwar lecture in, 184
Canham, Erwin, 152
Cannadine, David, 167
Carroll, Richard, 186
Carter, George, 98
Carter, Jimmy, 126, 163
Carter, Shirley, 98
Cater, Douglass, 188
Catholics: at Andover, 8; at Yale, 156
Catton, Bruce, 162
Center for International Studies (CIS),
    115–16
Central Intelligence Agency (CIA),
    115, 116
Chambers, Whittaker, 129
Chandler, Alfred D., Jr., 72–73, 79–82, 90,
    111, 112, 121, 267
Chandler, Fay, 73
Charpentier, Arthur, 195, 196
Chase, Mary Ellen, 124
Chauncey, Henry, 18, 64, 143, 153
Chauncey, Henry, Jr. "Sam," 143, 222,
    251, 267

Chayes, Abram, 22
Chessman, G. Wallace, 72
China, 131, 154
Christian Science Monitor, 256
CIA. *See* Central Intelligence Agency
Civil Rights Act of 1964, 202
Civil rights movement, 147, 175–76, 202,
    226; African American protest
    groups, New Haven, 229–30; *Bakke*
    case, 247, 248; Harvard housing
    controversy, 228–29
Civil Service Chronicle, 83
Clark, Annie, 139
Clark, Elias, 10, 139, 149
Clark, Thomas, 74
Clawson, Peggy Hinchman, 80
Cleaver, Eldridge, 219
Cleaver, Kathleen, 219
Clinton, Bill, 123
Cobb, Frank, 125
Coeducation: at Hotchkiss, 179; at Yale,
    204, 205, 206
Coffin, William Sloane, Jr., 138, 175–76,
    181, 183, 185
Cold War, 116, 172, 173, 222
Cole, Donald, 152
Colley, Linda, 167, 257
Columbia University, 246
Commager, Henry Steele, 90, 144, 163
Commonwealth lectures, University
    College, London, 186–87
Communism, 82, 178; anti–communist
    sentiments, post–World War II, 87,
    129–31, 151–52; at Harvard, 33; Wallace
    and, 237
Communist Manifesto, The (Marx and
    Engels), 151
Compton, Karl T., 104
Computer technology, in libraries,
    193, 195
Conant, James B., 20, 22, 31, 110, 232, 248
*Concept of Equilibrium in American Social
    Thought, The* (Russett), 145
Containment, doctrine of, 173
Continuing education: at Aspen
    Institute, 151–52, 191, 196–98;
    biographical documentaries, 266;

Buckingham seminars, Cambridge,
    98–99; at Sloan School of Industrial
    Management, 109
Coolidge, Calvin, 3
Cooper, Richard, 238
Corporatism, 172
Council on Priorities and Planning,
    Yale, 256
Cox, Archibald, 222, 229, 248
Cox, Constance Buffum, 95
Cox, Hugh, 131
Croly, Herbert, 172, 173
Cronon, William, 244
Cullman, Joe, 179
Curtin, Phyllis, 168
Curtis, Charles, 89

Dahl, Robert, 203, 204
Daley, Radley, 195
Dallek, Robert, 264
Dalrymple, Willard, 98
Dalzell, Robert F., Jr., 144, 145, 258
Danger and Survival (Bundy), 237
*Daniel Webster and the Trial of American
    Nationalism* (Dalzell), 144
Darrid, Diana Douglas, 138–39
Darrid, William (William Blum)
    (brother), 1, 35, 119, 138–39, 266
Davis, David Brion, 185
Dean, Howard, 147
Dean of students, role of, 73
Debating team, Andover, 11, 17
Deconstructionists, 255
Defense Department, U.S., 100
DeMan, Paul, 255
Democratic Party, 148
de Santillana, Giorgio, 99
Destroyer escort (DE), 42
Deutsch, Karl, 114–15
Diggers, 196, 197
Disruption of the American Democracy, The
    (Nichols), 85
Divisional committees, at Yale, 255
Doctor (title), 3–4
Documentaries, biographical, 266
Donnelly, Francis, 153–54
Douglas, Jean Wallace, 237

Drinan, Robert F., 253
Drug culture, at Yale, 207
Dudley Hall, Harvard, 73
Duffey, Joe, 189
Duhig, Charles W., 73
Dunham, Bill, 155, 156
Dunlop, John, 231

Eastland, James O., 130, 131, 132
Ebert, Robert, 217
Eccles, Marriner, 127, 133
Economic history, 260
Edith and Woodrow (Levin), 124
Egypt, 243
Eisenhower, Dwight D., 116, 131, 132
Eliot, T. S., 16
Embersits, Jack, 207–8, 224
Emerson, Ralph Waldo, 56, 227
Employment Act of 1946, 260
Encryption devices, 42
English history, instruction in, 261
Eros and Civilization (Marcuse), 101
Ethnicity, and progressive politics, 86
European American Studies meeting,
    Oslo, 171–72

Fairbank, John K., 154, 214
Fairlie, Henry, 242
Fanton, Jonathan, 144, 240
Farnsworth, Dana, 98
Federal government, academics'
    involvement in, 100–101
Field, Bernice, 195
Field, Jim, 28
Finley, John, 217
Fischer, Fritz, 170
Food, politics of, 244
Foord, Archibald, 160
Ford, Henry, II, 179
Ford, Mimi, 97
Ford, Truman Mitchell "Mike," 22, 35,
    36, 97
Forrestal, James, 67, 68
France, 160, 161, 170
Franklin D. Roosevelt and the New Deal
    (Leuchtenburg), 146
Freedom from Fear (Kennedy), 177

Freedom of the press: and Roosevelt's
    libel suit against the New York
    World, 79
Freeman, Douglas S., 74
Freidel, Frank, 134
Freud, Sigmund, 16
Freund, Paul, 214, 217
Friedman, Francis, 103
Frisch, David, 103
From the Morgenthau Diaries (Blum), 128,
    132–35, 177
Fuess, Claude Moore, 3, 8, 19
Fussell, Paul, 265

Gabriel, Ralph, 118, 119
Galbraith, John Kenneth, 103, 123, 178,
    188–89
Gardner, John, 218
Gates, Henry Louis, Jr. "Skip," 206
Gatzke, Hans, 157
Gay, Peter, 182, 185
General Education in a Free Society
    (Conant), 110
Germany, 160–61, 168–71
Giamatti, A. Bartlett, x, 251–52, 254–57,
    262
GI Bill, x, 61, 62, 76
Gilmore, Myron, 30–32, 34, 56, 62–66, 70,
    97, 106, 170, 214, 247, 267
Gilmore, Sheila, 96, 97, 170
Ginsberg, Allen, 207
Gladwyn, Lord, 169
Gnomes, 201
Goethals, George W., 97
Goheen, Robert, 218
Golden, Judah, 156
Goldman, Eric, 122, 150, 173
Goodman, William B., 242
Graduate teaching, 262–63
Graham, Sandra, 228, 229
Grasso, Ella, 235
Gray, Charles, 112, 247
Gray, Hanna Holborn, 246–51
Grayson, David, 143
Greenberg, David, 147
Griswold, A. Whitney, 137, 138, 141, 142,
    147, 150, 151, 153, 155–61

Gropius, Walter, 94
Guam, 34, 57, 64
Guffey, Joseph, 74
Gummere, Richard, Jr., 12

Hacker, Louis, 178
Hall, John W., 157, 158, 168, 257
Hall, Robin, 158
Halsey, William Frederick, Jr., 54, 65
Handlin, Mary, 97
Handlin, Oscar, 35, 62, 72, 76, 97, 110, 124, 213, 214
Handlin, Ruth, 97
Hansen, Alvin, 110
Harbridge House, 100
Harris, Charles, 55, 58
Harrison, Gilbert, 189
Harsch, Joseph, 256
Hartford Courant, 236
Harvard Corporation, 211–19, 232–36, 243, 245, 252; and *Bakke* case, 248; and search for university president, 230–32
Harvard Crimson, 236
Harvard Investment Company, 234
Harvard University, 20, 21; anti-Semitism at, 22–23, 103; Blum's graduate studies at, 71–77; Blum's honorary degree from, 252; Blum's Phi Beta Kappa address at, 227–28; Blum's undergraduate studies at, 20–37; commencement (1970), 228–29; commencement (1971), 232; communists on faculty of, 82; corporate responsibility at, 233–34; disposal facility and power plant, 234; diversity in admissions policy, 248, 266; émigré instructors at, 27; faculty of, 23–36; honorary degrees awarded by, 233; housing controversy at, 228–29; Jewish faculty members at, 230; residential houses of, 26; search for president of, 230–32; student unrest at, 211, 216, 217; World War II and, 33–34
Harvard University Press, 78, 110
Hawley, Ellis, 146
Hayes, Bart, 14

Hellenic Center, Washington, D.C., 216
Henderson, L. J., 31
Henning, Basil and Alison, 224
Henry Adams Club, Harvard, 72
Hepburn Act of 1906, 121
Herrin, Judith, 166
Hersey, John, 168, 223, 227
Hesburgh, Ted, 233
Hewlett, Richard, 131–32
Hexter, Jack, 185
Hicks, John D., 122
Hindoo (ship), 51–52
Hiss, Alger, 86, 129
History: American, 17–18, 261; fashion in scholarship, 259–61; induction in study of, 15; learned societies, 86; as profession, 1, 69–70; professors of, x; revisionism, ix; rewards in study of, 267; uncertainty principle in, 147–48; writing of, 84, 92, 120, 135
Hobbes, Thomas, 24
Hocking, Ernest, 31
Hodgson, Godfrey, 253
Hofstadter, Richard, 90, 136, 169, 172
Holborn, Hajo, 154, 157, 160, 170, 186
Holden, Betty, 170
Holden, Reuben "Ben," 138, 170, 223
Holmes, Frederic L., 108
Holocaust, the, 264–65
Holt, Michael, 183
Holton, Gerald, 214
Holweg, Bethmann, 170
Homans, George, 79
Hoover, Herbert, 138
Horne, F. J., 64, 65, 67, 68
Hotchkiss School, 178–79
Houghton, Mifflin, 88–89, 91
House, E. M., 124, 138
House Un-American Activities Committee, 87
Hughes, Stuart, 214
Hull, Cordell, 133
Humphrey, Hubert, 190

Ickes, Harold, 177
Ignatius, Paul and Nancy, 100
Imperialism, American, 172

Imperial presidency, 163
Industrial Workers of the World
    (IWW), 87
*In My Time: A Medley of Andover
    Reminiscences* (Fuess, editor), 19
International Monetary Fund (IMF), 178
Isolationism, 25
Italy, 170, 256
Iwo Jima, 57, 58, 60

Jackson, Pat, 96
Jaeger, Werner, 27
James, William and Julie, 197
Jenks, Jeremiah W., 260
Jews: at Andover, 4, 7–9; on Harvard
    faculty, 230; Holocaust, the, 264–65;
    as members of Harvard Corporation,
    212, 214; at MIT, 103; and Roosevelt's
    policy, 178; at Yale, 155–56
Joe Tumulty and the Wilson Era (Blum),
    88–89, 91–92
John F. Kennedy Library, Boston, 256
Johnson, Gerald W., 91
Johnson, Lyndon B., 169, 187, 188, 202,
    253, 254, 257, 264
Johnson, Warren, 74
Jones, Ernest, 16
Jones, Howard Mumford, 90
*Journal of Abnormal and Social
    Psychology*, 74

Kahn, Herman, 130, 195–96
Kahn, Louis, 141
Kaiser, Bob, 147
Kalman, Laura, 258
Kane, Keith, 211, 212, 213, 215
Kantor, Rosabeth, 253
Kaplan, Ben, 214, 215, 217–18
"Katahdin" (Thoreau), 55
Katz, Milton, 95, 96, 99, 214, 227
Katz, Vivian, 96, 98
Keeney, Barnaby Conrad "Barney,"
    26–30, 33, 154
Kenefik, J. Gordon, 195
Kennan, George, 173
Kennedy, David M., 177, 258

Kennedy, John F., 96, 132, 168, 169
Kennedy, Mary, 95
Kennedy, Robert F., 189, 190, 202, 222
Kent, Robert B. and Barbara, 97
Kent State University, Ohio, 224
Kernan, Alvin, 209
Kerr, Chester, 155, 189, 254, 256, 257
Kerr, Joan, 189
Kerry, John F., 147
Kessen, Bill, 209, 210, 240
Keynes, John Maynard, 260
Killian, James R., 104, 113, 116
Kimball, Warren F., 256–57
Kindelberger, Charles, 134
King, Ernest J., 64, 65, 67, 68
King, Martin Luther, Jr., 202, 222
Kiphuth, Delaney, 139, 149
Kissinger, Henry, 265
Knox, Bernard, 216
Knox, Frank, 67, 68
Kopkind, Andrew, 177
Krieger, Leonard, 155–56
Kuhn, Thomas, 219
Kuttner, Stephan, 156

LaFollette, Robert, 189
Lamar, Howard R., 140, 161, 179–80, 182,
    185, 251
Lamport, Felicia (Mrs. Ben Kaplan), 214,
    218
Langer, William, 214
Language courses, at Yale, 262
LaPiana, George, 27
Larrabee, Eric, 22
Laslett, Peter, 166
Latin America, 44–45
League of Nations, 91–92, 125
Lee, Frank, 168
Lee, Richard, 153
Lend-lease program, 177
Leonard, Arthur W., 16, 17
Leopold, Richard W., 34, 35, 36, 64, 70, 76,
    80–81, 112, 125, 154, 267
Letters of Theodore Roosevelt, The, 75–76,
    78–91, 120–22
Leuchtenburg, William, 146

Leviathan (Hobbes), 24
Levin, Phyllis Lee, 124
Levin, Rick, 253
Liberty, Justice, Order (Blum), 88, 241, 265–66
Libraries, 190–96, 198–200
Library Journal, 265
Library of American Biography series, 124
Library of Congress, Blum's research in, 74, 78, 79
Lichten, Bill, 246
Lieberman, Joseph, 147
Liebert, Fritz, 192, 195
Lilley, William, III, 144
Lindblom, Charles E., 123, 159
Lindsay, John V., 123, 147
Link, Arthur S., 75, 91, 122, 124, 125, 150
Lippmann, Walter, 172, 173, 254, 256–57
Lloyd, Henry Demarest, 172
Lockwood, Betty, 226–27
Lockwood, Theodore, 112, 226
Lodge, Henry Cabot, 122
London, England, 187
Long, Breckenridge, 178
Longworth, Alice Roosevelt, 89–90
Lopez, Robert, 156
Lovett, "Uncle Sid," 228
Lowell, A. Lawrence, 22
Lowell textile manufacturers, Mass., 144–45
Lynd, Staughton, 183–84, 185

MacArthur, Douglas, 227
McCarthy, Eugene, 189–90, 197
McCarthy, Joseph, 82, 96, 132
McFeely, William, 163, 267
McGovern, George, 235–36
MacIlwain, Charles, 27–28
MacLeish, Archibald, 20, 265
MacMullen, Ramsey, 182
McNaughton, John, 100
Mahan, Alfred Thayer, 173
Mahoney, Thomas, 106
Mailer, Norman, 22
Maine, McCarthy's campaign in, 189–90
Malone, Dumas, 86, 87

Manalia, Tony, 48
Mandatory retirement, 253, 263
Manhattan Project, 131
Mansfield, Harvey, 266
Marbury, William, 211, 212, 213
Marcuse, Herbert and Inge, 100–101
Mariana Islands, 57
Marshall, Thurgood, 176
Marshall Islands, 56
Martz, Louis, 194
Marx, Karl, 151
Marxism, 30, 31, 220
Mason, Edward, 217
Massachusetts Institute of Technology (MIT), 75–76, 78, 82, 103–19; and Center for International Studies, 115–16; classified research at, 82–83; 115–16; core curriculum, 110–15, 261, 262; meritocracy of, 103; new math and new physics developed at, 153
Massachusetts Young Democrats, 95
Mathias, Anne, 244
Mathias, Peter, 165, 167, 244
Mauve Decade (Beer), 70
May, Georges, 156, 186, 208, 209, 210, 220, 251
Mayer, Jane, 147
Mayo, Bernard, 87
Mellon, Paul, 200, 216
Merk, Frederick, 28–29, 35, 56, 62, 69, 71, 72, 76, 80, 81, 90, 142, 147, 214
Merriman, John, 257
Merriman, Roger, 23–24, 25, 35
Middle class, American, 173
Midshipman schools, USN, 38–39, 39–41
Miles Corporation, 255
Miller, John Perry, 160, 163
Miller, R. H., 177
Miller, William, 110
Millikan, Max, 115
Mills, Kenneth, 220, 226, 227
Mind in the Making, The (Robinson), 15
Minorities: at eminent universities, 249. *See also* African Americans
Mirror, The (Andover literary magazine), 11

Mississippi Valley Historical Society, 86

Moore, Barrington and Betty, 100–101

Morgan, Edmund S., x, 137–40, 142, 154–63, 167, 180, 181, 183, 186, 257, 266, 267; forged letter sent to, 250; and Lynd, 184, 185; and undergraduate regulations, 209–10

Morgan, Helen, 139, 158, 161, 250

Morgenthau, Henry, Jr., 117, 126–34, 168, 177, 178

Morgenthau, Henry, III, 128

Morgenthau, Joan, 129

Morgenthau, Robert, 129, 130

Morgenthau diaries, 126–35, 166, 177

Moriarty, Thomas J., 216

Morison, Elting E., 63–68, 70, 71, 75–84, 87, 88, 90, 110, 117, 119, 121, 152, 168, 214, 246, 267; at MIT, 103–5, 108, 109, 111, 113, 116; at Yale, 182–83

Morison, Robert, 153, 241

Morison, Samuel Eliot, 63, 69, 71

Mott, Neville, 168

Moyers, Bill, 188

Munich, University of, 160–61

Murchison, John, 179

Muskie, Edmund S., 190

National Endowment for the Humanities (NEH), 187, 190

National Experience, The (textbook), 146, 162–63

National Guard, 187, 223

National Video Resources, 266

National Youth Administration, U.S., 33

Nativism, 87

Naval law, 42, 54

Naval logistics, 63–70, 267

Navy, U.S., 33, 34, 36, 38–61

NEH. See National Endowment for the Humanities

New Deal, 134, 254, 260

New Freedom (Wilson's program), 86

New Haven, Conn., 138, 139, 153–54, 219, 222, 223, 229–30, 256

New Jersey, reform movement in, 86

New Left, 172, 173, 188, 194, 197

New math and new physics, 153

New Republic, 147, 177, 189, 242

Newsweek, 242

New World, The (Hewlett and Anderson), 132

New York City, 9–10

New Yorker, The, 90, 147

New York Herald Tribune, 90

New York Times, 90, 124, 134, 147, 177, 214, 253, 256, 263

New York World, 74, 79

Nicholas, Herbert, 160, 187, 243–45

Nichols, Roy F., 85

Nickerson, Albert, 211, 212, 215, 216, 229, 230, 231, 234, 236

Nimitz, Chester William, 57

Nixon, Richard M., 163, 221–22, 224, 236, 263

Nixon Materials Project, National Archives, 264

Northern Ireland, 171

Norway, 172

O'Connor, Sandra Day, 253

Oliphant, Herman, 134

Oliver, Frederick Scott, 70, 71

Olsen, A. William, Jr., 178–79

O'Neill, William, 263–64

Organization of American Historians, 86, 154

Osterweiss, Rollin, 156

Ottemiller, John, 192, 194, 201

Our Young Folks (magazine), 123

Owen, David, 71, 76, 86, 87, 97, 136

Owen, Louise, 97

Oxford University, England, 241, 243–45

Palme, Olaf, 233

Palmer, A. Mitchell, 87

Palmer, Robert R., 136, 185

Panama Canal, 44

Pareto, Vilfredo, 31, 32, 85

Parrington, Vernon, 35

Parrish, Michael E., 258

Parsons, Talcott, 81

Partial retirement, 253, 257

Pataki, George, 147

Patrol craft (PC), 42, 44

Patterson, James T., 263
Paul, Randolph, 134
PC 616, Blum's service on, 42–60
Pearl Harbor attack (1941), 33
Pelikan, Jaroslav, 238
People of Plenty (Potter), 140
Pepke, Mrs. Walter "Pussy," 152
Perkins, Elliot, 62–63
Perry, Ralph Barton, 30, 32
Pevsner, Nicholas, 166
Phased retirement, 253, 257
Phi Beta Kappa, 36
Phillips Academy, Andover, Mass., 1–2;
    anti-Semitism at, 8; athletics and
    sports at, 4, 10, 11; Blum's legacy
    from, 19, 266; campus of, 7, 94;
    diversity at, 266; faculty of, 11–18;
    history of, 3; objectives of, 11; values
    and traditions of, 3–4
Phillips Exeter Academy, N.H., 4
Phinney, Frederick and Eleanor, 97–98
Pierson, George Wilson, 119, 136–40, 150,
    151, 154–58, 180, 181, 224, 257
Pierson, Letitia "Letty," 140, 158, 167
Plumb, J. H., 167
Political economy, 260, 261
Political history, 259, 260, 261
Politics, 85–86; in 1944, 236; in 1948, 82; in
    1952, 82, 96; in 1972, 235–36; three
    types of, 221–22
Pollak, Kathy, 139
Pollak, Louis, 139, 183, 207, 248, 253
Pollak, Nancy, 244
Poor, Henry Varnum, 81
Populism, 172
Porter, Bill, 45–50
Potter, David M., 88, 119, 138, 139, 140,
    142, 144, 157, 160
Poverty: in Egypt, 243; in Latin America,
    44–45
Powell, Lewis, 248
Powell, Thomas Reed, 97
*Power and Responsibility: Case Studies in
    American Leadership* (festschrift,
    Kennedy and Parrish, editors), 258
Price, Martin, 249
Price of Vision, The (Wallace diaries), 237

Primary and secondary education, new
    approaches to, 152–53
Princeton University, 125, 150
Pringle, Henry, 84, 91, 122
Process of Economic Growth (Rostow), 115
Progressive Party, 189
Progressive Presidents, The (Blum), 188,
    253–54
Progressivism, 71, 85, 86, 121, 122, 123, 172
Promise of America, The (Blum), 166, 171,
    173, 177
*Public Philosopher: Selected Letters of
    Walter Lippmann* (Blum), 256–57
Public Records Office, London, 244
Public service, 147
Pulleyn, Jack, 9–10
Pullin, William, 162
Pumpkin Papers, 129
Pusey, Nathan Marsh, 22, 210–18, 227,
    229, 230, 232
Putnam, George, 234

Q clearance, 131
Queen's University, Northern Ireland, 171

Racial issues. *See* African Americans;
    Civil rights movement
Rackley, Alex, 219
Radcliffe College, 35
Radicalism, American, 197
Rae, John, 106, 111
Randolph, A. Philip, 233
Reagan, Ronald, 163
Red Scare, 86–87
Reform movement, 85, 86, 121, 122, 123
Reich, Charles, 197
Religion, progressive politics and, 86
Republican Party, 131, 132, 221–22
Republican Roosevelt, The (Blum), 92, 97,
    109, 110, 121, 122, 123, 242
Reynolds, Lloyd, 209
Rice, Sylvia, 80
Richardson, Elliot, 218, 233
Ripley, William C., 260
Roberts, Michael, 171
Robinson, James Harvey, 15, 16
Rockefeller, David and Peggy, 236

Rockefeller Foundation, 114
Rogers, Rutherford D. "Rudy," 196,
    201–2, 205, 223
Rome, Italy, 170
Roosevelt, Eleanor, 133, 134, 147
Roosevelt, Franklin D., 55–56, 63, 68, 128,
    132, 133, 134, 178, 242, 253; foreign
    policy of, 168, 170–71; and the
    Holocaust, 264–65
Roosevelt, Franklin D., Jr., 42
Roosevelt, Theodore, 189, 253, 254, 260;
    academic and intellectual interests of,
    83–84; Blum's evaluation of, 121–22;
    Blum's undergraduate lectures on,
    146–47; letters of, 75–76, 78–91,
    120–22; nativist sentiments of, 87; and
    social and political reform, 85–86
Roosevelt and Morgenthau (Blum), 178
Roosevelt Memorial Association, 89
Root, Elihu, 122
Rose, Willie Lee, 163
Rosovsky, Henry, 251
Rostow, Eugene V., 188
Rostow, Walt W., 115, 116
ROTC (Reserve Officers Training
    Corps), 202–5, 216
Rough Riders, 146
Round Table (journal), 71
Russett, Cynthia Eagle, 145
Ryerson, Ellen Gluck, 143, 253

Salvemini, Gaetano, 27
Samuelson, Paul, 103, 115
Sawyer, Charles, 14
Schlesinger, Arthur, Sr., 72
Schlesinger, Arthur, Jr., 69, 70, 97, 117,
    122, 126, 127, 132, 162, 163, 168, 169,
    190, 214, 219, 264–67
Schmidt, Benno, 257–58
Schmoke, Kurt, 220
Scholarship, in 1950s, 120
School of Design, Harvard, 217
Schorske, Carl, 24–25, 264
Schumpeter, Joseph, 27
Science courses, at Yale, 261–62
SDS. *See* Students for a Democratic
    Society

Seale, Bobby, 219–21
Security clearance, at MIT, 115, 116
Seibold, Louis, 74
Senior societies, 148–49
Sevareid, Eric, 152
Seymour, Charles, 124, 138
Shakespeare and the Nature of Man
    (Spencer), 106
Shannon, William V., 91
Shape of the River, The (Bok and
    Bowen), 248
Siegfried, Andre, 91
Silver, Alison, 147
Sims, Everett, 162
Sims, William S., 64, 81
Sit-in, at Yale library, 199
Slichter, Charles, 211, 215
Sloan School of Industrial Management,
    MIT, 109
Smith, Gaddis, 157, 180
Smith, Lacey Baldwin, 111–12
Smith, Steve, 190
Snow, C. P., 112
Social class, politics and, 85, 86
Social Gospel, 12
Social history, 259
Society of Fellows, Harvard, 219
Socrates, trial of, 152
Solomon, Barbara, 73–74, 227
Solomon, Peter, 74
Solomon Islands, 53, 54, 55
Solow, Robert, 103, 166, 167, 231
Sorenson, Ted, 132
South Africa, 233, 251
Spanish-American War, 146
Sparks, David, 195
Spence, Jonathan, 144, 180, 181
Spencer, Theodore, 106
Stagflation, 207
Stampp, Kenneth, 118, 119, 162, 267
Stark, Harold R., 65
Steele, Ronald, 254
Steffens, Lincoln, 86
Sterling Memorial Library, Yale, 193, 194,
    198, 199–200
Sterling Professor, at Yale, 256
Stevens, Jerry, 251

Stevenson, Adlai E., 82, 96, 132

Stewart, Zeph, 158, 214

Stimson, Henry L., 13, 20, 81, 127, 133, 177, 237

Stone, Robert, 216, 234

Stratton, Julius "Jay," 82, 104, 105, 114, 117–18, 119

Strayer, Joseph, 112

Students for a Democratic Society (SDS), 183, 188, 203, 204, 207, 210, 228

Student unrest and protests, 175–76, 181, 188, 193–94, 197, 202–5, 224–25, 226, 251, 262; at Harvard, 211, 216, 217; and Seale murder trial, 219–24; "strike" at Yale, 220–22; Wright Hall takeover, 207–10; Yale library sit-in, 199

Submarine chaser (SC), 42, 44

Submarine Chaser Training Command (SCTC), 41

Supreme Court, U.S., 252; Bakke case, 247–48

Susman, Helen, 233

Taft, Horace, 238, 239–40, 254

Tanis, James, 192, 194, 195, 196, 198

Taylor, Charles, 176–77, 184, 191–96, 198, 201–3, 208, 212, 213, 238

Teachers, age of, 262–63

Tear gas, 223, 224

Tedder, Lord, 167

Temporary Student Employment (TSE), at Harvard, 33, 35

Tenure, 155, 174, 180–81, 184, 249, 255, 263

Terrie, Henry, 10

Theodore Roosevelt Association, 78

Thomas Aquinas, St., 106–7

Thompson, Benjamin and Mary, 93–94

Thompson, Leonard, 185

Thomson, Keith, 240

Thoreau, Henry David, 55, 56

Ticknor and Fields, 256

Times Literary Supplement, 266

Timothy Dwight College, Yale, 182

Tobacco stock, Harvard's ownership of, 234

Tobin, Jim, 209, 235, 245–46

Todd, Lord, 168

Triffin, Robert, 168

Trinity College, Hartford, Conn.: Blum's honorary degree from and commencement address at, 226–27

Trinkaus, J. P., 220, 222, 224

Truman, Harry S., 82, 86

TSE. See Temporary Student Employment

Tuchman, Barbara, 214

Tumulty, Joseph P., 70–77, 84, 85, 86, 88, 89, 91, 124

Tumulty, Joseph P., Jr., 70, 74

Turner, Henry A., Jr., 180

Tutorial system, at Harvard, 26, 29–30

Tuttle, Gordon, 10

Typhoon, 58–59

"Undergraduate Regulations," 210

Undergraduate teaching, 262

United Nations, 95, 244

United States in World Affairs, The (Rae and Mahoney), 106

University College, London, 186–87

U.S. Naval Logistics in the Second World War (Ballantine), 64

Vance, Cyrus, 222

Van Sinderen, Albert, 192

Vietnam War, 222, 227, 236; opposition to, 175–76, 183, 187, 188, 189, 202, 207, 224, 226–28

Vineyard Map, 200

Vosper, Robert, 196

Voting Rights Act of 1965, 202

V Was for Victory (Blum), 206, 241–42, 264–65

Wagoner, George, 10

Wallace, Henry A., 82, 237–38

Wallace, Ilo, 237

Walsh, Jack, 9, 10

Walworth, Arthur, 138

Ward, William, 173

War Refugee Board, 178

Washington Monthly, 265

Washington Post, 100, 147, 236

Watergate scandal, 236

Watson, Dick, 179
Watson, Tom, 172
Weathermen, 219, 222
Weaver, Howard, 184
Wechsler, Ann, 189
Weisman, Steve, 147
Weisskopf, Victor, 99, 100, 103, 113
When M. I. T. Was Boston Tech
    (Burchard), 104
"Where Have All the Heroes Gone?"
    (Blum's speech), 227
White, Harry Dexter, 129–31, 178
White, Ted (PC officer), 45, 48, 50–55
White, Theodore H., 213, 214
Whitehead, Alfred North, 30–31
Whiteman, Harold, 149
Whitten, Larry, 199–200
Widener Library, Harvard, 78
Wiener, Norman, 113
Wigglesworth, Hope Williams, 79, 80
Wild, Payson, 36
Wilder, Thornton, 1
Wilkinson, John, 208, 209, 251
Williams, Colia, 207
Williams College, 117
Wilson, Edmund, 90
Wilson, Thomas, 110
Wilson, Woodrow, 27, 71, 72, 74, 75, 84,
    85, 86, 91, 92, 110, 147, 253, 254; Blum's
    biography of, 124–26; Blum's
    evaluation of, 124–26
Winks, Robin, 180
Wolfe, Thomas, 55–56
Wolff, Robert Lee, 213, 214
Women: at elite educational institutions,
    249, 266; students at Yale, 142, 206; on
    Yale faculty, 157, 248, 249
Wood, Leonard, 87
Woodrow Wilson School of Public
    Affairs, Princeton, 150
Woodward, Bob, 147, 236
Woodward, C. Vann, 69, 140, 157, 158,
    162, 172–73, 185, 187, 188, 221, 233, 257,
    266, 267
Woodward, Glenn, 157, 158, 172
World War I, 125, 170; and nativist
    sentiments, 87

World War II, 20, 21, 25, 32–35, 178, 267;
    Blum's service in, 38–60; D–E day, 50;
    food shortages, 244; heroes of, 227;
    home front during, 236–37, 241–42;
    Pacific theater, 50, 52–60
World War II veterans, x–xi, 72, 73
Wright, Arthur, 144, 157, 158, 181, 193
Wright, Frank Lloyd, 94
Wright, Mary C., 144, 157, 158, 180–81
Wyatt, Joe Billy, 234
Wylie, Craig, 88–89, 110
Wyzanski, Charles, 219

Yale College, Dean of, 156
Yale Daily News, 199, 210, 236
Yale Review, 138, 265
Yale University, 21, 29, 119, 207–10; Blum
    as chairman of history department
    at, 173–74, 176–80, 186, 187; Blum as
    director of libraries at, 190–96,
    198–202; Blum-Pelikan committee,
    238–39; Blum's introduction to,
    136–42; Brewster named president of,
    161; British graduate students at,
    159–60; budgetary and financial
    concerns of, 182, 184–85, 192, 194, 198,
    200, 201, 207, 238–40, 254; committees,
    186, 248–49, 253, 254, 255; Council on
    Priorities and Planning, 256; course
    graders at, 146; diversity at, 204, 206,
    266; energy conservation at, 254–55;
    faculty recruitment at, 181–83, 248;
    Giamatti as president of, 251–52,
    254–57; Gray as acting president of,
    246–51; mandatory retirement at,
    253; manners of students at, 148;
    and New Haven protest groups,
    229–30; phased retirement at, 253;
    publication standard at, 249; radical
    faculty at, 183; requirements and
    recommendations at, 261, 262;
    ROTC controversy at, 202–5; Russian
    Studies program at, 182; Schmidt as
    president of, 257–58; and Seale murder
    trial, 219–21; search for new president
    of (1977), 250–51; student unrest and
    protests at, 175–76, 181, 188, 193–94,

197, 199, 202–5, 207–10, 220–25, 251;
summer semesters at, 239–41; tenure
at, 155, 174, 180–81, 184, 249, 255;
women at, 142, 204, 205, 206, 248, 249;
and workers' strike at, 251
Yale University Press, 155, 200, 254
*Years of Discord: American Politics and
Society, 1961–1974* (Blum), 263–64

Yergin, Daniel, 203
Yesterday's Children (anthology), 123–24
Young Communist League, at
Harvard, 33

Zimmerman, P. D., 242
Zink, Pamela. *See* Blum, Pamela Zink